Objective Fictions

Objective Fictions
Philosophy, Psychoanalysis, Marxism

Edited by Adrian Johnston, Boštjan Nedoh
and Alenka Zupančič

EDINBURGH
University Press

Edinburgh University Press is one of the leading university presses in the UK. We publish academic books and journals in our selected subject areas across the humanities and social sciences, combining cutting-edge scholarship with high editorial and production values to produce academic works of lasting importance. For more information visit our website: edinburghuniversitypress.com

© editorial matter and organisation Adrian Johnston, Boštjan Nedoh and Alenka Zupančič, 2022
© the chapters their several authors, 2022

Edinburgh University Press Ltd
The Tun – Holyrood Road, 12(2f) Jackson's Entry, Edinburgh EH8 8PJ

Typeset in 10/14 Ehrhardt by
Cheshire Typesetting Ltd, Cuddington, Cheshire

A CIP record for this book is available from the British Library

ISBN 978 1 4744 8932 4 (hardback)
ISBN 978 1 4744 8934 8 (webready PDF)
ISBN 978 1 4744 8935 5 (epub)

The right of Adrian Johnston, Boštjan Nedoh and Alenka Zupančič to be identified as the editor of this work has been asserted in accordance with the Copyright, Designs and Patents Act 1988, and the Copyright and Related Rights Regulations 2003 (SI No. 2498

Contents

Acknowledgments	vi
Notes on Contributors	x

Introduction: Beyond the Nominalism-Realism Divide: Objective Fictions from Bentham through Marx to Lacan
Adrian Johnston, Boštjan Nedoh and Alenka Zupančič — 1

1. Marx's Theory of Fictions — 13
   Slavoj Žižek

2. Is Surplus Value Structured Like an Anamorphosis? Marx, Lacan and the Structure of Objective Fiction — 24
   Boštjan Nedoh

3. Shades of Green: Lacan and Capitalism's Veils — 45
   Adrian Johnston

4. From the Orderly World to the Polluted Unworld — 64
   Samo Tomšič

5. The Genesis of a False Dichotomy: A Critique of Conceptual Alienation — 85
   Cara S. Greene

6. Nietzsche's Critique of Objectivity and Its 'Tools' — 105
   Aleš Bunta

7. Tips and Tricks: Remarks on the Debate between Badiou and Cassin on 'Sophistics' — 124
   Peter Klepec

8. On Rumours, Gossip and Related Matters 144
   Mladen Dolar

9. 'There is no such thing as the subject that thinks': Wittgenstein and Lacan
   on Truth and the Subject 165
   Paul M. Livingston

10. The Awful Truth: Games and Their Relation to the Unconscious 183
    Amanda Holmes

11. The Objective Construction: Freud and the Primal Scene 198
    Tadej Troha

12. (From the Lie in the Closed World to) Lying in an Infinite Universe 217
    Frank Ruda

13. A Short Essay on Conspiracy Theories 232
    Alenka Zupančič

Index 250

Acknowledgements

Part of the research in this volume is funded by the Slovenian Research Agency under the research programme P6-0014 'Conditions and Problems of Contemporary Philosophy', the research project J6-9392 'Problem of Objectivity and Fiction in Contemporary Philosophy' and the bilateral cooperation project BI-US/18-10-026 between the Research Centre at the Slovenian Academy of Sciences and Arts, Institute of Philosophy, and the Department of Philosophy, University of New Mexico, USA.

As the editors of this volume, we would like to thank all contributing authors for accepting our invitation and contribute outstanding chapters. We are also grateful to Edinburgh University Press, especially to Carol Macdonald, Sarah Foyle and Kirsty Woods, and the production team, for making this volume possible.

Adrian Johnston, Boštjan Nedoh and Alenka Zupančič
Albuquerque and Ljubljana, March 2021

Notes on Contributors

Aleš Bunta is a Research Fellow at the Research Centre of the Slovenian Academy of Sciences and Arts, Institute of Philosophy, Ljubljana, and a lecturer at the ZRC SAZU Postgraduate School. He is the author of numerous *paper*s and three books in Slovene: *To Annihilate Nothing?* (Analecta, 2007), *The Magnetism of Stupidity: Plato, Erasmus of Rotterdam, Alan Ford* (Analecta, 2010; Croatian translation: Ljevak, 2012) and *A-cogito* (Analecta, 2016).

Mladen Dolar is Professor and Senior Research Fellow at the Department of Philosophy, University of Ljubljana. His principal areas of research are psychoanalysis, modern French philosophy, German idealism and art theory. He has lectured extensively at universities in the USA and across Europe and is the author of over 150 papers in scholarly journals and collected volumes. Apart from fourteen books in Slovene his book publications include most notably *A Voice and Nothing More* (MIT 2006, translated into nine languages) and *Opera's Second Death* (with Slavoj Žižek, Routledge, 2001, also translated into several languages). His new book *The Riskiest Moment* is forthcoming with Duke University Press. He is one of the founders of the 'Ljubljana Lacanian School'.

Cara S. Greene is a 4th year PhD student in the Philosophy Department at the University of New Mexico in Albuquerque, New Mexico. In 2015, Cara received a Master's degree in Critical Theory and the Arts from the School of Visual Arts in New York City, with a focus on Aesthetics and Social Theory. In 2012, Cara received a Bachelor's degree from Colorado College with a major in Philosophy and a minor in Psychoanalysis. Her philosophical areas of specialisation include Nineteenth- and Twentieth-Century Continental Philosophy, Critical Theory, Psychoanalysis and

Phenomenology. She is currently working on a dissertation on Hegel and modern sacrifice.

Amanda Holmes is an Assistant Professor in the Philosophy Department at the University of Applied Arts, Vienna. Her work is situated at the intersection of psychoanalysis and philosophy. She received her PhD in Philosophy from Villanova University in 2020 and has authored numerous *paper*s on desire, language and being. She is currently drafting her first book project, tentatively titled *Lacanian Erotology*.

Adrian Johnston is Chair of and Distinguished Professor in the Department of Philosophy at the University of New Mexico at Albuquerque and a faculty member at the Emory Psychoanalytic Institute in Atlanta. His most recent books are *Irrepressible Truth: On Lacan's 'The Freudian Thing'* (Palgrave Macmillan, 2017), *A New German Idealism: Hegel, Žižek, and Dialectical Materialism* (Columbia University Press, 2018) and *Prolegomena to Any Future Materialism, Volume Two: A Weak Nature Alone* (Northwestern University Press, 2019). With Todd McGowan and Slavoj Žižek, he is a co-editor of the book series *Diaeresis* at Northwestern University Press.

Peter Klepec is a Research Adviser at the Research Centre of the Slovenian Academy of Sciences and Arts, Institute of Philosophy, Ljubljana. His main areas of research are contemporary French philosophy, German idealism and Lacanian psychoanalysis. He is the author of many *paper*s or essays and of three books in Slovene: *On the Emergence of the Subject* (ZRC, 2004), *Profitable Passions. Capitalism and Perversion 1* (Analecta, 2008; Serbian translation: Biblioteka Theoria, 2016) and, most recently, *Matrices of Subjection. Capitalism and Perversion 2* (Analecta, 2019).

Paul M. Livingston teaches philosophy at the University of New Mexico in Albuquerque. He is the sole author of four books, most recently *The Logic of Being: Realism, Truth, and Time* (Northwestern University Press, 2017), and the co-author, with Andrew Cutrofello, of *The Problems of Contemporary Philosophy* (Polity, 2015). His current project is a logical investigation of the problem of the one and many, primarily as it occurs in analytic philosophy, Platonism and Indo-Tibetan Madhyamaka thought.

Boštjan Nedoh is a Research Fellow at the Research Centre of the Slovenian Academy of Sciences and Arts, Institute of Philosophy, Ljubljana. He is the co-editor (with Andreja Zevnik) of the volume *Lacan and Deleuze: A Disjunctive Synthesis* (Edinburgh University Press, 2017) and the author of the book *Ontology and Perversion: Deleuze, Agamben, Lacan* (Rowman & Littlefield International, 2019).

Frank Ruda is Senior Lecturer in Philosophy at the University of Dundee, Scotland. With Rebecca Comay he is the author of *The Dash – the Other Side of Absolute Knowing* (MIT Press, 2018), and with Agon Hamza and Slavoj Žižek of *Reading Marx* (Politiy, 2018) and *Reading Marx* (Polity, 2021). He is also the author of several monographs, including *Abolishing Freedom: A Plea for a Contemporary Use of Fatalism* (Nebraska University Press, 2018) and *Indifference and Repetition* (2022).

Samo Tomšič holds a PhD in Philosophy and is a Research Associate at the Humboldt University Berlin, Germany and visiting professor at the University of Ljubljana, Slovenia. His research areas comprise psychoanalysis, structuralism, political philosophy and epistemology. He is the author of *The Capitalist Unconscious: Marx and Lacan* (Verso, 2015) and *The Labour of Enjoyment, Towards a Critique of Libidinal Economy* (August Verlag, 2019).

Tadej Troha is a Research Fellow at the Research Centre of the Slovenian Academy of Sciences and Arts, Institute of Philosophy, Ljubljana, and an Assistant Professor at the Department of Educational Sciences, Faculty of Arts, University of Ljubljana. His research interests include Freudian and Lacanian psychoanalysis, ethics, political philosophy and modernist literature. He is the author of two books in Slovene: *Neither Miracle Nor Miracle* (Analecta, 2009) and *Interventions into the Irreversible* (Analecta, 2015).

Slavoj Žižek holds a PhD in Philosophy at the University of Ljubljana and in Psychoanalysis at the Université Paris VIII, and is Senior Researcher at the Department of Philosophy, University of Ljubljana and International Director at the Institute for Humanities, University of London. His latest publications include *Hegel in a Wired Brain* (Bloomsbury, 2020) and *Pandemic 2: Chronicles of a Time Lost* (Or Books and Polity Press, 2020).

Alenka Zupančič is a Slovene philosopher and social theorist. She is a Research Advisor at the Research Centre of the Slovenian Academy of Sciences and Arts, Institute of Philosophy, Ljubljana. She is also professor at the European Graduate School in Switzerland. Notable for her work on the intersection of philosophy and psychoanalysis, she is the author of numerous *paper*s and books, including *Ethics of the Real: Kant and Lacan* (Verso, 2000), *The Shortest Shadow: Nietzsche's Philosophy of the Two* (MIT Press, 2003), *Why Psychoanalysis: Three Interventions* (NSU Press, 2008), *The Odd One In: On Comedy* (MIT Press, 2008) and, most recently, *What is Sex?* (MIT Press, 2017).

Introduction: Beyond the Nominalism-Realism Divide: Objective Fictions from Bentham through Marx to Lacan

Adrian Johnston, Boštjan Nedoh and Alenka Zupančič

WHEN IT COMES to questions of objectivity in current philosophical debates and public discourse, we are witnessing the re-emergence and growing importance of two classical, opposed approaches: nominalism and (metaphysical) realism. Today's nominalist stances, by absolutising intersubjectivity, are moving towards the abandonment of the very notion of truth and objective reality. By contrast, today's realist positions, including those bound up with scientific discourse, insist on the category of the 'object-in-itself' as irreducible to any kind of subjective mediation. However, despite their apparent mutual exclusivity, both nominalism and realism, paradoxically yet not surprisingly, coincide regarding one point: they both imply an absolute and clean separation between the domains of objectivity and subjectivity, between the 'object-in-itself' and subjective mediation, and, ultimately, between truth and fiction.

From the point of view of the history of philosophy, it could be said that the opposition between nominalism and (metaphysical) realism can be – at least to some extent – traced back to the very origins of philosophy. If a necessary condition of the Platonic theory of Ideas as ideal forms was the exit from the cave as the realm of shadows, this very same exit actually laid the ground for the classical metaphysical distinction between two neatly separated words, namely that of appearances and that of truth/essence. Whether the main achievement of Plato's allegory of the cave was to provide the concept of Idea/truth, or the invention of fiction – in the sense that the Idea constitutes the very measure with respect to which we are able to recognise the fictitious world of the cave's shadows as fictitious – is of secondary importance. What is probably most interesting is that Socrates was, in fact, the first philosophical 'victim' of the opposition he set up. As Mladen Dolar shows in his essay in this volume, Socrates may well be the most ferocious advocate of truth, yet this did not prevent him from being convicted on the basis of rumours and gossip, which are by definition without any precise (subjective) bearer – 'the rumour has IT', as Dolar puts it, referring to the Freudian impersonal speech of the unconscious. Yet, as the case of Socrates's trial shows, fictitious entities like rumours and gossip, despite them being fictions in the sense that they do not claim to refer to factual truth (rumour is a rumour), they nevertheless have the objective status of elements that truly structure the existing reality; to some extent they are even the products of this same reality. This is why they deserve to be called *objective fictions*. As such, they are perhaps even more true than the truth of the gods of metaphysics, if we consider their fatal consequences for Socrates.

Despite this poignant reminder of the high price that philosophy paid for ignoring the power of objective fictions, contemporary nominalist and realist trends both seem to continue to ignore it – and, hence, to repress the fundamental deadlock traversing their own past rather than addressing it.

Differently from these prevailing trends which presuppose a clear-cut distinction between objectivity (object, truth) and subjectivity (subject, fiction), or else aim at abandoning this distinction altogether and declaring everything that takes place as 'objective', the main conceptual figure of this volume is *objective fiction*. This figure does not simply blur the lines between the two categories, but draws our attention to the antagonistic, *contradictory* character of objective reality itself as something objective.

Thus the term 'objective fiction' refers not only to fictions and similar phenomena, which constitute the necessary integral parts of either forms of knowledge or objective reality, parts without which this very same knowledge or reality would disintegrate. More importantly, this term also refers to fictions that are the products of this objective reality itself. Recall the Marxist concept of 'commodity fetishism' or, on a different level, Lacan's definition of the big Other (*qua* symbolic order) as that 'which has a body and does not exist':[1] these fantasmic entities are not simply subjective illusions nor subjective mediations, but constitute the core of the structure of objective *and* subjective reality themselves, their short-circuit. This means that these entities are the effects of a negativity – contradictions and gaps – within reality itself, and one cannot simply remove them from reality without the latter disintegrating.

The structure of objective fictions is articulated and elaborated in this volume by relying mainly on those *materialist* theoretical traditions (Marxism and psychoanalysis *in primis*) which never accepted the straightforward distinction between the spheres of subjectivity and objectivity, or between fiction and truth, but instead prioritised the concepts of *universality* and *contradiction* as *sublations* of both domains. As such, these traditions are irreducible to the nominalism-realism divide. This perhaps might be regarded as a crucial distinctive feature of a truly materialist concept: in prioritising the structural paradoxes or contradictions of objective reality (of which the subject and subjective as well as the fictitious and fictional are integral parts), a sharp distinction between objectivity and subjectivity, as well as between truth and fiction, is simply inoperative.

In the remainder of this introduction, we will try to outline the basic structure and logic of objective fiction via a discussion triangulating three thinkers: Marx, Lacan and Bentham. Indeed, as will become apparent in a moment, Bentham's *Theory of Fictions* not only foreshadows core features of this volume's conceptual leitmotif (i.e. objective fictions). Benthamite philosophy also surprisingly establishes core connections between both Marxist and Lacanian approaches to the topic of fictions, with these two orientations being central for the chapters to follow here.

In fact – and to be more precise – Lacan functions as a marriage broker bringing together the odd couple of Bentham *avec* Marx. What makes this Lacan-facilitated rapprochement between Bentham and Marx odd (i.e. surprising) is Marx's scathing hostility towards Bentham's utilitarianism, with its philosophical (mis)treatments of socio-economic, political and legal phenomena.

Two mentions of Bentham in the first volume of *Das Kapital* succinctly and powerfully convey Marx's acidic scorn for Benthamite utilitarianism. Marx, at the end of Part Two ('The Transformation of Money into Capital') of his 1867 *magnum opus*, famously inserts Bentham's name into a sarcastic characterisation of capitalism's marketplaces, including its job markets. Bentham enjoys the dubious honour of being both the only proper name and the last term of the series consisting of the preceding terms 'Freedom, Equality, Property . . .'[2] Marx treats Bentham's name as synonymous with the horrifically pitiless selfishness of Dickensian England.

Later in *Capital, Volume One*, a long footnote contained in Chapter Twenty-Four heaps derision on Bentham's head.[3] Marx dismisses Benthamite utilitarianism as a crude ideological false naturalisation of the capitalist interests peculiar to modern industrialism. At the end of this lambasting of Bentham, Marx concludes, 'I should call Mr. Jeremy a genius in the way of bourgeois stupidity.'[4] Bentham ingeniously, although unintentionally, lays bare the mindlessly brutal greed of industrial England's ruling class.

Yet, despite Marx's pronounced aversion to Bentham, Lacan's psychoanalytic reflections on the latter's 1813–15 *Theory of Fictions* disclose an unexpected cross-resonance between Marx and Bentham. Specifically, Lacan enables a link to be established between Benthamite 'fictions' (about which more will be said shortly) and Marxian 'real abstractions'. Although the phrase 'real abstractions' typically is credited to Alfred Sohn-Rethel,[5] it nicely captures a motif readily discernible in Marx's own writings.[6] This motif is nothing other than what Žižek, in his contribution opening this volume, labels 'Marx's Theory of Fictions', a title fortuitously calling to mind Bentham's *Theory of Fictions* (and, in 1993's *Tarrying with the Negative*, Žižek provides a lucid examination of Lacan's reading of this Bentham[7]).

Borrowing a phrase from Hegel's *Science of Logic*, one fairly could say that capitalism in its virtual entirety is, for Marx, a 'realm of shadows'.[8] Or, in still more Hegelian language that Marx himself deploys, the capitalist universe is an 'inverted world' (*verkehrte Welt*). In this topsy-turvy place where seemingly everything is upside-down, subjectivity appears in the guise of objectivity (through the 'thingification' [*Verdinglichkung*] of reification), objectivity appears in the guise of subjectivity (via the fetishisms of capital and commodities treating lifeless things, instead of labouring subjects, as the active agents of the capitalist mode of production) and, in general, various fictions replace realities.

However, these Marxian fictions are limited neither to illusory-*qua*-epiphenomenal surface appearances, as the hollow lies of capitalism's ideologies, nor to the epistemology of the historical materialist analysis of capitalism, with the abstract theoretical categories of its critique of political economy. That is to say, these fictions are not mere matters of ideological and/or critical thinking (along the lines of a strict separation between thinking and being). Rather, they are concrete components integral to the very being of capitalist reality in and of itself. They must be recognised as part and parcel of the inventory of the social ontology of capitalism.

Within the capitalist socio-economic system, relations between persons really are (and do not just seem to be) reduced to relations between things; labour really does become abstract in the form of available, fungible, de-skilled bodies with nothing but quantities of purchasable time; individuals really are reduced to the status of simple bearers (*Träger*) or personifications of trans-individual class roles; and inhuman circuits of capital flows really do escape from control by those conjuring with them. In short, such abstractions as are involved with fetishism, reification, alienation and the like are all-too-real aspects of life under capitalism. Hence they are real abstractions. Or, as per the title of the present volume, these ideological and theoretical fictions are (also) 'objective fictions'. As Lacan would put it, these fictions have legs; they march in the streets (*à la* Lacan's pointed rebuttal of the May '68 slogan 'Structures don't march in the streets').[9] Capitalism's fictions walk among us, sometimes even walking about as us, with them impersonating us and/or us impersonating them.

But what about Lacan and the connection he makes possible between Marx and Bentham? At this juncture, a selective parsing of Bentham's *Theory of Fictions* is requisite before turning to Lacan's comments on this work. In line with the prevailing sensibilities of early-modern British philosophy, Bentham adheres to a specific constellation of philosophical positions. His utilitarianism, encompassing ethics, politics and law, is bound up with an empiricist epistemology as well as a nominalist ontology. An awareness of Bentham's combination of utilitarianism, at the level of practical philosophy, with both empiricism and nominalism, at the level of theoretical philosophy, is necessary for an appreciation of the contents of his *Theory of Fictions*.

Lacan repeatedly stresses that the Benthamite notion of the fictitious is inseparable from and indispensable to utilitarianism.[10] He portrays Bentham as pushing utilitarianism to 'its logical extreme',[11] including in *Theory of Fictions* specifically.[12] However, Lacan's remarks here aside – they will come up again below – the likely initial impression for a first-time reader of *Theory of Fictions*, especially one unfamiliar with the rest of Bentham's corpus, is of a doctrine pushing nominalism to its logical extreme.

For Bentham's hyper-nominalist ontology, the domain of true reality is extremely small and restricted. Only tangible 'substances' perceived in the (supposed) immediacy of the here and now as individuated objects of the senses are deemed by Bentham to be 'real entities'. The vastly wider scope of everything else presumably under the sun would be, in one way or another, fictitious.

A perusal of Bentham's *Theory of Fictions* reveals that, for the author, any general concept, category, class or set over and above nominalism's sensory-perceptual particulars counts as a 'fiction'. Hence a far-from-exhaustive list of Benthamite fictional entities would include: qualities distinct from and predicable of a plurality of particular substances;[13] time as the omnipresent milieu of all unique happenings;[14] existence as the universal status of any and all beings as merely existing;[15] modal categories (possibility, necessity, contingency, etc.);[16] nature as designating the entirety of the physical universe;[17] common nouns grouping together innumerable individuals; prescriptive/normative terms for values, principles, ideals and the like; and anything else that is not an individuated sensible thing perceived by conscious experience in the *hic et nunc*. Bentham's strict adherence to nominalism compels him to broaden the notion of the fictitious to cover a mind-bogglingly wide range of topics.

Given the dizzying array of fictional entities in Bentham's *Theory of Fictions*, one already senses that Bentham cannot conflate the fictitious in his broad meaning with the deceptive. Indeed, he explicitly notes that far from all fictions in his sense are deceptions.[18] Lacan underscores this point in his comments on Bentham's account of the fictional.[19]

Early on in *Theory of Fictions*, Bentham tightly tethers the fictitious to the linguistic. Perhaps not by coincidence, it is a linguist, the great structuralist Roman Jakobson no less, who alerts Lacan to Bentham's *Theory of Fictions*.[20] Bentham, in line with his nominalism, asserts that, 'To language, then – to language alone – it is, that fictitious entities owe their existence; their impossible, yet indispensable, existence.'[21] He subsequently characterises the fictitious as 'a necessary resource'.[22] Even later, Bentham maintains:

> By *fictitious entities* are here meant, not any of those which will be presented by the name of *fabulous*, i.e. imaginary *persons*, such as *Heathen Gods*, *Genii*, and *Fairies*, but such as *quality – property* (in the sense in which it is nearly synonymous to *quality*), *relation*, *power*, *obligation*, *duty*, *right*, and so forth. Incorrect as it would be if the entities in question were considered as being, in point of reality, upon a footing with *real* entities . . . the supposition of a sort of *verbal* reality, so to speak, as belonging to these fictitious entities is a supposition without which the matter of language could never have been formed, nor between man and man any converse carried on other than such as hath place between brute and brute.[23]

Bentham's distinction between the fictitious and the fabulous neatly maps onto Lacan's distinction between the Symbolic and the Imaginary respectively.[24] From the (problematic) perspective of a hard-nosed, unromantic utilitarian, it would seem that humanity could very well do without the fabulous-Imaginary. Such unreal products of the picture-thinking of daydreaming, fantasising, etc. ostensibly lack the sort of concrete use-value (i.e. 'utility') privileged by utilitarianism's cold calculations of costs and benefits. These creations of the imagination would be nothing more than whimsical frippery played with by children and artists. Yet, even prior to the advent of psychoanalysis and its crucial contributions to a critical reassessment of the fiction-reality contrast, the classical Marxist theory of ideology already suggests that fabulous entities are not without their significant usefulness for established realities (in the case of historical materialism, economically based social orders).

In relation to what is conveyed by Bentham in the preceding block quotation, Lacan latches onto the idea of the '*verbal* reality' of fictional (as distinction from fabulous) entities.[25] Following Bentham's tethering of the fictional to the linguistic, Lacan observes that Benthamite fictions are to be situated 'at the level of the signifier'.[26] Again, Bentham's fictional entities should be located within the Lacanian register of the Symbolic. Just as Lacan identifies properly human subjects as 'speaking beings' (*parlêtres*), with socio-symbolic mediation constitutive of humanity as different-in-kind from animality, so too does Bentham already propose that the '*verbal* reality' of languages' fictional entities transforms the voiceless, grunting animal (i.e. 'brute') into the loquacious, gregarious human (i.e. 'man').

Midway through the passage just quoted from *Theory of Fictions*, Bentham further nuances matters by indicating that the fictional shares features with both the fabulous and the real. Like fabulous entities, fictional entities are unreal measured against nominalism's (restrictive) standard of reality. But, like real entities, fictional entities are invaluable and irreplaceable for the practical tasks of navigating both natural and social realities. As seen, Bentham insists on linguistic fictions' 'impossible, yet indispensable, existence' and them being 'a necessary resource'. Later on in *Theory of Fictions*, when addressing political and legal entitlements and obligations, he describes the fictitious entity 'right' as 'a fiction so necessary that without it human discourse could not be carried on'.[27] Bentham's 'discourse' arguably is cognate with the later Lacan's '*discours*' as designating not just language and linguistic intercourse, but the 'social links' (*liens sociaux*) of institutions, practices and relationships with which languages are inextricably intertwined.[28]

Fiction-facilitated practicalities, especially of a social sort, are precisely what Bentham's utilitarianism prioritises. In the same preceding quotation, over half the examples Bentham gives for fictitious entities (i.e. '*power, obligation, duty, right*') pertain to state and juridical domains. Indeed, Bentham's initial impetus for composing his *Theory of Fictions* comes from his consideration of 'legal fictions' specifically.[29] Thus the Lacanian emphasis on the strong bond between utility and fiction for Bentham is quite justified. Relatedly, as Lacan's favourite book,[30] Oscar Bloch and Walther von Wartburg's *Dictionnaire étymologique de la langue française*, documents, the French word '*jouissance*' carries with it the legal connotation of a property owner's right to use what he/she owns.[31] Lacan explicitly invokes this strand of the etymology of *jouissance*, enjoyment *qua* usufruct, as involved in his own metapsychological employment of this word.[32]

In *Seminar XI* (*The Four Fundamental Concepts of Psychoanalysis* (1964)), Lacan mentions in passing that Freud himself, in both his theory and practice, relies on constructs akin to fictions *à la* Bentham.[33] Lacan has in mind specific moments in Freud's later work. In 1933's *New Introductory Lectures on Psycho-Analysis*, Freud confesses:

> The theory of the instincts [*Die Trieblehre*] is so to say our mythology [*unsere Mythologie*]. Instincts [*Die Triebe*] are mythical entities [*mythische Wesen*], magnificent in their indefiniteness [*Unbestimmtheit*]. In our work we cannot for a moment disregard them, yet we are never sure that we are seeing them clearly.[34]

Contemporaneous with this confession, Freud, in a letter to Albert Einstein, writes:

> It may perhaps seem to you as though our theories are a kind of mythology [*eine Art von Mythologie*] . . . But does not every science [*Naturwissenschaft*] come in the end to a kind of mythology like this? Cannot the same be said to-day of your own Physics?[35]

And, in 1937's 'Analysis Terminable and Interminable', he portrays analytic metapsychology in its entirety as a 'witch', quoting from Part One, Scene Six of Goethe's *Faust* in so doing ('We must call the Witch to our help after all!'):

> We can only say: 'So muss denn doch die Hexe dran!' – the Witch Metapsychology [*Die Hexe Metapsychologie nämlich*]. Without metapsychological speculation and theorizing – I had almost said 'phantasying' [*Phantasieren*] – we shall not get another step forward.[36]

Central aspects of what one could call 'Freud's Theory of Fictions' are on full display in these quoted remarks. He goes so far as to depict metapsychology as a whole, the overarching conceptual framework for all of psychoanalysis including its clinical labours, as a system of speculative fantasies or theoretical mythologies, namely a network of fictions.

Yet, in a likely unintended and tacit echoing of Bentham's *Theory of Fictions*, this same Freud emphasises the unavoidability and indispensability of these speculative fantasies for both the theory and practice of analysis. Hence Freud's metapsychological concepts are fictitious entities in Bentham's precise sense (i.e. as neither fabulous nor real entities). Furthermore, Bentham almost certainly would concur with Freud when the latter surmises that even the most rigorous empirical, experimental sciences of nature, such as the mathematised physics epitomised by Einstein himself with its hypothetical formal models, themselves are built up on the basis of fictional entities serving as grounding categories and concepts for these disciplines (apropos modern natural science, recall that Bentham treats time, nature, etc. as fictional entities). Finally, in good Benthamite fashion, Freud foregrounds the precious utility of his metapsychological fictions, his foundational analytic mythologies and fantasies.

The immediately preceding risks prompting one to conclude that, for Freud, 'the Witch Metapsychology' is theoretically legitimate and practically necessary only at the subjective-epistemological level of the theorising and practising analyst. However, as witnessed above with respect to Marx, the fictitious entities of the historical materialist critique of (capitalist) political economy are not just intellectual abstractions at the epistemological level of thinking, but also are real abstractions at the ontological level of being. Likewise, in the case of Freud, the fictitious entities of psychoanalytic metapsychology are as much woven into the concrete lived existences of analysands and all human subjects (*qua parlêtres*) as they are baked into the reflections of those subjects who happen to be analytic thinkers and clinicians. As with Marx's fictions, so too with Freud's: they are objective-ontological-real, not merely subjective-epistemological-ideal, fictions.

Lacan implicitly makes this same point about the objectivity of Freudian fictitious entities in another of his glosses on Bentham. In *Seminar XX* (*Encore* (1972–73)), he employs his psychoanalytic appropriation of Bentham's *Theory of Fictions* to argue that subjects as such (i.e. as speaking beings enmeshed in the social links of discourses) utilise the fictitious entities that are the signifiers of the socio-linguistic symbolic order as means to the end of *jouissance*.[37] Combining the Lacanian renditions of both Bentham and Marx, one could say that, for this Lacan, the utility of signifiers resides in their *jouissance*-value.

Another issue Lacan raises with respect to Bentham's *Theory of Fictions* involves bringing this Bentham into connection with one of Lacan's central psychoanalytic theses. In both *Seminar VII* (*The Ethics of Psychoanalysis* (1959–60)) and *Seminar XVI* (*From an Other to the other* (1968–69)),[38] he ties the fictitious as per Benthamite utilitarianism to his one-liner according to which, 'every truth has the structure of fiction' (*toute vérité a une structure de fiction*).[39] In the '*verbal* reality' of the analysand's free-associational monologues, the core truths of the unconscious usually reveal themselves in the form of fictions. Unconscious truth articulates itself in the intricately configured language of dreams, fantasies and lies, among other phenomena constituting familiar parts of the day-to-day details of the analyst's clinical work.

The present volume could be encapsulated with a complementary inversion of Lacan's aphorism having it that 'truth has the structure of fiction': fiction has the structure of truth. More precisely, objective fictions organise and sustain what is taken to be reality in all its nitty-gritty concreteness. As already indicated above, and as will be amply illustrated throughout the contributions to this volume (contributions addressing such figures as Kant (Greene), Nietzsche (Bunta), Wittgenstein (Livingston), Koyré (Tomšič, Ruda) and Badiou (Klepec) in addition to Bentham, Hegel, Marx, Freud (Troha) and Lacan), these fictions come in an array of guises: not only dreams, fantasies and lies but also artistic and cultural products, commodity and sexual fetishes (Johnston), games of myriad sorts (Holmes), unverified but always circulating rumours impacting our lives (Dolar), the rhetorical manipulations of sophistry (Klepec), values both economic and ethical (Nedoh), and even the conspiracy theories proliferating in today's all-too-non-epiphenomenal virtual reality of social media (Zupančič), among other subjects.

As per Bentham's hyper-nominalism and its linkages to Marxian real abstractions via Lacan's commentaries on the *Theory of Fictions*, very little of what human beings count as 'reality' is free of fictions. In fact, quite the contrary – the fictitious makes up the vast bulk of what we inhabit as the concretely real. In the standard, commonsensical impression of the fiction-reality pair, the fictitious is taken to be subjective and marginal by comparison with the real as objective and central. This volume reveals that the exact opposite is actually the case.

At the heart of Hegel's philosophy lies a well-known intellectual sensibility: when an established conceptual opposition oscillates, when its poles reverse positions and/or blur into each other, this opposition needs to be overcome in the manner of a sublation (*Aufhebung*). The opposition between metaphysical realism and nominalism originates with the ancient Greeks, becomes central to the Medievals and continues on through modernity up until today. But, combining the just-mentioned Hegelian sensibility with the Bentham-Marx-Lacan triangulation as laid out in the preceding, the opposition between metaphysical realism and nominalism is ripe for a renewed effort at being sublated after Hegel's own attempts to sublate it.

Bentham's pushing of nominalism to its extremes results in a theory to the effect that the realities of human knowledge, institutions and relationships are shot through with fictions indispensable for all theory and practice. The Benthamite-utilitarian real world in all its tangible weight is what it is thanks to the shining through within it of ideal beings (i.e. fictitious entities) existing and accessible only in and through linguistic and conceptual mediums. Portrayed thusly, Bentham, with his *Theory of Fictions*, unwittingly brings about the dialectical coincidence of the opposites of nominalism and metaphysical realism – with the latter's classical Platonic allegory of the cave, theory of forms/ideas and doctrine of participation being uncannily and inadvertently echoed in Bentham's hyper-nominalist account of fictitious entities. Both poles of the traditional ontological realism-nominalism dichotomy converge in a thesis according to which what we (mis)take to be really real in truth relies on the subtle participation of abstractions discernible solely via careful theoretical scrutiny. This convergence signals an imperative to sublate the very dichotomy between nominalism and metaphysical realism. This sublation, however, can be achieved only in a materialist way: by thinking objective fictions as the effects of negativity (contradictions and gaps) within reality itself. The present volume's chapters are united in being contributions to the forging of a new theory of objective fictions rising to the challenge of this precise task in the contemporary conjuncture.

Notes

1. Jacques Lacan, *The Seminar of Jacques Lacan, Book XVII: The Other Side of Psychoanalysis, 1969–70*, ed. Jacques-Alain Miller, trans. Russell Grigg (New York: W. W. Norton, 2007), p. 66. This peculiar structure of the Other as locus of the inscription of truth is what enables that 'everything of that order, the false, even lies [. . .] only exist on the foundation of truth' (p. 187). This actually repeats Lacan's point made in *Seminar XI* that we can lie/deceive by (half-)saying the truth, as in the famous Jewish joke where one Jew tells another that he is catching the train to Lemberg: 'Why are you telling me you are going to Lemberg, the other replies, since

you really are going there, and that, if you are telling me this, it is so that I shall think that you are going to Cracow?' (Jacques Lacan, *The Seminar of Jacques Lacan, Book XI: The Four Fundamental Concepts of Psychoanalysis, 1964*, ed. Jacques-Alain Miller, trans. Alan Sheridan (New York: W. W. Norton, 1977), p. 139.
2. Karl Marx, *Capital: A Critique of Political Economy, Volume One*, trans. Ben Fowkes (New York: Penguin, 1976), p. 280.
3. Marx, *Capital, Volume One*, pp. 758–9.
4. Marx, *Capital, Volume One*, p. 759.
5. Alfred Sohn-Rethel, *Intellectual and Manual Labour: A Critique of Epistemology*, trans. Martin Sohn-Rethel (London: Macmillan, 1978), pp. 6–8, 17, 20–1, 28–9, 57, 60–1, 74, 77–8.
6. Karl Marx, *Critique of Hegel's Doctrine of the State*, *Early Writings*, trans. Rodney Livingstone and Gregor Benton (New York: Penguin, 1975), p. 161; Karl Marx, *Grundrisse: Foundations of the Critique of Political Economy (Rough Draft)*, trans. Martin Nicolaus (New York: Penguin, 1973), pp. 85, 88, 100–2, 104–5, 142–6, 157, 164, 331, 449–50, 831–2; Karl Marx, *A Contribution to the Critique of Political Economy*, ed. Maurice Dobb, trans. S. W. Ryazanskaya (New York: International, 1970), pp. 30–1, 49; Marx, *Capital, Volume One*, pp. 739, 909; Karl Marx, *Capital: A Critique of Political Economy, Volume Two*, trans. David Fernbach (New York: Penguin, 1992), p. 185; Karl Marx, *Capital: A Critique of Political Economy, Volume Three*, trans. David Fernbach (New York: Penguin, 1981), pp. 275, 596–7, 603.
7. Slavoj Žižek, *Tarrying with the Negative: Kant, Hegel, and the Critique of Ideology* (Durham, NC: Duke University Press, 1993), pp. 85–8.
8. G. W. F. Hegel, *The Science of Logic*, trans. George di Giovanni (Cambridge: Cambridge University Press, 2010), 21.42 (p. 37).
9. Lacan, *Seminar XVII*, pp. 14–55.
10. Jacques Lacan, *The Seminar of Jacques Lacan, Book VII: The Ethics of Psychoanalysis, 1959–60*, ed. Jacques-Alain Miller, trans. Dennis Porter (New York: W. W. Norton, 1992), p. 242; Jacques Lacan, *Le Séminaire de Jacques Lacan, Livre XVI: D'un Autre à l'autre, 1968–69*, ed. Jacques-Alain Miller (Paris: Éditions du Seuil, 2006), p. 190; Jacques Lacan, *The Seminar of Jacques Lacan, Book XX: Encore, 1972–73*, ed. Jacques-Alain Miller, trans. Bruce Fink (New York: W. W. Norton, 1998), pp. 3, 58.
11. Jacques Lacan, *The Seminar of Jacques Lacan, Book II: The Ego in Freud's Theory and in the Technique of Psychoanalysis, 1954–55*, ed. Jacques-Alain Miller, trans. Sylvana Tomaselli (New York: W. W. Norton, 1988), p. 9.
12. Lacan, *Séminaire XVI*, p. 190.
13. Jeremy Bentham, *The Theory of Fictions*, in C. K. Ogden, *Bentham's Theory of Fictions* (New York: Harcourt, Brace, 1932), p. 19.
14. Bentham, *The Theory of Fictions*, pp. 20–1.

15. Bentham, *The Theory of Fictions*, p. 50.
16. Bentham, *The Theory of Fictions*, p. 51.
17. Bentham, *The Theory of Fictions*, p. 134.
18. Bentham, *The Theory of Fictions*, p. 118.
19. Lacan, *Seminar VII*, p. 12; Lacan, *Séminaire XVI*, p. 190.
20. Lacan, *Seminar VII*, p. 12.
21. Bentham, *The Theory of Fictions*, p. 15.
22. Bentham, *The Theory of Fictions*, p. 73.
23. Bentham, *The Theory of Fictions*, p. 137.
24. Žižek, *Tarrying with the Negative*, p. 87.
25. Lacan, *Seminar XX*, p. 118.
26. Lacan, *Seminar VII*, p. 228.
27. Bentham, *The Theory of Fictions*, p. 118.
28. Lacan, *Seminar XVII*, pp. 12–13; Jacques Lacan, *The Seminar of Jacques Lacan, Book XIX: . . . or Worse, 1971–72*, ed. Jacques-Alain Miller, trans. A. R. Price (Cambridge: Polity, 2018), pp. 30, 131–3, 205; Lacan, *Seminar XX*, pp. 17, 30, 54; Jacques Lacan, *Le Séminaire de Jacques Lacan, Livre XXI: Les non-dupes errent, 1973–74* (unpublished typescript), 12/11/73, 1/15/74, 4/9/74, 5/21/74.
29. Bentham, *The Theory of Fictions*, pp. 141–50.
30. Lacan, *Séminaire XVI*, p. 179.
31. Oscar Bloch and Walther von Wartburg, *Dictionnaire étymologique de la langue française* (Paris: Presses Universitaires de France, 2016, 4e tirage), p. 352.
32. Jacques Lacan, *The Seminar of Jacques Lacan, Book VI: Desire and Its Interpretation, 1958–59*, ed. Jacques-Alain Miller, trans. Bruce Fink (Cambridge: Polity, 2019), p. 105.
33. Lacan, *Seminar XI*, p. 163.
34. Sigmund Freud, *Gesammelte Werke* (*GW*), ed. E. Bibring, W. Hoffer, E. Kris and O. Isakower (Frankfurt: S. Fischer, 1952), *GW* 15: 101; Sigmund Freud, *The Standard Edition of the Complete Psychological Works of Sigmund Freud* (*SE*), 24 volumes, ed. and trans. James Strachey, in collaboration with Anna Freud, assisted by Alix Strachey and Alan Tyson (London: Hogarth Press and the Institute of Psycho-Analysis, 1953–74), *SE* 22: 95.
35. *GW* 16: 22; *SE* 22: 211.
36. *GW* 16: 69; *SE* 23: 225.
37. Lacan, *Seminar XX*, pp. 58–9.
38. Lacan, *Séminaire XVI*, p. 190.
39. Jacques Lacan, *Le Séminaire de Jacques Lacan, Livre VII: L'éthique de la psychanalyse, 1959–60*, ed. Jacques-Alain Miller (Paris: Éditions du Seuil, 1986), p. 21; Lacan, *Seminar VII*, p. 12.

| Marx's Theory of Fictions
Slavoj Žižek

THERE ARE IN Marx's *Capital* long passages which deal with the necessary role of fiction in capitalist reproduction, from commodity fetishism as a fiction which is part of social reality itself to the topic of fictitious capital introduced in *Capital, Volume Two* and elaborated in *Capital, Volume Three*. The three volumes of Capital reproduce the triad of the universal, the particular and the individual: *Capital, Volume One* articulates the abstract-universal matrix (concept) of capital; *Capital, Volume Two* shifts to particularity, to the actual life of capital in all its contingent complexity; *Capital, Volume Three* deploys the individuality of the total process of capital. In recent years, the most productive studies of Marx's critique of political economy have focused on *Capital, Volume Two* – why? In a letter sent to Engels on 30 April 1868, Marx wrote:

> In Book 1 [...] we content ourselves with the assumption that if in the self-expansion process £100 becomes £110, the latter will find *already in existence in the market* the elements into which it will change once more. But now we investigate the conditions under which these elements are found at hand, namely the social intertwining of the different capitals, of the component parts of capital and of revenue (= s).

Two features are crucial here, which are the two sides of the same coin. On the one hand, Marx passes from the pure notional structure of capital's reproduction (described in *Volume One*) to reality, in which the capital's reproduction involves temporal gaps, dead time, etc. There are dead times that interrupt smooth reproduction, and the ultimate cause of these dead times is that we are not dealing with a single reproductive cycle, but with an intertwinement of multiple circles of reproduction which are never fully coordinated. These dead periods are not just an empirical complication but an immanent necessity; they are necessary for reproduction, but they complicate the actual life of capital.[1] On the other hand, fiction intervenes here (in the guise of fictitious capital, whose notion is further elaborated in the third volume of *Capital*); fiction is needed to overcome the destructive potential of complications, delays, dead periods, so that, when we pass from pure logical matrix to actual life, to reality, fiction has to intervene.

The second volume of *Capital* focuses on the problem of realising surplus value, disrupted first and foremost by time and distance. As Marx put it, during its circulation time, capital does not function as productive capital and therefore produces neither commodities nor surplus-value: capital's circulation generally restricts its production time and hence its valorisation process. This is why industry is increasingly clustered outside of urban centres close to motorways and airports in order to streamline circulation.

Another implication is the growing role for a credit system that enables production to continue throughout the circulation process. Credit can be used to bridge the gap in situations where surplus value has not yet been realised and under conditions where capitalists expect future consumption of their goods and services. This may seem like rather a banal point, but it has real consequences for how the economy functions, illuminating a systemic reliance on fictitious capital (although Marx introduced this term later, in *Capital, Volume Three*). Money values backed by yet unproduced or sold goods and services are thus the essential lifeblood of capitalism, rather than an eccentric or irregular consequence of an otherwise self-reliant system: in order to function as capital, money must circulate, it must again employ labour-power and again realise itself in expanded value. Let's take an industrialist who has enough money in his bank account so that he can retire and live off the interest: the bank must *loan* his capital to another industrialist. The industrialist who has borrowed the money must service the loan, i.e. pay interest, out of the profits he makes. The sum of money on the market is thus redoubled: the retired capitalist still owns his money, and the other capitalist also disposed of the money he borrowed. But, as the class of speculators, bankers, brokers, financiers and so on grows, as is inevitably the case wherever the mass of capital in a country reaches a sufficient scale, the bank finds that it is able to loan out *far more* than it has deposited in its vaults. Speculators can sell products that they do not possess; 'the right kind of person' is good for credit even when they have nothing. Note how trust, i.e. interpersonal relations, re-enters the scene here, at the level of what appear to be the utmost impersonal financial speculations: the ability of the bank to make unsecured loans is dependent on 'confidence':

> In this way, the money form produces not only impersonal relations of domination but at the same time produces interpersonal forms of domination as fictitious

capital exists as a form of appearance of value not on the basis of the substance of abstract labour that produces the subject-object inversion, but through interpersonal forms of domination that promise future production of value as substance. / Therefore, there is a different kind of subjection working on the bearers of fictitious capital which is on the basis of an interpersonal relation forged through a contract.[2]

Thus one and the same unit of productive capital may have to support not just the one retired industrialist who deposited his savings with the bank, but *multiple* claims on one and the same capital. If the bank accepts one million from our retiree, but loans out on the basis of it ten million to multiple borrowers, each of the multiple owners of this ten million has *equal* claim to that same value of the originally deposited one million – this is how *fictitious capital* comes about. At times of expansion and boom, the mass of *fictitious capital* grows rapidly; when the period of contraction arrives, the bank finds itself under pressure and calls in its loans, defaults occur, bankruptcies, closures, share prices fall, and things fall back to reality – fictitious value is wiped out. This brings us to a formal definition of fictitious capital: it is *that proportion of capital which cannot be simultaneously converted into existing use-values*. It is an *invention* which is absolutely necessary for the growth of real capital; it is a fiction which constitutes the symbol of confidence in the future. Or, as Rebecca Carson résumés this entire movement: 'Non-capitalist variables become formally subsumed through circulation, making them necessary for the reproduction of capital, yet they are variables nonetheless necessarily exterior, described by Marx as "interruptions" within the movement of capital.'[3]

What this means in socio-economic terms is that we should unconditionally avoid any notion of Communism as an order in which fictions no longer reign over actual life, i.e. in which we return to actual life. As Hardt and Negri repeatedly insisted, there is an unexpected emancipatory potential in the craziest speculations with fictive capital. Since valorisation of the working force is the key aspect of capitalist reproduction, we should never forget that in the sphere of fictitious capital there is no valorisation, no market exchange of commodities and no labour that produces new value – and because, in a capitalist society, personal freedom is grounded in the 'free' exchange of commodities, inclusive of labour power as a commodity, the sphere of fictitious capital no longer demands personal freedom and autonomy; direct interpersonal relations of subordination and domination return in it. It may appear that this reasoning is too formal, but one can elaborate this in a more precise way: fictitious capital involves debt, and being indebted limits personal freedom; for the workers, debt is involved in the (re)production of their workforce itself, and this debt limits their freedom to bargain for a work contract.

So where here is any emancipatory potential? Elon Musk proposed a mega-algorithm program that would manage our investments better than any stockbroker company, allowing ordinary people to invest small sums under the same conditions as billionaires. The idea is that, when this program is freely available, it will lead to a more fair distribution of wealth. Although the idea is problematic and ambiguous, it does indicate the ultimate nonsense of stock exchange games. If a mega-algorithm can do the work better than humans, stock exchanges could become an automatic machine – and, if this works, private ownership of stocks will also become useless, since all we'll need will be a gigantic AI machine for the optimal allocation of resources. This is how the extreme of financial capitalism can open up an unexpected path to Communism.

However, fictions operate in the space of what Lacan called the big Other, the symbolic order, and there is a fundamental difference between a subject's alienation in the symbolic order and the worker's alienation in capitalist social relations. We have to avoid the two symmetrical traps which open up if we insist on the homology between the two alienations: the idea that capitalist social alienation is irreducible since the signifying alienation is constitutive of subjectivity, as well as the opposite idea that the signifying alienation could be abolished in the same way Marx imagined the overcoming of capitalist alienation. The point is not just that the signifying alienation is more fundamental and will persist even if we abolish the capitalist alienation – it is a more refined one. The very figure of a subject that would overcome the signifying alienation and become a free agent who is master of the symbolic universe, i.e. who is no longer embedded in a symbolic substance, can arise only within the space of capitalist alienation, the space in which free individuals interact. Let's indicate the domain of this symbolic alienation with regard to Robert Brandom's attempt to elaborate 'the way to a postmodern form of recognition that overcomes ironic alienation. This is the recollective-recognitive structure of trust.'[4] For Brandom:

> [This] may be the part of [Hegel's] thought that is of the most contemporary philosophical interest and value. That is partly because he attributes deep political significance to the replacement of a semantic model of atomistic representation by one of holistic expression. [. . .] It is to lead to a new form of mutual recognition and usher in the third stage in the development of Geist: the age of trust.[5]

'Trust' is here trust in the ethical substance (the 'big Other', the set of established norms) which doesn't limit but sustains the space of our freedom. Referring to Chomsky, Brandom gives his own reading of the classic distinction between negative freedom and positive freedom: negative freedom is the freedom from predominant norms and obligations which can lead only to universalised ironic distance towards all positive regulations (we shouldn't trust them, they are illusions masking particular interests), while positive freedom is the freedom whose space is opened up and sustained by our adherence to a set of norms. As Chomsky pointed out, language enables an individual who inhabits it to generate an infinite number of sentences – this is the positive freedom of expression provided by our acceptance of the rules of language, while negative freedom can lead only to ironic alienation. But, is the freedom of irony, of ironic distance, also not a form of positive freedom grounded in a deep acquaintance with the rules? Is something like ironic alienation not inherent to those who really inhabit a language? Let's take patriotism: a true patriot is not a fanatical zealot, but somebody who can quite often practise ironic remarks about his nation, and this irony paradoxically vouches for his true love of his country (when things get serious, he is ready to fight for it). To be able to practise this kind of irony, I have to master the rules of my language much more deeply than those who speak it in a flawless, non-ironic way. One can even say that to really inhabit a language implies not just knowing the rules, but knowing the meta-rules which tell me how to violate the explicit rules; it doesn't imply making no mistakes, but making the right kind of mistakes. And the same goes for the manners that hold together a given closed community – this is why, in the old times, when there were still schools to teach ordinary people how to behave in high-class society, these schools were, as a rule, an abominable failure: no matter how much they taught you the rules of behaviour, they were not able to teach you the meta-rules that regulate the subtle transgressions of the rulers. And, speaking about expressive subjectivity, one also can say that subjectivity appears in speech only through such regulated violations – without them, we get a flat, impersonal speech.

And, what if we imagine Communism in a similar way: as a new ethical substance (a frame of rules) that enables positive freedom? Maybe this is how we should reread Marx's opposition of the kingdom of necessity and the kingdom of freedom: Communism is not freedom itself, but the structure of a kingdom of necessity that sustains freedom, the principal commitment to a Cause which makes all my transgressive pleasures possible. In other words, we shouldn't imagine Communism as a self-transparent order with no alienation, but as an order of 'good' alienation, of our reliance on a thick invisible cobweb of regulations sustaining the space of our freedom. In Communism, I should be led to 'trust' this cobweb *and ignore it*, focusing on what makes my life meaningful. This constitutive alienation in the symbolic substance is missing in Kohei Saito's *Karl Marx's Ecosocialism*,[6] the latest, most consistent attempt to think humanity's embeddedness in nature without regressing into dialectical-materialist general ontology. In his search of a pre-capitalist foundation of human life, he posits the process of metabolism between nature and humans as the ground on which the process of Capital is based. This metabolism was distorted by

Capital, which parasitises on it, so that the basic 'contradiction' of capitalism is the one between natural metabolism and capital – nature resists capital, it poses a limit to capital's self-valorisation. The task of Communists is thus to invent a new form of social metabolism which will no longer be market-mediated but organised in a human (rationally planned) way. That's why Saito is profoundly anti-Hegelian: his axiom is that Hegelian dialectics cannot think the natural limits of Capital, namely that the self-movement of Capital cannot ever fully 'sublate'/integrate its presupposed natural base:

> Marx's ecology deals with the synthesis of the historical and transhistorical aspects of social metabolism in explaining how the physical and material dimensions of the 'universal metabolism of nature' and the 'metabolism between humans and nature' are modified and eventually disrupted by the valorization of capital. Marx's analysis aims at revealing the limits of the appropriation of nature through its subsumption by capital. (p. 68)

Marx does not talk about subsumption under capital in abstract formal terms. He is interested in how this subsumption is not just a formal one, but gradually transforms the material base itself: air gets polluted, deforestation, land is exhausted and rendered less fertile, etc. Saito is right to see in this rift the basic 'contradiction' of capitalism: once social production is subsumed under the form of the self-valorisation process of Capital, the goal of the process becomes capital's extended self-reproduction, the growth of accumulated value. And, since the environment ultimately counts as just an externality, destructive environmental consequences are ignored, they don't count:

> [C]apital contradicts the fundamental limitedness of natural forces and resources because of its drive toward infinite self-valorization. This is the central contradiction of the capitalist mode of production, and Marx's analysis aims at discerning the limits to this measureless drive for capital accumulation within a material world. (p. 259)

Ecology is thus for Saito in the very centre of Marx's critique of political economy, and this is why, in the last decades of his life, Marx was extensively reading books on the chemistry and physiology of agriculture. (The reason why Marx turned to the physiology and chemistry of agriculture is clear: he wanted to study the life process of metabolism without falling into the trap of conceiving life that precedes capital in the terms of a Romantic 'vital force'.) Saito's central premise is that THIS 'contradiction' cannot be grasped in the Hegelian terms – this is why he mockingly mentions that Western Marxism 'primarily deals with social forms (sometimes with an extreme fetishism of Hegel's *Science of Logic*)' (p. 262). But we cannot get rid of Hegel in such an easy way. When Marx wrote that the ultimate barrier of capital is capital itself (in *Capital, Volume Three*, Chapter 15, entitled 'Exposition of the Internal Contradictions of the Law') – 'The *real barrier* of capitalist production is *capital itself* ('*Die wahre Schranke der kapitalistischen Produktion ist das Kapital selbst*') – we should be precise in the Hegelian sense and clearly distinguish *Schranke* from *Grenze*: *Grenze* designates an external limitation while *Schranke* stands for the immanent barrier of an entity, for its internal contradiction. Say, in the classic case of freedom, the external limitation of my freedom is the freedom of others, but its true 'barrier' is the insufficiency of this notion of freedom which opposes my freedom to the freedom of others – as Hegel would have put it, this freedom is not yet true freedom. And the whole point of Marx is that capital is not just externally limited (by nature, which cannot be exploited indefinitely) but immanently limited, limited in its very concept.

Which mode of relating to Hegel should then an ecologically oriented Marxism assume today? When Chris Arthur says that 'it is precisely the applicability of Hegel's logic that condemns the object as an inverted reality systematically alienated from its bearers',[7] he thereby provides the most concise formulation of 'Hegel's logic as the logic of capital': the very fact that Hegel's logic can be applied to capitalism means that capitalism is a perverted order of alienation. Or, as John Rosenthal put it, 'Marx made the curious discovery of an object domain in which the inverted relation between the universal and the particular which constitutes the distinctive principle of Hegelian metaphysics *in fact* obtains': 'The whole riddle of the "Marx-Hegel relation" consists in nothing other than this: [. . .] it is precisely and paradoxically the *mystical* formulae of Hegelian "logic" for which Marx finds a rational scientific application.'[8] In short, while, in his early critique of Hegel, Marx rejected Hegel's thought as a crazy speculative reversal of the actual state of things, he was then struck by the realisation that there is a domain which behaves in a Hegelian way, namely the domain of the circulation of Capital.

Recall the classic Marxian motif of the speculative inversion of the relationship between the Universal and the Particular. The Universal is just a property of particular objects which really exist, but when we are victims of commodity fetishism it appears as if the concrete content of a commodity (its use-value) is an expression of its abstract universality (its exchange-value) – the abstract Universal, the Value, appears as a real Substance which successively incarnates itself in a series of concrete objects. That is the basic Marxian thesis: it is already the effective world of commodities which behaves like a Hegelian subject-substance, like a Universal going through a series of particular embodiments.

In Marx's reading, the self-engendering speculative movement of Capital also indicates a fateful limitation of the Hegelian dialectical process, something that eludes Hegel's grasp. It is in this sense that Lebrun mentions the 'fascinating image' of Capital presented by Marx (especially in his *Grundrisse*): 'a monstrous mixture of the good infinity and the bad infinity, the good infinity which creates its presuppositions and the conditions of its growth, the bad infinity which never ceases to surmount its crises, and which finds its limit in its own nature.'[9] This, perhaps, is also the reason why Marx's reference to Hegel's dialectics in his 'critique of political economy' is ambiguous, oscillating between taking it as the mystified expression of the logic of Capital and taking it as the model for the revolutionary process of emancipation. First, there is dialectic as the 'logic of capital': the development of the commodity-form and the passage from money to capital are clearly formulated in Hegelian terms (capital is money-substance turning into self-mediating process of its own reproduction, etc.). Then there is the Hegelian notion of proletariat as 'substance-less subjectivity', i.e. the grandiose Hegelian scheme of the historical process from pre-class society to capitalism as the gradual separation of the subject from its objective conditions, so that the overcoming of capitalism means that the (collective) subject re-appropriates its alienated substance. The Hegelian dialectical matrix thus serves as the model of the logic of capital as well as the model of its revolutionary overcoming.

So, again, which mode of relating to Hegel should an ecologically oriented Marxism assume today: Hegelian dialectics as the mystified expression of the revolutionary process; as the philosophical expression of the perverted logic of Capital; as the idealist version of a new dialectical-materialist ontology? Or should we simply claim (as Althusser did) that Marx only 'flirted' with Hegelian dialectics, that his thinking was totally foreign to Hegel? There is another one: a different reading of Hegel's dialectical process itself that leaves behind the predominant notion of this process as the process of gradual subjective appropriation of substantial content. Already decades ago, in the early years of modern ecology, some perspicuous readers of Hegel noted that Hegelian idealist speculation does not imply an absolute appropriation of nature – in contrast to productive appropriation, speculation lets its Other be, it doesn't intervene in its Other. As Frank Ruda pointed out,[10] Hegel's Absolute Knowing is not a total *Aufhebung* – a seamless integration of all reality into the Notion's self-mediation; it is much more an act of radical *Aufgeben* – of giving up, of renouncing the violent effort to grab reality. Absolute Knowing is a gesture of *Entlassen*, of releasing reality, of letting-it-be to stand on its own, and, in this sense, it breaks with the endless effort of labour to appropriate its Otherness, the stuff that forever resists its grasp. Labour (and technological domination in general) is an exemplary case of what Hegel calls 'spurious infinity'; it is a pursuit which is never accomplished because it presupposes an Other to be mastered, while philosophical speculation is at ease, no longer troubled by its Other.

This brings us back to the topic of fiction. Does this gesture of releasing reality, of letting-it-be to stand on its own, mean that we accept reality as it is in itself, outside the network of symbolic fictions? Here things get more complex. For Hegel, the form of this 'letting-it-be' is knowledge, scientific knowledge (in his sense of the word) which doesn't mess with its object but merely observes its self-movement. What scientific knowledge observes is not its object in itself but the interaction between in-itself and our fictions, where fictions are an immanent part of the in-itself – and it is the same with Marx for whom, if we subtract fictions, social reality itself disintegrates. Today's experimental science, however, displays a stance towards its object which is the opposite of Hegel's: not a stance of impassively observing the object's self-movement in its interplay with fictions, but the stance of actively intervening in its object and its technological manipulation, even creating new objects (through biogenetic mutations), which simultaneously aims at how this object is in itself, independently of our interaction with it. Let's take brain science, the exemplary case of today's science: neurobiologists and cognitive scientists like to undermine our common sense of being autonomous free agents with the claim that subjective freedom is a fiction – in reality, in itself, our brain processes are fully determined by neural mechanisms. The Hegelian answer to this is that yes, freedom is immanently linked to fiction, but in a more subtle way – to quote a well-known passage from the 'Preface' to Hegel's *Phenomenology of Spirit*:

> The activity of dissolution is the power and work of the *Understanding*, the most astonishing and mightiest of powers, or rather the absolute power. The circle that remains self-enclosed and, like substance, holds its moments together, is an immediate relationship, one therefore which has nothing astonishing about it. But that an accident as such, detached from what circumscribes it, what is bound and is actual only in its context with others, should attain an existence of its own and a separate freedom – that is the tremendous power of the negative; it is the energy of thought, of the pure I.[11]

The power of the Understanding is the power of tearing apart in one's mind what in reality belongs together – in short, the power to create fictions. One should be attentive to a key detail in the quote from Hegel: this power is not just the basic form of human freedom; it is the power of 'separate freedom' acquired by an object itself when it is torn out of its living context and thus obtains a separate existence of its own. But is this power active only in our mind while reality remains the same in itself? In other words, are we dealing with a new version of Sartre's opposition between the reality of being-in-itself and consciousness as the vortex of being-for-itself? We should recall here Marx's definition of human labour from Chapter 7 of *Capital, Volume One*:

> A spider conducts operations which resemble those of the weaver, and a bee would put many a human architect to shame by the construction of its honeycomb cells. But what distinguishes the worst architect from the best of bees is that the architect builds the cell in his mind before he constructs it in wax. At the end of every labour process, a result emerges which had already been conceived by the worker at the beginning, hence already existed ideally.[12]

These imaginings – fictions – are, of course, not just in the worker's head; they emerge out of the socio-symbolic interaction of workers, which presupposes the 'big Other', the order of symbolic fictions. So how does the 'big Other' relate to (what we experience as) external reality? This is THE basic philosophical problem – and, at this point, we should stop.

Notes

1. Incidentally, the same holds for market competition: a participant in it never disposes of complete data about supply and demand which would enable him/her to make the optimal decision, and this incompleteness (the fact that individuals are compelled to decide without full information) is not just an empirical complication – it is (to put it in Hegelese) part of the very notion of market competition.
2. Rebecca Carson, 'Time and Schemas of Reproduction' (manuscript).
3. Carson, 'Time and Schemas of Reproduction'.
4. Robert Brandom, *A Spirit of Trust: A Reading of Hegel's Phenomenology* (Cambridge, MA: Harvard University Press, 2019), p. 501.
5. Brandom, *A Spirit of Trust*, p. 506.
6. Kohei Saito, *Karl Marx's Ecosocialism* (New York: Monthly Review Press, 2017). Numbers in brackets refer to the pages of this book.
7. Luca Micaloni and Christopher J. Arthur, 'The Logic of Capital. Interview with Chris Arthur', *Consecutio Rerum*, vol. 3, no. 5 (2018), p. 482 (available online at: <https://www.academia.edu/38109734/The_Logic_of_Capital._Interview_with_Chris_Arthur> last access 28 January 2021).
8. Quoted from <https://www.academia.edu/3035436/John_Rosenthal_The_Myth_of_Dialectics_Reinterpreting_the_Marx-Hegel_Relation>.
9. Gerard Lebrun, *L'envers de la dialectique* (Paris: Editions du Seuil, 2004), p. 311.
10. See Frank Ruda, *Abolishing Freedom: A Plea for a Contemporary Use of Fatalism* (Lincoln, NB: University of Nebraska Press, 2016).

11. G. W. F. Hegel, *Phenomenology of Spirit* (New York: Oxford University Press, 1977), pp. 18–19.
12. Karl Marx, *Capital. Critique of Political Economy, Volume One*, trans. Ben Fowkes (London: Penguin, 1976), p. 284.

2 Is Surplus Value Structured Like an Anamorphosis? Marx, Lacan and the Structure of Objective Fiction
Boštjan Nedoh

Neoliberalism and Human Capital as Symptoms of Foucault's 'Historical Nominalism'

Although the main purpose of this contribution[1] is to unfold the concept of objective fiction by relying on Marx's critique of political economy and Lacan's psychoanalytic theory, it is nevertheless worth beginning at the very opposite end, namely at the end, which is, epistemologically speaking, as distant as possible from both Marx and Lacan. Indeed, this end is Michel Foucault's 'historical nominalism'.[2] Specifically, I will begin by examining the way in which Foucault's nominalism is reflected in his own critical (mis)reading of Marx in his 1978–79 seminar *The Birth of Biopolitics*,[3] which does not only totally dismiss Marx's labour theory of value and his concept of labour power, but in turn gives undeserved theoretical credit to neoliberal authors such as Theodore Schulz and Gary Backer, and particularly to neoliberal theories of 'human capital' as an antipode to Marx's concept of labour power. To be sure, Foucault expressed a very ambiguous attitude toward Marx and his critique of political economy throughout his *oeuvre*, which oscillated from harsh critique to admiration.[4] In this respect, it could be said that the seminar *The Birth of Biopolitics*, dedicated to the exploration of modern liberal governmentality, belongs to the former rather than to the latter. Therein Foucault outlines a very harsh critique of both classical political economy and Marx's critique of political economy, whereby the main conceptual tool of Foucault's critique is represented by the neoliberal concept of 'human capital' as the 'opposite extreme' of Marx's concept of labour power. According to Foucault, the concept of 'human capital' is to be grasped precisely as some kind of 'remedy' for a fundamental deficiency of both classical political economy and Marx's critique thereof.

As is known, the key point of this alleged deficiency is that, contrary to their rhetoric, classical political economy and Marx's critique thereof never actually really dealt with the concept of labour in their analyses of the capitalist politico-economic system and that, within this theoretical tradition, labour actually remained 'unexplored'. As Foucault himself says:

> Of course, we can say that Adam Smith's economics does begin with a reflection on labor, inasmuch as for Smith the division of labor and its specification is the key which enabled him to construct his economic analysis. But apart from this sort of first step, this first opening, and since that moment, classical political economy has never analyzed labor itself, or rather it has constantly striven to neutralize it, and to do this by reducing it exclusively to the factor of time.[5]

According to Foucault, the original sin was thus already committed with Smith's political economy, which ignored or overlooked the significance of concrete and diverse phenomenal forms of labour and reduced the entire question of this concept to its temporal component, that is abstract labour, whose measure is labour time. This conception of Foucault's intensifies a few pages later in the same lecture, when he places Marx on the same level of political economy by confronting his key differentiation between labour and labour power, which the concept of abstract labour is based on, with the alleged neoliberal reproach that the abstraction of labour does not originate in capitalism itself as a historical process, as Marx claimed, but is supposed to be a pure ideological phantasm of Marx's philosophy itself:

> Now, say the neo-liberals [. . .] what is responsible for this 'abstraction'? For Marx, capitalism itself is responsible; it is the fault of the logic of capital and of its historical reality. Whereas the neo-liberals say: The abstraction of labor, which actually only appears through the variable of time, is not the product of real capitalism, [but] of the economic theory that has been constructed of capitalist production. Abstraction is not the result of the real mechanics of economic processes; it derives from the way in which these processes have been reflected in classical economics. And it is precisely because classical economics was not able to take on this analysis of labor in its concrete specification and qualitative modulations, it is because it left this blank page, gap or vacuum in its theory, that a whole philosophy, anthropology, and politics, of which Marx is precisely the representative, rushed in.[6]

Presupposing this absence of a serious analysis of the concept of labour in classical political economy and in Marx, Foucault then focuses on the neoliberal theory of human capital, which he presents as the epistemological breakthrough that is supposed to fill in or compensate for the lack of analysis. If we sum this up somewhat broadly: in contrast to classical political economy and the critique thereof, which reduced the problem of labour to the undifferentiated use of labour power or to abstract labour measured by labour time, the theory of 'human capital' is supposed to enable a differentiation of abstract labour into its qualitatively different concrete phenomenal forms. As Foucault continues, 'seen from the side of the worker, labor is not a commodity reduced by abstraction to labor power and the time [during] which it is used',[7] rather, in neoliberal economic analyses, a human being becomes the 'opposite extreme of a conception of labor power', an active 'entrepreneur of himself',[8] and is therefore forced to engage in *increasing the value of himself as capital*: 'This is true to the extent that, in practice, the stake in all neo-liberal analyses is the replacement every time of *homo oeconomicus* as partner of exchange with a *homo oeconomicus* as entrepreneur of himself, being for himself his own capital, being for himself his own producer, being for himself the source of [his] earnings.'[9]

Wherein lies the problem of Foucault's conception, the interest-free crediting of neoliberalism and especially the theory of human capital, which is supposed to represent an antipode to Marx's labour theory of value and the concept of abstract labour? Why does Foucault acknowledge the pertinence and epistemological innovativeness of these distinctly anti-speculative theories? It seems that we should seek the reason for Foucault's benevolence towards neoliberals primarily in what Thomas Flynn named Foucault's 'historical nominalism', whose fundamental feature is precisely the rejection of universality and generality. In this way, Foucault not only categorically rejects the Hegelian-Marxian concept of universal history, but thus also overlooks the tectonic consequences of the historical processes that by their nature and structure are universal and general. Specifically, capitalism valorises the cultural specificities of commodities and the qualitative specifics of concrete labour, but it does so precisely through elements that are universal (the wages system, commodity fetishism, etc.). According to Foucault, who here is acting something like a messenger of neoliberals, such 'universals' are actually merely theoretical constructs and not products of the capitalist social structure or the historical dynamics of capitalism. In other words, Foucault overlooks that Marx's critique of political economy was not created on a blank page represented by the absence of the analysis of the concept of labour in its concrete phenomenal forms, so as a sort of symptomatic displacement of trauma.[10] On the contrary, Marx's critique of political economy and the labour theory of value were created *on the basis* of his explicit critique of the concept of labour, or, more precisely, the capitalist mystification of labour that functions as a necessary ideological supplement to abstract labour, which, together with the abstraction of labour, is actually produced by capitalism itself. Put differently, Marx's introduction of the concept of abstract labour measured by labour time, which functions as the cunning of reason behind the backs of concrete workers who 'do not know' that, in the exchange, they equate their products precisely on the basis of 'real abstraction', is only one side of his labour theory of value. The other side is that the concrete producers 'do not know' about real abstraction (or if we take into account the Freudian theory of fetishism that complements that of Marx, they 'disavow' the abstraction) precisely due to the ideological supplement represented by the mystification of labour, that is, because the use of their labour power, which they hire out to an employer against payment, appears to them as labour itself or the value of labour itself (which corresponds precisely to the neoliberal definition of human capital as adopted by Foucault). As Marx says: 'The value or price of the labouring power takes the semblance of the price or value of labour itself.'[11]

The key consequence of the fact that the use of labour power takes 'the semblance of the price or value of labour itself', that is that the wage takes the semblance of all created value, is precisely the disavowal of the exploitation of labour power, not in the subjective moralistic sense, but rather in the objective sense of this exploitation, which Marx calls 'surplus labour', being objectively necessary for the production of surplus value, which leads to profit. That is why Marx says that the historical specificity of capitalism as an economic system based on wage labour lies in 'surplus labour', which is 'unpaid labour' in which surplus value originates, necessarily seeming 'to be paid labour': 'This false appearance distinguishes *wages labour* from other *historical* forms of labour.'[12]

Here we come to the second and perhaps even more important reason behind Foucault not only putting Marx and neoliberals on the same scales, but ultimately tipping the scales of their epistemological power in favour of the latter. For both neoliberals and Foucault's 'historical nominalism', it is unthinkable that the 'false appearance' or the fiction that Marx talks about would be produced by the dynamics and the historical/objective reality or *discourse* (to anticipate Lacan's discussion below) of capitalism itself; they can only be a product of Marx's philosophical or anthropological imagination. Put differently, Foucault – perhaps surprisingly, yet quite evidently – insists on a quite clear dividing line between the external objective reality of capitalism and (Marx's) subjective discourse about this reality, which is why he ultimately cannot analytically capture the conceptual dimension not simply of fiction, but of *objective fiction*, which best suits the 'false appearance' as the main element of the ideological mystification of wage labour in capitalism.

In fact, objective fiction does not simply refer to a subjective illusion or even 'false consciousness' in Marx's sense, which is opposed to the actual objective reality 'out there'. After all, this division represents a quite classical metaphysical apparatus within which there is a clear dividing line between external objects and the subject of consciousness that the objects stand before. Marx's 'false appearance', which is at the core of the mystification of wage labour, corresponds to objective fiction not simply because, as such, it has real effects, that is because it effectively mystifies or conceals unpaid/surplus labour, which, within wage labour, is precisely the fund of abstract labour in which surplus value originates, but much more because it is produced by the objective reality of capitalism itself or the capitalist discourse as the social bond and not simply by Marx's philosophy, as Foucault claims in his nominalistic spirit.

Below I will first take a more detailed look at the specific structure of the 'false appearance' in Marx, while, in the concluding part, I will try to further connect this structure with Lacan's concept of anamorphosis and the concept of the social hieroglyphic, which can be found in both Lacan and Marx.

The Value of Labour and Surplus Value

In a well-known and extensively discussed passage of *Seminar XVII*, Lacan says:

> Something changed in the master's discourse at a certain point in history. We are not going to break our backs finding out if it was because of Luther, or Calvin, or some unknown traffic of ships around Genoa, or in the Mediterranean Sea, or anywhere else, for the important point is that on a certain day surplus *jouissance* became calculable, could be counted, totalized. This is where what is called the accumulation of capital begins.[13]

Much has been written about the 'homology' between Marx's surplus value and Lacan's surplus *jouissance*, which constitutes the core of the above-cited passage.[14] However, at least one point of this homology has remained substantially less illuminated and conceptualised than others. It is worth asking how 'on a certain day' surplus *jouissance* began to count. What is the 'logic' of this counting and especially under what conditions does surplus *jouissance* begin to count and add up as surplus value?

Lacan's and Marx's answers to the above question are basically the same; they are only articulated differently. But the answer is also in both cases two-fold. Let us begin with Lacan. As he himself mentions at the beginning of the cited passage, the condition of the counting of surplus value is a change in the master's discourse, which, as Alenka Zupančič has repeatedly noted,[15] refers precisely to the separation of knowledge from labour. Recall that the starting point of Lacan's theory of discourses is the master–slave dialectic, which is at the core of the discourse of the ancient master.[16] This discourse is characterised by *jouissance* and knowledge being on the side of the slave and not the master (the essence of the master is 'that he does not know what he wants'[17]), with both elements (*jouissance* and knowledge) being immanently co-dependent in the form of the slave's practical knowledge (*savoir-faire*). According to Lacan, the modern age is marked by the discursive break, which is based on the spoliation of the slave's knowledge: the modern knowledge on which capitalism is based is scientific knowledge or *episteme* (S_2).[18]

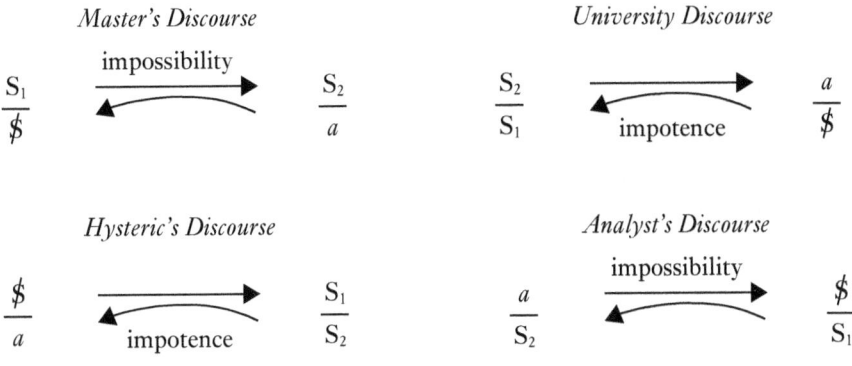

Figure 2.1 The Four Discourses of Lacan

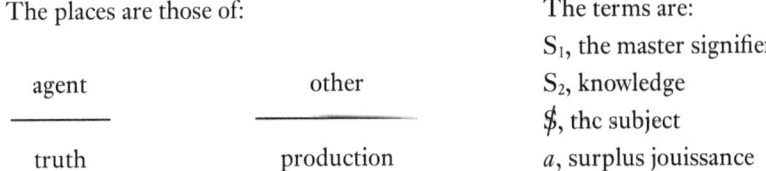

Figure 2.2 Places and Terms in Lacan's Discourses

In comparison to the ancient *savoir-faire*, the fundamental characteristic of *episteme* is that it is separated from the slave's labour and as such transferable. That has important implications of course: by taking the place of the agency of the university discourse, knowledge must disavow labour as its truth, whereby the form of this disavowal is a constant valorisation of the surplus created precisely by so-called 'surplus labour'. As Lacan emphasises, what the ancient slave is spoliated of here is not his or her labour or simply the products of his or her labour, but his or her knowledge as *savoir-faire*.[19] It is precisely in this discursive constellation or with this discursive shift from the master's discourse to the university discourse that labour, separated from knowledge, begins to function as a real loss or entropy,[20] which is precisely the fund of labour time that, according to Marx, is the source of surplus value. Put differently, labour becomes separated from labour time and takes the form of a 'stain' within knowledge, something that must necessarily be concealed if knowledge as *episteme* is to function as an agency of discourse.

Here, Marx's answer to the problem of the counting of surplus value is quite compatible with Lacan's, only that Marx formulates it in historical terms: the condition of the counting and production of surplus value is the separation of men from their means of production at the end of the feudal epoch. It is this separation that further enables the capitalist as the owner of capital to find in the market workers as the possessors of labour power, characterised by having nothing to sell in the market 'except their labouring power, their working arms and brains'.[21] Both are formally/legally free and equal persons who sign an employment contract, by which the worker as the possessor of labour power makes his or her labour power available to the owner of capital for a determined (not unlimited) time and payment (wage). The spontaneous, ideological understanding of this situation is the following: labour creates value, by which the owner of capital covers all the costs (in addition to the worker's wage, also all other production costs, such as machines, raw materials, etc.), and must then sell the products or services at a higher price, with the difference between the selling price and the costs being precisely surplus value, which gives rise to profit. According to this explanation, surplus value emerges in the process of exchange or circulation, and not in the process of production. However, such is actually not the case. In 'Wages, Price and Profit', Marx is categorical about this: 'To explain, therefore, the *general nature of profits*, you must start from the theorem that, on an average, commodities are *sold at their real values*, and that *profits are derived from selling them at their values*, that is, in proportion to the quantity of labour realized in them.'[22]

What does it mean that profit is already derived from selling products at their real values without all the surcharges that the owner of capital can or cannot afford in view of the (monopolistic or competitive) market position of his or her products? In answering this question, we have to step onto the terrain of the labour theory of value. In the market, the products of labour are sold or exchanged for the universal equivalent (money) because the same amount of abstract or simple human labour measured by abstract or simple labour time is realised therein. In addition to money, labour is one of the forms of 'real abstraction' produced by capitalism.[23] With the use of human labour, the value of raw materials and other means of production whose value is constant ('constant capital') is *transferred* to the products, while, as a special commodity, labour power has the specific characteristic that, besides its own value, which is expressed in wages or the value of its own reproduction, it also *adds* to the new products a surcharge or additional value (which is why Marx names this part of capital reserved for the purchase of labour power 'variable capital', since its value multiplies in the process of production).

By being used, labour power reproduces all the past value of the raw materials used thereby and the means of production and the value of itself as labour power, while adding a surcharge to all this. The surcharge is created due to what Marx calls 'surplus labour'. Surplus labour is precisely the difference between the labour time spent on the reproduction of value, including the reproduction of the value of labour power (wages), and the entire labour time for which the worker has hired out his or her labour power. The value or the price of labour power is always smaller than the value of the performed labour. Put differently, a worker does not work only during the labour time in which he or she creates the value that is equivalent to the value of his or her wages, but also during the additional or surplus labour time in which he or she creates (surplus) value that exceeds the reproduction of all other value. It is precisely this surplus labour that is the source of surplus value, which, in Marx, is further divided into interest, rent – and profit. That is why the rate of surplus value and the rate of profit depend especially on the proportion between the value or price of labour power and the value that labour power creates in the production process:[24] the higher the value of labour power (wages), the lower the final rate of profit, and vice versa, but the value of labour power will never be equal to the created value – in that case, the rate of profit would be zero. It is precisely this difference between the two values that Marx calls 'exploitation', which is completely formal, objective and independent of the subjective feeling of exploitation – it exists where there is surplus labour, which exists wherever there are capitalist relations of production, regardless of the workers subjectively 'feeling' exploited or not.

With these basic elements of the buying and selling of labour power, the abstraction of labour and surplus labour, which constitute the system of wage labour, we obtain not only two, but (all) three (necessary) elements of the capitalist accumulation of capital: (1) the reproduction of value (of raw materials and labour power); (2) the production of surplus value (surplus labour time); and (3) what Marx calls the 'semblance of labour', which is precisely the ideological supplement necessary for the ideological reproduction of the capitalist relations of production. We will now examine this supplement in more detail.

We mentioned that the source of surplus value is surplus labour, which Marx correctly notes is 'unpaid labour'. But to this, Marx immediately adds that the peculiarity of the wages system and, let us add, of the ideological success of capitalism, which is based on wage labour, is precisely that '*unpaid labour* seems to be *paid labour*': 'Although one part only of the workman's daily labour is *paid*, while the other part is *unpaid*, and while that unpaid or surplus labour constitutes exactly the fund out of which *surplus value* or *profit* is formed, it seems as if the aggregate labour was paid labour. This false appearance distinguishes *wages labour* from other *historical* forms of labour.'[25] Marx believes that the first reason for this 'false appearance', according to which the '*value or price of the labouring power* takes the *semblance of the price or value of labour itself*',[26] should be sought in the known time lag between the production process of creating value and the payment of the workers' wages, which are paid out only *after* the (weekly or monthly) cycle in the production process has been completed.

But this is not the only reason – or rather it consists of two parts. The second and perhaps even more important reason that produces the anamorphic objective fiction according to which the value of labour power or a wage takes the semblance of the value of labour itself is that in capitalism – as opposed to the previous historical forms of labour – the paid and unpaid portions of labour are not formally separated. They are part of the same abstract labour time (and space); there is no objective or external dividing line between them that would enable one to differentiate between paid and unpaid labour or the hours a worker spends on the production of value that is equivalent to his or her wages and surplus labour appropriated by the owner of capital. The structure of surplus labour is the same as the structure of entropy mentioned by Lacan in his example of descending and ascending a hill with a weight on one's back: if we take into account only the signifiers of energetics, then the calculated work is zero even though we know that real work was performed, that is a real loss of energy took place.

This specific characteristic of wage labour, which produces the mentioned 'false appearance', becomes even clearer the moment Marx compares it to the other two historical forms of labour – slavery and feudalism: in slavery, even paid labour appeared to be unpaid labour (slaves worked for free, the costs of their reproduction were limited only to their daily physical reproduction, but the owners had to buy them beforehand), while, in feudalism, labour intended for the reproduction of the serfs and their families was temporally and spatially separated from the labour they performed for their feudal masters. The peculiarity of the wages system on which capitalism and the production of surplus value are based lies precisely in it merging the paid and unpaid portions of labour time, thereby producing the appearance that all performed labour is paid labour, meaning that, during the entire labour time, workers produce the value that they are later paid for by their wages. The objective existence of unpaid labour is manifested only on the unconscious *Other scene*; in the persistence of surplus value within the capitalist knowledge as a stain – without unpaid labour, there would be no surplus value and consequently no profit. The key point here is that the semblance of labour does not emerge outside the framework of capitalist production or in the ideological superstructure (which includes human rights and the observance of contractual and legal relations, which the purchase and sale of labour power are based on), but is produced by the relations of production themselves or the wages system. Precisely because this (false) appearance originates not in the ideological apparatuses outside production, but in the mode of production itself, it corresponds to the term 'objective fiction' – a fiction or appearance that is not simply a consequence of a false subjective view, but is produced by objective reality or the *discourse* of capitalism itself. Ideology is already inscribed in the social base. It is precisely due to the appearance according to which unpaid labour seems to be paid labour, that is due to the ideological mystification of labour, that surplus value in capitalism can come to count, or, to be precise, that the symbolic ideological constellation, in which surplus value begins to count and becomes calculable, is reproduced.

To summarise, we can say something along these lines: in order for surplus value to count and be calculable, it is necessary for an owner of capital to find in the market a formally free possessor of labour power or a worker, so they can conclude a legally valid contractual relation between two free subjects. However, the necessary ideological supplement that reproduces the power of contractual relations and, at the same time, conceals the asymmetry in the social power of labour and capital is precisely the mystification or the appearance of labour according to which the contractual value of labour power (wages) necessarily appears as the entire amount of the created value.

At this point, we come across a question that is crucial in all respects, that is the question of the precise structure of 'false appearance', and the related question of how Marx even manages to see the difference between paid and unpaid or surplus labour within the structure of appearance that precisely erases the difference. In short, how does Marx trace, within the entire labour time, in which there is no manifest difference between the work hours during which the value of labour power is reproduced and the hours that constitute surplus labour time, the difference between two separate segments, the second of which (surplus labour) is the source of surplus value?

If we anticipate a bit, we can say that, at first sight, the structure of 'false appearance' and Marx's conception of it are reminiscent of Lacan's conceptualisation of anamorphosis as the structure of the gaze within the field of vision, which Lacan develops while considering the famous 'stain' (in the form of a human skull) in Holbein's masterpiece *The Ambassadors* (1533). If we assume the already well-documented homology between psychoanalysis and historical materialism,[27] and if we presuppose that 'anamorphosis is the screening of the object a',[28] that is the way the lack appears in the field of vision, then we can say that, within the capitalist production process, surplus value (in the form of surplus labour) homologically appears precisely in the form of anamorphosis.

It seems that, to a large extent, surplus value corresponds precisely to the stain in the painting which is characterised by the fact that when we acknowledge that a stain is a meaningful image, we lose the rest of the painting. Yet in Marx's and Lacan's 'parallactic' approach, the very deciphering of the stain as an image-meaning is insufficient insofar as their approaches consist precisely in highlighting the place of the subject in the painting or in the production process – which, after all, is what differentiates their materialistic theory of the subject from other theories. In what follows, we will therefore first focus on the anamorphic structure of surplus value itself, and then also on the place of the subject within this structure.

The Structure of Surplus Value: From Anamorphosis . . .

Lacan provides his first more extensive analysis of the phenomenon of anamorphosis in Holbein's *The Ambassadors* (1533) in *Seminar VII*, where he points out, among other things, that anamorphosis is a distinctly modern phenomenon. It appears especially in sixteenth- and sevententh-century European painting, which, in the structural sense, follows the changes in the field of modern science, especially geometry and the discovery of the 'geometrical laws of perspective'.[29] According to its basic definition, anamorphosis is a spatial illusion or 'any kind of construction that is made in such a way that by means of an optical transposition a certain form that was not visible at first sight transforms itself into a readable image. The pleasure is found in seeing its emergence from an undecipherable form.'[30] The anamorphic painting technique thus introduces an additional twist to the classical painting techniques, for, by including a stain in the painting or constructing a painting within a painting, it produces a materialisation of the void on an extimate surface, which is extimate precisely because two spaces come together on the same surface and thereby become twisted and curved, so that the 'outside' and the 'inside' appear on the same curved surface and are no longer separated from each other. As has been said many times, the main point of anamorphosis developed by Lacan in *Seminar XI*, based on the paradoxical 'stain' in Holbein's *The Ambassadors*, is that the gaze is the 'object',[31] that is it does not belong to the subject that stands opposite external objects, but, as such, belongs to the painting itself or the geometrical field of the visible. The gaze is not a medium of cognition, but is something that the subject encounters in the painting in the transition from the whole painting to an unclear stain (as a painting within a painting), which, with the change in perspective, turns out to be a human skull. The price to be paid is, of course, losing the rest of the painting the moment the stain turns out to be an image-meaning. Lacan's emphasis here, however, is not so much on the fact that, with the change in perspective, the stain changes into a meaningful image, but on the gaze as the *objet petit a* being an external/objective materialisation or a representative of the subject as the lack of being. Put differently, *objet petit a* is the way the subject is inscribed in the field of the visible. This point was developed by Mladen Dolar in his extensive and detailed study of anamorphosis:

> What is at stake here is not the notion of representation, which is always a representation for a subject, namely, that which is put before him (*vor-stellen*).

> Possessing the function of the screen, the stain is like a stand-in for the gaze: the objectal external 'representative' of the subject and its desire, and it has ultimately the same structure as the notorious *Vorstellungsrepräsentanz* in the field of language and the signifier, that is, as a representative of representation. The stain is a stand-in for a structurally missing representation (the signifier of the missing signifier), which makes the whole field of representation dependent upon it. The ersatz of the stain is structurally missing but this stand-in is on the same level as other representations, standing in for the impossibility of ever closing, delimiting or totalizing the field of representation. Representation is non-whole, not-all, because of the inscription of the subject for whom something is represented in the field of representation itself. There is a short-circuit.[32]

In light of Dolar's passage, we could say that, in the field of the visible, the *objet petit a* (as the phallic object) is what the phallic signifier (as the signifier of *jouissance*) is in the field of language. They both represent the subject in their respective fields and, as such, represent the surplus that appears in the place of the structurally absent original satisfaction. They are not representations *for* the subject, but stand-ins for or representatives *of* the subject in the field of language and the field of the visible. In the field of the visible, the subject, as the lack of being, is inscribed in the painting together with his or her desire through the representation of the gaze as the *objet petit a*. It is this structure that enables the satisfaction of desire and the production of what Lacan calls surplus *jouissance* from a successful deciphering of the stain.

The stain in Holbein's painting can function as a screen or a 'stand-in for the gaze' because it corresponds to the basic characteristic of the *objet petit a* in Lacan, that is it is actually an anti-image since it does not have its specular image or otherness.[33] Lacan's point here thus lies not simply in the satisfaction gained from a successful deciphering of the unclear image or stain, but rather that, in so doing, one already transforms the stain into a positive image, thereby losing its very function as the one existing merely as a disturbing or detotalising moment in the painting, and not as separated from it in any way. For the stain is not the *other image*, an autonomous entity, which breaks into the field of the visual from the outside, but the *other of the image* or painting, an internal short-circuit of the field of vision itself. The success of deciphering the stain as a positive image already conceals the fact that the field of the visible is detotalised at the ontological level and not on the ontic level. That is why, as was already mentioned, Lacan's key point about the phenomenon of anamorphosis does not lie in deciphering the enigmatic stain itself, but in articulating the stain as a stand-in for the subject in the painting. Put differently, the gaze as an object belongs to the geometrical field of the visible, and as such is also a marker for the place of the subject's inscription in the painting itself. The subject and the object are no longer separated in the sense of the interior and the exterior of the painting, but belong to the same field as its effects.

It seems that surplus value in Marx has exactly the same structure as the anamorphic stain in Holbein's *The Ambassadors*. Even more, it seems that, at the level of the painting, *The Ambassadors* even directly visualises this structural paradox. It does so not only at the level of the structural relation between the stain and the entire painting that we have discussed thus far, but also at the level of the depicted figures, whereby *The Ambassadors* visualises the real of the structure in both senses of the word. The painting depicts nothing other than modern scientific knowledge itself (two ambassadors surrounded by instruments of knowledge and technical tools characteristic of modern science), which is precisely the knowledge that is established with the spoliation of the slave's practical knowledge (*savoir-faire*), that is with the separation of knowledge from the slave's labour. This separation simultaneously transforms the labour itself, which, with this discursive break or change in the master's discourse, as Lacan says, acquires the form of entropic surplus labour, which Lacan marks with *objet petit a*. One of Lacan's points regarding surplus labour as entropic loss is precisely that it becomes invisible from the viewpoint of modern knowledge: in descending and ascending a hill along the same path, the signifiers of energetics say that no work was performed. In the same way, when looking at the painting as a whole, the human skull appears as a stain. And perhaps it is no coincidence that, in *The Ambassadors*, surplus labour, which is the source of surplus value and surplus *jouissance*, is depicted precisely by a stain that, with a change of perspective, obtains the image of a human skull, which is, of course, the classical image of death. In this respect, in *The Ambassadors*, the stain as the materialisation of the surplus (surplus value and surplus *jouissance*) is depicted precisely by a skull as a metaphor of the death drive, which is materialised in the gaze as the *objet petit a* in the painting. However, the point here lies not in deciphering the stain/surplus, whereby we would lose the rest of the painting, but rather in the fact that, as in the case of entropy, the stain emerges only with(in) the painting itself and does not exist independently thereof.

We come across precisely the same point as to the production of surplus value in Marx, who claims that, in the production process, surplus value is produced as its surplus and not as an autonomous, independent entity. If surplus labour is the fund of abstract labour time, from which there derives surplus value, then we shall say that this amount of labour time is not an independent amount and that, at the phenomenal level, it cannot be clearly separated from the amount of time used for the reproduction of the value of labour power. In the case of producing surplus value, we should rather say that surplus labour sticks to abstract labour precisely as its internal stain, an internal short-circuit that cannot be visually separated from the entire amount of abstract labour, but rather functions as a purely formal internal discursive surplus over the signifying articulation through which capitalist production is organised. If surplus value was only an extra-discursive addition, then this form of exploitation would rather correspond to the pre-capitalist feudal form of labour and not to the wages system on which capitalist production is based. And it seems that one of the main ideological features of the infinite accumulation of capital is nothing other than a constant attempt at deciphering this traumatic stain: the owners of capital constantly reinvest surplus value, and thereby attempt to increase the volume of production and consequently accumulation, while the owners of labour power decipher it precisely by recognising in it a positive image, the image of their own value of labour power, which is nothing other than the false appearance, according to which the value of labour power appears as the value of labour itself. In this constellation, Marx, just like Lacan, was able to avoid the temptation to decipher the essence of the value, which leads to the positivisation of the stain of surplus value, precisely because he found in the production of the stain a stand-in for the subject and not simply an enigmatic meaning of the value of concrete labour. The deciphering rather corresponds to what the theories of human capital did and what in the end constitutes the core of the mystification of value. Put differently, both Marx and Lacan analyse and articulate the stain as an effect of the structure (of the relations of production in Marx and discourse in Lacan) and not as a 'hard' extra-discursive reality that is supposedly independent of discursive mediation.

In this regard, the anamorphic structure of surplus value in the field of the visible is homologous to the metaphor of the social hieroglyphic, which Marx and Lacan both employ to explain the logic of capitalist production on the one hand and the logic of the signifier on the other. In the last section, we will take a more detailed look at the structural homology between anamorphosis and the hieroglyphic.

... to the Social Hieroglyphic

Let us return for a moment to the mentioned spoliation of the slave's knowledge, which, according to Lacan, is the constitutive gesture that causes the transition from the master's discourse to the university discourse as the primary form of the capitalist social bond. Lacan says that spoliation transforms a serf into a wage labourer, who begins to function as a 'unit of value'.[34] In the discourse of the ancient master, knowledge was on the side of the slave/the other, and it referred to 'know-how' (*savoir-faire*), thus practical knowledge of the production of goods that brought pleasure to the master who did not have such knowledge. The renouncement of direct *jouissance* by the slave produced surplus *jouissance*, surplus satisfaction in the place of the structural absence of satisfaction. The 'spoliation of knowledge', which, according to Lacan, brings about the quarter turn of the discourse that transforms knowledge from the slave's practical 'know-how' to the so-called epistemic or scientific knowledge, while, at the same time, transferring it to the side of the master, simultaneously causes a shift of the surplus *jouissance* to the manifest level of discourse, while, in the place of production, a split subject begins to be produced.

In this context, the emergence of a wage labourer as a 'unit of value' (*objet petit a*) in the discursive place of the other is nothing but Lacan's translation of Marx's real abstraction, that is abstract social labour measured by abstract labour time ($S_2 \rightarrow a$), on which the system of wage labour and the production of surplus value are based, while the structural place of the other itself is characterised by the fact that, in the market or the sphere of circulation, an owner of capital buys labour power, which sells nothing other than precisely labour power. In other words, a labourer is inscribed in the discourse as a 'unit of value' insofar as he or she is spoliated of his or her substantial particularity, thus labour power, whose concrete use counts merely as abstract labour. If a labourer were inscribed in the discourse as 'human capital' and not as labour power, then there would be no surplus labour and no surplus value.

Here we come to the key consequence of the fact that a labourer counts as a 'unit of value' merely in the regime of capitalist knowledge. For, in the place of production, this counting begins to produce a split subject ($a/\$$ on the right side of the university discourse). We will now try to examine in more detail the relation between the 'counting' of value on the one hand and the production of the split subject on the other by drawing on the metaphor of the social hieroglyphic, which not only figures as a term in both Marx and Lacan, but also has an identical meaning in both, regardless of their different theoretical contexts, and, as such, provides an entry into their materialistic theory of the subject. In *Capital*, immediately after the famous 'they do this without being aware of it', by which Marx refers to the cunning of reason that operates behind the backs of the producers of commodities and implies the real abstraction, which means that the commodities are exchanged for an equal quantity of abstract human labour materialised in each of them, he adds the following: 'Value, therefore, does not have its description branded on its forehead; it rather transforms every product of labour into a social hieroglyphic.'[35]

How, then, can we decipher the 'mystery' of commodities as a social hieroglyphic? The spontaneous and therefore ideological approach taken by classical political economy consists in trying to decipher the direct meaning of such a hieroglyphic, that is in searching for and then translating its concrete meaning from an ancient language into a present-day language or from the silent language of commodities into human language. Marx indeed sees the reason for such a spontaneous approach in commodity fetishism, which induced classical political economy to deal with the concrete content of commodities instead of their formal determinations, that is with the value form itself. The latter is precisely what differentiates Marx's critique of political economy from classical political economy. That is why, in deciphering the mystery of the social hieroglyphic named commodity, Marx focuses precisely on the value form of commodities: what determines the exchange value and thus the equivalence of mutually exchangeable commodities is the equal amount of abstract human labour materialised therein, which is measured by abstract labour time. And because the value of commodities is determined by abstract labour, this implies the difference we highlighted above between the value created by labour power and the value of this labour power itself, whose social expression is a wage. What, therefore, stands behind the commodity form is the subject as the result of this difference: the social antagonism or logical contradiction between labour and capital derives from the fact that the more value labour produces, proportionally the less it gains through wages. And the 'proletariat' as a social subject *qua* symptom is precisely the effect of this difference.[36]

The key point of Marx's critique of political economy thus lies not in it deciphering the direct meaning of concrete commodities, their substantial mystery, but in analysing the commodity form to find the structural cause of commodity production and the counting of surplus value on the one hand and the subject as the effect of this same production process on the other (recall, in Lacan's university discourse, that the barred subject is located in the structural place of production).

We find exactly the same point in Lacan's case of hieroglyphics, by which he explains his well-known definition of the signifier:

> Now, what is a signifier? I have been drumming it into you long enough not to have to articulate it once again here. A signifier is that which represents a subject. For whom? – not for another subject, but for another signifier. In order to illustrate this axiom, suppose that in the desert you find a stone covered with hieroglyphics. You do not doubt for a moment that, behind them, there was a subject who wrote them. But it is an error to believe that each signifier is addressed to you – this is proved by the fact that you cannot understand any of it. On the other hand you define them as signifiers, by the fact that you are sure that each of these signifiers is related to each of the others. And it is this that is at issue with the relation between the subject and the field of the Other. The subject is born in so far as the signifier emerges in the field of the Other. But, by this very fact, this subject – which, was previously nothing if not a subject coming into being – solidifies into a signifier.[37]

The point of the incomprehensible hieroglyphic thus lies not in us deciphering its hidden meaning, but in the hieroglyphic, in the form of signifiers, implying its subject, the subject as the effect of a certain signifying articulation. At this point, it seems that the hieroglyphic has an anamorphic form homologous to the stain in the field of the visible. It is a signifying representative of the subject, its marker in the field of language. So, it is not a matter of a direct meaning and the deciphering thereof, but of an unstable symbolic structure, whose internal torsion is materialised in the surplus value/stain, which does not exist independently, outside the signifying system.

Again, we find a similar point in Marx's analysis of the commodity form: surplus value sticks as an internal stain/surplus to the value that transforms commodities into social hieroglyphics and equates them on the basis of the equal amount of abstract human labour materialised therein. As such, surplus value is a material representative of the subject and his or her abstract labour, which is characterised precisely by the fact that it is not private-individual labour, but social labour, 'registered' in the field of the big Other. The subject is therefore an effect (not a condition)[38] of the production and counting of surplus value. In other words, the subject, as such, is nothing other than an effect of the constitutively lacking (primordially repressed) signifier,[39] due to which surplus *jouissance* or surplus value is formed as a discursive surplus in the place of the lacking signifier. The unary trait, or the master-signifier (S_1), whose fundamental characteristic is that it repeats itself, makes the subject 'solidify into a signifier', which can be read in the sense that, as a 'unit of value', the labourer counts in the regime of the capitalist symbolic constellation sutured by the singular signifier. It is precisely this suture that conceals from the subject the fact that he or she does not exist as capital, but merely as a substantial nothingness, that is as a stain and not as a deciphered image of his or her own value, which is precisely the phantasm on which the idea of human capital is based.

To bring this contribution to a close, we can only briefly add that Marx's insistence on eliminating the wages system as such and not simply on increasing the value of labour power within this system implies precisely his insistence on the structural primacy of the discourse over the stain alone, while the temptation we should resist is precisely the satisfaction in deciphering it, in isolating the stain from its structural causes. The goal of the new politico-economic constellation that Marx calls communism is thus neither the deciphering of the stain, which merely reproduces the existing field of the visible (the relations of production), nor a naive attempt at erasing the stain, but a different, new articulation of the relation between the stain and the entire painting. Communism as a stain that becomes the painting itself?

Notes

1. This chapter is a result of the research programme P6-0014 'Conditions and Problems of Contemporary Philosophy', the research project J6-9392 'The Problem of Objectivity and Fiction in Contemporary Philosophy' and the bilateral cooperation project BI-US/18-20-026 'Objectivity beyond the Subject-Object Dichotomy: Fiction, Truth, Affect' between the Research Centre of the Slovenian Academy of Science and Arts and the University of New Mexico, which are funded by the Slovenian Research Agency.
2. Relying on Paul Wayne's conception of 'historical nominalism', Thomas R. Flynn described Foucault's approach to history as nothing other than 'an attempt to draw the full conclusions from a consistently nominalistic position'. Thomas R. Flynn, *Sartre, Foucault, and Historical Reason* (Chicago and London: University of Chicago Press, 2005), p. 31.
3. See Michel Foucault, *The Birth of Biopolitics, Lectures at Collège de France, 1978–79*, trans. Graham Burchell (Basingstoke: Palgrave, 2008).
4. One of the most concise and rigorous recent studies of Foucault's ambiguous relation to Marx can be found in Zdravko Kobe, 'Foucault's Neoliberal Post-Marxism', in *Lacan Contra Foucault*, ed. Nadia Bou Ali and Rohit Goel (London and New York: Bloomsbury, 2019), pp. 161–209.
5. Foucault, *The Birth of Biopolitics*, pp. 219–20.
6. Foucault, *The Birth of Biopolitics*, pp. 221–2.
7. Foucault, *The Birth of Biopolitics*, p. 224.
8. Foucault, *The Birth of Biopolitics*, p. 225.
9. Foucault, *The Birth of Biopolitics*, p. 226.
10. As a side note, we should mention – in the context of Foucault's misreading of Marx in the seminar *The Birth of Biopolitics* – one pretty astonishing coincidence with his misreading of Freudian psychoanalysis in the first volume of *The History of Sexuality*: in fact, as Alenka Zupančič has shown (see Alenka Zupančič, 'Biopolitics, Sexuality and the Unconscious', *Paragraph*, vol. 39, no. 1 (2016), pp. 49–64), Foucault dismisses Freudian psychoanalysis as a 'technology of biopolitics' without ever mentioning the concept that represents Freud's greatest discovery: the unconscious. Likewise, in the seminar *The Birth of Biopolitics*, Foucault develops a critique of Marx without ever mentioning any of the latter's three fundamental concepts, namely the value form, surplus value and commodity fetishism. Taking into account any of these three concepts, one can only dismiss 'human capital' as a discursive element of the ideological mystification of labour.
11. Karl Marx, 'Wages, Price and Profit', in *Wage Labour and Capital and Wages, Price and Profit* (Paris: Foreign Language Press, 1976/2020), p. 89.

12. Marx, 'Wages, Price and Profit', p. 89.
13. Jacques Lacan, *The Seminar of Jacques Lacan, Book XVII: The Other Side of Psychoanalysis*, ed. Jacques-Alain Miller, trans. Russell Grigg (London and New York: W. W. Norton, 2007), p. 177; hereafter cited as *Seminar XVII*.
14. The 'homology' at stake has been discussed in detail, especially by Alenka Zupančič and Samo Tomšič. See, for example, Alenka Zupančič, 'When Surplus Enjoyment Meets Surplus Value', in *Jacques Lacan and the Other Side of Psychoanalysis: Reflections on Seminar XVII*, ed. Russell Grigg (Durham, NC and London: Duke University Press, 2006), pp. 155–78; Samo Tomšič, *The Capitalist Unconscious: Marx and Lacan* (London and New York: Verso, 2015); Samo Tomšič, *The Labour of Enjoyment: Toward a Critique of Libidinal Economy* (Cologne: August Verlag, 2019); Samo Tomšič, 'Psychoanalysis, Capitalism, and the Critique of Political Economy: Toward a Marxist Lacan', in *Jacques Lacan: Between Psychoanalysis and Politics*, ed. Samo Tomšič and Andreja Zevnik (London and New York: Routledge, 2016), pp. 146–63.
15. See Zupančič, 'When Surplus Enjoyment Meets Surplus Value', pp. 155–78.
16. For an overarching assessment of the 'mastery' in Lacan's theory of the four discourses, see Peter Klepec, 'On the Mastery in the Four "Discourses"', in *Jacques Lacan between Psychoanalysis and Politics*, ed. Samo Tomšič and Andreja Zevnik (London and New York: Routledge, 2016), pp. 115–30.
17. Lacan, *Seminar XVII*, p. 32.
18. Figures 2.1 and 2.2 can be found in Jacques Lacan, *The Seminar of Jacques Lacan, Book XX: Encore*, ed. Jacques-Alain Miller, trans. Bruce Fink (W. W. Norton, 1998), pp. 16 and 17.
19. See Lacan, *Seminar XVII*, p. 32.
20. Recall Lacan's example of entropy:

    I defy you to prove in any way that descending 500 meters with a weight of 80 kilos on your back and, once you have descended, going back up the 500 meters with it is zero, no work. Try it, have a go yourself, and you will find that you have proof of the contrary. But if you overlay signifiers, that is, if you enter the path of energetics, it is absolutely certain that there has been no work. When the signifier is introduced as an apparatus of *jouissance*, we should thus not be surprised to see something related to entropy appear, since entropy is defined precisely once one has started to lay this apparatus of signifiers over the physical world. (Lacan, *Seminar XVII*, p. 49)

    To be sure, the 'real loss' in the form of surplus work, which is precisely the main source of surplus value, does not pre-exist the 'overlaying' of the signifiers of energetics on it, but is the effect of this discursive operation, that is, as Lacan does not fail to point out in this passage, it emerges only after the apparatus of signifiers (knowledge) is laid over the physical world or nature.

21. Marx, 'Wages, Price and Profit', p. 84. Indeed, according to Marx, the separation of men from their means of production, which leads to the distinction between the owner of capital or capitalists and the possessors of labour power or workers, originates in what he calls the 'primitive accumulation of capital' (see Karl Marx, *Capital. A Critique of Political Economy, Volume One*, trans. Ben Fowkes (London: Penguin, 1976), pp. 873–940), that is, the privatisation of the means of production in the historical passage from feudalism to capitalism. This is why in 'Wages, Price and Profit' Marx proposes an even more radical term: 'Original Expropriation' (Marx, 'Wages, Price and Profit', p. 84).

22. Marx, 'Wages, Price and Profit', p. 82.

23. Labour as 'real abstraction', that is, as 'social labour', and not as a transhistorical invariable, is nowadays again the subject of theoretical debates. For more on this, see a recent intervention by Slavoj Žižek: "Is Abstract Labor Universal?", available at: <https://thephilosophicalsalon.com/is-abstract-labor-universal/#_ednref6> (accessed 20 January 2021). As far as money as 'real abstraction' in capitalism is concerned, money obviously existed in historical formations prior to capitalism. However, as Arthur Bradley has recently shown, relying on Marx's famous footnote in *Capital*, where he discusses Aristotle's distinction between the close order of the household (*oikonomia*) and chrematistics' conception of money as something that can be created anew, which transforms the economy into a potentially endless process, capitalism breaks with the Aristotelian essentially naturalistic and ontological conception of money, which considered the capacity to create the money as conceived by chrematistics to be 'unnatural'. In capitalism, the question of money as a 'real abstraction' is not even posed in terms of 'nature' but in terms of 'use'. See Arthur Bradley, 'Human Interests', *Theory, Culture and Society* (forthcoming).

24. *The rate of surplus value*, all other circumstances remaining the same, will depend on the proportion between that necessary to reproduce the value of the labouring power and the *surplus time* or *surplus labour* performed for the capitalist. It will, therefore, depend on the *ratio in which the working day is prolonged over and above that extent*, by working which the working man would only reproduce the value of his labouring power, or replace his wages. (Marx, 'Wages, Price and Profit', p. 88)

25. Marx, 'Wages, Price and Profit', p. 89.
26. Marx, 'Wages, Price and Profit', p. 89.
27. See Tomšič, *The Capitalist Unconscious*.

28. Mladen Dolar, 'Anamorphosis', *S: Journal of the Circle for Lacanian Ideology Critique*, vol. 8 (2015), p. 129.
29. Jacques Lacan, *The Seminar of Jacques Lacan, Book VII: The Ethics of Psychoanalysis*, ed. Jacques-Alain Miller, trans. Dennis Porter (London and New York: W. W. Norton, 1992), p. 140; hereafter cited as *Seminar VII*. See on this also Lorenzo Chiesa, 'Exalted Obscenity and the Lawyer of God: Lacan, Deleuze, and the Baroque', in *Lacan and Deleuze: A Disjunctive Synthesis*, ed. Boštjan Nedoh and Andreja Zevnik (Edinburgh: Edinburgh University Press, 2017), pp. 145–7.
30. Lacan, *Seminar VII*, p. 135.
31. Jacques Lacan, *The Seminar of Jacques Lacan, Book XI: The Four Fundamental Concepts of Psychoanalysis*, ed. Jacques-Alain Miller, trans. Alan Sheridan (London and New York: W. W. Norton, 1998), lessons 6–9, pp. 67–121; hereafter cited as *Seminar XI*.
32. Dolar, 'Anamorphosis', p. 130.
33. 'A common characteristic of these objects as I formulate them is that they have no specular image, in other words, no alterity' (Jacques Lacan, 'Subversion of the Subject and the Dialectic of Desire in the Freudian Unconscious', in *Écrits: The First Complete Edition in English*, trans. Bruce Fink (London and New York: W. W. Norton, 2006), p. 693).
34. Lacan, *Seminar XVII*, p. 81.
35. Marx, *Capital*, p. 167.
36. See, on this, the already canonical discussion by Slavoj Žižek, *The Sublime Object of Ideology* (London: Verso, 1989), Ch. 1, pp. 10–53.
37. Lacan, *Seminar XI*, pp. 198–9.
38. Precisely because the subject is placed at the level of effect and not at the level of the condition of possibility, we are dealing in Marx and Lacan with a materialist and not simply a transcendental theory of the subject. See on this Samo Tomšič, 'Towards a New Transcendental Aesthetics?', in Michael Friedman and Samo Tomšič (eds), *Psychoanalysis: Topological Perspectives* (Berlin: Transcript, 2016), pp. 95–124. However, for 'transcendental materialism' as a 'synthesis' of the materialist and transcendental approach, see Adrian Johnston's three-volume *Prolegomena to Any Future Materialism* (Evanston, IL: Northwestern University Press, 2013 (Vol. 1) and 2019 (Vol. 2)).
39. On the structural primacy of primal repression or the repression of the first signifier, which causes the symbolic order to run according to the principles of metaphor and metonymy, see the ground-breaking book by Alenka Zupančič, *What Is Sex?* (Cambridge, MA: MIT Press, 2017).

3 Shades of Green: Lacan and Capitalism's Veils
Adrian Johnston

THE TENTH AND final session (16 June 1971) of Jacques Lacan's *Seminar XVIII: Of a Discourse That Would Not Be a Semblance* (1971) contains a now well-known assertion. On that occasion, Lacan claims that Karl Marx is responsible for inventing, albeit *avant la lettre*, the specifically psychoanalytic concept of the symptom.[1] In this context, Lacan promptly identifies Marx's analysis of money in connection with commodity fetishism as the site of this proto-Freudian innovation within the Marxian corpus.[2]

Of course, in psychoanalysis, all sorts of phenomena can count as symptoms in the Freudian sense: dreams, parapraxes, slips of the tongue, compulsive repetitions, apparently somatic ailments, etc. Yet Lacan, taking his lead from the first volume of *Das Kapital*, repeatedly focuses on fetishes as exemplary analytic symptoms. Several times, he posits an equivalency (or, at least, significant overlapping) of usage of the term 'fetishism' between Marxism and psychoanalysis.[3]

Lacan's crediting of Marx with inventing the concept of the symptom as it subsequently comes to feature in Freudian psychoanalysis understandably focuses on the symptom of commodity fetishism as per *Capital, Volume One*. However, Lacan ignores the fashions in which this fetishism reaches a peak at which it reveals its purified essence only in the third volume of *Das Kapital* (with Marx's reflections on money as 'interest-bearing capital' (IBC)). A psychoanalytic engagement with commodity fetishism as per Volume Three allows both: one, for correcting certain inaccuracies in Lacan's reading of Marx as well as, two, further nuancing and validating Lacan's core intuitions about fetishism as a point of convergence between Marxism and psychoanalysis. Moreover, Freudian and Lacanian analytic considerations apropos sexual fetishism furnish a set of cautionary considerations regarding the prospects for overcoming commodity fetishism – and, along with it, capitalism itself as a mode of production. In light of Sigmund Freud's and Lacan's analyses of fetishism and its defences, 'curing' commodity fetishism, although far from impossible, looks to be a much more daunting and difficult task than traditional Marxism seems to anticipate. Marxists might need to be much more patient than they would expect to be about the eventual dissolution of capitalistic fetishism. Although fetishes are fictions, deceptive illusions mesmerising those in their thrall, they nonetheless are stubbornly objective, namely real abstractions with all-too-concrete efficacy and consequences.

As early as *Seminar V: Formations of the Unconscious* (1957–58), Lacan zeros in on 'the fetishistic value of gold'.[4] In *Seminar VI: Desire and Its Interpretation* (1958–59), he identifies Marx's miser, the hoarder of gold, as the paradigmatic fetishist.[5] Likewise, in *Seminar XVI: From an Other to the other* (1968–69), money is spoken of as the 'enigmatic . . . fetish *par excellence*'.[6]

At this same moment in the sixteenth seminar, Lacan makes a mistake in his discussion of money *à la* Marx. He contends that, for Marx, money has no use-value.[7] This is erroneous on two levels. First, if currency in its physical form (i.e. as metal, paper, etc.) is at issue, the tangible qualities of currency indeed possess use-value(s). With metallic coins, one can scratch off lottery tickets, perform flips to decide between binary alternatives ('heads or tails?'), pry certain things open, and so on. And, if one chooses to do so, one can write on bills, turn them into paper airplanes, light cigars with them and the like. These are examples of uses that coins and bills possess by virtue of their character as particular kinds of material objects. Moreover, these use-values are distinct from their roles in facilitating the exchange of other commodities. Hence, money as currency indeed has use-values apart from exchange-values.

Second, there is money as interest. What Marx calls 'interest-bearing capital' is defined by him as money insofar as it possesses the potential to produce more money.[8] In other words, IBC is money with the use-value of giving rise to surplus-value, with the rate of interest as the market price for this particular use-value.[9] Perhaps Lacan overlooks this second type of use-value with which money (as capital) is endowed due to his apparent neglect of Marx's discussions of commodity fetishism and interest specifically in the third volume of *Capital*. Lacan's musings about commodity fetishism seem to be limited to references to the first volume alone.

I wish to overcome this limitation by extending the Lacanian treatment of Marxian commodity fetishism to cover this fetishism as it completes itself via IBC as per *Capital, Volume Three*. Doing so promises to enrich an appreciation of the psychoanalytic mechanisms of repression (*Verdrängung*) and disavowal (*Verleugnung*) especially. But, in order to attain these enrichments, a more detailed engagement with Lacan's account of fetishism is necessary.

Fetishism receives the greatest amount of Lacan's attention during the period of his teaching from the mid-1950s through the early 1960s. The fourth (*The Object Relation* (1956–57)), fifth, and sixth seminars contain the majority of his comments on this topic. However, a handful of remarks on fetishism are scatted across subsequent years of *le Séminaire*.

First of all, Lacan repeatedly depicts fetishism as epitomising the libidinal economics of human subjectivity in general. More precisely, Lacan associates fetishism with what is at the heart of his distinctive conception of 'desire' (*désir*). In the same contexts during which he discusses fetishists and their fetishes, he emphasises the essential, inherent perversity of human desire as such[10] (in Lacan's footsteps, Octave Mannoni, in his classic 1963 essay on fetishism, '*Je sais bien, mais quand même . . .*', likewise anchors fetishism, with its mechanism of disavowal (*Verleugnung*),[11] in the ostensibly trans-historical make-up of Lacanian desire[12]). At these moments, Lacan also crowns fetishism 'the perversion of perversions'[13] and maintains that, 'All of desire's objects are fetishistic in character.'[14] He portrays fetishism as 'a particularly fundamental example of the dynamic of desire.'[15] Lacan likewise casts the fetish object as a 'milestone of desire' (*borne miliaire du désir*).[16]

Very much in the spirit of the 'return to Freud' of the 1950s, Lacan carefully grounds his own account of fetishism in Freud's writings on the topic. In the 1927 essay 'Fetishism,' Freud states the following apropos his central thesis having it that fetish objects are stand-ins for the absent feminine penis, ersatz things designed specifically to ward off castration anxiety:

> When now I announce that the fetish is a substitute for the penis, I shall certainly create disappointment; so I hasten to add that it is not a substitute for any chance penis, but for a particular and quite special penis (*eines bestimmten, ganz besonderen Penis*) that had been extremely important in early childhood but had later been lost. That is to say, it should normally have been given up, but the fetish is precisely designed to preserve it from extinction. To put it more plainly: the fetish is a substitute for the woman's (the mother's) penis . . .[17]

This 'particular and quite special penis' is nothing other than the impossible, non-existent maternal phallus (i.e. 'the woman's (the mother's) penis'). Lacan endorses Freud's core thesis concerning fetishism here.[18] And, insofar as those sexed female by definition do not have penises, a feminine phallus, as precisely what fetish objects are disguised substitutes for, is akin to a square circle. Like a square circle, it is a fiction sustainable only in and through linguistic symbolisations.[19]

For Lacan, who appropriately focuses on Freud's '*bestimmten, ganz besonderen*

Penis', the only sort of 'castration' feminine subjects, the mother included, can undergo is of a symbolic sort. Why? As I explain elsewhere:

> In . . . the mid-1950s, Lacan introduces a tripartite schema of negatives on the basis of his register theory. More precisely, in recasting Freud's ideas with regard to castration, he distinguishes between 'privation' (as Real, an incarnate non-presence dwelling in material being in itself), 'castration' (as Symbolic, a deficit created in reality by the interventions of sociolinguistic mediators), and 'frustration' (as Imaginary, a representational confusion of Real privation and/or Symbolic castration as deprivations and obstacles gratuitously imposed from without – to the extent that the Imaginary misrecognizes the Real as the Symbolic and vice versa, frustration reacts to privation as castration and to castration as privation).[20]

I subsequently add:

> . . . biologically female human organisms, in the (material) Real, are not 'missing' a penis or anything else; they simply are as they are. With regard to the dimension of the Lacanian Real pictured as the presupposed plenum of asubjective incarnate being, there are no absences or lacks. Instead, with respect to the matters at issue in the psychoanalytic castration complex, there are, from this angle, just vaginas and penises. The vagina is not the absence of a penis, since trying to situate these organs vis-à-vis each other in this way is, according to Lacan's register theory, a category mistake in which a comparison between proverbial apples and oranges is subreptionally transformed into a binary opposition between having and not having, one and zero, plus and minus, and so on.[21]

I continue:

> But, of course, Freud and Lacan both consider the committing of this category mistake, in which penises and vaginas go from being apples and oranges to becoming presences and absences, to be a near-inevitability during ontogenetic subject formation as taking shape within still-reigning phallocentric symbolic orders. In Lacan's rendering of the castration complex, the inscription of lacks in the Real by the Symbolic – it is only through symbolization that something can be said to be missing, strictly speaking – establishes the very distinction between privation and castration per se. As regards a biological female, privation would be the fact that having a vagina entails not having a penis (as the Spinozistic-Hegelian ontological principle has it, *omnis determinatio est negatio*, or 'all determination is negation'). This privation is transubstantiated into castration proper if and only if such

determination-as-negation is symbolised as itself a non-determination, namely, as an absence relative to a specific corresponding presence (in elementary formal-logical terms, when a difference between A and B is reinscribed as a contradiction between A and not-A). According to Lacan, 'castration' is intrinsically Symbolic – for him, it is always 'symbolic castration' – both for these reasons, as well as because the castration complex epitomises the more general existential ordeal of the living human creature being subjected to the overriding and overwriting dictates of the big Other as symbolic order with its overdetermining significations.[22]

The theoretical-conceptual triad of privation-castration-frustration I gloss in these passages is presented by Lacan primarily in *Seminar IV*, which itself also contains his single most sustained set of reflections on fetishism. The missing maternal phallus central to both Freud's and Lacan's interpretations of fetish objects is the object of specifically symbolic castration as per Lacan and his trinity of privation, castration and frustration.

Indeed, Lacan again and again denies that the phallus of the fetishist has to do with the Real or Imaginary penis (as the object of privation or frustration respectively).[23] Instead, the missing maternal phallus ultimately at stake in all instances of fetishism as per psychoanalysis is the one created and sustained *ex nihilo* by the signifiers involved with symbolic castration. This special phallus is Symbolic in (second) nature.[24] Accordingly, fetish objects are and have to do with the artificial and false (*factice*).[25] In one of Lacan's earliest pieces to appear in English, 1956's 'Fetishism: The Symbolic, the Imaginary and the Real' (co-authored with Wladimir Granoff and contemporaneous with Lacan's fourth seminar), the connection between fetishes and Symbolic signifiers is stressed throughout.[26]

Also in *Seminar IV*, in the section Jacques-Alain Miller entitles 'The Fetish Object' (a section consisting of three consecutive sessions, 30 January, 6 February and 27 February 1957), Lacan speaks of the symbolic order as giving rise to 'the desire for the impossible' ('*le désir de l'impossible*').[27] During this same seminar session (27 February 1957), he relatedly asserts that fetishism, 'the perversion of perversions', has nothing(ness) as its object ('*l'objet est exactement rien*').[28] As I noted a moment ago, this same Lacan views fetishism as displaying the distilled essence of human *désir tout court*. Moreover, Lacanian desire consistently is linked to a libidinal dynamic involving absence, lack, nothing(ness), etc.

The fetishist's desire is governed by the missing maternal phallus. This desired thing is a contradictory, unreal (non-)object sustained as a point of reference only in and through symbolisation. Thus fetishism brings out in especially sharp relief the essence of desire in general as fixated upon signifier-marked impossibilities and inexistences. This explains both Lacan's association of the phallus and the fetish object with the Platonic *ágalma* in *Seminar VIII: Transference* (1960–61)[29] as well as his equation of the fetish with *objet petit a* as cause of desire in *Seminar X: Anxiety* (1962–63).[30]

In a fortuitous turn of phrase, the Lacan of the fourth seminar refers to the phallus as '*la monnaie majeure*' (major currency).[31] This might very well be an intentional wording, given that the Lacan of this period soon proceeds to link his discussion of analytic fetishism with commodity fetishism *à la* Marx (as involving money, gold and the like). At this juncture, though, I want to pause briefly in order to draw a comparison between the missing maternal phallus as per Lacan and Marx's account of interest in the third volume of *Das Kapital*.

Already in *Capital, Volume One*, in the second half of the first paragraph of 'The Fetishism of the Commodity and Its Secret', Marx employs the example of a wooden table to bring out the weirdness of commodities, these apparently banal objects, within capitalism. He famously states:

> The form of wood, for instance, is altered if a table is made out of it. Nevertheless the table continues to be wood, an ordinary, sensuous thing (*ein ordinäres sinnliches Ding*). But as soon as it emerges as a commodity, it changes into a thing which transcends sensuousness (*ein sinnlich übersinnliches Ding*). It not only stands with its feet on the ground, but, in relation to all other commodities, it stands on its head (*auf den Kopf*), and evolves out of its wooden brain grotesque ideas, far more wonderful than if it were to begin dancing of its own free will.[32]

Arguably, the symbolised non-entity that is the absent feminine phallus underlying fetishism and its peculiar objects is of a degree of sense-transcending strangeness comparable to Marx's wooden table *qua* commodity. What is more, commodity fetishism, according to Marx, reaches its definitive apotheosis in the form of IBC.[33] As IBC, money gives the impression of being uniquely capable of sustaining the dynamic of M-M', namely self-valorisation as the production of surplus-value *ex nihilo*. An object that seems to behave as a subject, an inert, lifeless product of human artifice that looks as though it spontaneously engages in an auto-enhancing frenetic movement of self-multiplication – is this not at least as fantastical as maternal phalli? When functioning as IBC, money appears more than any other commodity (whether wooden tables or whatever else) 'to begin dancing of its own free will'. Interestingly, Norman O. Brown performs the Freudian gesture of tethering interest as money-breeding money to childhood fantasies about faeces – 'Money is inorganic dead matter which has been made alive by inheriting the magic power which infantile narcissism attributes to the excremental product.'[34] Brown soon adds that, 'Money inherits the infantile magic of excrement and then is able to breed and have children.'[35]

That said, and before addressing Lacan's fashions of linking analytic and Marxian fetishisms, another facet of the Lacanian rendition of the fetish object is important for me to highlight. In the three sessions of *Seminar IV* entitled 'The Fetish Object', Lacan brings to the fore the figure of the veil (*le voile*) or curtain (*le rideau*). The function of veiling is crucial to Lacan's speculations about fetishism.[36]

Lacan declares that, 'The curtain is . . . the idol of absence.'[37] What he means by this is that the fetish object can be traced back to the last thing the young fetishist-to-be sees before this little person's vision confronts the maternal Other's lack of a phallus. This classic Freudian narrative explains, for instance, the prominence of shoe fetishism, since the mother's shoe is something seen by the small child's gaze ascending up her legs just prior to it alighting upon her genital region. For Lacan, the fetish is 'a substitute, a monument'[38] – 'The fetish is a *Denkmal*.'[39] That is to say, the fetish object memorialises for the fetishist the moment right before the crossing of the threshold into a registration of 'castration' and/as sexual difference.[40]

During the fourth seminar, Lacan utilises a reference to the medium of film so as to further concretise his linkage between the fetish and the curtain/veil. He describes the fetish object as arising from the sudden stoppage of a filmed sequence in which a frame immediately prior to the frames containing the scene of the missing maternal phallus is frozen in place. This frozen frame becomes the template for the subsequent fetish object(s). Moreover, with the freezing of the film at a moment preceding the scene of 'castration', the frozen frame operates as a sort of veil covering the missing phallus. Similarly, since this same frame is part of a longer sequence, it is a metonymic fragment standing for the whole filmed episode that reaches its denouement in the confrontation with the maternal Other as deprived of the phallus.[41]

The fetish object, like a screen memory[42] as well as other types of analytic symptoms, simultaneously reveals and conceals that against which it serves as a defence. Analytic symptoms are repressions and, at the same time, returns of the repressed. As a stand-in, the fetish object conceals the maternal phallus for which it substitutes. As a monument, the fetish object reveals its repressed (or, rather, disavowed) origins, memorialising its roots for those with eyes to see and ears to hear.

Curtains and veils likewise both conceal and reveal. On the one hand, they cover over something hidden behind them. On the other hand, through this same covering, they suggest a number of possible presences or absences on their nether sides. Curtains and veils encourage those they confront to project various things into the indeterminate beyonds they shroud. Lacan's well-known recounting, in *Seminar XI: The Four Fundamental Concepts of Psychoanalysis* (1964), of the *trompe l'oeil* painting contest between Zeuxis and Parrhasios nicely makes this point.[43] What is more, the curtain/veil serves to maintain a desire-sustaining distance between desire itself and its corresponding object.[44]

Marx, in his characterisations of IBC as the apogee of capitalistic fetishism, employs the German adjective '*äußerlichste*' (most superficial) to characterise this fetishism.[45] Marx's positing of a maximal superficiality in the fetishism of M-M' entails a dialectics weaving together surfaces and depths as well as visibilities and invisibilities. Lacan's parsing of the analytic fetish object as a curtain/veil that simultaneously both obscures a beyond (as a kind of repression) as well as bears witness, like a monument or memorial, to what it obscures (as a sort of return of the repressed) arguably elucidates the type of superficiality at work in Marxian commodity fetishism as culminating in IBC. If the fetishist's object is an analytic symptom par excellence, then the place where Marx perhaps most strikingly anticipates the symptom in the analytic sense (an anticipation Lacan, as seen, attributes to him) is in the treatment of interest in the third volume of *Das Kapital*.

IBC's M-M' is the fetishised seventh veil of capitalism. IBC, as the culmination of commodity fetishism, is the surface, or even the iceberg's tip, on which the revealing return of the repressed perversely coincides with the most concealing repression. On the revealing hand, M-M' renders visible the truth that capitalists accrue surplus-value as something for nothing, without themselves contributing productive labour. Yet, on the concealing hand, M-M' renders invisible the truth that labour, not capital, produces all values. IBC hides this truth behind its opposite, namely the diametrically opposed false appearance according to which capital itself, as self-valorising value, is the mother of all values.

In *Seminar V*, Lacan initiates a process of interweaving the Marxian and psychoanalytic theories of fetishism. Inspired by Marx, he holds up the example of gold as a paradigmatic avatar of human desire.[46] Gold historically embodies and epitomises currency as the universal equivalent, namely the one commodity exchangeable for all other commodities. In Lacan's terms, this makes gold, as the emblem of exchange-value, a Symbolic facilitator of a *désir* sliding indefinitely from commodity to commodity. Gold-*qua*-money is the signifier of desire's inherent tendency to drift metonymically, restlessly and ceaselessly from object to object.[47]

Soon after this, in *Seminar VI*, Lacan consequently insists that commodity fetishism is to be situated in his register of the Symbolic. He contends that Marx's version of fetishism depends upon the logic of the signifier as decoded by Lacanian psychoanalysis.[48] Yet Lacan's conceptions of desire and Symbolic signifiers avowedly are meant to be trans-historical. In the spirit of Freudian metapsychology, Lacan is committed to a perspective according to which psychoanalysis can and does pinpoint psychical-subjective structures and dynamics common to all humans in all times and places. Moreover, Lacan even insists on the trans-historical status of core analytic concepts right when referencing Marx on money and commodity fetishism. Considering Marx's historicising bent, this is rather perplexing.[49]

The question of just how much of a historiciser Marx is or is not is itself very tricky. On my reading of him (as developed elsewhere), he is not automatically and unqualifiedly opposed to hypothesising trans-historical forces and factors. Indeed, certain components of his own historical materialism look as though they need to function as transcendental-type possibility conditions for history and its myriad phenomena.[50]

Yet, at least when it comes to commodity fetishism, Marx almost certainly would be resistant to Lacan's gestures of wrapping it up with a desire purportedly inherent to humanity's *Gattungswesen*. Marx defines commodities such that they are objects peculiar to capitalism alone. Furthermore, although interest as money breeding money shows up in various historical modes of production, IBC as money breeding surplus-value through lending to commercial/industrial (i.e. productive) capital (as M-C-M') also is peculiar to capitalism alone. IBC is different from interest yielded by lending to traders or consumers.

At the same time, Marx might be willing to acknowledge that the more general logic of interest as M-M' (i.e. as operative in lending to consumers, merchants and capitalists alike) goes from being a freak exception prior to capitalism (as it indeed is portrayed by Aristotle,[51] for instance) to becoming the normalised rule under the reign of finance capital. Nonetheless, given the difference-in-kind between a consumerist desire oriented toward use-values (as C-M-C') and a properly capitalist desire oriented toward exchange/surplus-values (as M-C-M'),[52] the Lacanian move of annexing capitalistic commodity fetishism to desire as a universal, trans-historical category risks obscuring more than it illuminates.

Despite such dangers, Lacan's analytic meditations on commodity fetishism nevertheless also subtly enhance the sense in which, according to Marx, fetishism entails relations between persons showing up in the guise of relations between things. To be more exact, Lacan links fetish objects, including Marxian commodities, to his notion of *le désir de l'Autre* (the Other's desire). He proposes that the exchanged objects of commodity fetishism signify this desire.[53] Blending together Marx's and Lacan's wordings, this would be to say that fetishised commodity-objects are things substituting, memorialising or standing-in for Others and the subject's (fraught non-)relationships with them. But what, precisely, does this mean? And what are its implications for Marxism and/or psychoanalysis?

I would suggest that money, as the commodity par excellence *qua* universal equivalent, could be appropriately labelled in hybrid Marxian-psychoanalytic terms as 'the self-cleaning fetish'. This phrase might initially call to mind symptomatic compulsive hand washing. However, I am referring with this label instead to capitalist money as laundering itself. Although money is not really self-valorising – it appears so only through capital's illusory eclipsing of the productivity of the labour power it exploits – it certainly looks to be self-laundering under capitalism.

In fact, at this juncture, three different modes of capitalistic money's self-laundering ought to be identified. First, there is the ideology of the level playing field of job markets wherein capital and labour meet and negotiate fair-and-square employment contracts. In particular, there is the myth of a day's wages for a day's work. Obviously, this myth uses a false equivalence between the quantity of monetary remuneration for labour performed and the quantity of time spent in performing said labour. Money as wages thereby, within the frame of this fiction, conceals capitalism's structurally necessary exploitation of labour power in the guise of surplus unpaid labour as surplus-value appropriated gratis by capital.

Second, there is the difference between rate of surplus-value and rate of profit. The rate of surplus-value calculates this value in relation to variable capital only. By contrast, the rate of profit calculates surplus-value in relation to total capital (i.e. variable plus constant capital). Hence, looking at surplus-value as profit makes it seem as though capital is extracting much less from labour than it is in actuality.[54] Worse still, the notion of profit tends to be ideologically packaged as 'wages of superintendence' and/or 'profit of enterprise', namely income genuinely earned by capitalists performing specialised sorts of their own labour.[55] The members of the bourgeoisie sweat too. They truly deserve just compensation.

Third, there are the illusions emanating from money as IBC. Such money capital is indeed the apex of commodity fetishism. It presents the fiction of a golden egg laying more golden eggs – and this without either goose or goose-rearing farmer. IBC is the divine miracle, the immaculate conception, of surplus-value enhancing itself *ex nihilo*, without productive labour or any living subjective agency whatsoever. M-M' is akin to a thingly version of Baron Munchausen, money pulling itself up ever higher by nothing but its own hair. A person performing such a feat just once is fantastical enough. An inert object doing so ad infinitum is beyond belief. Yet interest fetishism is precisely belief in this fantastical thing, this incredible fiction. Such belief in the power of self-multiplying money launders (i.e. represses) acknowledgment that labour, not capital, is the sole and ultimate source of all use-, exchange- and surplus-values.

But, even if one discovers and comes to see through all three of these self-laundering operations of capitalism's money, such insight alone is not enough. The Enlightenment article of faith having it that knowing the truth is itself already liberating fails to hold in Marxism and psychoanalysis, and especially in cases of both commodity and analytic fetishism. Freud's and Lacan's analyses of fetishism are particularly helpful in further elucidating and buttressing Marx's long-standing thesis according to which theoretical critique (i.e. the 'weapon of criticism') is no substitute for corresponding practical action (i.e. the 'criticism of weapons').[56]

Marx starts distinguishing himself from the Left Hegelian fellow travellers of his youth in concluding that purely intellectual attacks by themselves are insufficient for revolutionary change.[57] Psychoanalysis, particularly in relation to commodity fetishism as per the mature Marx, is of great assistance in reinforcing this feature of Marx's position. However, as will be seen, this assistance might be so great as to indicate that, at a bigger-picture level, Marx was too sanguine about the nearness of capitalism's demise. In this manner, psychoanalysis might prove to be a dangerous, albeit crucial, supplement for (classical) Marxism.

One of the peculiarities of fetishism, according to psychoanalysis, is its distinctive defence mechanism. Freud identifies 'disavowal' (*Verleugnung*) as fetishism's signature way of dealing with castration *qua* the absence of the maternal phallus.[58] Freudian *Verleugnung* entails a 'divided attitude' (*zweispältige Einstellung*).[59] Mannoni famously encapsulates this divided attitude of the disavowing fetishist with the mantra '*Je sais bien, mais quand même . . .*'[60] The division is between the affirmation of castration (i.e. Freud's '*die Behauptung*'[61] and Mannoni's 'I know full well') and its denial (i.e. Freud's *Verleugnung* and Mannoni's 'but nonetheless . . .'). Lacan describes this cleavage of mindset as an ambivalence characteristic of the fetishist.[62] Freud himself even goes so far, in two texts from the end of his life (*An Outline of Psycho-Analysis*[63] and 'Splitting of the Ego in the Process of Defence',[64] both from 1938), as to connect disavowal as fetishistic *Verleugnung* with a splitting of the ego (*Ichspaltung*) into irreconcilable portions.[65] Consistency definitely is not a hobgoblin of fetishistic minds.

The perversions in general are difficult to treat clinically. Since perverse subjects enjoy their symptoms, they tend not to seek out treatment of their own volition. If they present for an analysis (or for non-analytic psychotherapy), often it is because they are being pushed into doing so either by law enforcement or a spouse threatening divorce. The prognosis for a reluctant, coerced analysand is never good.[66] Analysands tend to be sufficiently motivated to endure the hardships of the analytic process only if and when their symptoms become, on balance, more unsatisfactory than satisfactory, thereby loosening and diminishing their libidinal investments in these symptoms. Only faltering pathologies and failing defences promise therapeutic successes.

But, with fetishism in particular, as a species of the genus perversion, the difficulty for analysis is even greater still. Freud, near the end of his 1927 piece on the subject, notes of fetishisms with pronounced disavowal that, 'A fetish of this sort, doubly derived from contrary ideas, is of course especially durable' ('*Ein solcher Fetisch, aus Gegensätzen doppelt geknüpft, hält natürlich besonders gut*').[67] The fetishist's divided attitude, with its 'contrary ideas', enables the fetishist to defang and render ineffective the analyst's interpretations of his/her (but almost always his) perverse symptoms through a sort of intellectual acceptance of the repressed – with intellectual acceptance as a manoeuvre in which the return of the repressed redoubles the initial repression, rather than undoing it. As per Mannoni, to each analytic interpretation, the fetishistic analysand can (and usually does) respond with a version of 'I know full well' (*Je sais bien*). Thereby, no interpretive bullseyes stick.

Then there is the corresponding disavowal of this same knowledge (of castration, sexual difference and the impossible, non-existent feminine phallus[68]) in the style of the fetishist's immediately ensuing 'but nonetheless . . .' ('*mais quand même . . .*'). This negating 'nonetheless' typically occurs not so much in (conscious) thoughts and words, but, instead, crystallised in the form of the fetish object itself[69] (and the enacted sexual behaviour accompanying it, in which female genitalia are sidelined). The fetish object is a prosthetic believer. That is to say, it is as though this privileged thing does the believing in the feminine phallus for the fetishist.

The fetishistic subject thus is permitted to not believe that he really, unconsciously believes what is consciously 'known full well' to be absurd, disgusting, disturbing, horrifying, incomprehensible, nonsensical, ridiculous, traumatic, etc. Through the fetish, belief is de-psychologised and objectified, preserved in being ossified and held manipulably, manageably at arm's length. In this case, spirit really is a bone, with the fetishist's disavowed belief (spirit) re-materialising as the fetish object (bone). Even for professional analysts, it is remarkably challenging to disabuse people of beliefs they do not believe they have – although these people sometimes even literally are holding these beliefs in their hands while denying they retain them.[70]

The opening paragraph of 'The Fetishism of the Commodity and Its Secret' indicates that the commodity fetishist too does not believe in the 'metaphysical subtleties and theological niceties' materialised within both commodities themselves as well as the commodity fetishist's externalised behaviour toward them on society's marketplaces. As Marx comments in the first sentence of this most famous section of *Capital, Volume One*, 'A commodity appears at first sight to be an extremely obvious, trivial thing.'[71] Convincing a commodity fetishist that he/she, in his/her efficacious public conduct, does not actually relate to commodities as 'obvious' and 'trivial' poses similar challenges to analysing a sexual fetishist.

The same might hold for IBC, the capitalist commodity fetish par excellence. IBC's fetishist fetishises the peculiar commodity that is money capital. Some of these interest fetishists perhaps know full well that money by itself does not really engender more money, but nonetheless . . . when they lend out their money, it tends to return to them in an amount larger than that initially lent. Even if they personally do not believe in money-breeding money, why would they stop loaning it if they keep receiving M' from others in exchange for M? If others are fools enough to continue doing this, they too would be fools in turn were they to stop taking advantage of this persisting social fact.

The cynically enlightened financial capitalist safely can bank on others desiring money and believing in its seemingly magical powers to grow on its own despite its lifeless artificiality. Borrowing more language from Mannoni, this jaded rentier does not 'believe in magic' but rather believes in 'a magic of belief' (i.e. others' beliefs and, ultimately, the beliefs of a faceless, indeterminate Other).[72] The idle speculator conjures up his income from this very magic. Why cease enjoying others' symptoms? Why not live off of the easy, effortless con-artistry of capitalising on 'a magic of belief'? Why not make a career out of being a professional compulsive gambler playing with other people's money in casinos ranging from national stock markets to on-line day-trading websites?

Lacan – and Mannoni following him – furnishes valuable assistance here. The Lacanian approach to commodity fetishism brings into theoretical consideration the desires and beliefs of others.[73] In the case of Marx's commodity fetishist, one can imagine 'curing' an individual commodity fetishist in a two-step process. First, he/she is somehow or other finally brought to recognise and admit that he/she in truth does indeed subscribe to a host of 'metaphysical subtleties and theological niceties'[74] apropos those objects that are commodities. Second, this commodity fetishist is then converted into being a thoroughgoing critic of these now-avowed beliefs, wholeheartedly denouncing them as fictitious, ideological, illusory, insidious and so on.

Yet, even for such a 'cured' commodity fetishist, if others around him/her still go on behaving in fashions conforming to commodity fetishism, then the surrounding socio-economic system (i.e. the capitalistic symbolic order, capital as big Other) compels him/her likewise to perseverate in commodity-fetishistic behaviour. He/she thus is not effectively cured after all. In general, one believes in money because one believes that others believe in money; this is a second- and third-hand belief, not a first-person one. Hence, if, for instance, a 'cured' IBC fetishist remains convinced that others are convinced of the wondrous self-multiplying powers of money capital as M-M', then he/she is not even really cured of his/her fetishism in the first place.

What is more, the others to whom the disillusioned commodity fetishist relates hypothetically could themselves also, as individuals, be disabused of commodity fetishism too. But, so long as each 'cured' subject relates to the others as if these others are not cured, then commodity fetishism strangely persists as an effective socio-economic reality to which nobody subjectively adheres in terms of first-person belief. Everyone being cured is not enough. Everyone has to believe that everyone else has been cured too – and, even then . . . An anonymous Other, perhaps nowhere instantiated amongst society's subjects taken merely as an aggregate of individuals interrelating, is enough to sustain commodity fetishism. So long as 'They believe,' all singular subjects are free to take themselves to be disbelievers while continuing to produce and reproduce really existing commodity fetishism as the external socio-economic system of capitalism.[75]

Freud's 1927 underscoring of the 'especially durable' ('*halt . . . besonders gut*') quality of the fetish is worth noting again at this point. Bringing Lacan and Mannoni to bear on Marx makes this Freudian observation especially resonant with commodity fetishism as I have parsed it in the immediately preceding paragraphs. The durability of commodity fetishes, IBC included, now can be more profoundly appreciated.

Initially, commodity fetishists do not believe that they fetishise commodities ('For me, commodities are extremely obvious, trivial things'). If they come to realise and see through their (previously unconscious) beliefs in 'metaphysical subtleties and theological niceties', they likely continue to believe that others continue to believe in such subtleties and niceties. In so doing, they compulsively reproduce their own commodity fetishism in what really counts, namely their actions. Furthermore, if even these others themselves also have self-consciously disinvested in the ideology of commodity fetishism, this still is insufficient to deactivate and dissolve the reality of commodity fetishism so long as each subject (mis)attributes investment in this fetishism to others (or to the spectral Other as a ghostly presence both everywhere and nowhere at once). Like the Freudian fetish, commodity fetishism is surprisingly stubborn.

When all is said and done, commodity fetishism as per Marx is grounded in and amounts to the objective (and not subjective) alienation in which, under capitalism, it truly is the case that persons and their social relations are governed by things and things' exchange relations. Unless and until social control is (re)asserted over the palpably concrete invisible hand of commodities and their market interactions, commodity fetishism will persist uncured. Minus the anti-capitalistic, materialist criticism of weapons, no anti-fetishistic, idealist weapon of criticism will deal commodity fetishism the *coup de grâce*. As Marx puts this:

> The religious reflections of the real world (*Der* religiöse Widerschein *der wirklichen Welt*) can . . . vanish only when the practical relations of everyday life between man and man, and man and nature, generally present themselves to him in a transparent and rational form (*die Verhältnisse des praktischen Werkeltagslebens den Menschen tagtäglich durchsichtig vernünftige Beziehungen zueinander und zur Natur darstellen*). The veil is not removed (*streift nur ihren mystischen Nebelschleier ab*) from the countenance of the social life-process (*Gestalt des gesellschaftlichen Lebensprozesses*), i.e. the process of material production, until it becomes production by freely associated men (*frei vergesellschafteter Menschen*), and stands under their conscious and

planned control. This, however, requires that society possess a material foundation (*eine materielle Grundlage*), or a series of material conditions of existence (*eine Reihe materieller Existenzbedingungen*), which in their turn are the natural and spontaneous product of a long and tormented historical development (*einer langen und qualvollen Entwicklungsgeschichte*).[76]

The first sentence of this passage has deep roots in Marx's thinking, going back to some of his earliest writings (most notably, the opening paragraphs of his 1843–44 essay 'A Contribution to the Critique of Hegel's Philosophy of Right. Introduction'[77]). My psychoanalytic reflections on commodity fetishism suggest that a qualification be appended to these remarks from the first volume of *Capital*: Alas, the 'social life-process (*Gestalt des gesellschaftlichen Lebensprozesses*), i.e. the process of material production' can survive and continue on, at least for a long while, after the removal of the veil (or, more in line with Marx's German here, the dissipation of the mystical mist (*mystischen Nebelschleier*), the ideological veil of fog).

As Slavoj Žižek expresses this caveat, Marx's old formula for ideology, 'They do not know what they are doing, but they are doing it nonetheless,' needs to be counterbalanced by a new formula for ideology having it that, 'They know full well what they are doing, but they are doing it nonetheless.'[78] The history of capitalism after Marx's death in 1883 and up through the present has rendered utterly implausible the Bible-borrowed Enlightenment confidence according to which, 'Know the truth, and the truth will set you free.' Analytic sexual fetishism, more than any other psychopathological phenomenon, drives home the power of commodity fetishism, and the entire mode of production with which it is inseparably enmeshed, to endure even after its dirty secrets have been publicly aired.

Marx writes above of future social trajectories having to undergo 'a long and tormented historical development' ('*einer langen und qualvollen Entwicklungsgeschichte*') in order to bring about the dismantling of the capitalist mode of production (and, with it, of the materialised fetishism of commodities). The psychoanalytic perspective on fetishism does not (at least not necessarily) contradict the idea that such development might eventually come to pass. Perhaps, at some point on the road ahead, the calibration of satisfactions and dissatisfactions with the social symptoms that are commodity fetishes will tilt decisively in the direction of dissatisfaction for a critical mass of capitalism's subjects. But, in the meantime, an early-twenty-first-century Lacano-Marxist reassessment of commodity fetishism forecasts an even longer, more tormented historical development ahead than Marx himself somewhat optimistically expected. As for the sexual fetishist's analyst, so too for the historical materialist critic of commodity fetishists: patience is a virtue. A new communist patience is urgently needed.[79]

Notes

1. Jacques Lacan, *Le Séminaire de Jacques Lacan, Livre XVIII: D'un discours qui ne serait pas du semblant, 1971*, ed. Jacques-Alain Miller (Paris: Éditions du Seuil, 2006), p. 164.
2. Lacan, *Séminaire XVIII*, pp. 164–5.
3. Jacques Lacan, *The Seminar of Jacques Lacan, Book VI: Desire and Its Interpretation, 1958–59*, ed. Jacques-Alain Miller, trans. Bruce Fink (Cambridge: Polity, 2019), p. 478; Jacques Lacan, *Le Séminaire de Jacques Lacan, Livre XIV: La logique du fantasme, 1966–67* (unpublished typescript), 4/12/67.
4. Jacques Lacan, *The Seminar of Jacques Lacan, Book V: Formations of the Unconscious, 1957–58*, ed. Jacques-Alain Miller, trans. Russell Grigg (Cambridge: Polity 2017), p. 62.
5. Lacan, *Seminar VI*, pp. 312–13.
6. Jacques Lacan, *Le Séminaire de Jacques Lacan, Livre XVI: D'un Autre à l'autre, 1968–69*, ed. Jacques-Alain Miller (Paris: Éditions du Seuil, 2006), p. 285.
7. Lacan, *Séminaire XVI*, p. 285.
8. Karl Marx, *Capital: A Critique of Political Economy, Volume Three*, trans. David Fernbach (New York: Penguin, 1981), pp. 459–60, 464–5, 473.
9. Marx, *Capital, Volume Three*, p. 517.
10. Jacques Lacan, *Le Séminaire de Jacques Lacan, Livre IV: La relation d'objet, 1956–57*, ed. Jacques-Alan Miller (Paris: Éditions du Seuil, 1994), p. 165; Lacan, *Seminar V*, p. 68.
11. Sigmund Freud, *Gesammelte Werke*, ed. E. Bibring, W. Hoffer, E. Kris and O. Isakower (Frankfurt: S. Fischer, 1952), *GW* 14: 316; Sigmund Freud, *The Standard Edition of the Complete Psychological Works of Sigmund Freud*, 24 volumes, ed. and trans. James Strachey, in collaboration with Anna Freud, assisted by Alix Strachey and Alan Tyson (London: Hogarth Press and the Institute of Psycho-Analysis, 1953–74), *SE* 21: 156.
12. Octave Mannoni, 'I Know Well, but All the Same . . .', trans. G. M. Goshgarian, *Perversion and the Social Relation*, ed. Molly Anne Rothenberg, Dennis A. Foster and Slavoj Žižek (Durham, NC: Duke University Press, 2003) pp. 80–1.
13. Lacan, *Séminaire IV*, p. 194.
14. Lacan, *Seminar VI*, p. 312.
15. Lacan, *Séminaire IV*, p. 165.
16. Lacan, *Séminaire IV*, p. 381.
17. *GW* 14: 312; *SE* 21: 152.
18. Lacan, *Seminar V*, pp. 210, 263, 329.
19. Adrian Johnston, 'Non-Existence and Sexual Identity: Some Brief Remarks

on Meinong and Lacan', *Lacanian Ink: The Symptom*, no. 3, Fall/Winter 2002, <http://www.lacan.com/nonexistf.htm>.

20. Adrian Johnston, *Prolegomena to Any Future Materialism, Volume Two: A Weak Nature Alone* (Evanston, IL: Northwestern University Press, 2019), p. 204.
21. Johnston, *Prolegomena to Any Future Materialism, Volume Two*, pp. 218–19.
22. Johnston, *Prolegomena to Any Future Materialism, Volume Two*, p. 219.
23. Johnston, *Prolegomena to Any Future Materialism, Volume Two*, pp. 152, 170, 175.
24. Lacan, *Séminaire IV*, pp. 152, 158; Lacan, *Seminar V*, pp. 212–13.
25. Lacan, *Séminaire IV*, p. 170.
26. Jacques Lacan and Wladimir Granoff, 'Fetishism: The Symbolic, the Imaginary and the Real', *Perversions: Psychodynamics and Therapy*, ed. Sandor Lorand and Michael Balint (New York: Gramercy, 1956) pp. 265–76.
27. Lacan, *Séminaire IV*, p. 183.
28. Lacan, *Séminaire IV*, p. 194.
29. Jacques Lacan, *The Seminar of Jacques Lacan, Book VIII: Transference, 1960–61*, ed. Jacques-Alain Miller, trans. Bruce Fink (Cambridge: Polity, 2015), pp. 140–1.
30. Jacques Lacan, *The Seminar of Jacques Lacan, Book X: Anxiety, 1962–63*, ed. Jacques-Alain Miller, trans. A. R. Price (Cambridge: Polity, 2014), pp. 102–3.
31. Lacan, *Séminaire IV*, p. 159; Patrick Avrane, *Petite psychanalyse de l'argent* (Paris: Presses Universitaires de France, 2015), p. 33.
32. Karl Marx, *Karl-Marx-Ausgabe: Werke-Schriften-Briefe, Band IV: Ökonomische Schriften, erster Band*, ed. Hans-Joachim Lieber, *Das Kapital: Kritik der politischen Ökonomie, erster Band*, ed. Hans-Joachim Lieber and Benedikt Kautsky (Darmstadt: Wissenschaftliche Buchgesellschaft, 1962), p. 46; Karl Marx, *Capital: A Critique of Political Economy, Volume One*, trans. Ben Fowkes (New York: Penguin, 1976), pp. 163–4.
33. Marx, *Capital, Volume Three*, pp. 515–17, 523–4, 596, 609, 955, 968; Karl Marx, *Theories of Surplus-Value, Part III: Volume IV of Capital*, ed. S. W. Ryazanskaya and Richard Dixon, trans. Jack Cohen and S. W. Ryazanskaya (Moscow: Progress Publishers, 1971), p. 453.
34. Norman O. Brown, *Life Against Death: The Psychoanalytical Meaning of History*, 2nd edn (Hanover, NH: University Press of New England, 1985), p. 279.
35. Brown, *Life Against Death*, p. 279.
36. Lacan, *Séminaire IV*, pp. 155–6; Guy Rosolato, 'Étude des perversions sexuelles à partir du fétichisme', in Piera Aulagnier-Spairani, Jean Clavreul, François Perrier, Guy Rosolato and Jean-Paul Valabrega, *Le désir et la perversion* (Paris: Éditions du Seuil, 1967), pp. 20–1.
37. Lacan, *Séminaire IV*, p. 155.

38. Lacan, *Séminaire IV*, p. 156.
39. Lacan, *Séminaire IV*, p. 156.
40. Mannoni, 'I Know Well, But All the Same . . .', p. 70.
41. Lacan, *Séminaire IV*, pp. 157, 165, 194.
42. Lacan, *Séminaire IV*, pp. 157–8.
43. Jacques Lacan, *The Seminar of Jacques Lacan, Book XI: The Four Fundamental Concepts of Psychoanalysis, 1964*, ed. Jacques-Alain Miller, trans. Alan Sheridan (New York: W. W. Norton, 1977), pp. 103, 111–12.
44. Lacan, *Seminar VI*, p. 439.
45. Karl Marx, *Karl-Marx-Ausgabe: Werke-Schriften-Briefe, Band VI: Ökonomische Schriften, dritter Band*, ed. Hans-Joachim Lieber, *Das Kapital: Kritik der politischen Ökonomie, dritter Band, drittes Buch*, ed. Hans-Joachim Lieber and Benedikt Kautsky (Darmstadt: Wissenschaftliche Buchgesellschaft, 1964), p. 156; Marx, *Capital, Volume Three*, p. 515.
46. Lacan, *Seminar V*, p. 62.
47. Lacan, *Seminar V*, p. 62.
48. Lacan, *Seminar VI*, p. 313.
49. Lacan, *Seminar VI*, pp. 312–13.
50. Adrian Johnston, 'Meta-transcendentalism and Error-First Ontology: The Cases of Gilbert Simondon and Catherine Malabou', *New Realism and Contemporary Philosophy*, ed. Gregor Kroupa and Jure Simoniti (London: Bloomsbury, 2020), pp. 171–5.
51. Aristotle, *Politics*, trans. C. D. C. Reeve (Indianapolis: Hackett, 1998), lines 1257a–1258a (15–18).
52. Adrian Johnston, 'From Closed Need to Infinite Greed: Marx's Drive Theory', *Continental Thought and Theory: A Journal of Intellectual Freedom*, special issue 'Reading Marx's *Capital* 150 Years On', ed. Mike Grimshaw and Cindy Zeiher, vol. 1, no. 4, October 2017, pp. 270–346.
53. Lacan, *Seminar VI*, pp. 478–9.
54. Karl Marx, *Grundrisse: Foundations of the Critique of Political Economy (Rough Draft)*, trans. Martin Nicolaus (New York: Penguin, 1973), p. 767; Marx, *Capital, Volume Three*, pp. 267, 400; Marx, *Theories of Surplus-Value, Part III*, p. 459; Rudolf Hilferding, *Finance Capital: A Study of the Latest Phase of Capitalist Development*, ed. Tom Bottomore, trans. Morris Watnick and Sam Gordon (London: Routledge & Kegan Paul, 1981), p. 150; Roman Rosdolsky, *The Making of Marx's 'Capital'*, trans. Pete Burgess (London: Pluto Press, 1977), pp. 369–70.
55. Marx, *Capital, Volume Three*, pp. 503–4, 506, 968; David Harvey, *A Companion to Marx's Capital, Volume Two* (London: Verso, 2013), p. 200.
56. Karl Marx, 'A Contribution to the Critique of Hegel's Philosophy of Right.

Introduction', *Early Writings*, trans. Rodney Livingstone and Gregor Benton (New York: Penguin, 1975), p. 251.
57. Marx, 'A Contribution to the Critique of Hegel's Philosophy of Right', pp. 243–5; Karl Marx, *Economic and Philosophical Manuscripts, Early Writings*, trans. Rodney Livingstone and Gregor Benton (New York: Penguin, 1975), p. 395; Karl Marx, 'Theses on Feuerbach', trans. S. Ryazanskaya, *Karl Marx: Selected Writings*, ed. David McLellan (Oxford: Oxford University Press, 1977), pp. 156–8; Karl Marx and Friedrich Engels, *The Holy Family, or Critique of Critical Criticism: Against Bruno Bauer, and Company*, trans. Richard Dixon and Clemens Dutt (Moscow: Progress Publishers, 1975), pp. 66–7, 103, 105, 118, 148.
58. *GW* 14: 316; *SE* 21: 156; Rosolato, 'Étude des perversions sexuelles à partir du fétichisme', pp. 10–11.
59. *GW* 14: 316; *SE* 21: 156.
60. Mannoni, 'I Know Well, But All the Same . . .', pp. 70–1.
61. *GW* 14: 316; *SE* 21: 156.
62. Lacan, *Séminaire IV*, p. 166.
63. *GW* 133; *SE* 23: 202–3.
64. *SE* 23: 275–8.
65. Rosolato, 'Étude des perversions sexuelles à partir du fétichisme', pp. 15, 18, 20.
66. Adrian Johnston, *Badiou, Žižek, and Political Transformations: The Cadence of Change* (Evanston, IL: Northwestern University Press, 2009), pp. 101–2.
67. *GW* 14: 316; *SE* 21: 157.
68. Rosolato, 'Étude des perversions sexuelles à partir du fétichisme', pp. 9–11, 18.
69. Mannoni, 'I Know Well, But All the Same . . .', pp. 70–1.
70. Mannoni, 'I Know Well, But All the Same . . .', p. 90; Johnston, *Badiou, Žižek, and Political Transformations*, pp. 117–18.
71. Marx, *Capital, Volume One*, p. 163.
72. Mannoni, 'I Know Well, But All the Same . . .', p. 88.
73. Avrane, *Petite psychanalyse de l'argent*, pp. 25–6.
74. Marx, *Capital, Volume One*, 1976, p. 163.
75. Mannoni, 'I Know Well, But All the Same . . .', pp. 77–8, 91; Johnston, *Badiou, Žižek, and Political Transformations*, p. 88.
76. Marx, *Das Kapital, erster Band*, p. 57; Marx, *Capital, Volume One*, p. 173.
77. Marx, 'A Contribution to the Critique of Hegel's Philosophy of Right', pp. 243–5.
78. Slavoj Žižek, *The Sublime Object of Ideology* (London: Verso, 1989), pp. 29, 33.
79. Johnston, *Badiou, Žižek, and Political Transformations*, pp. 35–6, 53.

4 From the Orderly World to the Polluted Unworld
Samo Tomšič

It's the difference between what works and what doesn't work. What works is the world. The real is what doesn't work. The world goes on, it goes round – that's its function as a world. To perceive that there is no such thing as a world – namely, that there are things that only imbeciles believe to be in the world – it suffices to note that there are things that make the world (*monde*) revolting (*immonde*), if I may say so.[1]

The End of the World and the Growth of Knowledge

If we are to believe Alexandre Koyré, modernity began with the end of the world.[2] This event was certainly less spectacular than in any of our modern-day science fiction scenarios. At first glance a discreet incident, the end of the world took place in the framework of modern physics: an epistemic event, which restructured the space of scientific thinking, by introducing into the human conception of reality a feature it did not know before, the infinite. The end of the world meant above all the end of reality's finitude. Infinite space and the cosmological world picture were mutually exclusive.

This scientific development comprised a methodological shift that Koyré considered to be at the core of the revolutionary sequence stretching from Copernicus via Galileo to Newton, the mathematisation of chance and thus the extension of mathematics and geometry to those spheres of physical reality that premodern, Aristotelian physics considered non-mathematisable, 'generation and corruption'. If premodern science was above all a 'science of being' then the modern one slowly but surely established itself as a 'science of becoming'. Needless to say, this scientific revolution at the same time triggered resistance from the guardians of the old order, in which science and religion were supposed to form an alliance. One merely needs to recall that Giordano Bruno, the first proper philosophical advocate of infinity of worlds, and Nicolai Copernicus, the founder of modern heliocentrism, were both condemned and the former sentenced to death. Faced with the same penalty, Galileo had to revoke his scientific findings, while Descartes was intimidated enough to carefully censor his writings and refrained from publishing his treatise on the world. As Freud eventually phrased it, modern physics inflicted a wound to human self-love by bringing down its ultimate expression, the construction of a closed and ordered totality governed by the principle of beauty. Following upon both Freud and Koyré, Lacan commented on the premodern conception of reality in the following manner: 'The word cosmos preserved its sense, which leaves its trace in the diverse ways we speak about cosmos, we speak of cosmetics . . . Cosmos is what is beautiful. It is made beautiful – by what? In principle by what we call reason.'[3]

However, while early modern physics may have exposed that reality is ultimately a result of libidinal investment – or with the Freudian vocabulary, an extension of the pleasure principle – it did not entirely disrupt the libidinal link between reality, reason and beauty. The mechanistic worldview, initiated by Cartesian dualism and perfected by Newtonian physics, implemented an updated version of epistemic cosmetics.[4] Still, the expansion of mathematics abolished the cosmological divide between the superlunary sphere of invariable geometrical and mathematical truths ('heavens') and the sublunary sphere of variable and therefore non-mathematisable processes ('earth'). It may not have entirely abolished the projection of rational order onto the real, but it did demonstrate in its own manner that the real resists totalisation. Hence Lacan's remark that one should not loose sight of the difference between what works and what doesn't work, between worldly reality and the unworldly real. In post-Newtonian physics, the intertwining of 'disfunctioning' and 'functioning' became increasingly central, and consequently the last remainders of the world were slowly but surely removed from the field of knowledge.

Leaving aside any discussion of whether the epistemological shift from the closed world to the infinite universe was a radical break, what in any case followed was a thorough transformation of the way the symbolic order intervenes into the physical and biological processes. Perhaps it would be more precise to identify this shift with the movement from complete reality to the incomplete real or from the functional being to the dysfunctional becoming. In any case, what was introduced was an entirely new discursive regime, or a continuous development, which reached a tipping point in high modernity. This became concrete, above all, with mathematics. Integral mathematisation of reality does not imply that nothing is left outside the grasp of mathematics, but rather that scientific methods and procedures, the combination of formalisation and experimentation, succeed in actualising the symbolic in the real. This actualisation does not take place in a neutral manner, in other words it does not leave the real unaltered – in difference precisely to premodern physics and astronomy, which projected subjective fictions onto the objective world, thus fabricating the fantasy of stable and complete reality. The real may not have fitted into the world-picture, but this discrepancy did not alter the logic of fictionalisation or 'imaginary organisation' (Lacan). To recall merely the most prominent example, the Ptolomeian system of epicycles was continuously revised and complicated in order to account for all the observable irregularities in the movement of heavenly bodies.

What irreversibly changed with modernity is that fictions themselves unfold their productive potential. In doing so they assume a real status and become independent from the human subject. One crucial aspect of the modern scientific revolution is tied to the shift from subjective to objective fiction, and more specifically from representation to production. This feature of epistemic productivity is incorporated in the German term *Wissenschaft* (science), a composition of creation (*schaffen*) and knowledge (*Wissen*). Modern science is constituted as an epistemic economy, and more precisely an accumulative regime of knowledge,[5] whose main concern is to extract knowledge from the real. One can therefore also say that modern science is extractivist in its essence.

This epistemic mode of production comprises an element that was still unfamiliar to premodern science, an unprecedented form of knowledge whose defining feature is growth: 'surplus-knowledge'.[6] This objectification of knowledge in the guise of a growing, dynamic surplus makes of science a virtually endless accumulative process, which is in stark contradiction to the fantasy of closed world. It is this surplus-knowledge that turns modern science into an effective objective fiction with a grand future: 'For me the only true, serious science worth following is science fiction. The other, official science with its altars in the laboratories gropes its way forward without reaching any happy medium. And it has even begun to fear its own shadow.'[7] Modern science is thus internally bound to science fiction, which is truly revolutionary in its active manipulation of the real, precisely by means of objectified fictions, and official science, which still remains anchored in some kind of empiricism and therefore the centrality of human observer, and which is moreover intimidated by the unleashed power of fictions in the epistemic field. The emergence of scientific anxiety is therefore not simply attached to the intertwining of science with fictionality, but to the objectivity and efficiency of fiction, as well as to the fact that the accumulative regime of knowledge runs its own course, making scientists appear somewhat powerless, impotent and even clueless.

It is no chance that Lacan formulated these lines in the mid-1970s, when the debates concerning the unrestrained character of the natural sciences reached its peak, eventually leading to the proliferation of ethical committees whose task was to come up with regulative frameworks for scientific experimentation. The atom bomb provided a major cause of anxiety toward natural sciences, the fabrication of potentially lethal viruses and the then still fresh prospect of genetic manipulation another. With the detachment of science from its 'official' framework a second ending of the world began to announce itself, this time in the guise of an actual extinction of the 'world-building animal' (Heidegger's name for humanity) and potentially the erasure of life in general: 'That would be a true triumph. It would mean that humanity would truly have achieved something – its own destruction. It would be a true sign of the superiority of one being over the others. Not only its own destruction, but the destruction of the entire living world.'[8] This second ending of the world may itself be a fantasy, but with productive fiction at the core of science it becomes increasingly impossible to tell whether this fantasy is in the process of implementation or not. It is not so much natural science as such, but rather objective fiction, which seems to run amok.

One point in Lacan's sarcasm is worth considering, namely the continuity between the unforeseeable consequences of autonomous science or 'science fiction' and the ideal that it brought into existence, the domination of nature. This ideal was spelled out both in Francis Bacon, the presumable utilitarian *avant la lettre*, and in Descartes, the founder of modern rationalism. Its Cartesian version ambiguously reflects the displacement initiated by the modern regime of knowledge:

> For these notions have made me see that it is possible to attain knowledge which is very useful in life, and that unlike the speculative philosophy that is taught in the schools, it can be turned into a practice by which, knowing the power and action of fire, water, air, stars, the heavens, and all the other bodies that are around us as distinctly as we know the different trades of our craftsmen, we could put them to all the uses for which they are suited and thus make ourselves as it were the masters and possessors of nature. This is not only desirable for the discovery of a host of inventions (*infinité d'artifices*) which will lead us effortlessly to enjoy the fruits of the earth and all the commodities that can be found in it, but principally also for the preservation of health, which is without doubt the highest good and the foundation of all the other goods of this life.[9]

The combination of mathematics and technology allows humans to shape and alter their relation to nature. Although Descartes frames it as that of mastery and possession, 'as if' marks an ambiguity in this relation. More importantly, for Descartes the aim of this relation remains linked to some kind of 'social value' ('preservation of health') and only in the next move to the reification of nature (enjoyment of natural 'commodities'). In the latter respect, science actively contributes to the extractivist tendencies of the capitalist organisation of production. While the Cartesian framework contains an essential tension between the epistemic and economic signification of domination over nature, another tension is internal to science itself: science as an autonomous accumulative process, in which knowledge is generated for the sake of knowledge, and science as a social process, in which production of knowledge relates to the preservation and improvement of human existence. It is no way an exaggeration to conclude that, if the second case provides us with a social vision of science, the first case points toward an anti-social dimension of knowledge for the sake of knowledge or surplus-knowledge. It is this second dimension that causes anxiety, if not only to scientists themselves, more generally to the human subject as such.

Needless to say, the coded truth behind the fantasies of the total extinction of humanity and planetary devastation concerns the suspicion that the accumulative regime of knowledge and the extractivist regime of valorisation, 'science fiction' and fictitious capital foster active indifference toward the human subject and toward the preservation of life. The scandal of modern science lies in its progressive alienation from and of the human subject. Koyré indicated this in his own manner by repeatedly insisting that, since Galileo, natural sciences no longer explain the way reality appears to the conscious human observer. Furthermore, modern science mobilises 'the power and action', as Descartes writes, of material processes in order to fabricate a manifold of *artifices*, materialised artificialities or fictions, which in their own manner challenge the human perception of reality. To repeat, modern science is an effective manipulation of the real by means of fictions, and what Descartes calls 'mastering of nature' ultimately means its active yet unforeseeable transformation. If Descartes's main contribution consisted in grounding an accumulative regime of knowledge, this suggests that the substantial epistemic economy deviates from the practical knowledge of the craftsmen. By introducing an unprecedented movement into knowledge (growth), science effectively detaches itself from use-value, which still predominated in the 'science of artisans or of engineers'.[10] By subverting the relation between use-value and epistemic-value (homologous to the economic notion of exchange-value) natural sciences constitute themselves as autonomous, self-reproductive processes. They fabricate objects, which change their function: 'all the instruments of astronomy before Galileo were instruments of observation; they were moreover instruments of measurement (...) of simply observable facts. In a sense they were still tools, whereas the Galilean instruments (...) are instruments in the strongest sense of the term: they are incarnations of theory.'[11] These inventions of theory or fictions materialised correlate to a real that does not appear and is therefore not reducible to 'observable facts' or objects of sensuous experience. Experimentation is not to be conflated with experience; it is an epistemic practice characteristic of the accumulative regime of knowledge. Furthermore, what

Descartes calls scientific *artifices* and Koyré 'incarnations of theory' comprise not only technological objects, but also and moreover epistemic objects, whose 'ontological' status intersects with economic objects, commodities and value. Both types of objects are embedded in a system in which the essential activities to be pursued are, respectively, the growth of value and the growth of knowledge.[12]

From Scientific to Economic Amnesia

Lacan was extensively preoccupied with this deviation of science from the human subject, not least in the remark according to which modern science rests on a foreclosure of the subject, its radical rejection. The distinction between 'science fiction' and 'official science' is formulated in this critical horizon. One could say that 'official science' remains at its core a 'human science', whereas 'science fiction' reveals at the heart of scientific modernity the emergence of something like an 'inhuman science'.

Heidegger at one point caused controversy when he stated, 'science does not think',[13] since thinking for him comprises the production of meaning, the paradigmatic example of which is poetic language. Moreover, for Heidegger, thinking always comprises a world-building (*weltbildend*) activity, which is why in his view humans and animals are separated by an unbridgeable ontological gap. Contrary to the thinking and therefore world-building 'animal', animals proper are world-poor (*weltarm*) and therefore do not think. Mathematics does not think either, not so much because it would be world-poor since it is not an 'animal activity', but rather because it is 'world-dismantling'.[14] In this respect, mathematics stands on the opposite margin of the symbolic order, as a language deprived of meaning. Indeed, if mathematics is world-dismantling rather than world-building, it appears in sharp contradiction with the poetic activity of world making. At first glance, Heidegger's dictum 'science does not think' seems to resonate with Lacan's distinction between 'science fiction' and 'official science' – it targets something like the hidden truth behind official science. At the same time, Heidegger's dictum is not immune to the alarmism that Lacan criticised in scientists themselves. Moreover, Heidegger's phrase can be contrasted with Lacan's critical remark from his famous writing 'Science and Truth' (a title that could be interpreted as 'Science and Fiction'): 'the fact is that science, if one looks at it closely, has no memory. Once constituted, it forgets the circuitous path by which it came into being; otherwise stated, it forgets a dimension of truth that psychoanalysis seriously puts work.'[15]

Lacan makes a more nuanced epistemological claim about scientific thinking by asserting that the natural sciences are characterised by a structural amnesia. Instead of asserting the all too simple – not to say wrong – dichotomy between science and thinking, the claim 'science forgets' exposes in scientific thinking an example of the impasse, tension and resistance that characterises thinking in general: thinking without a stable central instance, which can only achieve its stabilisation under the condition that it represses its internal impasses, but in doing so constitutes itself as a conflicted intellectual process.[16] Lacan's evocation of the anxiety of scientists exemplifies a return of the scientific repressed, certainly in the guise of fearing the unforeseeable consequences of epistemic accumulation, but also as the return of the rejected subject, disturbing and disrupting the integration of science in the capitalist obsession with surplus-production. One could turn around Heidegger by saying that science forgets that it thinks – since thinking is what it does most intensively in moments of crises. In the sequence of solidification of a scientific paradigm (to put it with Thomas Kuhn) science 'domesticates' thinking, and this domestication is an essential component of the epistemic mastering of nature. In this process, science does not assume a metaposition, but equally falls on the side of the domesticated. To continue with Kuhn, it becomes normal science and a procedure of normalisation in thinking. In other words, it becomes integrated in the capitalist mode of production, where it can unfold its revolutionary potential without actively interfering with the capitalist organisation of social and subjective reality for the ultimate aim of extracting surplus-value.

Another level of oblivion that grounds modern science concerns the conviction that, by abolishing its dependency on the human observer, it unfolds in a neutral space of thinking. As long as it was still centralised by the human gaze, scientific knowledge was contaminated by subjective fictions, fabricating sexuated cosmologies and thus extending what Freud called the pleasure principle to non-human registers of reality.[17] One could say that this expansion stood for an innocent and somewhat comical attempt at 'dominating' nature. However, when Koyré remarked that modern physics explains the real with the impossible, he pinpointed a thorough displacement of the relation between fictions and the real. To repeat, by rejecting the subject from knowledge, science became objective fiction, which moreover unleashed the productive potential of fictions. Early modern physics replaced sexuated cosmologies with *extractivist metaphysics*, where the primary and ultimate goal consists in gaining an epistemic surplus-product from material processes in nature.[18]

Lacan's aforementioned evocation of science fiction should not be understood as an anticipation of the vulgar postmodern view, according to which every reality, including the scientific one, is a result of discursive performativity. Instead, the notion of science fiction wants to acknowledge the specific ontological scandal that accompanies the detachment of fiction from the 'human observer':

> In effect, it is, all the same, necessary not to forget that it is characteristic of our science not to have introduced a better and more extensive knowledge of the world

but to have brought into existence, in the world, things that did not in any way exist at the level of our perception ... The space in which the creations of science are deployed can only be qualified henceforth as the *in-substance*, as the *a-thing, l'achose* with an apostrophe – a fact that entirely changes the meaning of our materialism.[19]

An important aspect of the statement 'science forgets' thus concerns the ontological scandal of epistemic production. Science must not be conflated with simple cognition; this is where pragmatic and analytic epistemologies fall short, for the accumulative regime of knowledge does not mean 'progress in cognition' (the latter being at best 'scientific ideology', to use Canguilhem's expression). If producing surplus-knowledge is indeed the main activity of modern science, the applicability of this knowledge lies elsewhere. Rather than expanding cognition it widens the horizon of the appropriation of nature and is therefore embedded in another expansive process, the 'absolutisation of the market',[20] the actual name for the 'infinite universe' that resulted from the epistemic end of the world. Science demolished the fantasy of the world not only by abolishing the hierarchical order between the stable superlunary sphere and the unstable sublunary sphere, but also by introducing in the world things that violate the sensuous regime of perception. This detail is more important than it may seem. Lacan does not simply say that these things did not exist at all – otherwise his statements such as 'energy is a numeric constant' would indeed point toward something like a performative theory of scientific production.[21] By contrast, Lacan radicalises Koyré's thesis, according to which the main concern of modern science is not 'saving the phenomena' or, in other words, keeping the scientific description of the real in accordance with human perception. Natural sciences are no longer concerned with 'appearing for' (the conscious human subject). Rather than engaging in 'phenomenology' (science of appearance), they practice 'phenomenanalysis' (decomposition of appearances) and have little concern for 'demonstrating' the existence of the world in terms of a consistent totality of appearances.

When Lacan eventually introduced the term *immonde*, he strove to grasp the dynamic fusion of epistemic and economic fictions with the physical and biological real. *Immonde* has hardly anything in common with the world of ontologically stable substances and things.[22] Just like commodities according to Marx, the creations of science are equally 'sensuous suprasensuous things', operating in a register where it is increasingly difficult to distinguish between the symbolic and the material. This is where epistemic production most overtly intersects with the economic production:

> And these tiny objects little *a* that you will encounter when you leave, there on the footpath at the corner of every street, behind every window, in this abundance of these objects designed to be the cause of your desire, insofar as it is now science

that governs it – think of them as lathouses ... The lathouse has absolutely no reason to limit its multiplication.[23]

Lathouse is another peculiar Lacanian neologism, which can be linked to *immonde*. The word alludes to Greek terms *aletheia* (truth) and *ousia* (substance or essence). Lacan keeps *lethe* (oblivion), thus referencing Heidegger's speculative etymology of the Greek term for truth. For Heidegger, truth comprises the interplay of unveiling and veiling, remembering and forgetting. If modernity is characterised by the proliferation of 'lathouses' this suggests that reality is continuously expanded with objects whose essence or substance is void. Again, science does not, according to this somewhat pessimistic reading, expand cognition; in this regard it emancipates itself not only from the human subject but also from any potential 'use-value'. It merely has epistemic-value, where the main stake consists in producing knowledge for the sake of knowledge that is reinvested in scientific discourse in order to keep the 'multiplication of lathouses' going.

The amnesia, which makes of science a 'success story', constantly progressing in the extraction of surplus-knowledge, is not without resonance with a problem that Marx brought forward in his critique of classical political economy. Economics, too, is marked by historical amnesia and blindness for the intricacies accompanying objective fiction. Marx, for instance, demonstrates this economic amnesia by restating the problem of 'primitive accumulation'. Under this term, classical political economists strove to construct a fictitious prehistory of capitalism, thus forging an ahistorical myth, according to which capitalism was brought into existence by the economic sacrifices of the proto-capitalist elite, by its 'renunciation of enjoyment'.[24] This myth that Marx mockingly compares to the function of original sin in religion represses the historical genesis of capitalism, a history of violence, which accompanied the implementation of the capitalist mode of production and moreover continues sustaining it in the present. Marx's historical narration focuses on the expropriation of rural population and more generally on the expropriation of individuals of their bodies.[25] At the same time, Marx leaves the space open for conceiving primitive accumulation in terms of present-day violence: economic, colonial, sexual and environmental. More generally, then, primitive accumulation stands for the violent extraction of epistemic, economic and libidinal surplus from bodies and environments.

Another crucial aspect of political-economic amnesia concerns its blindness for the role of objective fictions in the ongoing dismantling of subjectivised bodies, social bonds and environmental orders through the extractivist tendencies of the capitalist system. The most popular excerpt in *Capital*, where this blindness is exposed, is the section on commodity fetishism. Throughout the volume, Marx argues that political economy repeatedly demonstrates its misunderstanding of objective fiction, when it makes of value a substantial feature of commodities, of money as a self-breeding entity and of capital an automatic subject. Fetishisation of value then signals that political economy operates on the level of appearance, and in doing so continues pursuing the premodern epistemic ideal of 'saving the phenomena' on the modern 'phenomenon' of objective and seemingly automatic growth of value. For Marx, in turn, value must be desubstantialised, hence his simple yet crucial insistence that value is a social relation, or to be more precise an anti-social relation, given that sociality in capitalism consists of the interdependency between destructive violence and extraction of surplus. Consequently the history of capitalism is ultimately a history of the augmentation of violence, which obtains its systematised expression in the production of a devastated reality, precisely the one that Lacan calls *immonde*. This is also where the epistemic end of the world and the economic dismantling of environmental and social systems intersect.

From Surplus to Waste

The French word *immonde* means 'filthy', 'disgusting' and 'revolting', pointing toward pollution and corruption of orderliness. Simultaneously, Lacan relates *immonde* to the difference between the functioning of reality and the disfunctioning of the real. Although modern science broke with the ancient conceptions of cosmological order, it introduced a new mode of taming the real's 'disfunctioning'.[26] The role that the 'imaginary organisation' played by means of geometry in this process in antiquity has been replaced by mathematics, the symbolic science par excellence. The sequence spanning from Galileo to Newton stands for a process in which a properly modern mechanistic worldview is fabricated. Descartes's reduction of materiality to pure extension remains exemplary of this epistemic shift. From the body every irregularity and disturbance is removed, until corporeality appears subjected to stable geometrical laws and linear causality. At the other end of the early modern scientific revolution, Newton proposed his vision of a clockwork universe, from which its Creator could withdraw, since reality was made to work without His constant supervision and intervention. The mechanistic *mundus* survived subsequent revolutions in physics, and it is easy to understand why this is the case. It reflects a regime of knowledge, whose main achievement consists in the passivisation of matter, a procedure which turned out to be crucial for implementing economic valorisation and commodification.

To return to *immonde*, the term signifies a specific negation of the world, the unworld. The prefix 'un-' relates to the 'world' similarly as in *unbewusst* (unconscious) or *unendlich* (infinite). In all cases 'un-' does not simply negate consciousness, finitude and worldliness, but rather pinpoints their unstable character, the fact that finitude, reality and consciousness are from within traversed by a disturbance. Their out-of-joint feature obtains a thingly expression, as Lacan explicitly suggests: 'there are things that only imbeciles believe to be in the world', things that corrupt the world's consistency and through their very presence 'in the world' make it appear unworldly. One can only speak of the world in the way cosmology did under the condition that one blends out these problematic things, which literally prevent the world from existing. The opposite of *immonde* is therefore *Weltanschauung* (worldview).

Weltanschauung evokes the centrality of human gaze and the activity of looking (*schauen*), as well as the intellectual faculty of intuition (*Anschauung*). In *Critique of Pure Reason*, Kant famously distinguished between empirical or sensuous intuitions that are given through organs of perception, and pure intuitions, which precede every sensuous experience and stand for a priori forms of intuition: space and time. These pure intuitions belong solely to the subject and sustain what in Lacanian terms can again be called imaginary organisation of the real. Kant understands pure intuitions as representations, applied to sensuous perceptions as structuring operations, which introduce their own kind of order in the material given through experience. When Lacan speaks of things that are not part of the world he may create the impression of simply repeating the Kantian distinction between phenomena and noumena, thus conflating his concept of the real with the Kantian thing in itself. Lacan, however, vehemently rejected such equation:

> It is not even remotely Kantian. I make that quite clear. If there is a notion of the real, it is extremely complex and in that sense it is not graspable, not graspable in a way that would constitute a whole. It would be an incredibly anticipatory notion to think that the real constitutes a whole. As long as we haven't verified it, I think we would do better to avoid saying that the real in any way whatsoever forms a whole.[27]

In the Kantian scenario the thing in itself operates as an ontological stabiliser, if one may say so, preventing the absurd scenario in which appearance would not relate to anything outside itself. It is the necessary assumption in order to envision reality as stable, ordered and complete. The thing in itself turns out to be the exact opposite of the 'extreme complexity' of the real; it is extremely simple, since it is ultimately nothing but the pure assumption of externality and objectivity. Of course, Kant equally criticised the speculations of cosmology regarding the completeness and totality of the world. His account of cosmological antinomies is a retrospective look at the notion of world from an epistemic paradigm, in which the world no longer stands for an operative epistemic fiction. However, the critical point of Lacan's self-differentiation from Kant concerns the status of the thing in itself as a regulative border and as an assumption of pure objectivity, which continues to reproduce the ontological thesis of reality's completeness. It is its presumable withdrawal from reality that is problematic, and Lacan's main effort in his critique of Kant's theory of cognition is to point out the existence of things, which are in themselves yet do not match the Kantian divide on phenomena and noumena because they are, precisely, epistemic and economic fabrications, fictions objectified. In distinction to the thing in itself, the existence of 'lathouses' does not have to be assumed, since they impose themselves, for instance by causing desire (to link back to the earlier quote, where Lacan links the scientific 'lathouse' with object *a*, the object-cause of desire). The very presence of these hybrid objects – both material and symbolic – demonstratively corrupts the worldliness of the world, again not because they would be withdrawn or absent from the world or unreachable for thinking, but because they are very much thinkable and present. Their very presence demonstrates the ontological incompleteness and instability of the real.

It is no coincidence that, after differentiating between the real and thing in itself, Lacan references a forgotten debate between the mathematician Émile Poincaré and the philosopher Émile Boutroux regarding the ontological status of natural laws. A few years ago, Boutroux's name re-emerged from oblivion in the polemics around Quentin Meillassoux's speculative realism. It was Boutroux who first authored the idea of the contingency of natural laws, albeit not in Hume's sense, where natural laws reflect human habit and chance remains external to these laws.[28] Contrary to Hume's scepticism, Boutroux argued that the real follows a law which is neither invariable nor sustained by some kind of intrinsic necessity. In order to sustain his point on the dysfunction and incompleteness of the real, Lacan comments, 'it is not at all clear to me why the real would not allow for a law that changes'.[29] Hence, the real is not simply without law, chaotic or anarchic. It is both organised and unstable. One could say that, in contrast to the cosmological idea of the complete, homeostatic and equilibrated, in short functioning world, post-Newtonian physics and modern biology conceive the real in terms of organised disequilibrium. Or, as Lacan simplifies the point, the real does not work, in other words the mechanistic world picture does not hold. The mechanistic philosophy reinvented the premodern paradigm of worldliness, which was now sustained with ongoing mathematical formalisation rather than with imaginary 'cosmetics'.[30]

This brings us back to the second meaning of *immonde*, the revolting or polluted world, the world populated not only with epistemic objects, but also with those that confront us with the destructive consequences of modern extractivist metaphysics, of the capitalist mode of production and its corresponding mode of enjoyment.

Here the surplus-object immediately turns out to be the central objective fiction of modernity.

Lacan at some point argued that there was a homology between the economic category of surplus-value and what he called surplus-enjoyment. The latter attempted to translate the German *Lustgewinn* (yield in pleasure), with which Freud named the libidinal 'side product' of mental activities and processes. The homology between both surplus-products, the mental and the social evolves around the fusion of material and symbolic, objectivity and fiction. At the same time it strives to pinpoint a common problematic of psychoanalysis and critique of political economy, the destructive consequences of the emergence of this new type of object in reality.

The object in question is characterised by the fact that it contains movement. This feature is expressed in the double meaning of the French term *plus* (surplus), which depending on the context can mean 'more' and 'no more'. The equivocity points out that this specifically modern object, in which lack and surplus are fused, in the same move causes satisfaction and dissatisfaction.[31] Its condition of possibility is the symbolic register in the triple guise of linguistic value (language), economic value (social production) and epistemic value (knowledge). Furthermore, its objective status signals that the surplus must not be dismissed as subjective illusion or fantasy, just like the capitalist demand of surplus-value must according to Marx not be viewed as mere 'individual mania'.[32] The surplus is a fiction, which, while dependent on the existence of the human subject, turns against the latter. The subject finds itself in the status of an inner exclusion from the object. One could equally say that the surplus-object is that part of the subject which is detached from the latter, autonomised and endowed with logic and life of its own.

In can be recalled in passing that Lacan proposed three examples of the fusion of the material and symbolic, which are not to be conflated: *agalma*, Thing and object *a*. These objective fictions are unambiguously discussed in relation to different historical epochs. *Agalma* is contextualised in Plato's dialogue *Symposium*, and more specifically in Alcibiades's speech in praise of Socrates. Alcibiades insists that Socrates possesses a treasure, which is enclosed in his interior, Socrates's body being merely an unattractive shell containing this love worthy object. *Agalma* implies an interior which is separated from exterior. Further, the Thing is exemplified in the context of medieval troubadour lyrics and concerns above all the status of the Lady, who is depicted as a transcendent, unreachable object of the poet's desire. The only relation with this exteriority is language, notably poetry, by means of which the troubadour expresses his praise to the Lady-Thing and in doing so unites desire, love and enjoyment. Interior and exterior are again sharply distinguished, except that the object now stands for an absolute outside. Coming finally to object *a*, Lacan makes clear that this specifically modern surplus-object requires a different topology. Object *a* is situated at the very border between inside and outside, blurring the distinction between both orders. It is this blurring that introduces the necessary dynamic, which makes the object appear as endowed with growth (hence 'surplus' in the sense of 'more').

It is equally important that in their theories of surplus-object, Marx and Freud both argue that work is the only way of linking with this surplus: social work when it comes to surplus-value and unconscious work when it comes to surplus-enjoyment.[33] But work is also the process, in which the object is lost the moment it is produced (and it is continuously produced): surplus-value joins capital, thus making it grow, while surplus-enjoyment is consumed by the drive, thus inciting its demand for more.

The three types of objective fiction, the ancient, the medieval and the modern, show that we are dealing with three types of unreachable: immanence, transcendence and torsion. However, only in relation to the object *a* do we find the crucial dynamic – accumulation – which makes of object *a* an object of growth. And to repeat, the driving force of growth is the link between lack and surplus, the two interdependent aspects of *plus* in surplus-value and surplus-enjoyment, even if this link in the case of enjoyment does not comprise quantitative increase or accumulation. Nevertheless, what is crucial is the combination of satisfaction and dissatisfaction.

However, there is a flipside of growth, which already played a crucial role in Marx and which concerns the modern transformation of subjectivity into an abject: surplus-population. The latter stands for redundant subjectivity without a social bond, in difference, say, to the industrial proletariat, who is still embedded in the capitalist social bond through work. Differently put, work is the process by means of which the proletariat is held in the position of inner exclusion from surplus-population. Looking at the matter from this double angle, the proletariat and surplus-population, the social character of capitalism is anything but certain. The continuous increase of surplus-value and the pursuit of proverbial economic growth in themselves do not contribute to the construction of the social, insofar as we understand under the social a shared political space, in the constitution of which everyone can participate. Contrary to this scenario, capitalist 'sociality' appears to be anti-social to the core, organised around the imperative of economic competition, generation of resentment and finally an essential redundancy brought to the point in the very category of surplus-value. One could also recall the familiar Marxian point that capitalism introduces a 'social relation' between things rather than between subjects and that the ultimate goal of production is the self-valorisation of capital – an asocial activity if there ever was one.[34]

In a somewhat surprising remark, Lacan insisted that capitalism is not simply good for nothing – it is the things that it does that are good for nothing,[35] in other words, they have no social value because they remain within the exclusive horizon of economic valorisation, where augmentation of value remains its own purpose. To repeat, the self-valorisation of capital is fundamentally an anti-social activity. If the actions of capitalism are good for nothing, while capitalism is good for one thing in particular, augmentation of profit, this means that its actions necessarily aim at dismantling the social,[36] since it is this dismantling that conditions the extraction of surplus-value from the social fabric, the living bodies and the environment. In doing so, capitalism constantly demonstrates that the social was never guaranteed and should never be taken for granted. This is also the core of Marx's turn toward the notion of communism, which at its most basic signifies an open-ended struggle for the prevalence of the social over the anti-social, not for reconstructing another 'closed world', hence no nostalgia for premodernity, but for inventing a common political space, which will no longer be organised around the production of surplus in its double guise of sublime object and repulsive object, object and abject.

The fragility of social bonds was also Freud's major concern in his later works, notably in *Civilisation and Its Discontent*. There, Freud once again speaks of 'culture' in general, but what he actually reflects on is the enforced globalisation of capitalism, and particularly its war- and crisis-ridden dynamic. For this violent cultural condition, inscribed in the individual's mental apparatus in the guise of the super-ego and its cruelty, Freud argues that it causes general discontent, unrest or malaise (all three words come together in the German *Unbehagen*). In this feeling, or perhaps rather systemic affect, which sums up the way humans experience the impossible and unjust systemic demands, the human subject intuits the actual status it assumes in view of the capitalist system: of exploitable material from which surplus-value shall be extracted until its body and mind reach the point of exhaustion. Writing on the eve of the economic crisis (1929) which accelerated the course of events leading to the Second World War, Freud outlines his 'cosmological' vision of the conflict between Eros and the death-drive. In this context, the death-drive begins to signify a univocally destructive and anti-social force.[37] While Eros stands for the force that binds, i.e. sustains the social, the death-drive does not simply stand for a force that dissolves the social bonds, but rather bends them so that they sustain solely the satisfaction of the drive. In this respect, capitalism 'liberates' the anti-social potential of the drive, and in doing so indeed lays the foundations for something that deserves to be called the 'society of death-drive',[38] a paradoxical 'anti-social social' condition embedded in a process of self-dissolution.

Finally, the anti-sociality of capitalism can be further exemplified in the flipside of surplus-production, which is the production of waste. Lacan once made a peculiar remark, according to which 'civilisation is waste, *cloaca maxima*',[39] thereby referencing one of the world's earliest sewage systems in ancient Rome. It may seem as if Lacan saw in sanitation the ultimate marker of civilisation or an expression of perplexity humans feel when they confront their own waste. But this is not the entire point. Lacan proposes a properly Hegelian infinite judgment: civilisation does not simply produce waste as some kind of reminder of the repressed tie between nature and culture. Rather, civilisation must be understood from its extreme point, the abject, where it becomes itself indistinguishable from waste, this eminently cultural object, which today more than ever functions as a disturbance in nature and culture alike, reminding humans not only that they are not mastering nature but moreover that they are living in a system of production, which is increasingly running amok.

Elsewhere, Lacan elaborates his infinite judgment more thoroughly:

Because as far as we know all the other animals that exist do not encumber the earth with their waste (*déchets*), while it is altogether singular that everything man makes always ends up as waste. The only thing that preserves a little bit of dignity are the ruins, but get out of your shells all the same and you will notice the number of broken cars that are piled up in places, and you will realise that wherever you put your foot, you put it somewhere, where people have tried in every possible manner to recompress old waste in order to not be submerged by it, literally. This is quite a business! It's a whole business of organisation, right? Of imaginary organisation, if one may say so.[40]

Sewer removes waste out of sight, and in doing so contributes to the 'imaginary organisation' of reality. For this reason, the sewer is already a phenomenon of the closed and orderly world of premodernity. There is no cosmos without sewage. Thus medieval geocentrism was not simply an expression of 'human self-love', as Freud would put it. The sublunary sphere was the realm of imperfection, and so to speak a register of reality, where all the waste of the world accumulated. Earth was, indeed, *cloaca maxima*. Lacan's infinite judgment, which defines the highest (culture) with the lowest (waste), obtains a different twist in capitalism, where waste is no longer removed out of sight, does not vanish into some imagined nowhere, but is accumulated in the new paradigm of worldliness, the polluted unworld, reflecting the ongoing overproduction and overpopulation that marks the epoch of capitalism. As said, Marx's notion of surplus population already explicitly suggested that human beings, too, are increasingly becoming part of waste.

In the end, the epistemological shift from the 'closed world' to the 'infinite universe' appears as the shift from *cloaca maxima* to the polluted unworld, where worldliness and pollution are fused. The only world that capitalism is able to construct is a filthy unworld, in which the accumulated waste signals the boundless systemic and subjective enjoyment in the anti-social society implemented and sustained by capitalism. Lacan's concept of object *a* exposes the two-faced redundancy of the surplus-product, the fusion of value and trash, sublime object and repulsive abject. Waste, too, is fiction materialised, or rather what remains of enjoyment as its repulsive material residue. One could also say that waste reveals the true status of surplus-enjoyment and surplus-value. Behind their sublime objectivity, which fuels the fetishisation of objects of value and of enjoyment, both surplus-products ultimately describe verbal and economic trash. Neither surplus-enjoyment nor surplus-value serves any purpose; their entire 'social' value consists in keeping the capitalist self-valorising and overproducing machinery running.

One could recognise in the term *immonde* a peculiar anticipation of the environmental breakdown, which is today impossible to ignore. Of course, Lacan's point is not that science and capitalism corrupted some actually existing natural whole – this corruption took place on the subjective level – but rather that the accumulation of waste, this inevitable and necessary side effect of the capitalist organisation of production around the insatiable systemic demand for surplus-value, increases the instability of the already unstable environmental order. In other words, it demonstrates the instability, processuality and alterability of natural systems, and in doing so provides us with the catastrophic example of the blurring of the distinction between nature and culture. *Immonde* ultimately stands for the indistinction between both orders and obtains an iconic representation in the continents of waste emerging and expanding in the oceans across the globe. If the premodern cosmos was reality 'made beautiful by reason' then the modern unworld is reality made revolting by capital.

Still, capitalism never ceased to behave like the premodern world, insofar as it compulsively runs its course. In short, capitalism works, and it works all too well. It just might be the most functional order in the history of humanity. But contrary to everything that its advocates may argue, whether liberal or conservative, neoliberal or social-democratic, capitalism works against humanity. It has never been and never will be an order that would deserve to be described as social.

Notes

1. Jacques Lacan, 'Triumph of Religion', in *The Triumph of Religion, Preceded by Discourse to Catholics*, trans. Bruce Fink pp. 61–2 (trans. modified); *Le triomphe de la religion* (Paris: Seuil, 2005), p. 76. The author acknowledges the support of the Cluster of Excellence *Matters of Activity. Image Space Material* funded by the Deutsche Forschungsgemeinschaft (DFG, German Research Foundation) under Germany's Excellence Strategy – EXC 2025 – 390648296.
2. Koyré does not say this literally, but this is the direct conclusion that can be drawn

from his narration of the gradual shift, first in philosophy (notably with Giordano Bruno) and then in natural science (with René Descartes and Isaac Newton) from the paradigm of the closed world to that of the infinite universe. See Alexandre Koyré, *From the Closed World to the Infinite Universe* (Baltimore: Johns Hopkins University Press, 1968).

3. Jacques Lacan, 'Ouverture de la section clinique', *Ornicar?*, vol. 9 (1977), p. 7.
4. At this point another classic from the history of science can be cited, E. J. Dijksterhuis, *The Mechanization of the World Picture* (Oxford: Oxford University Press, 1961).
5. 'With Descartes knowledge, scientific knowledge is constituted on the mode of production of knowledge. Just as an essential stage of our structure that one calls social but is in fact metaphysical, and which is called capitalism, is accumulation of capital, the relation of the Cartesian subject to this being, which is affirmed in it, is founded on the accumulation of knowledge' (Jacques Lacan, *Le Séminaire, livre XII, Problèmes cruciaux pour la psychanalyse* (unpublished), 9 June 1965). Knowledge does not grow automatically, but requires an alienated subject that in Descartes obtains the expression of methodological doubt. More generally, modern science and capitalist economy share the link between alienation and production. The feature of growth is absent in premodern cosmologies, where only desperate refinement of the adopted world-picture takes place, as in the abovementioned case of Ptolomeian epicycles.
6. Jean-Claude Milner, 'Le savoir comme idole', *Cahiers d'Études Lévinassiennes*, no. 5 (2006), p. 337. The Marxist implications of surplus-knowledge were recently elaborated by Slavoj Žižek, *Incontinence of the Void* (Cambridge, MA: MIT Press, 2017), p. 162ff.
7. Jacques Lacan, 'There can be no crisis of psychoanalysis', available at: <https://www.versobooks.com/blogs/1668-there-can-be-no-crisis-of-psychoanalysis-jacques-lacan-interviewed-in-1974> last accessed: 29 December 2020). In line with this, Lacan declares science to be an impossible profession, together with government, education and psychoanalysis.
8. Lacan, 'Triumph of Religion', p. 60.
9. René Descartes, *Discourse on Method*, trans. Ian Maclean (Oxford: Oxford University Press, 2006), p. 51; *Oeuves complètes*, Vol. III, *Discours de la Méthode et Essais* (Paris: Gallimard, 2009), p. 122.
10. Alexandre Koyré, *Études d'histoire de la pensée scientifique* (Paris: Gallimard, 1973), p. 167.
11. Koyré, *Études*, p. 59.
12. However, we would end up in epistemic fetishism if we were to remove alienated subjectivity from the picture. Similarly political economy amounted to economic fetishism when it blended out value as a social relation, rather than a positive quality

of objects themselves. When Lacan in the late 1960s declared science to be a social link – hence comprising an exploited subjectivity, which intersects with the one sustaining the capitalist production – he overtly turned against the fetishisation of science that could still be suspected in Koyré's framing. Lacan's theory of science in terms of a social link and consequently of knowledge as a social relation thus inevitably comprises a 'critique of epistemic economy'. I deal with this term and context more extensively in forthcoming paper.

13. See Martin Heidegger, *Vorträge und Aufsätze* (1954) (Stuttgart: Klett-Cotta, 2004), p. 127.
14. I should add that Heidegger does not frame his critique of mathematics in this manner; it is my own reading of Heidegger's interpretation.
15. Jacques Lacan, *Écrits: The First Complete Edition in English*, trans. Bruce Fink (London and New York: W. W. Norton, 2006), p. 738.
16. At this point we can recall the classical Freudian point that repression and return of the repressed are not to be separated. Repression is ultimately a failed action, which merely displaces a problem rather than resolves it.
17. It would be wrong to assume that modern epistemic constructions escape sexuation. The crucial difference is that premodern sexuated cosmologies evolved around the idea of homeostatic pleasure and sexual relation, whereas now they comprise the increase of pleasure and sexual non-relation. If Lacan recognised in surplus-value the economic name for enjoyment of the capitalist system (systemic enjoyment), then surplus-knowledge stands for enjoyment of modern science (epistemic enjoyment). Furthermore, as long as science thinks of matter in passive terms, it reproduces the premodern sexuation of reality, coded in the very ideal of domination of nature. For the relevant critical account of the link between passive matter and femininity, see the classic by Judith Butler, *Bodies That Matter* (New York: Routledge, 1993), pp. 23–55.
18. Needless to add, modern extractivist metaphysics comprises two other components, production of surplus-value in the economic sphere and production of surplus-enjoyment in the subjective sphere.
19. Jacques Lacan, *The Seminar of Jacques Lacan, Book XVII: The Other Side of Psychoanalysis*, trans. Russell Grigg (London and New York: W. W. Norton, 2006), pp. 158–9; hereafter cited as *Seminar XVII*.
20. Jacques Lacan, *Le Séminaire, livre XVI, D'un Autre à l'autre* (Paris: Seuil, 2006), p. 37. In the same lecture we read: 'Knowledge has nothing to do with work. But in order to clarify something in this matter, there has to be a market, a market of knowledge. Knowledge has to become a commodity' (p. 39). Knowledge is coextensive with the regime of value and epistemic quantification of reality with economic valorisation.

21. The full statement goes as follows: 'Because energy is not a substance which, for example, improves or goes sour with age; it's a numerical constant that a physicist has to find in his calculations, so as to be able to work' (Jacques Lacan, *Television*, trans. Joan Copjec (London and New York: W. W. Norton, 1990), p. 18.)
22. Milner, for instance, distinguishes between 'matter without qualities', which is specific for the modern epistemic and economic regime, and 'qualities without matter', which can be linked to the world of appearances and the conscious observer. He furthermore translates 'matter without qualities' with 'exchange-value' and 'qualities without matter' with 'use-value'. See Jean-Claude Milner, *Constats* (Paris: Gallimard, 2002), p. 120.
23. Lacan, *Seminar XVII*, p. 159.
24. See Karl Marx, *Capital, Volume One*, trans. Ben Fowkes (London: Penguin Books, 1990), p. 873. The term 'renunciation of enjoyment' is used by Lacan in *Seminar XVI* and can be interpreted as a reaction to Marx's discussion of the so-called abstinence theory of the capitalist (Marx, *Capital*, p. 738–41). Marx himself uses the term 'renunciation of pleasure' that Lacan, not by chance, declares to be at the core of 'modern morality' (Lacan, *D'un Autre à l'autre*, p. 109).
25. This is why primitive accumulation is important for a critique of colonialism and for radical feminist theory, most prominently in Silvia Federici, *Caliban and the Witch. Women, the Body and Primitive Accumulation* (New York: Autonomieda, 2004).
26. As soon as one takes a closer look at the phenomena which make the world, one confronts a much more inconsistent and dysfunctional structure of reality. This is what Lacan aims at when he somewhat vaguely remarks that the real is what does not work, in other words that the real is an unstable structure which could potentially be described as disfunctioning – of course, again from the viewpoint of human observers, who continue approaching the real from the perspective of a functioning world.
27. Lacan, 'Triumph of Religion', pp. 80–1.
28. Boutroux's thesis on the contingency of natural laws has been mobilised by Catherine Malabou in her critique of Meillassoux. Malabou deduces from Boutroux the notion of gradual contingency, hence contingency as process (one could also say metamorphosis or mutation) rather than occurrence (as, precisely, in Hume, Kant and Meillassoux). See Catherine Malabou, *Before Tomorrow. Epigenesis and Rationality* (Cambridge: Polity Press, 2018).
29. Malabou, *Before Tomorrow*, p. 81.
30. The real is a disturbance, even if this disturbance is only minimal. This is also the point of the banal sounding remark that the real does not constitute totality or is non-all. One should not dismiss the banality of Lacan's statement, since it draws attention to an ongoing resistance against the real, a resistance that defines human thinking and that can be pinpointed also in Kant's transcendental aesthetics. The pure forms

of intuition, Euclidian space and linear time, play an essential role in the constitution of an ordered and complete vision of the real. Lacan's repeated insistence that we need to elaborate a new transcendental aesthetics, which will be in accordance with our contemporary science, therefore requires thinking all the things that make the world unworldly.

31. Although Lacan was unaware of it, it is certainly more than just a happy coincidence that Marx and Freud both named the force that constantly demands more of the surplus-object the drive (*Trieb*).
32. See Marx, *Capital*, p. 739. Marx remarks that the main achievement of the modern capitalist consists in its transformation of the miser's drive of enrichment into the capitalist drive of self-valorisation. While the former drive appears as 'individual mania', the latter introduces a 'rational' yet 'fanatic' regime of production. Hence, the capitalist link between production of surplus-value, exploitation and violence.
33. For a well-pointed account of the unconscious work, see Mai Wegener, 'Why should dreaming be a form of work?', in *Jacques Lacan Between Psychoanalysis and Politics*, ed. Samo Tomšič and Andreja Zevnik (London: Routledge, 2016), pp. 164–79.
34. That is the point of the 'fetishist' mystification of capitalist anti-sociality: 'the relationships between the producers, within which the social characteristics of their labours are manifested, take on the form of a social relation between the products of labour' (Marx, *Capital*, p. 164). Hence, instead of a social bond between the subjects we have a pseudo-social bond between commodities, from which subjectivity is rejected. Not only modern science but capitalism, too, are grounded on a foreclosure of the subject and of the social bond along with it.
35. Lacan, *D'un Autre à l'autre*, p. 239.
36. According to Wendy Brown, the political imperative of neoliberalism is: 'Society must be dismantled.' See Wendy Brown, *In the Ruins of Neoliberalism* (New York: Columbia University Press, 2019). One could expand this imperative to the broader history of capitalism.
37. For the discussion of an earlier, more ambiguous understanding of the death-drive in Freud's *Beyond the Pleasure Principle*, see Alenka Zupančič, *What Is Sex?* (Cambridge, MA: MIT Press, 2017), pp. 94–106.
38. I borrow the term from Todd McGowan.
39. Jacques Lacan, 'Conférences et entretiens dans des universités nord-américaines', *Scilicet*, nos. 6–7 (1976), p. 61. Dominique Laporte's *History of Shit* (Cambridge, MA: MIT Press, 2000) is an expanded commentary of this Lacanian 'infinite judgment'.
40. Jacques Lacan, *Le Séminaire, livre XXI, Les non-dupes errent* (unpublished, 9 April 1974).

5 The Genesis of a False Dichotomy: A Critique of Conceptual Alienation
Cara S. Greene

THOUGH MODIFIED VERSIONS of realism and conceptualism[1] persisted throughout the history of Western philosophy in various guises, these perspectives now seem to be operative in partisan discourse across the political spectrum. The mainstream conceptualist view upholds the primacy of 'concepts' and 'discourse' over and above 'things', as the 'reality' of objects is dependent upon their conceptual recognition and meaningful use in language. The mainstream realist view claims that the objects that lie behind or underneath concepts are more important than their conceptual representations, as these linguistic categories must refer to at least one real object or state of affairs for the concept to be useful. Importantly, these ideological realists and conceptualists maintain the superiority of either a concept's formal linguistic pole or its objective pole. Both the self-aware proliferation of disinformation on the right as well as the popularity of neologisms on the left express conceptualist tendencies – they value the 'word' over the 'thing' – as both conspiracy theorists and certain representatives of postmodernism would agree that the establishment of new concepts and relative standards of truth are means to overcome biased and anachronistic notions of objectivity. Alternatively, the right-wing mythologisation of an idealised national past as well as the left-wing isolation of identity categories both express commitments to realism, insofar as both traditionalism and personal identity rely on the existence of referents that have meaning and ontological weight outside of purely conceptual discourse. In turn, conceptualism and realism have migrated out of the halls of academia and into the public forum. Though conceptualists and realists on both sides of the aisle are (more or less) committed to their respective positions in good faith, the presupposed division between word and thing that undergirds both perspectives is taken as given: the independence of concept and object is merely assumed to be the true structure of language. On the contrary, for dialectical philosophers – thinkers like Hegel, Marx, Lacan and others – the schism of signifier and signified is not an a priori metaphysical feature of language but is rather the character of concepts in the paradigm of formal logic.[2] In truth, the abstract linguistic and concrete substantial are mutually generative rather than strictly opposed. Nonetheless, even though there's a rich philosophical precedent of recognising the true dialectical nature of concepts, the false dichotomisation of word and thing continues to flourish in spite of it. While it seems puzzling that philosophers and ideologues alike continue to uphold this dichotomy, Marx's materialist thesis sheds light on the staying power of these one-sided perspectives: the reason this bifurcated picture of concepts prevails today is not due to the intellectual profundity of these two positions. Rather, the debate perseveres because the opposition of word and thing is a real abstraction, or a philosophical representation of the separation of individual qualitative use and formal quantitative exchange under capitalism.

Nonetheless, this hypothesis – that the mutual exclusivity of abstract concept and concrete particular is a product of capitalist infrastructure – does not imply that the *distinction* between word and thing is unique to capitalist society. Most of the Western philosophical tradition maintained the separation of the conceptual and the real; Plato himself recognised that the discovery of Truth hinged upon the division of the immaterial philosophical dialectic and worldly reality. In other words, both the linguistic separation of concept and object and the metaphysical separation of ideal and material precede capitalist society, and in turn, cannot be hastily dismissed as a modern illusion. Rather, the problem with the persistence of conceptualist and realist tendencies, as premised on the isolation of concepts from their objects and the subordination of one to the other, has to do with these perspectives' isomorphism to the apparent mutual exclusivity of the form and content of commodities, and the ideological effects of this material fact. Commodities manifest either as numerical names – exchange values – *or* as concrete things – use values – but never simultaneously.[3] In accordance with this incompatibility vis-à-vis commodities, people in capitalist society relate to objects in two separate registers: either I am a private consumer of my property or I am participating in the social exchange of commodities. The reification of this social bifurcation has psychological consequences, articulated by Adorno and Horkheimer thus:

> The formalism of this principle [of non-contradiction] and the entire logic established around it stem from the opacity and entanglement of interests in a society in which the maintenance of forms and the preservation of individuals only fortuitously coincide. The expulsion of thought from logic ratifies in the lecture hall the reification of human beings in factory and office.[4]

While the law of non-contradiction is a neutral *philosophical* position, capitalism's commodification of all things proliferates endlessly and indiscriminately; as a result, logic's either/or thinking overflows its ideal boundary into the empirical world and the two become entangled. Put differently, the separation of ideal concept and real object has gotten out of hand, insofar as the dichotomy between them becomes a naturalised ontological presupposition that upholds the partition between governing macro-level structures and private individuals subject to them. As Adorno and Horkheimer imply, the opposition of functionary 'worker' and idiosyncratic 'person' is not simply a logical distinction, as who I am on the job 'formally' and who I am off the job 'informally'. It is a *real* distinction – an objective fiction – that obfuscates my agency at work and conceals the true relation between my job title and who I am. This 'false consciousness', supported by the presupposed division of names and things, causes individuals to become genuinely 'alienated' from themselves, other people and the conditions of their own lives: a state of affairs that becomes their fate, one they seem to have no control over.[5]

Thus, even though the relationship between the philosophical positions of conceptualism and realism to capitalist exchange is not self-evident, materialist analysis reveals that the alienation of the concept and the alienation of the worker reflect one another, the former via superstructure and the latter via infrastructure. The conceptual separation latches onto the ontological dichotomy of subjects and objects, a perfect ideological storm that allows the status quo to remain unchecked and detaches 'private' individuals from the dominant concepts and categories that determine their lives. In order to recognise the relation between the subject and the symbolic order, we must contextualise the acceptance of conceptualism and realism – as well as the metaphysical false dichotomy of universal and particular – in both philosophical and historical terms, as intellectual-ideological bedfellows with capitalist commodity exchange.

In what follows, I will locate the historical origin of the debate between conceptualists and realists in the medieval debate between nominalists, realists and conceptualists, and summarise the differences between these positions. I will then track the development of realism and conceptualism out of the Middle Ages through Kant's idealist conception of concepts in the *Critique of Pure Reason*. Next, I will outline Hegel's dialectical critique of the Kantian concept, but conclude – alongside Sohn-Rethel – that the Hegelian dialectical concept failed to capture that all things, including concepts, appear dichotomous under capitalism. Next, I will detail the ways in which the division of word and thing mimics the mutual exclusivity of exchange and use. Finally, I will explain how Marxist Psychoanalysis has the unique capacity to expose the connection between the concept, the objective world and the individual, and in turn reveal our subjective participation in the creation of the objective 'terms' of our lives.

Both conceptualism and realism emerged as responses to the problem of universals, a philosophical debate concerning the relationship between universals and particulars that has both metaphysical and linguistic dimensions. In ancient Greece, Plato's metaphysical realism took universals to be mind-independent Forms that were qualitatively different from the particular objects or phenomena that 'participate in' these Forms: the 'Dogness' of dogs exists independent of the particular animals that are dogs, as well as the minds of people who apply the concept 'dog' to the animals in question. However, it is impossible to explain how the self-contained Form of 'Dog' is the *truth* of dogs – i.e. the Form Dog's dog-character, Dog's *dogishness* – without positing another meta-Form that Dog participates in: a gesture that contradicts the independent nature of the Form in the first place.[6] As a response to the inconsistency of this 'extreme' realist position regarding universals, Aristotle advanced a 'strong' realist position, in which universals exist, but only within the particular or individual: a dog's 'Dogness' is a quality alongside other qualities like brownness and furriness. For both versions of realism, the proposition 'Spot is a dog' points to the existence of the universal 'Dog', though for Plato, the universal is a stand-alone entity, whereas for Aristotle, the universal is inseparable from particulars. In the Middle Ages, the Christian Scholastics incorporated Platonic and Aristotelian realist positions regarding universals into Christian theological debates on topics like the limitedness or limitlessness of God and the connection between the human mind and the divine mind. For medieval realists like Walter of Mortagne and Johannes Duns Scotus, not only were universals independent of thinking subjects, but universals were the only 'true' things in existence. Yet, due to the Scholastics' belief in the direct relation between the particular spiritual subject and the universal divine, Scholastic realism understood universals as both metaphysical entities and as 'objective concepts',[7] ambiguating the connection between language and metaphysics.

Unlike realists, nominalists reject the existence of universals, asserting that universals are nothing more than linguistic conventions, relations between particulars or qualitative tropes. Some forms of nominalism are realist insofar as they uphold the independent existence of particulars – like Abelard's nominalism – while other forms of nominalism rejected the independent existence of both universals and particulars – like Ockham's nominalism. The latter more extreme form of nominalism inspired a third position, conceptualism, which fully abandoned the realist commitments of nominalism and realism: for a conceptualist, universals are neither existing independent things in themselves, nor are they objective features of particulars. Instead, the accurate relation of a universal concept to a thing – or more accurately, a representation of a thing – occurs within the mind: as such, the worldly or 'real' relation of universals and particulars is irrelevant. Though the Scholastics were generally unconcerned with the physical empirical world, Hegel notes that this oversight led to Scholasticism's undoing. Due to the significance of concrete reality in new secular intellectual domains like humanism and political science, 'the real world' encroached upon the abstract metaphysics of the feudal Christians, at which point philosophy or 'reason' heeded 'the necessity of setting to work on nature in order to obtain immediate certainty'.[8] During the Enlightenment, realism, nominalism and conceptualism were brought down to earth, and as a result, the parameters of the debate were redrawn on the ground. After abandoning the metaphysical realm of the Forms and the Christian heaven, realists and nominalists began to concern themselves with the natural sensible world, as represented by the empiricist and materialist sensibilities of thinkers like Hobbes and Diderot. Alternatively, thinkers expressing broadly 'conceptualist' views concerned themselves with the powers of subjective human reason, represented more or less by Descartes's solipsistic rationalism. As such, the realist perspectives of realism and nominalism and the anti-realist perspective of conceptualism expanded to address the relation between subject and object as well as the relation between the abstract and the concrete. Though the medieval debate on Forms and sensible particulars as well as the more modern debate regarding ideas and their objects both appear to concern the metaphysical problem of universals, these debates can usefully be seen as determined in part through the word-object question.

In the *Critique of Pure Reason*, Kant aimed to determine the role of the psyche in the acquisition of true knowledge of objective reality, which involved discerning the possibility of 'homogeneity' between concepts and intuitions. In the section titled 'The Schematism of the Pure Concepts of The Understanding', Kant attempts to explain the relationship between concepts of the understanding and objects in reality: how it's possible for an object to be 'subsumed' under a concept, or how a category is 'applied' to appearances.[9] In the 'Schematism', Kant's distinction between the pure concepts – or rules of thought – and empirical concepts – ordinary names that apply to specific classes – is vague, but in both cases, Kant notes that the interceding element between concepts of the understanding and sense-derived representations is the 'transcendental schema', a 'mediating representation' that is *both* 'intellectual' and 'sensible'.[10] Unlike the faculty of the imagination, which unifies sensibility in general into thinkable representations, the schema is a *product* of the imagination which 'provides a concept with its image'.[11] The schema is not concerned with the *general* translation of sense data into intellectual language, but it is what mediates between specific concepts and specific representations: it's what allows the 'given' dog Spot to be 'subsumed' under the intellectual concept 'dog'. However, Kant underscores that the schema *do not* bridge the divide between the objective world and the mind: the schema do not involve the direct communication between, say, the individual living dog Spot – born in 2004, has floppy ears and anxiety – and the concept 'dog'. Rather, empirical concepts only directly relate to the schema 'as a rule for the determination of our intuition in accordance with a certain general concept'.[12] In other words, Spot-ness is irrelevant to my accurate application of the empirical concept 'dog;' the only thing that the schema retrieves from intuition and gives to the Understanding is the fact that Spot is a four-footed thing, that Spot adheres to the 'rule' of the concept 'dog'. In Kant's words, 'dog' is not 'restricted to any single particular shape that experience offers me or any possible image that I can exhibit *in concreto*'.[13] Thus, though the schematism is more targeted than the general unifying function of the imagination, the schematism is *still* an inner synthesis of appearances under a category or judgment, with no real concern for the 'single particular shape that experience offers me': Spot is only intelligible to me because he's a dog. In turn, Kant refuses to posit a real connection between the concept and the singular empirical particular, but defaults to his position that this connection between the conceptual universal and its particular instantiations is immanent to subjectivity. Kant's understanding of concepts in the Schematism thus downplays those unique features of objects that distinguish them from others and ignores the question of the relation between representations and objects in themselves. In this way, Kant subordinates the particular 'thing' to the universal 'concept' and locates both of them within the domain of Reason. Though the former conclusion is a realist one, Kant's perspective can be understood as broadly conceptualist, albeit a different conceptualism from medieval conceptualism. Unlike medieval conceptualism, Kant stresses the indispensability of the manifold of sensible intuition for the cognition of objects. Nonetheless, Kant does retain the anti-realism of medieval conceptualism, as the meaningful dimension of experience that allows for a connection between 'word' and 'thing' to come about may have nothing to do with 'real' things.

Throughout his corpus, Hegel identified Kant's transcendental idealist conception of judgments as abstract and 'one-sided', as Kant alienates words and their referents. Unlike Kant, Hegel posited the identity of name and thing, insofar as he conceives a name as a linguistic expression of a thing (and vice versa): as a result, the two aspects cannot be detached or stratified. In Hegel's eyes, the concept is able to 'bridge the sensory and the suprasensory'.[14] Before diving into Hegel's analysis of concepts, we might detour through his 'Doctrine of Being' in his *Encyclopedia Logic* as a way to understand Hegel's conception of the relation between form and content – a distinction that will lay the dialectical foundation for Hegel's analysis of concepts.

Hegel observes that everyday consciousness believes it to be obvious that 'things are more than mere numbers'.[15] Of course, the Ten Commandments are much more than a collection of commandments that add up to the number ten; they have been the governing principles of Judeo-Christian life for thousands of years. Yet, the quantity of the commandments cannot be separated from their quality: the fact that their meaning involves much more than their number does not mean that the quantity of commandments is arbitrary or irrelevant. There is a scene in Mel Brooks's film *History of the World* in which Moses descends from Mount Sinai to present the Israelites with the Ten Commandments only after accidentally dropping a third tablet. If Moses hadn't broken the third tablet, the extra five commandments wouldn't simply be an expansion of the existing Ten Commandments; these extra commandments would alter the character of the prior commandments and fundamentally change the nature of Judeo-Christian theory and practice. It's also not the case that the existence of the extra five commandments would open the floodgates for God to send down countless other commandments. Rather, the formal or abstract characteristics of the commandments, including their order, wording and number, would necessarily affect the content of all the commandments: in this way, their content is connected to and limited by the form in which they were delivered to Moses. For Hegel, the distinction between general form and specific content does not involve the subordination of either feature: for Hegel, all division is relation.[16]

Later on, in the 'Doctrine of the Concept' in his *Encyclopedia Logic*, Hegel explains that concepts and judgments are isomorphic, as concepts – like judgments – have three distinct 'moments': universality, particularity and individuality. Hegel illustrates these moments using the concept 'horse': the concept's universal dimension is its animality, its particular dimension is its species (as not merely an animal but a horse) and its singular or individual dimension is that which distinguishes it from all other horses – it is *this* unique horse. Hegel explains that the universal moment of the concept is not simply the linguistic facade that stands apart from the empirical instantiation or meaning of the concept. Rather, the individual moment of the concept is the *self-mediation* of the universal concept, the concept's 'utterly concrete' negative – that is, determinate – unity with itself. On the other hand, the singular horse contains both its particularity as a horse as well as the animality that is its universality: to recall our earlier example, though the dog Spot is the concrete manifestation of the abstract concept 'dog', and is distinguished from the concept in and through its individuality, none of Spot's features can be divorced from the concept. In Hegel's parlance, the singular thing is the self-differentiation of the concept, *not* that which lies outside of it.[17] Though Hegel affirms the distinction of these moments, he doesn't favour the particular over and above the universal, or vice versa. At the same time, Hegel notes that these moments are 'held apart from one another by external reflection':[18] the appearance of the separation between 'word' and 'thing' is not a deception, it is rather an inalienable feature of rational experience of the world. However, the appearance of this division *is* an incomplete picture of the concept, the separation doesn't go all the way down: the universal, particular and individual are – in themselves – inseparable from and immanent to the formal concept, which actualises itself in its real idiosyncratic manifestations.

Thus, in his dialectical alternative to Kant's ideal 'one-sided' structure of concepts, Hegel implicitly identifies the problem with the separation of ideal conceptualism on the one hand and a materialist realism on the other, as they radically separate the moments of the concept and then assert the truth of one moment over and above the other. Theoretically, Hegel's exposition of the true holistic structure of concepts would allow 'modern philosophical consciousness' to recognise the absurdity of upholding either name *or* thing as the 'in itself' of concepts, and therefore move beyond this dualism. However, as evidenced by the staying power of the perspectives of conceptualism and realism, both in the domain of philosophy as well as in the background of popular ideological discourse, this Hegelian intellectual sublation hasn't occurred. *Geist* takes the 'external relation' of words and things at face value. While Hegel's 'Concept' presents a more accurate conception of the relationship between words and things, Kant's bifurcation of reality into subjective 'concepts' on one side and objective 'things' on the other continues to dominate our understanding of language over and above Hegel's dialectical conception. Yet the dominance of this dichotomous conception is not attributable to the *truth* of the Kantian picture over and above the *falsity* of the Hegelian one. Rather, it is due to the fact that Kant's dualism was – and still is – the theoretical reflection of a practical state of affairs, the theoretical scaffolding of a social nexus organised around the mutual exclusivity of commodity exchange and use. In other words, though Hegel outlined the actual relationship between a concept's moments – and in so doing, exposed the erroneous nature of the dichotomisation of word and thing – Hegel misunderstood the divide between language and referent to be a problem of consciousness, that could therefore be overcome philosophically. On the contrary, the staying power of vulgar conceptualism and realism and Kantian two-worlds metaphysics can be attributed to the fact that Kant's transcendental idealism functions as a philosophical mirror of the structure of reality under the conditions of capitalist exchange.

Because Hegel failed to recognise the tendency to oppose concepts and reality as an outgrowth of commodity-based society, Hegel's diagnosis of the problem with the Kantian concept remained on the level of idealist critique.[19] After Hegel, the Marxist tradition condemned this Hegelian misstep *ad nauseum*, often reducing Hegel's idealism to merely a modified inheritance of Kant's idealism. However, Alfred Sohn-Rethel, a Marxist intellectual on the fringes of the Frankfurt School of Social Research, developed a more nuanced historical materialist critique of the two main figures of German Idealism in his magnum opus *Intellectual and Manual Labour*. Sohn-Rethel attributed the failure of Hegel's philosophy to 'catch on' to the affinity between Kant's transcendental philosophy and the separation of exchange and use in commodity-based society. Though, by and large, Sohn-Rethel's study concerns the way that Kant's epistemological categories are 'abstractions' that naturalise the distinction between intellectual and manual labour, we can apply Sohn-Rethel's materialist thesis to the realm of concepts: in addition to providing superstructural support for the division and stratification of abstract and concrete labour, the philosophical prominence of two-worlds metaphysics (*à la* Kant) also leads to the alienation of concepts and objects.

As Marx outlines in *Capital, Volume One*, the commodity leads a double life: it exists to be used on the one hand, and to be exchanged on the other. A particular commodity can only be used once it 'drops out' of circulation, at which point it subsequently performs a specific function or 'satisfies a human need' in the life of the consumer.[20] For instance, you're not allowed to eat your groceries before proceeding through the checkout lane, but you're free to do so when you get home. However, before a commodity is purchased and taken off the market, it had a different character – a social, rather than private, character – insofar as the commodity exhibited the form of exchangeability that allowed it to be bought and sold alongside every other commodity. The commodity's universal social dimension – its price or 'money name' – allowed the commodity to be traded for a number of small paper bills of equal value (aka money).[21] How many bills constitute 'equal value' is determined by the specific quantity indicated on the commodity's numerical name-tag, which itself represents the amount of 'abstract human labour' required for the commodity's production.[22] Needless to say, evidence of the physical work that produced the commodity is also conspicuously absent from the commodity's 'private' life as a useful object as well as its stint in the realm of monetary exchange. Leaving the production of the commodity aside, Marx's insight here is that an object's use value and exchange value are 'mutually exclusive in time':[23] this phenomenon can be seen in the fact that a house cannot be lived in and 'exchanged' simultaneously – that's why realtors ask tenants to leave when they are showing the house to prospective buyers. This mutual exclusivity of formal or conceptual exchange and individual qualitative use is thus a social requirement – not an ontological feature of the object – that is internalised by the object via its commodity form.

Due to the fact that the commodity's 'concrete' existence as my property and its 'abstract' existence as a commodity cannot coexist, certain ways of thinking and behaving have been habituated to accommodate this separation. In turn, the 'actions' of buyers and sellers involved in exchange is social, concerned with trading their commodity for another commodity of equal value (the commodity of money), while the 'consciousness' of each person is private, concerned only with the commodity's singular existence as a useful object, the commodity's value *for them*. Hence, commodity buyers and sellers understand themselves to be private minds in the public sphere: in Sohn-Rethel's words, 'there *seems* to be nothing between the owners but segregation'.[24] The fact that the *one* commodity is, in a sense, a *two*, that is, exhibiting its formal quality and its useful quality in separate registers, the process of exchange also involves an 'abstraction' within and between individuals. In Sohn-Rethel's words:

> There are indeed two abstractions interlocked with each other. The first springs from the separation of exchange from use . . . The second operates within the very relationship itself, and results from the interplay of the exchanging parties as solipsistic owners. It attaches directly to the act of exchange itself.[25]

Hence, the exchange of commodities – that is, the essential activity that sustains modern life itself – gives rise to a peculiar kind of comportment, as well as a solipsistic conception of subjectivity that replicates the 'laws of exchange', in which reality is divided into private particular subjects and public universal objects.[26] By Sohn-Rethel's lights, capitalist society is thoroughly permeated by the abstraction of the commodity's separation of use and exchange, which inevitably engenders a philosophical conception of subjectivity that upholds this exclusivity of subjective reason and objective world, epitomised in Kant's transcendental subject and the separation of noumena and phenomena. In sum, Kant's 'ideal abstraction' of subjects and objects obscures its true origin, namely the 'real abstraction' of commodity exchange.[27]

While the structure of concepts was not explicitly the focus of Sohn-Rethel's analysis, his theory of real abstraction lends itself to our materialist analysis of the alienated concept. As we've already seen, concepts – like commodities – are 'divided' into signs and referents, the former fulfilling the formal universal role much like exchange value, and the latter fulfilling the particular or qualitative role much like use value. However, as Sohn-Rethel emphasises with regard to Kantian epistemology, this infrastructural division imprints itself on dominant conceptions of the world and ourselves via superstructural institutions like philosophy.[28] This structural assumption affects the ways we interact, conceive of ourselves and understand our relationship to reality: Marx called this state of affairs 'alienation'. Nevertheless, Sohn-Rethel's utilisation and elaboration of Marx's materialist premise implies that if capitalist relations of exchange were to be overcome, the unbridgeable chasm between word and thing – as well as 'private' subject and 'public' object – would follow suit. As Kantian-bourgeois epistemology also upholds these divisions, we can apply the same logic to the question of overcoming the opposition of the one-sided realist and conceptualist polarities. Due to the fact that this dichotomy reflects the socio-economic basis of capitalist society, rational *Aufhebung* will not allow us to move beyond the conceptualist-realist paradigm, as Hegel supposed. Rather, the only way for us moderns to transcend the limits of these perspectives would be through a total restructuring of the relations of production and exchange.

At the same time, overcoming the debate does not entail an impossible utopian reconciliation of subject and object, word and thing. Rather, it involves recognising the ways in which reason reifies or naturalises certain assumptions or viewpoints about itself and the world. In fact, Sohn-Rethel's critique of Kant's transcendental subjectivity overlooks a less obvious Kantian insight that is relevant to our guiding concern about the bifurcation of concepts: namely that all reflection necessitates a division between the subject and object of thought, though the fault line of this division is not determined a priori. In the 'Transcendental Dialectic', Kant explains that the judgment 'I think' is the 'vehicle of all concepts', insofar as concepts mediate the process of thought, which requires a thinker.[29] Kant notes that this judgment implies a distinction between two 'kinds of objects' of inner perception (or 'apperception'): at a minimum, I not only inwardly perceive myself as a thinking thing, but I also perceive the contentless thinking process, the transcendental condition for having thoughts and experiences. Kant continues that even without taking in any sense data, the 'I think' seems to generate transcendental predicates out of itself: like the judgment that the self is an immaterial substance; that it is qualitatively simple and incorruptible; that it is quantitatively single and thus the unity of my personality; that this self relates to possible objects in space and it thus has an interactive capacity, etc.[30] Kant then explains that these presupposed determinations are 'paralogisms' of pure reason, or false/misleading inferences based on the basic transcendental judgment 'I think'. For example, Kant notes that the assumption of subjectivity as an immaterial substance is 'merely inferred from the concept of the relation that all thought has to the I as the common subject in which it inheres'.[31] In other words, though we can posit that the representation 'I' accompanies all thought, we can't validly assume that 'substance' is predicated as a 'standing or abiding intuition', a persisting sense impression.[32] Kant thus recognises that we can grant Descartes's Archimedean 'I think, I am' to invest the 'I' with substantiality *only if* we resist the tendency to ascribe qualities like 'everlasting duration' to the concept of substance. Hence Kant observed that human beings *tend* to deduce certain predicates from the primary judgment 'I think', even though these inferences are unfounded. In other words, Kant stumbled upon an awareness that thought presupposes a minimal division or distinction between thinker and thinking, but that this ground-level differentiation of subject and object causes reason to push itself into the realm of speculative metaphysics and determinism.

The insight that Kant's oft-neglected account of split subjectivity offers us is twofold: first of all, that all thinking – the vehicle for concepts – indeed involves a division between 'I' and 'object of thought;' but second of all, this division cannot be further qualified: it is merely a primary division. In the 'Paralogisms', Kant does not necessarily imply that this 'split-ness' maps onto the division of word and thing, as he does in the 'Schematism'. What's more, Kant observed that reason commonly conceives of its split-ness in misleading and unsupported ways: we tend to misconstrue the nature of subjectivity by hypostatising certain beliefs about it. Yet, as evidenced by Kant's attempts in the first *Critique* to defend the separation of noumena and phenomena, Kant fails see that his essential idealisation of mind and world is itself a paralogism, as it quarantines the 'I' in cognitive-metaphysical reality without being able to sufficiently defend this determination.[33] The schism between ideal and material is unprovable within the bounds of transcendental idealism because Kant prohibits Reason from locating itself in the world. In truth, the hypostatisation of inner consciousness over and above external activity is ungraspable from within the 'contemplative' Kantian standpoint because it is an outgrowth of commodity exchange, not an internal feature of subjectivity.

Why salvage this Kantian insight into the minimal division of subjectivity, and what does it have to do with overcoming the ideological tendency to reify either word or thing? If the aim of this study is to problematise the 'alienation' of concepts, it bears repeating that there is indeed a separation between the particular individual 'thing' and universal category or 'concept'. The objective concepts I use to define myself will *always* be abstracted from the concrete dimensions of my unique subjectivity; the collapse or total reconciliation of both subject and world as well as ideal and material is an impossibility. However, capitalist reason upholds these divisions as *thoroughgoing* antagonisms without revealing that the fissure between form and content is not an essential ontological feature of reality but a historically established standard. As a consequence, ordinary consciousness is incapable of recognising that the negation of the abstract universal via the concrete particular conceals a relation between them. As such, the either/or of conceptualism and realism seems to be the only way to understand concepts as well as our participation in and creation of them. Moreover, it is not enough to either uncover the dialectical structure of concepts, as Hegel does via 'Doctrine of The Concept', or thoroughly historicise the schism between ideal and material, as Sohn-Rethel does in *Intellectual and Manual Labour*. The former is limited by its immanence to 'consciousness', and the latter is limited by its immanence to 'history', insofar as we understand these things as opposed, an understanding that we now recognise as an ideological outgrowth of capitalist exchange. Though there is indeed a difference between the abstract universal and the concrete particular, individual existence is inextricable from the macro-level 'objective' structures that determine it, and the naturalised categories that appear to be necessary are only viable through their empirical substantiation by and through the actions of individuals. If we acknowledge the historical origin of the spurious bifurcation of names and things, we can not only move past the one-sided reified perspectives of realism and conceptualism, but we will then have the capacity to discern our subjective participation in the creation of the objective world, and the ways in which linguistic categories enable and limit individual experience.

In the weeds of his analysis of the exchange abstraction, Sohn-Rethel comments that the influence of capitalist logic on the consciousness of individuals manifests in the way that:

> [people] in subservience often act to the advantage of those above them. They consider themselves to have acted in self-interest although in fact they have merely obeyed the laws of the exchange nexus. *Here is not the place to examine the superstructure of advanced capitalism, but a materialist social psychology of the future would certainly be strengthened by integrating the causal relationship between the abstractions of exchange and thought into the theories of Reich, Fromm, Marcuse, etc.[34]

Sohn-Rethel suggests that attempts to understand psychology under capitalism, as taken on by Freudo-Marxists like Reich, Fromm and Marcuse, should recognise that the fact that people organise their lives around and derive a sense of meaning from alienated labour and commodity exchange is not solely attributable to bourgeois brainwashing, but rather because we have unconsciously internalised the logic of 'the market' itself. Indeed, as Sohn-Rethel proposes in this footnote, Marxist Psychoanalysis is uniquely poised to discern the mutual interaction between language and people's lives and, moreover, Marxist Psychoanalysis *also* has the capacity to resist the materialist tendency to reduce all ideal phenomena to economic mechanisms. As a dialectical method premised on the notion that the 'outside world' and our 'inner consciousness' condition one another, Marxist Psychoanalysis affirms that the ideal and the material – as well as the conceptual and the real – cannot be fully integrated or fundamentally separated. Hence, over and above philosophical idealism and vulgar materialism, which reduce historical phenomena to the psyche and vice versa, Marxist Psychoanalysis is a practical method that is in a position to acknowledge that, while the abstraction of the individual thinker and the objective world is an inalienable feature of life, the extreme partitioning of word and thing is a social phenomenon – a liberatory recognition.[35]

As Paul Ricoeur established, Marx and Freud are hermeneuticists of suspicion: they both endorse that the way things seem must be probed to unearth the way things really are; the latter carries out this excavation via the psyche and the former via history, society and economics. However, as Hegel reminds us, both this delineation between mind and world *as well as* the supposition that appearances and essences are bivalent are themselves suspect assumptions. While the ideal-subjective and the material-social constitute the starting points of Psychoanalysis on the one hand and Marxism on the other, these two tracks inevitably converge, as both traditions are premised on the intertwinement of psychological and material-social life. What's more, neither Freud nor Marx disposes of the 'illusory' topsoil of their subject matter: the stories we tell about ourselves, like our surface-level understanding of our neuroses and the way others perceive us, are themselves the keys to unlocking the deeper and truer understanding of our relationship to ourselves and the world. Though the connection between Marxism and Psychoanalysis is often overlooked within these disciplines respectively, the tradition of Freudo-Marxism that Sohn-Rethel refers to brings out the ways in which each augments the other in indispensable ways. Specifically, I contend that the hybrid discipline of Marxist Psychoanalysis is an 'objective' historical materialist practice that incorporates rather than forecloses the study of the individual psyche: that is, it involves the fundamental interpenetration of the abstract universal and empirical particular and is therefore poised to uncover the true connection between words and things.

In his 1929 essay *Dialectical Materialism and Psychoanalysis*, Freudian communist Willhelm Reich analyses the compatibility of Marxism and Psychoanalysis in light of the proclamation of their incompatibility by adherents of bourgeois psychology and vulgar materialism. To prove the harmoniousness of Marxism and Psychoanalysis, Reich uses the dialectical psychoanalytic concept of the 'reality principle' as an illustrative example. In Freudian psychoanalysis, the 'pleasure principle' is a psychical force that seeks the satisfaction of drives and the attainment of pleasure. Alternatively, the 'reality principle' is a mediating psychical force that keeps the primal pleasure principle in check by modifying and suppressing it, so that the individual can still achieve enjoyment and satisfy their drives, but only in and through 'substitutive satisfactions' or socially acceptable pleasurable phenomena.[36] Reich notes, however, that the reality principle is not absolute: its regulations are shaped by the context that the individual exists within. The reality principle is therefore a primary, trans-historical psychical structure, as an indispensable 'bridge' that mediates between the singular psyche and its objective situation. At the same time, the contents of the reality principle change based on the particularities of that individual's context: the reality principle under feudalism is not the same as the reality principle under capitalism because the norms that emerged from those distinct socio-economic configurations were different. In turn, the reality principle is nothing other than the force of the universal within the particular – the world within the self. What's more, the reality principle is realised in and through language: the analysand narrates their own self-understanding to the analyst. In turn, a Marxist Psychoanalyst can bring out the fact that the analysand's self-understanding is simultaneously enabled and limited by the state of affairs that appears to be the case: that, for instance, the analysand's pathological desire to be 'successful' is a reflection of the version of 'success' they inherited from repressive parents and from capitalist society at large, which understands 'success' only in terms of one's position vis-à-vis commodity production and exchange. What's more, the concept of 'success' itself involves the mutual exclusivity of one's objective-economic dimension and one's particular private dimension, and prioritises the former. This recognition of the true structure of the language we use to talk about ourselves – that is, the relation of one's individual experience to the concepts that define us and vice versa – will allow the analysand to discern that universal concept of 'success' is nothing other than the ideological reflection of certain specific a posteriori social and material relations: there is no Platonic Form of 'success', though the concept does refer to a set of well-established associations. As evidenced by Marxist Psychoanalysis's dialectical understanding of the connection between the things we say and the conditions of our lives, as well as the fact that it takes the specific experience of the subject – rather than the abstract 'life of the mind' – as its starting point, Marxist Psychoanalysis as a hybrid discipline is better suited to study the integrated structure of concepts than straightforwardly philosophical and materialist analyses of language on their own.

Though the opposition of conceptualist and realist orientations is rooted in medieval and German Idealist philosophy, the do-si-do of capitalist exchange and its accompanying logic of mutual exclusivity allowed the segregation of abstract discourse and its meaningful content to appear natural. As a consequence, the dialectical relationship between discourse and life is obscured, so much so that it seems like one can either believe that abstract concepts generate reality or that empirical reality generates concepts. As such, ideological responses to the socio-economic status quo inevitably involve 'choosing a side', even though putting one's faith in the conceptual realm of theory *or* the concrete realm of practice fails to notice the ways that these registers are connected. By taking refuge in esoteric symbolism and discursive conjecture, the right-wing conspiracy theorist fails to see how these fictions conceal an ordinary and tragic situation in which the ruling class – not a hidden cabal of Jewish puppeteers – upholds a system that allows the few to flourish at the expense of the well-being of the many. Alternatively, some progressive groups' preoccupation with concrete action over and above abstract critique neglects the ways in which dominant belief systems permeate material life: pre-figurative political projects, for instance, understand their creation of concrete or 'real alternatives' to capitalism as practical expressions of equality and freedom without recognising the ways these ventures are saddled with the ideological baggage of the society these activists attempt to escape. As both of these viewpoints neglect either the real or the conceptual, they fail to see how each upholds the other. However, these naive responses to 'the way things are' are not the result of moral failings of individuals. Rather, these contemporary conceptualist and realist tendencies result from a system of social relations that reifies the division of abstract and concrete and obscures the mutual interconnection of language and world.[37]

Notes

1. In this *paper*, I use 'conceptualism' as roughly synonymous with 'linguistic constructivism', indicating that proponents of this view believe that concepts determine reality and reject the idea that concepts have fixed referents. Due to the fact that the various philosophical perspectives that prioritise concepts over and above real phenomena shift significantly over the course of history and contain critical differences between one another, I employ the concept of 'conceptualism' as an umbrella term, as 'linguistic constructivism' is a relatively modern philosophical orientation popularised by strains of poststructuralism.
2. Unlike a formal logical system which holds that A and –A cannot logically coexist, Hegel's dialectic, for instance, is premised on the concomitant interrelation of affirmation and negation, not their mutual cancellation. The distinct subject and predicate of a judgment – as well as the signifier and signified of a concept – already contain this insight: rather than being held apart as two extremes, the subject or concept 'comes out of itself' in its determination – its predicate or content is neither easily collapsed into nor entirely alien from it. In Hegel's words:

   > The firm principle that formal thinking lays down for itself here is that contradiction cannot be thought. But in fact the thought of contradiction is the essential moment of the concept. Formal thought does in fact think it, only it at once looks away from it and stating its principle it only passes over from it into abstract negation.

   George Willhelm Friedrich Hegel, *Encyclopedia of the Philosophical Sciences in Basic Outline, Part I: Science of Logic*, ed. Klaus Brinkmann and Daniel O. Dahlstrom (Cambridge: Cambridge University Press, 2010), 12.246, p. 745.
3. 'Though a commodity may, alongside its real shape (iron, for instance), possess an ideal value-shape or an imagined gold-shape in the form of its price, it cannot simultaneously be both real iron and real gold.' Karl Marx, *Capital, Volume One* (London: Penguin Books, 1990), p. 197.
4. Max Horkheimer and Theodor W. Adorno, *Dialectic of Enlightenment: Philosophical Fragments*, ed. Gunzelin Schmidd Noerr, trans. Edmund Jephcott (Stanford: Stanford University Press, 2002), p. 23.

5. Regarding this phenomenon, Lukács observes:

   > Bourgeois thought observes economic life consistently and necessarily from the standpoint of the individual capitalist and this naturally produces a sharp confrontation between the individual and the overpowering supra-personal 'law of nature' which propels all social phenomena. This leads both to the antagonism between individual and class interests in the event of conflict . . . and also to the logical impossibility of discovering theoretical and practical solutions to the problems created by the capitalist system of production.

   Georg Lukács, *History and Class Consciousness: Studies in Marxist Dialectics*, trans. Rodney Livingstone (Cambridge, MA: MIT Press, 1971), p. 63.
6. Plato and R. Allen, *Plato's 'Parmenides'* (New Haven: Yale University Press, 1997), 132a–b, p. 10.
7. Klima Gyula, 'The Medieval Problem of Universals', ed. Edward N. Zalta, in *The Stanford Encyclopedia of Philosophy*, 2017. Available at: <https://plato.stanford.edu/entries/universals-medieval/#Intr> (last accessed 18 January 2021).
8. Georg Willhelm Friedrich Hegel, *Hegel's Lectures on the History of Philosophy (Complete)*, trans. Elizabeth Sanderson Haldane and Frances H. Simon. (Lector House LLP, 2020), p. 555.
9. Immanuel Kant, *Critique of Pure Reason*, ed. and trans. Paul Guyer and Allen W. Wood (New York: Cambridge University Press, 1998), A138/B177, p. 272. For more on Kant's conception of concepts, see Michael Pendlebury, 'Making Sense of Kant's Schematism', *Philosophy and Phenomenological Research*, vol. 55, no. 4 (December 1995), p. 779.
10. Kant, *Critique of Pure Reason*, A138/B177, p. 272.
11. Kant, *Critique of Pure Reason*, B179–A140, p. 273.
12. Kant, *Critique of Pure Reason*, A141, p. 273.
13. Kant, *Critique of Pure Reason*, A141, p. 273.
14. This quote comes from Hegel's discussion of Pythagoras, who understood numbers to be 'the thought of the sensory itself' – not an abstraction from reality, but part and parcel with the 'essence' of the universe. We can extend this reading of number to understand the intimate and inextricable connection between concepts and what they express. See Hegel, *Encyclopedia of the Philosophical Sciences in Basic Outline, Part I: Science of Logic*. p. 166.
15. Hegel, *Encyclopedia of the Philosophical Sciences in Basic Outline, Part I: Science of Logic*, p. 166.
16. One might object that there are places in Hegel's corpus where he can be read as subordinating empirical content to the rational Idea, perhaps most notoriously in his final chapter on 'Absolute Knowing' in the *Phenomenology of Spirit*. This

interpretation would therefore conclude that Hegel is ultimately a capital-I idealist who absorbs the many into the one and the real into the conceptual. The problem with such a reading is that Hegel's Concept is thoroughly dialectical: it doesn't exist in a logical realm over and above the concrete world, as these registers are fundamentally unified. In Hegel's words, 'finitude and infinitude are inseparable. The finite is this transition, this self-transposition into infinity, and infinity at once consists in having the finite within it. Neither apart from the other holds the truth'. Georg Willhelm Freidrich Hegel, *Lectures on Logic,* trans. Karl Hegel and Clark Butler. (Bloomington: Indiana University Press, 2001), p. 111.

17. Hegel, *Encyclopedia of the Philosophical Sciences in Basic Outline, Part I: Science of Logic*, p. 238.
18. Hegel, *Encyclopedia of the Philosophical Sciences in Basic Outline, Part I: Science of Logic*, p. 240.
19. Lucio Colletti comes to a similar conclusion and uses it to challenge Marxists' affinity for Hegelian philosophy. In *Marxism and Hegel*, Colletti claims that, in spite of the fact that certain components of absolute idealism – like Hegel's ideas of 'Reason' and 'objectivity' – are fundamental to Marxism, Hegelian concepts like the Absolute and the Pure Idea are evidence of Hegel's resurrection of metaphysics, a domain fundamentally at odds with historical materialism. Moreover, Colletti holds that historical materialists justify their inclination toward Hegelian philosophy by retroactively reading Marxist materialism back into Hegel's idealism. On the contrary, Colletti believes that Hegelian Marxists have largely misinterpreted Kantian philosophy, condemning it as vulgar idealism, whereas Hegelian philosophy, which posits the identity of thought and being, more accurately represents the idealism that materialists reject. While the Hegelian Concept is not as simple as Colletti illustrates it to be – see footnote 16 – Colletti is correct to retrieve heterogeneity from the Hegelian Marxist dustbin, because, as Colletti implies, bourgeois thought's willful ignorance about and dismissal of material reality can be justified by the Hegelian motto that the real is rational. See Lucio Colletti, *Marxism and Hegel*, trans. Lawrence Garner (London: New Left Books, 1973), chapters IV–VI.
20. Marx, *Capital, Volume One*, p. 163.
21. Marx, *Capital, Volume One*, p. 203.
22. Marx, *Capital, Volume One*, p. 150.

23. The point is that use and exchange are not only different and contrasting by description, but are mutually exclusive in time. They must take place separately at different times. This is because exchange serves only a change of ownership, a change, that is, in terms of a purely *social status* of the commodities as owned property. In order to make this change possible on a basis of negotiated

> agreement the physical condition of the commodities, their *material status*, must remain unchanged, or at any rate must be assumed to remain unchanged.

Alfred Sohn-Rethel, *Intellectual and Manual Labour*, trans. Martin Sohn-Rethel (Atlantic Highlands, NJ: Humanities Press, 1978), pp. 23–4.
24. Sohn-Rethel, *Intellectual and Manual Labour*, p. 41 (emphasis mine).
25. Sohn-Rethel, *Intellectual and Manual Labour*, p. 46.
26. Sohn-Rethel, *Intellectual and Manual Labour*, p. 51.
27. Sohn-Rethel, *Intellectual and Manual Labour*, p. 62.
28. This position is also echoed by Adorno and Horkheimer in the *Dialectic of Enlightenment*, who note that Kant's reification of the universal in his 'Schematism' is directly tied to the reification of the impersonal subject over and above the individual person in capitalist society:

    > The true nature of the schematism which externally coordinates the universal and the particular, the concept and the individual case, finally turns out, in current science, to be the interest of industrial society ... Everything – including the individual human being, not to mention the animal – becomes a repeatable, replicable process, a mere example of the conceptual models of the system. Conflict between the administrating, reifying science, between the public mind and the experience of the individual, are precluded by the prevailing circumstances.

    Horkheimer and Adorno, *Dialectic of Enlightenment: Philosophical Fragments*, p. 65.
29. Kant, *Critique of Pure Reason*, A341/B399, p. 411.
30. Kant, *Critique of Pure Reason*, A344/B402, p. 413.
31. Kant, *Critique of Pure Reason*, A350, p. 416.
32. Kant, *Critique of Pure Reason*, A351, p. 417.
33. Hegel echoes this sentiment in his critique of Kantian idealism in 'The Certainty and Truth of Reason' section of the *Phenomenology of Spirit*:

    > This idealism is involved in this contradiction because it asserts the *abstract Notion* of Reason to be the True; consequently, reality directly comes to be for it a reality that is just as much *not* that of Reason, while Reason is at the same time supposed to be all reality. This Reason remains a restless searching and in its very searching declares that the satisfaction of *finding* is a sheer impossibility.

    Georg Wilhelm Friedrich Hegel, A. V. Miller and J. N. Findlay, *Hegel's Phenomenology of Spirit*, 30th edn (Oxford: Oxford University Press, 1979), para. 239, p. 145.

34. Sohn-Rethel, *Intellectual and Manual Labour*, p. 42.
35. Adrian Johnston comes to a similar conclusion in his *paper* 'Labour Theory of Suture', in which Johnston acknowledges Kant's split subject as a precursor to Marx's alienated worker and Lacan's zero-sum psychical structure. Johnston explains that, ultimately, the realisation of 'class consciousness' not only involves recognising the working class as the true motor of history – identifying the influence of the human in objective world – but also involves recognising certain transcendental features of the psyche, like the inner division of thinker and object of thought. In so doing, a subject or analysand can recognise the limits of their own self-mastery. Adrian Johnston, '"I am nothing, but I make everything": Marx, Lacan, and the Labour Theory of Suture', in *Parallax: The Dependence of Reality on Its Subjective Constitution*, ed. Dominik Finkelde, Christoph Menke, and Slavoj Žižek (London: Bloomsbury, 2021– forthcoming), p. 19.
36. Wilhelm Reich and Siegfried Bernfeld, *Dialectical Materialism and Psychoanalysis* (London: Socialist Reproduction, 1972), p. 24.
37. For invaluable feedback on earlier drafts of this *paper*, special thanks to Adrian Johnston, Paul Livingston and Ann Murphy.

6 Nietzsche's Critique of Objectivity and Its 'Tools'
Aleš Bunta

NIETZSCHE IS WIDELY recognised as one of the most radical and influential critics of objectivity.[1] Such an assessment is, of course, well founded: Nietzsche indeed questioned all of the known philosophical criteria of objective knowledge. Best known is probably his rejection of positivism as encapsulated in his famous thesis: 'No, facts is precisely what there is not, *only interpretations*.'[2] However, Nietzsche's critique was no less severe when it came to the concepts of universality and necessity, which constitute the criterion of objectivity in Kant and essentially also in Hegel. Furthermore, Nietzsche also argued against the very tendency towards objectivity in contemporary philosophy, which, in his opinion, is a false tendency in an essential meaning of the term. 'We are not thinking frogs, nor objectifying and registering mechanisms with their innards removed,' says Nietzsche about philosophers, and adds: 'Constantly, we have to give birth to our thoughts out of our pain and, like mothers, endow them with all we have of blood, heart, fire, pleasure, passion, agony, conscience, fate, and catastrophe.'[3]

It would nonetheless be wrong to assume, I believe, that Nietzsche's philosophy can be regarded as entirely dismissive of all aspects of the meaning of objectivity, or to presume that Nietzsche's philosophical orientation can be described in terms such as 'nominalism' or even 'correlationism'. To take the simplest possible example: Nietzsche's phrase 'God is dead.' Is this phrase not completely irreconcilable with what in contemporary philosophy is often referred to as the correlationist circle? The phrase 'God is dead' simply cannot be formally articulated in conjunction with the expression 'I think that': to say 'I think that God is dead' is in complete discord with the inner economy of Nietzsche's own use of the phrase 'God is dead,' which is supposed to echo and reverberate through our thoughts *regardless* of what we might think (of God's existence), almost as if it were some sort of emerging pure objectivity (passing through our thoughts regardless of what we are thinking).

Secondly, even at the level of his direct assessment of the value of objectivity, Nietzsche's view ultimately appears more biased than is usually conceded. At a late stage of his writing, he commenced developing an argument accusing philosophy of being, from its earliest beginnings on, deeply and almost systematically involved in what he rather spectacularly called *General-Ansturm gegen die Erkenntniß zu Gunsten der Moral*.[4] According to this thesis, many philosophers – including Socrates, Stoics, Epicureans, Indian philosophers and Kant – embarked on the venture of developing a 'theory of knowledge' exactly in order to impose boundaries on scientific objectivity, and thus to ensure that the field of morality was kept safe from any objective critique. In fact, one way of describing the very core of Nietzsche's critique of the objectivist tendency in contemporary philosophy is to say that Nietzsche's critique was directed precisely against what he considered to be the *last, nihilist stage* of this same philosophical 'general attack against knowledge' which from a certain point onwards triggered a backlash against philosophy.

And thirdly, one thing for certain – Nietzsche did not conduct his criticism of objectivity in the name of the equal validity of various subjective viewpoints, which is the way his famous theory of 'perspectivism' sometimes tends to be misunderstood. As a matter of fact, one of Nietzsche's major issues with objectivity resides precisely in the fact that, for Nietzsche, the modern urge to legitimise knowledge as 'objective' knowledge represents *a false counterbalance* to what he considered to be the inherently demagogical character of democracy. Nietzsche was – correctly or not – convinced that the modern urge to legitimise knowledge through the category of objectivity in fact emerged as a solution to the question of how to invent a type of knowledge that was best suited to the demands of democratic morality: a type of knowledge that would be as much as possible *non-intrusive* with regard to the democratic rule of opinions. In this sense, he perceived 'objectivity' almost as the properly democratic form of censorship that considerably narrows our perception of truth. Hence, at least in this particular context, it is therefore plausible to say that Nietzsche's critique of objectivism was in fact predominantly directed against the 'freedom' of subjective opinions (in the service of which 'objectivity' attained its current status) and not so much against the idea of objectivity itself.

The Problem with Critique

So, did Nietzsche actually carry out a *critique* of objectivity? The question is in a way rhetorical, yet that does not mean that the answer is simple.

The reason for this originates in a known but still somewhat surprising datum: Nietzsche did not appreciate criticism, especially not the philosophies that see their main scope in developing a critique of one type or another. For Nietzsche, a critique is a process that, in its essence and in all respects, is condemned to come to a halt halfway through. In the case of philosophical critiques, this means, among other things, that a philosophy that considers itself to be a critique strangely gets stuck in front of its own doors. A nice example of what I am talking about is one of Nietzsche's views on epistemology or the critique of knowledge:

> Philosophy reduced to 'theory of knowledge' is, in fact, nothing more than a tentative division of philosophy into epochs and a doctrine of abstinence: a philosophy which does not venture a step over the threshold and awkwardly *denies* itself the right to enter – that is philosophy at death's door, an end, an agony, something pitiful![5]

According to Nietzsche, philosophy reduced to the theory of knowledge, the critical justification of the conditions of knowledge, is thus condemned to take place on its outer edge until its dying breath. And this belief should be extended to the entire critical dimension of philosophy. Clearly, his general reservations regarding criticism did not prevent Nietzsche from criticising; it might even be better to ask what he did not criticise. Furthermore, at least in my opinion, Nietzsche was also one of the subtlest epistemologists – perhaps the only one that, in just one short parenthesis, managed to sum up the meaning of the word *to understand*. But all of this does not change the fact that Nietzsche claimed – just as he did for objectivity and with very similar words – that criticism is only a 'tool' that the philosophy of the future will have to be able to feel deep beneath itself:

> These philosophers of the future will demand not only of themselves critical discipline and every habit which leads to purity and strictness in things of the spirit: they could show them off as their own kind of jewellery – nonetheless, for all that they still don't wish to be called critics. It seems to them no small insult inflicted on philosophy when people decree, as happens so commonly today, 'Philosophy itself is criticism and critical science – and nothing else!' This evaluation of philosophy may enjoy the applause of all French and German positivists (– and it's possible that it would have flattered even the heart and taste of *Kant*: we should remember the title of his major works –): our new philosophers will nonetheless affirm that critics are the tools of the philosopher and for that very reason, the fact that they are tools, still a great way from being philosophers themselves![6]

Critics are thus only the 'tools of the philosopher' and precisely therefore, as tools, not in the least 'philosophers themselves'. For comparison: only a few pages before, in the same chapter of *Beyond Good and Evil* entitled 'We Scholars', which represents Nietzsche's most concise and systematic attempt at a critical evaluation of objectivity, Nietzsche writes the following on the 'objective man':

> The objective man is an instrument, an expensive, easily damaged and blunted tool for measurement and an artful arrangement of mirrors, something we should take care of and respect. But he is no goal, no way out or upward, no complementary human being in whom the *rest* of existence is justified, no conclusion – and even less a beginning, a procreation and first cause.[7]

The 'objective man' – a scholar, a scientist or a philosopher that sees in objectivity the greatest value of knowledge – is merely a 'tool' and even though this tool is a precious 'tool for measurement and an artful arrangement of mirrors, something we should take care of and respect', the 'objective man' too, he says, 'belongs in the hands of someone more powerful'.[8]

The parallel that Nietzsche's text draws between the role of critique and the role of objectivity is evident and what we actually need to ask is only whether this comparison may surprise us at all. There is no doubt that, at least since Kant, critique and objectivity have been revolving around the same axis. Actually, we cannot imagine a philosophical critique that would not strive towards the ideal of objectivity. A critique that declares itself to be speaking in the name of the truth, thus a critique that lets us know that it knows the truth, has been more or less reduced to the domain of obscurantists, fanatics and a matter of bad taste: objectivity is the guiding line, the criterion, the goal, the condition and the method of criticism. However, the dependence is not one-sided, of course: that which first even opens the dimension of objective knowledge is in all respects precisely critical thought. Only critical thought has the potential to justify the criteria of objective knowledge; only critical thought is capable of attaining the objective insight into the core of the problem in any concrete situation. So, if objectivity is the highest value of criticism, then critical thought has to be recognised as the only possible path leading to objective knowledge.

Criticism and objectivity are therefore intertwined in all possible ways; they lean towards one another, which is why, from this perspective, it comes as no surprise that Nietzsche also treats them in their interrelation. But, of course, after we add together Nietzsche's negative view of criticism, especially if it is perceived as the goal of philosophical activity, and the fact that criticism and objectivity are practically inseparably connected, the entire problem presents itself in a completely different light. I should actually say that this connection first leads us to the real beginning.

The first question that arises in relation to the above is precisely the following: Can Nietzsche's treatment of the problem of objectivity really be adequately defined as a critique? For Nietzsche, criticism and objectivity are two sides of the same tendency and can be got rid of only in the same package, as it were. And one thing that is clear here is that at least criticism cannot be got rid of with *criticism*. Obviously, we can critically discuss criticism, but we will thereby never achieve what Nietzsche expects from the philosophers of the future, who will be able to feel criticism 'beneath and behind' themselves. A 'critique of criticism' can take place, but it cannot be *completed*: between its progression and the goal it is supposed to achieve is a barrier, which ultimately consists of its own empty accumulation. Clearly, a completely different path leads to the set goal, one that takes a sweeping detour: the philosophers of the future will be able to look down on criticism only when they become the mysterious figures that Nietzsche calls the creators of new values. Then, together with doing things halfway, which criticism entails, the critical tendency will be overcome – but not as a result of a critical process, but because it will either simply die off or become included in this higher form of philosophical activity.

Nietzsche's critique of objectivity is not in completely the same position of course: we saw at the beginning that it contains enough concrete emphases – what is especially important here is that, according to Nietzsche, the theory of perspectivism can replace the universe of objectivity – to make it impossible to deny that, in a general sense, this critique does proceed in the direction of its completion. The question that actually arises in relation to it is rather this one: Are all the critical emphases actually a result of a *critique proper* or are they enabled by another type of philosophical operation that is external to criticism and perhaps takes place via a completely different path? We will see that, in this respect, a compromise is needed: what is generally called the 'critique of objectivity' includes elements of both criticism and genealogy, perspectival ontology and especially intra-philosophical politics. In short, the 'critique of objectivity' is, first and foremost, a name for a broader dispositive of approaches.

This does not mean, however, that there is no critique of objectivity in the narrower, strict sense of a philosophical critique. Quite the opposite: the critique of objectivity proper is probably even a paradigmatic case of Nietzsche's own critical method, which, at the operative level, already essentially differs from the type of critique employed by epistemologists when looking for the conditions of objective knowledge. In short, the critique of objectivity proper is part of a broader dispositive, and yet, taken in itself, it already offers a key distinction in relation to what it criticises.

What then appears to be its main problem? Why does the critique of objectivity in the narrower, epistemological sense seem impossible? The answer is more than obvious:

Because objectivity is the universal condition of every philosophical critique, this can only mean one thing – by calling into question the category of objectivity, a critique actually also *calls itself into question*. Put more simply: the critique of objectivity is a process that calls itself into question; it cannot proceed otherwise than by way of calling itself into question. It is caught in a loop that, in some other similar cases, Nietzsche names *Gegenbewegung*, counter-movement – which in this case refers to the fact that with every new item of knowledge the critique of objectivity destroys the conditions of its possibility, it acts *against itself*. And the other way around, of course: in its course, it embodies the object of its critique and thus again acts *against itself*.

This counter-movement that attacks the very viewpoint of the critique is crucial. We can undoubtedly claim that *Gegenbewegung*, an attack on the viewpoint of the critique, is not only a specific internal hindrance of the critique of objectivity, but, as Heidegger already suggested, should also be seen as one of the essential features of Nietzsche's philosophy in general.

I think this key specific of Nietzsche's philosophy, which already suggests one of the aspects of the theory of perspectivism, can be encapsulated by connecting two of his well-known arguments against the theorists of objective knowledge.

The first argument delineates Nietzsche's general view on the philosophical search for the foundations of certainty:

> It might seem as though I had evaded the question of 'certainty.' The opposite is true; but by inquiring after the criterion of certainty I tested the scales upon which men have weighed in general hitherto – and that the question of certainty itself is a dependent question, a question of the second rank.
>
> The question of values is more fundamental than the question of certainty: the latter becomes serious only by presupposing that the value question has already been answered.[9]

According to Nietzsche, the most general problem of the philosophical search for the foundations of certainty, which the tendency to justify objective knowledge doubtlessly belongs to, is 'that the question of certainty itself is a dependent question, a question of the second rank'. More fundamental than the question of certainty is the question of values, which Nietzsche clearly does not mean merely in the sense of an abstract greater value of this question, but rather the opposite: his thesis is that the *question of certainty in itself depends on answering the question of values*. A key contribution to the understanding of this thesis is undoubtedly Heidegger's ascertainment that, for Nietzsche, '[t]he essence of value is based on its being a viewpoint.'[10] That means that, for Nietzsche, the basic problem of the question of certainty is precisely the unanswered question of the viewpoint.

Let us therefore take a look at the second argument, which is evidently directed against Kant's transcendental justification of objective knowledge:

> That a world accessible to our organs is also understood to be dependent upon these organs, that we understand a world as being subjectively conditioned, is not to say that an objective world is at all possible. Who compels us to think that subjectivity is real, essential?[11]

Nietzsche's argument against the transcendental justification of objectivity thus foregrounds not the concept of the object, but the concept of the subject. And we can actually say that Nietzsche's entire approach to epistemology is characterised by the belief that the *final recipient* of knowledge – the one that knowledge is conveyed to, the one that is supposed to understand something at the end – is at least as problematic as the object.

Pierre Klossowski comprehensively showed that, for Nietzsche, *consciousness*, taken as a whole, is a kind of process of cerebral self-deception, which functions by projecting the unconscious impulses from which thoughts emerge inwards, into the 'centre of consciousness', which enables us – on the condition of the successful functioning of self-deception – to experience ourselves as a 'thinking self'.[12] The 'thinking self' – the subject of 'thought' with its seat in the consciousness – is therefore only and solely a sort of *dependent variable*. Or, put differently, because the 'subject of thought' is conditioned on the contingent functioning of the cerebral self-deception, it is clear that there is nothing universal or necessary about it.

But this is not yet the core of Nietzsche's argument taken as a whole. What Nietzsche might find more important than the mere emphasis on the subject of thinking being an effect of deception is *the correct evaluation* of this deception. We have to grasp that the deception performs a function that, *from the viewpoint of life*, is a thousand times more valuable than any knowledge: for there is no doubt that the effect of the cerebral self-deception that places consciousness at the centre of the body and 'thinking' at the centre of consciousness has to be considered one of the most essential conditions for the survival of the human species.

This new order of rank between knowledge and the higher value of deception is essential also and especially from an epistemological perspective. It is this revaluation of the relation between deception and knowledge that actually triggers the main question of Nietzsche's approach to the theory of knowledge, the question of the polyvalent function of all that we are used to unequivocally conceiving as our 'apparatus for acquiring knowledge'.

Nietzsche says that 'our apparatus for acquiring knowledge is not *designed* for "knowledge"'.[13] And we should actually ask: If the cerebral self-deception that enthrones the 'subject of thinking' is the essential condition for the survival of the human species, is it not even more probable then that what we are used to comprehending as the 'apparatus for acquiring knowledge' is first and foremost adapted precisely to the task of preserving this fundamental, but vulnerable illusion? For Nietzsche, understanding is only one of the simpler functions of the 'apparatus for acquiring knowledge', while its main task is the infinitely more complex permanent preservation of the central illusion, which, in the given circumstances, represents the condition for the survival of the species. This also means that the micro-evolution of consciousness, which Nietzsche describes in several places,[14] had to adapt our 'apparatus for acquiring knowledge' also to the tasks that are in all respects *opposite* to those we ascribe to understanding. To a much larger extent than to knowledge, the 'apparatus for acquiring knowledge' is adapted to preserving the 'subject of knowledge', to whom it must serve everything with which it can feed the subject's inner illusion. And the other way round: all that the 'subject of knowledge' comprehends as the *most indisputable facts of consciousness* – for example, the 'fact' of its intentional orientation towards the object – are most probably some kind of adaptations that, in combination with the cerebral self-deception and the structure of language, enable the preservation of the illusion that *is* the subject itself.

The real target of Nietzsche's critique of the transcendental justification of objective knowledge is thus not the transcendental subject, which, as the condition of experience, is, in its functioning, excluded from every experience. The main target of Nietzsche's attack is the most elementary internal fact of consciousness, which is the very starting point of Kant's transcendental project before it even begins: the internal fact that objects appear for consciousness. No matter how we look at it, Kant's justification of the possibility of objective knowledge is only an explanation of this internal fact. From Nietzsche's perspective, though, this 'fact' is merely one of the forms of the adaptation of consciousness to its most complex goal – maintaining the illusion of the subject. The intentionality of consciousness is a fact only in the structure of an illusion.

Nietzsche's argument against the transcendental critical justification of objective knowledge mentioned above can thus be reformulated in the following manner: the transcendental critique does correctly point out that the 'objective world' is merely the result of a subjective constitution of reality, but it remains blind to the fact of *objects appearing for consciousness* being only an internal element of the objective deception that constitutes the subject.

The Concept of *Rangverschiebung*

We would expect that the attack on the philosophical justifications of objective knowledge represents the very core of Nietzsche's critique of objectivity, or at least its basic starting point. But the reality is different, for, in his main texts in which he explicitly problematises the question of objectivity, the topic of the critique of the philosophical justifications of objective knowledge is almost completely absent – which can by no means be explained with the chronological sequence of the development of Nietzsche's philosophy, since both topics are, with greater or lesser emphasis, separately present in all of Nietzsche's major mature works.

The problem that Nietzsche tackles in his most concise discussions on objectivity, such as 'We Scholars' and 'On Immaculate Perception', is not the epistemological problem of the criteria of certainty, but the problem of the emergence of a certain *monopoly over the truth*. Under the common signifier of 'objectivity', this monopoly over the truth – let us add that it brings nothing good to the truth itself – was appropriated by a chimera made up of *method, value* and a special *human type*.

For the method, which represents the first part of the chimera's body, Nietzsche uses the term 'disinterested contemplation', which primarily serves him as a signifier for scientific objectivity. Value is objectivity, but no longer taken merely as an ideal of the scientific approach, but also and especially as a type of value that perfectly fits the criteria of contemporary democratic morality. The type of human being which represents the third indispensable part of the chimera's body is the already mentioned 'objective man', for whom Nietzsche has a host of other names in his vocabulary, which, at least at first sight, are not easy to connect in a sensible way: the 'objective man' is thus also a (deceivingly) 'pregnant moon', a 'tomcat on the rooftop who 'creeps around half-closed windows', a 'lecherous and jealous monk', 'an artful arrangement of mirrors', or even 'a slave'.

The role of the 'objective man' is essential for two reasons. Firstly, the 'objective man' is what we could call the *subjective condition* of the development of scientific objectivity. The 'objective man' is the specific and unique form of existence whose wholly *subjective* predispositions and specifics made it possible for the tendency towards scientific objectivity to develop and be realised within it: 'The objective man [. . . is] the ideal scholar, in whom the scientific instinct after thousands of total and partial failures all of a sudden comes into bloom and keeps flowering to the end [. . .].'[15] Nietzsche was convinced that the ideal of 'disinterested contemplation' and especially the will, discipline and renouncement needed for its realisation, could never have been sufficiently developed and established if this ideal itself had not fed on and grown from a specific pathology, which the 'objective man' inherited from the 'religious man' in an almost completed from. In *On the Genealogy of Morality*,

Nietzsche later named this pathology, which should also be considered a regime of power and a specific structure of the economy of pleasure, the 'ascetic ideal'.[16]

According to Nietzsche, the ideal of 'disinterested contemplation' – which in order to be realised demands that we search for ways to overcome the level of subjectively conditioned and motivated viewpoints, that we discover ways of looking at things from an unburdened, neutral viewpoint and consequently see them 'as they are', in short, that we discover the way of *subtracting oneself* from one's viewpoint – has, from the very beginning, a layer of falseness or fakeness attached to it and this fakeness is not merely superficial. In the case of the ideal of 'disinterested contemplation,' the point does not simply lie in a residue of subjective pathology hiding *behind* the ideal; quite the opposite: the *ideal itself*, thus the imperative of overcoming subjective pathologies, is *in itself* a form of the most extreme possible subjective pathology, which in a way feeds on the denial of its true (pathological) being.

If there is something false and fake about the ideal that grows from the denial of its true nature, then there is actually something *perverse* about the human type that creates its highest ideal from the denial of its actual impulses. This can at least partly explain the very picturesque address to 'objective men' that Zarathustra gives in 'On Immaculate Perception':

> Your spirit was persuaded to despise the earthly, but not your entrails; and they are the strongest part of you!
>
> And now your spirit is ashamed to do the bidding of your entrails, and out of its own shame it takes the paths that sneak and lie.
>
> 'For me what is highest' – thus speaks your lying spirit to itself – 'would be to look upon life without desire and not like a dog with its tongue hanging out:
>
> To be content in viewing, with dead will, without the grasp and greed of selfishness – cold and ashen grey in my whole body, but with drunken mooning eyes!
>
> To me the dearest thing would be' – thus the seducer seduces himself – 'to love the earth as the moon loves it, and to touch its beauty only with the eyes.
>
> And to me the immaculate perception of all things would be that I desire nothing from things, except that I might lie there before them like a mirror with a hundred eyes.' –
>
> Oh you sentimental hypocrites, you lechers! Your desire lacks innocence, and now therefore you slander all desiring![17]

The second essential aspect of the 'objective man' is that, within the new hierarchy established with the increase in the chimera's power, the 'objective man' becomes a direct antagonist of the philosopher. There is something distinctly difficult and also hard to understand about this antagonism. The antagonism between the philosopher and the 'objective man' is doubtlessly *both* true and real, on the one hand, and false, on the other. And for the problem to be even greater: this antagonism undoubtedly *becomes the truest precisely when its falseness culminates in the extreme*.

We do not describe this antagonism correctly if we simply say that the philosopher and the 'objective man' are competitors. According to Nietzsche, they are not competitors at all. Furthermore, what is essential for the philosopher's strategy in this struggle is to not accept this comparison or even the comparability itself.

We also present this antagonism wrongly if we say that, due to the general progress of science, the 'objective man' has overtaken the philosopher on the social ladder and overshadowed his old glory. According to Nietzsche, illusion is also at work in this seemingly irrefutable fact: despite all the progress of science, the real social power of scientists is very relative. Even more: Nietzsche argues that even the social power that science does have is almost entirely borrowed from the forces that are external to science and actually dominate it. The social power of the 'objective man' is not his autonomous power; it is a power bestowed on the 'objective man' by democratic morality so he can help it undermine the authority of considerably more ambitious and more aggressive forces, such as philosophy and religion, which actually want to rule people's opinions and occupy them. The power in whose name science is supposed to surpass the philosopher thus originates in the philosopher himself as a reaction to him and his will to dictate new values. In this aspect, too, it is essential for the philosopher to not fall for the appearance of 'facts', the appearance of reality.

But wherein lies the reality of the described antagonism? The philosopher and the 'objective man' are not competitors in the sense of one overtaking the other on the social ladder; their confrontation is much deadlier: it is a confrontation about who will occupy the *position of the philosopher*.

> The declaration of independence of the scientific man, his emancipation from philosophy, is one of the subtler effects of the order and confusion in democracy: today the self-glorification and self-exaltation of the scholar stand in full bloom everywhere and in their finest spring – but that is still not intended to mean that in this case self-praise smells very nice. 'Away with all masters!' – that's what the instinct of the rabble wants here, too, and once science enjoyed its happiest success in pushing away theology, whose 'handmaiden' it was for so long, now it has the high spirits and stupidity to set about making laws for philosophy and to take its turn playing the 'master' for once – what am I saying? – playing the *philosopher*.[18]

The antagonism thus culminates in a confrontation of biblical proportions, in which the philosopher and the 'objective man' compete for the philosopher's very place, a confrontation that threatens the philosopher with being replaced by his counterfeit practically from within. And it is precisely this escalation of the antagonism that – contrary to the antagonism itself, in which, according to Nietzsche, we should predominantly see a construct of the interests of democratic morality – is actually *real*. For Nietzsche, the real core of the antagonism, the threshold through which this constructed, seeming antagonism *turns into a reality*, is the internal struggle between the philosopher and the form of the 'objective man' that has actually become the dominant form in philosophy and which Nietzsche calls the 'philosophical labourer'. 'I insist on the following point: people should finally stop confusing philosophical labourers and scientific people in general with philosophers – that in this particular matter we strictly assign "to each his due" and do not give too much to the former and much too little to the latter.'[19]

Let us try to unfold this heretofore merely sketched topology of the problem in more detail and in all its dimensions:

Nietzsche began his key text 'We Scholars' by saying that its goal is to intervene in what he names *Rangverschiebung*, a 'shift in rank ordering,' in the relation between science and philosophy.

> At the risk that moralizing here also will show itself to be what it always has been – that is, an unabashed *montrer ses plais*, as Balzac says – I'd like to dare to stand up against an unreasonable and harmful shift in rank ordering [*Rangverschiebung*] which nowadays, quite unnoticed and, as if with the clearest conscience, threatens to establish itself between science and philosophy.[20]

Nietzsche's text thus performs three tasks at once: it interprets the process of a real change, but the goal of this interpretation is doubtlessly motivated by an effect – the goal of this interpretation is to intervene in what it interprets, to change the course of the change it anticipates. The interpretation itself must take on this triple task of representation, anticipation and intervention.

Already in its first step – at the level of its stance – Nietzsche's text is thus evidently strictly opposed to the ideal of 'disinterested contemplation'. But we must ask in what way such an intervention of interpretation into a very real change, which the shift in the rank ordering of science and philosophy definitely is, is even possible.

We have already suggested the basic answer: *Rangverschiebung* in the relation between science and philosophy is doubtlessly a real process, but we must by no means overlook that the basis of this process is the *operation of appearance that obtains being only through the inadequacy of philosophy's reaction to it.* In other words, *Rangverschiebung*, the shift in rank ordering, is in itself first and foremost an aggressive interpretation that certainly changes reality, yet essentially does not rest on facts but rather on the capability to create an appearance of facts. It is precisely at this level that one can engage in an open duel therewith and try to cut off the inflow of appearance, on which it rests, into reality.

Having determined the status of Nietzsche's approach, let us now try to determine more firmly the position that objectivity has in relation to the shift in the rank ordering between science and philosophy. The position of objectivity is essentially twofold. According to Nietzsche, the first thing we should see in the rise of objectivity – in all its variants, including the philosophical discussions on the justification of objective knowledge – is the *essential symptom* of *Rangverschiebung* itself. In short, the rise in the value of objectivity must first be grasped as a reaction to the 'real' that the rise in the significance of science in relation to philosophy doubtlessly produces. On the other hand, objectivity is nevertheless also more than merely a symptom. Objectivity also belongs to the order of reasons that triggered the shift in the rank ordering, but – and this is essential – *not* in its primary form, thus not as the methodological basis of scientific progress, which is supposed to ensure science an increasing social importance, but in the *form of its other metamorphosis*, thus as the social value that – in the form of embodying the affinity between taking neutral views and the formal equality of all opinions – seals the alliance between democratic morality and science to the detriment of philosophy.

This is precisely where we have to place the basic breakthrough of Nietzsche's interpretative intervention. *Rangverschiebung* could never have been *realised*, could never have passed from appearance into being if philosophy had not made the wrong diagnosis and mistaken the true drive of *Rangverschiebung* for a false one, if it had not mixed up two heads of the chimera. After it sensed that it was losing its primacy over science, philosophy made the wrong diagnosis of this change: it overestimated the real reach of the social power of science and underestimated, if not even entirely overlooked, the hidden alliance between the scientific drive and democratic morality – the 'instincts of the rabble', as Nietzsche calls it – the alliance that, in the strongest sense, is embodied precisely by the double, chimeral nature of objectivity. So philosophy first made the mistake of taking the antagonism with science too seriously; it accepted the non-existing competition and tackled it by trying to *appropriate objectivity itself*, in which it rightly saw the drive of the progress of science, but also overlooked that its progress *is not* what actually gives science its social power. Philosophy thus became obsessed with objectivity – it began discovering unknown depth in it and wanted to make something immensely complex out if it, something philosophical, something that belongs only to it, to philosophy. It thus began to *limit* itself increasingly more *to epistemology*, with which it was supposed to either discover the foundations of its own objectivity or explain scientific objectivity; it began to close itself in it and thus to systematically wane. It was due to its own excessive fascination with objectivity, which Nietzsche thinks is nothing special – for him, objectivity is only strict discipline, which perfectly suits the psychological make-up of the 'objective man'; it is no more and no less than the (albeit rare) capability 'to be able to read off a text as a text without interposing an interpretation'[21] – that philosophy exhausted and brought itself to the point where it became weak enough and at the same time *similar enough to science* for science to actually be able to *justifiably and really* rise above it:

> From a general point of view, it may well have been more than anything else the human, all-too-human, in short, the paltriness of the newer philosophy itself which most fundamentally damaged respect for philosophy and opened the gates to the instincts of the rabble. We should nonetheless confess the extent to which, in our modern world, the whole style of Heraclitus, Plato, Empedocles, and of whatever all those royal and splendid hermits of the spirit were called is disappearing. Considering the sort of representatives of philosophy who nowadays, thanks to fashion, are just as much on top as on the very bottom – in Germany, for example, the two lions of Berlin, the anarchist Eugen Dühring and the amalgamist Eduard von Hartmann – an honest man of science *is entitled* to feel with some justice that he is of a better sort, with a better descent. In particular, the sight of these mish-mash philosophers who call themselves 'reality philosophers' or 'positivists' is capable of throwing a dangerous mistrust into the soul of an ambitious young scholar: they are, in the best of cases, scholars and specialists themselves – that's clear enough – they are, in fact, collectively defeated, *brought back* under the rule of science. At some time or other they wanted *more* from themselves, without having any right to this 'more' and to its responsibilities – and now, in word and deed, they represent in a respectable, angry, vengeful way the *lack of faith* in the ruling task and masterfulness of philosophy. But finally – how could it be anything different? Science nowadays is in bloom, and its face is filled with good conscience, while what all new philosophy has gradually sunk to – this remnant of philosophy today – is busy generating suspicion and ill humor against itself, if not mockery and pity. Philosophy reduced to 'theory of knowledge' is, in fact, nothing more than a tentative division of philosophy into epochs and a doctrine of abstinence: a philosophy which does not venture a step over the threshold and awkwardly *denies* itself the right to enter – that is philosophy at death's door, an end, an agony, something pitiful! How could such a philosophy –*rule*![22]

On the whole, Nietzsche's intervention against *Rangverschiebung* thus proceeds in three directions and can be summed up in three theses:

1. Despite the fact that *Rangverschiebung*, the shift in the rank ordering of the relation between philosophy and science, has already paved its way from appearance to being, took over the institutions and itself began to tailor reality, the fate of philosophy is still in its own hands. As a consequence of the toxic bite of the lowest of the chimera's heads (the one reeking of the 'rabble'), philosophy fell in love with the chimera's second head (objectivity as the basis of scientific progress) and, due to the effects of the love spell, assimilated to this head – to the extent that it went through a metamorphosis and *itself turned into the chimera's third head* – the 'objective man'. But if we make philosophy sober up, if we confront it with the fact that the shift in rank ordering *became a reality* only and solely because of its own wrong diagnosis – its belief that the shift is driven by the progress of science and not the political 'natural balance' between taking objective, neutral viewpoints and the formal equality of all opinions – then we can still pull philosophy out of the chimera's hold almost unscathed. It is true that *Rangverschiebung* will leave its mark at the level of institutions, but, for Nietzsche, that is only a minor problem. As opposed to science, which can exist only in the form of this or that social organisation, the *creation of new values* is a task that actually benefits from a degree of social isolation, solitude and detachment from the academic world. It is much more important that in this way – with a correct explanation of the roles that the chimera's individual heads play – the philosopher can stop *tragically mistaking himself for his counterfeit*, stop seeing in himself a subgenre of the 'objective man' and start allotting to objectivity the role that befits it, i.e. the role of a doubtlessly useful and necessary tool, but a tool that is nevertheless no more than that: a tool of philosophy and *not* its ideal.
2. The antagonism between philosophy and science is actually nothing but a *mask and a means* – both in one – of another antagonism, *the antagonism between philosophy and democratic morality*. According to Nietzsche, the prestige that contemporary democratic society awards to the scientific man, the appearance that he has overgrown the philosopher, must primarily be understood as a sort of advance payment that the 'objective man' receives in his account in return for his readiness to play the game of *the amount he received actually also belonging to him*. The impression that science has surpassed and overgrown philosophy needs to be got rid of once and for all, which can be done by taking a clear enough look at the fact that the 'objective appearance' of surpassing and overgrowing is *merely a means* with whose help the shift in the rank ordering *abducted* its own real being and *not* the real being itself.

3. According to Nietzsche, the reason that, despite the prestige that contemporary society awards him, the 'objective man' should be seen as a rather weak force is that the social power of science is always placed in a *dependence* on other types of power:

> No! Do not come to me with science when I am looking for the natural antagonist to the ascetic ideal, when I ask: 'Where is the opposing will in which its *opposing ideal* expresses itself?' Science is not nearly independent enough for that, in every respect it first needs a value-ideal, a value-creating power, in whose *service it can believe* in itself, – science itself never creates values. Its relationship to the ascetic ideal is certainly not yet inherently antagonistic; indeed, it is much more the case, in general, that it still represents the driving force in the inner evolution of that ideal.'[23]

For Nietzsche, science, which by itself is not capable of creating values, is thus essentially a dependent force; a force that is *incapable* of independent antagonism. At first it leaned on philosophy, but, through the process of *Rangverschiebung*, it entered into an alliance with democratic politics, within which its position only became weaker. In contemporary democratic society, science undoubtedly represents a counterweight to the chaos of the pluralism of opinions, but, by itself, it simply does not have the instruments to directly intervene in it; it depends on democratic politics and thus indirectly on the same pluralism of opinions it is supposed to counterbalance. It is ascribed the role of a supervisor with his hands tied. One of the main reasons, if not even the main reason, for Nietzsche's belief that, according to 'the laws of the order of rank',[24] philosophy remains and will remain above science is precisely that, as opposed to the essential dependence of the social power of science, philosophy is the force that, in the long term, through *creating values* – by performing its own inner philosophical task – *independently and directly* also acts as a political, socially transformative force that does not have to lean on anyone.

I believe it is almost impossible for Nietzsche's threefold diagnosis not to arouse mixed feelings. On the one hand, we cannot but acknowledge that, at a time when it was not so evident, he in a visionary way predicted the radical overturn in the hierarchy between philosophy and science. On the other hand – and I think this is almost completely inevitable – Nietzsche's solutions, especially his emphasis on preserving the leading role of philosophy, give the impression of an escape from the 'real' of this tectonic shift. Precisely here, however, a question arises that enables us to enter the process of *Rangverschiebung* as protagonists.

The dilemma is crystal clear: is our assessment really more objective than

Nietzsche's vision, or is it merely given from the *value viewpoint of the 'objective man'* that *Rangverschiebung* has imprinted in our way of thinking?

There is no doubt that – in the 140 years that separate us from the period in which Nietzsche made his diagnosis – science has made exceptional advances. But we are actually interested in the question of the *criterion* according to which one can claim that science has surpassed and overgrown philosophy. This criterion has not changed since Nietzsche's time: it is the utilitarian doctrine in line with which the category of social significance is placed in a relation of simple equality with the concept of direct social benefit. The problem of the utilitarian evaluation does not, of course, lie in ascribing too much to science; the problem of this doctrine lies in the fact that its predomination has practically erased *that which actually is the social purpose of philosophy*. While listing the 'prejudices' due to which philosophy lost its respect in the eyes of science, Nietzsche pointed out the 'colour blindness of the utilitarian man, who sees nothing in philosophy other than a series of *refuted* systems and an extravagant expense from which no one "receives any benefit"'.[25]

According to Nietzsche, this erasure of purpose and the social significance of philosophy originates in the deepest antagonism of Western civilisation. The principle of evaluation that takes place under the overarching value of utility, i.e. the evaluation that answers the question of what purpose something should serve, is for Nietzsche the quintessence of what he names 'slave morality': 'Slave morality is essentially a morality of utility.'[26] 'Slave morality' is not only a political category but, as Deleuze probably best explained, also includes an ontological dimension: 'slave morality' refers to the 'triumph of reactive forces'; it represents the criterion of negative selection that ascribes *value* only to those forces that, through their 'utility', are *subordinate* to something else, while it consigns all other (active) forces to oblivion.[27]

In its essence, at the level of its being, philosophy belongs to a diametrically opposed principle of evaluation, which Nietzsche names 'aristocratic' evaluation. The opposition between both types of evaluation is perhaps best expressed by Nietzsche's remark: 'The essential thing in a good and healthy aristocracy, however, is that it feels itself not as a function (whether of a monarchy or of a community) but as its *significance* and highest justification.'[28]

The above sentence must in no way be understood in the sense of philosophy being an end in itself – we have seen that, according to Nietzsche, philosophy (worthy of the name) very much strives and rushes towards a break, an effect, an objective. In a way, we could say almost the opposite: philosophy – and in Nietzsche something similar goes for the entire 'higher culture' – *must* experience itself as the highest purpose of society in order for it to even *be able* to take on its task: philosophy *must proceed from absolute self-affirmation*, so it can, *through itself and in the form of itself*, delineate new horizons.

Notes

1. This contribution was written in the framework of the scientific project J6-9392 'The Problem of Objectivity and Fiction in Contemporary Philosophy' and the programme P6-0014 'Conditions and Problems of Contemporary Philosophy', financed by the Slovenian Research Agency. An earlier version of this paper was published in Slovene in the journal *Filozofski vestnik* (Ljubljana: ZRC, 2020).
2. Friedrich Nietzsche, *The Will to Power*, trans. Walter Kaufman and R. J. Hollingdale (New York: Vintage Books, 1968), p. 267, para. 481.
3. Friedrich Nietzsche, *The Gay Science*, trans. Walter Kaufman (New York: Vintage Books, 1974), pp. 35–6, para. 3.
4. Friedrich Nietzsche, *Nachgelassene Fragmente 1887–1889, Kritische Studienausgabe Herausgegeben von Giorgio Colli und Mazzino Montinari* (Berlin and New York: Verlag de Gruyter, 1980), p. 324.
5. Friedrich Nietzsche, *Beyond Good and Evil*, trans. Ian Johnston (Arlington, VA: Richer Resources Publications, 2009), p. 110, para. 204.
6. Nietzsche, *Beyond Good and Evil*, pp. 121–2, para. 210.
7. Nietzsche, *Beyond Good and Evil*, p. 115, para. 207.
8. Nietzsche, *Beyond Good and Evil*, p. 113, para. 207.
9. Nietzsche, *The Will to Power*, p. 322, paras 587–588.
10. Martin Heidegger, *Off the Beaten Track*, trans. Julian Young and Kenneth Haynes (Cambridge: Cambridge University Press, 2002), p. 170.
11. Nietzsche, *The Will to Power*, p. 313, para. 583.
12. Pierre Klossowski, *Nietzsche and the Vicious Circle*, trans. Daniel W. Smith (London: Continuum, 1997), pp. 18–27.
13. Nietzsche, *The Will to Power*, p. 273, para. 496.
14. For instance: 'Consciousness – beginning quite externally, as coordination and becoming conscious of "impressions" – at first at the furthest distance from the biological center of the individual; but a process that deepens and intensifies itself, and continually draws nearer the center.' Nietzsche, *The Will to Power*, p. 274, para. 504.
15. Nietzsche, *Beyond Good and Evil*, p. 113, para. 207.
16. For one of the most incisive analyses of the economy of the ascetic ideal, see Alenka Zupančič, *The Shortest Shadow. Nietzsche's Philosophy of the Two* (Cambridge, MA, and London: MIT Press, 2003), pp. 46–62.
17. Friedrich Nietzsche, *Thus Spoke Zarathustra*, trans. Adrian del Caro (Cambridge: Cambridge University Press, 2006), p. 95.
18. Nietzsche, *Beyond Good and Evil*, p. 108, para. 204.
19. Nietzsche, *Beyond Good and Evil*, p. 122, para. 211.

20. Nietzsche, *Beyond Good and Evil*, p. 108, para. 204.
21. Nietzsche, *Will to Power*, p. 266, para. 479.
22. Nietzsche, *Beyond Good and Evil*, pp. 109–10, para. 204.
23. Friedrich Nietzsche, *On the Genealogy of Morals*, trans. Carol Diethe (Cambridge: Cambridge University Press, 2007), p. 113, para. 25.
24. Nietzsche, *Gay Science*, p. 334, para. 373.
25. Nietzsche, *Beyond Good and Evil*, p. 109, para. 204.
26. Nietzsche, *Beyond Good and Evil*, p. 183, para. 260.
27. For the connection between science and the 'triumph of reactive forces', see Gilles Deleuze, *Nietzsche and Philosophy*, trans. Hugh Tomlinson (London and New York: Continuum, 2002), p. 66.
28. Nietzsche, *Beyond Good and Evil*, p. 177, p. 258.

7 Tips and Tricks: Remarks on the Debate between Badiou and Cassin on 'Sophistics'

Peter Klepec

IN OUR TIMES – defined by populism, fake news, charlatans of all sorts and general scepticism as to the authority of reason – it seems that a debate on the sophists is not only in order, but perhaps more urgent than ever.[1] The popular and dominant view on sophistics has always been that it entails the deliberate use of false arguments with the intent to trick: according to this view, sophistics is really sophistry. Today we seem to be more than ever surrounded by sophists as fallacious reasoners whose sole aim is to trick and deceive. They tend to corrupt and disorient people; their role in the current economic, political and systemic crisis is important, even huge. However, is this a fact, a truth or a fiction? How is 'sophistics' related to trickery, to truth and to fiction? Is not its pejorative name, 'sophistry', a fiction produced and 'fixed' primarily by two prominent figures, Plato and Aristotle? This fiction is really a 'fixion', to use Lacan's pun; it is a 'fix(at)ion' of fiction – the decided and accepted fabrication of a past and of a common history. A fact is therefore a fabrication, a *fictum* that one decides to fix, which in our case 'fixes', sets, determines, prescribes our common understanding of 'sophistics'. In this sense, one might say that here we will simply try to follow and develop the consequences from a hint in Lacan saying: 'It is not a question of disputing authority, but of extracting it from fiction.'[2] The debate on (contemporary) sophistics/sophistry in its relation to philosophy between two French philosophers and collaborators, Alain Badiou and Barbara Cassin, is in our view centred precisely on that. Below, we will present a couple of comments and remarks regarding this issue.

What today we call 'sophist' has its own historical correlate, or rather counterpart, i.e. the pre-Socratic or rather pre-Platonist thinkers from the fifth century BC.[3] Thanks to many researchers of the history of thought, from Guthrie, Kerferd and Schiappa to Detienne, Jacqueline de Romilly and, last but not least, Barbara Cassin, we now know that the view of ancient sophistics was subsequently severely distorted by Plato and Aristotle.

> It is probable that the historical and intellectual importance of the sophists is now generally recognised to a much greater degree than was once the case. It is hardly a matter of dispute that they taught and discussed grammar, linguistic theory, moral and political doctrines, doctrines about the gods and the nature and origin of man, literary analysis and criticism, mathematics, and at least in some cases the elements of physical theory about the universe. But were they philosophers? This is still not generally admitted. It depends partly on the definition of philosophy. Here the ghost of Platonism is still active.[4]

So, starting with Plato and Aristotle, the sophists became identified with fallacious reasoners, deceptors and tricksters. Even more, Plato and Aristotle are mainly responsible for the fact that we seem to understand the sophists as a coherent school of thought, despite their many individual differences, and that 'sophistics' is today primarily understood as 'sophistry', i.e. as something intentionally deceptive, trickish, imposturous and reckless. With one single aim apparently: to deceive, to disorient and in the end to rule. In accordance therewith, Plato's dialogues present the rather hostile views of the sophists as 'hunters of young people and money', 'traders of false knowledge', 'traders in spiritual things', 'traders in words' and 'athletes in the sport of words'. For Plato, the sophists do not really offer any true knowledge but only various opinions of things. Because of that, Plato sought to distinguish the sophists from philosophers, arguing that a sophist is a person who makes his or her living through deception, whereas a philosopher is a lover of wisdom who searches for pure truth. Truth versus opinion, semblance versus a true, real thing, corruption versus virtue – that, according to Plato, is in essence the whole story of the relation between philosophy and sophistics (or rather sophistry). In a similar vein, Aristotle later points out that 'the art of the sophist is the semblance of wisdom without the reality, and the sophist is one who makes money from an apparent but unreal wisdom.'[5] The art of the sophists, for Aristotle, is therefore 'a kind of art of money-making from a merely apparent wisdom.'[6]

Without going too far or too deep into the many interesting details of the debate – such as the status of instruction for money[7] and of the 'price of the truth'[8] – we should note first that the debate itself is in a way limited and distorted. Why? By the time of Plato and Aristotle, the major figures of sophistics had already passed (Protagoras, Gorgias, Prodicus, Hippias, Trasymachus, Lykophron, Callicles, Antiphon, and Cratylus). Being dead, they simply were not only not able to discuss anything, even worse, their theses, points and arguments were only fragments:

Few of the sophists' own works have survived, and most of these only secondhand; their works – or portions of their works – have been incorporated into the works or collections of later writers. And the earliest surviving accounts of the sophists are often hostile to the characters, views, or practices. Plato's dialogues provide some of the most fully developed portraits of the older sophists, but his bias is clear: Plato wants to discredit their ideas, if not their character. Thus to recover the thinking of the sophists, scholars must often read through or against the texts in which that thinking is presented.[9]

In addition, if we take into account that their greatest opponents (Plato and Aristotle, namely) mediated to us these very fragments, we can easily understand why the negative view of the sophists was so influential and persistent for so long.

Nevertheless, why is the figure of the sophist so important for Plato and Aristotle? Obviously, it was very important. Koyré, for instance, emphasises that 'critique of the sophists – Plato's *bête noire* – fills up half of his *oeuvre*'.[10] Or, as Svoboda points out: 'Nearly a third of the Platonic corpus, for example, consists of conversations between Socrates and one or more of the elder sophists or of lengthy analyses of their teachings and their implications. No other Athenian author devotes this much attention to the sophists.'[11] Wherein lies the importance of the sophists not only for Plato's philosophy, but also for philosophy as such? Despite their slippery status, they seem to be a kind of necessary interlocutor, something that Deleuze and Guattari call a 'conceptual persona'. Obviously, not only is 'Socrates [. . .] the principal conceptual persona of Platonism',[12] as Deleuze and Guattari note, but that status should be ascribed to the 'sophists' as well. For what is a 'sophist' (in Plato), if not the following:

> The conceptual persona is not the philosopher's representative, but, rather, the reverse: the philosopher is only the envelope of his principal conceptual persona and of all other personae who are the intercessors [*intercessurs*], the real subjects of his philosophy. Conceptual personae are the philosopher's 'heteronyms', and the philosopher's name is the simple pseudonym of his personae. [. . .] The philosopher is the idiosyncrasy of his conceptual personae. The destiny of the philosopher is to become his conceptual persona or personae, at the same time that these personae themselves become something other than what they are historically, mythologically, or commonly (the Socrates of Plato, the Dionysus of Nietzsche, the Idiot of Nicholas of Cusa.[13]

Via and through Plato and Aristotle, the sophists indeed became 'something other than what they are historically, mythologically, or commonly'. However, why were they later repeatedly resurrected in so many different historical contexts? Their role as conceptual personae was mainly limited to being strawmen par excellence, a deviation that serves negatively as a warning as to which way of thinking one has to avoid. We had to wait until Hegel for this negative image of sophistics to be corrected. It was namely Hegel for whom the sophists became the true 'masters of Greece'. For Hegel they were not only important Greek pedagogues and teachers, but also politically powerful and dominant through the power of language. However, after Hegel the debate on sophistics was not over, quite the contrary. Why such a fury and fuss about sophistics and the sophists when they were long gone? 'Who's Afraid of the Sophists?' – to cite the title of a chapter in Barbara Cassin's recent book.[14] What is the main problem here – their attitude or their link to power, the (rhetorical and linguistic) means they were not afraid to deploy or their elusive nature? The latter, by the way, is proven masterfully in Plato's dialogue *Sophist*, a text which for Badiou is 'the greatest text in the history of philosophy'.[15] Is the main problem perhaps that they are 'masters', 'rival masters'? Be that as it may, the fact is that in post-Hegelian philosophy a debate with the sophists continues. The main reason is that we still perceive of the sophists as our contemporaries: 'If there is any consensus to be found among their defenders (and their enemies as well), it is the constantly mutating view that *the sophists are our contemporaries* – whether that makes them Enlightenment rationalists, eminent Victorians, cynical *fin de siècle* perspectivists, analytical moral philosophers, or, most recently of all, postmodernists.'[16] Nevertheless, what makes the sophists *our contemporaries*? Their supposedly general deceptions, fakes and fallacies? Recall that in Plato a sophist is already a fake; he or she resembles a philosopher 'as the wolf does the dog', as it stands in Plato's *Sophist* (231b). Even more, faking, pretending, deceiving are the tricks of their trade – sophistics for Plato is nothing but 'expertise in producing appearances' (236c).[17] Moreover, if we take into account that the English word 'appearance' here stands for Greek *phantasma*, one could say that, for Plato, the sophist is already someone whose business is illusion, fiction.[18] Even more, the sophist is seen as someone who produces and intensifies a 'plague of fantasies', to use Žižek's terminology. Not only as an agitator, but also as a demagogue, a rabble-rouser.[19]

That mobs, masses and rabble are specifically modern phenomena and a problem for modern as well as contemporary political philosophy is well established;[20] that mob rallies, in our time of the rise of populisms, are perceived as dangerous and perilous is not in doubt either. However, why are the sophists seen predominantly as demagogues and rabble-rousers? Because they use rhetoric?[21] Why are the sophists always connected to all kinds of disorientations? Why is there such a consensus even among our contemporaries as radically different as Allan Bloom, Vacláv Havel, Joseph Moreau, François Furet and Alain Badiou, as Cassin shows, 'that sophistics should be a prime target'?[22] Do we have to choose? Why? What is the choice about? Recall that in Plato's *Sophist* in the end we get two types of sophist: one 'a sincere imitator' and the other 'an insincere one' (268a). The elusive nature of the sophist demands that a choice be made. Is choosing the only option? It is at this point that many of the above-mentioned questions, dilemmas and choices are related to the above-mentioned recent debate on sophistics between Badiou and Cassin. Do we have to choose between their different views on sophistics, too? Or should, perhaps, the whole debate on sophistics be started and pursued on very different premises?

Perhaps it would be useful to add, even before we proceed to look more closely at Badiou's and Cassin's arguments on sophistics, some additional remarks. We have already mentioned a link between sophistics and trickery. This link, to put it bluntly, was never black and white, although we are frequently forced to think about sophistics in that way: sophistics was never just trickery, swindle, and imposture, yet it was never blameless in that regard either. In the English language today 'sophistics' or rather 'sophistry' is one of many synonyms of the word 'trickery' and also an indicator of the context the word 'sophistics' is usually associated with. However, the terms 'sophistics' and 'sophistry' are not identical and have counterparts in the German language, '*Sophistik*' and '*Sophisterei*'. The first term refers to doctrines taught by the 'sophists', i.e. the historical Greek thinkers from the fifth century BC, while the second designates the deviations associated with them. In a similar vein, the classic and yet still widely used French philosophical dictionary of André Lalande, *Vocabulaire technique et critique de la philosophie*, differentiates between two major meanings of the substantive 'sophistics': the first concerns a specific intellectual attitude of the Greek sophists, while the second is used to designate a 'philosophy of verbal reasoning, lacking solidity and seriousness', or sophistry.[23] One could say that in English a similar distinction is made by other means, that is via the 'distinction between "fallacy," which designates an error in reasoning that has all the appearances of truth, and "sophism," which denotes additionally an intention to deceive, with the difficulty that "fallacy" is the received translation for medieval *sophisma*, which is more ambiguous.'[24] There are therefore many ways of understanding one particular word, in our case 'sophistics', especially if we approach it from the perspective of different languages. How do we shift from one language to another? How do we translate from one into another? Here we encounter a problem of translation, we simply cannot translate everything, there are always certain impossibilities. These are not the result of translating between various languages, but have to do with a singular language as well. Furthermore, language is never just a language, it is never just a means of communication, but also a product of a certain culture, yet never entirely imprisoned in it, mastered, controlled or owned by it. Since 'a world opens up in a completely different manner via a certain language',[25] there are always multiple languages and multiple worlds as well.

If Barbara Cassin has any lifelong professional commitment, it is a commitment to subtleties (of a text/language): these subtleties are always linked with certain impossibilities internal to a language or to a text, and cannot be either abolished or bypassed by translation into other languages – hence the idea of untranslatability. The *Dictionary of Untranslatables* is a long-term project of Cassin's; it is in fact a group project, and a great achievement (and success). It is also a joint philosophical and political (European) project:

> Multiplicity is to be found not only among languages but within each language. A language, as we have considered it, is not a fact of nature, an object, but an effect caught up in history and culture, and that ceaselessly invents itself – again, *energeia* rather than *ergon*. So the *Dictionary*'s concern is constituted by languages in their works, and by the translations of these works into different languages, at different times. The networks of words and senses that we have sought to think through are networks of datable philosophical idioms, placed by specific authors in particular writings; they are unique, time-bound networks, linked to their address (exoteric or esoteric), to their level of language, to their style, to their relation to tradition (models, references, palimpsests, breaks, innovations). Every author, and the philosopher is an author, simultaneously writes in a language and creates his or her language [. . .]. The untranslatable therefore is also a question of case by case. Finally, there is multiplicity in the meanings of a word in a given language. As Jacques Lacan says in *L'Étourdit*, 'A language is, among other possibilities, nothing but the sum of the ambiguities that its history has allowed to persist.'[26]

That is perhaps, by the way, not a bad suggestion to consider here – 'sophistics' as the sum of the ambiguities that its history has allowed to persist? One of these ambiguities of 'sophistics' certainly pertains to its link with 'deception' – are the 'sophists' simply 'tricksters'? Why is trickery so often associated with sophists? Obviously because of their infamous knowledge of language and rhetoric. They are always praised as masters of language; however, the trouble is that language and speech do not and cannot have the Master. For Lacan, a human being is a speaking being, yet does not master speech or language. Lacan, despite many changes throughout his work, never changes on one particular point: there is no Trickster, no big Manipulator or Master who pulls the strings. There is no Master, yet there are masters. However, even here a master is always an intersubjective effect, or better, it is an effect *produced by occupying a certain place*. In the end, for Lacan – following Hegel here – the figure of the master is a figure of an impostor and dupe. Recall that for Hegel the sophists are 'the masters of Greece', yet the very same Hegel devalued the figure of the Master: after Hegel there is 'a radical decline of the function of the master, a function that obviously governs all of Aristotle's thought and determines its persistence over the centuries. It is in Hegel that we find expressed an extreme devalorisation of the position of the master, since Hegel turns him into the great dupe, the magnificent cuckold of historical development.'[27] Moreover, if historically the picture of the sophists was distorted by Plato and Aristotle, this distortion was precisely because of the struggle as to who is a true master. The recent debate between Badiou and Cassin is centred precisely at this point – without being invoked explicitly.

The debate itself is not only about sophistics, it touches upon many and various topics, from Heidegger to Lacan,[28] and it would be impossible to examine it here more closely. The debate has recently been commented on from the point of view of later Lacan,[29] yet we will try to tackle it here from a very different point of view. We will leave aside many other topics this debate is also about, such as the problem of knowledge (matheme), the relation between philosophy and sophistics along the axis man-woman, formulas of sexuality, etc. We will try to provide here only the general stakes, arguments and premises of Badiou and Cassin's debate about philosophy and sophistics.

Let us first begin by pointing out what Badiou and Cassin in general agree on. They both agree that the great enemy is the One, they are both strongly against Aristotle, they both agree that another, non-Heideggerian hi/story of the beginnings of philosophy and of the pre-Socratics is needed, and they both agree on the importance of Lacan's psychoanalysis for contemporary thought. Here, at the point of Lacan, they rather unsurprisingly disagree – while for Badiou Lacan is a most notorious anti-philosopher,[30] for Cassin he is the most notorious contemporary sophist;[31] while Badiou stresses the importance of univocity and matheme in later Lacan, Cassin seems to favour homophony and equivocity, etc.[32] This setting is quite typical. Both Cassin and Badiou at every point of their debate and controversy regularly present us, the readers, with a choice to be made: one has to choose, a decision has to be taken, they claim. Therefore, it is not surprising that a similar 'either-or' choice awaits us in debating 'sophistics' and 'philosophy'. Should we accept it?

A general problem is that in that way the debate on 'sophistics' from its very beginnings is permeated by rivalry, competition and struggle. From the perspective of philosophy, sophistics is not only seen as its negative alter ego, but as its bad, even perverse double. The stakes are high and they involve a debate as well as many charges of duplicity, fallacy, etc. As any reader of Lacan knows, rivalry and competition, together with narcissism, aggression, illusion, fixation, etc., pertain to the Imaginary. In the Imaginary struggle prevails, and that struggle is defined by choice, even a lethal vel (i.e. choice, in Lacan's sense): either you or me. For a long time Lacan used all that together with a passage from Hegel's *Phenomenology of Spirit* known as the 'master-slave dialectic'. The latter importantly influenced not only him, but the entire contemporary twentieth-century French philosophy.[33] Even to the point that Deleuze and Guttari in their *What Is Philosophy?* claimed that, historically, philosophy is possible only within a circle of friends. However, 'it is even more difficult to know what *friend* signifies, even and especially among the Greeks.'[34] So, every friendship is also a rivalry, and in that sense philosophy always had its rivals, from sociology to today's advertising. Who, then, is a sophist – a friend (whose friend?), a rival or even an enemy? Or a rival master (but a false one, of course)? The debate on sophistics as a whole, and therefore not only the debate between Badiou and Cassin, in this sense indeed circulates around this fixion/fiction of the master. Perhaps it is time to extract it from that context; following Lacan saying that here, too, 'it is not a question of disputing authority, but of extracting it from fiction.'[35]

In what sense? In the sense that every fiction, to use again Lacan's pun, is a fixion, a fiction that fixates sophistics as sophistry in our case, and, this happened in our case with Plato, which fixates the opposition between philosophy and sophistics. Badiou, as Plato's most infamous contemporary defender, repeats here the Platonist gesture of delimitation. For Badiou, philosophy from its very beginnings is opposed to sophistics. Philosophy has to be delimited from sophistics, yet for Badiou 'nothing is more philosophically useful to us than contemporary sophistics'. While philosophy 'ought never yield to anti-sophistry extremism', it loses itself whenever 'it harbors the dark desire to do away with the sophist once and for all.' For Badiou, an attitude defines the true dogmatism of philosophy: 'the claim that the sophist, because he is like the perverse double of the philosopher, ought not to exist. No, the sophist must instead be assigned to his place.' Therefore, 'the ethics of philosophy essentially inheres in retaining the sophist as adversary, in conserving the *polemos*, or dialectical conflict. The disastrous moment occurs when philosophy declares that the sophist ought not to be, the moment when it decrees the annihilation of its Other.'[36] Therefore, despite sharp criticism of sophistics, Badiou retains the figure of the sophist:

> From the outset, the sophist has been philosophy's enemy brother, its implacable twin. Deep in its historicist malaise, philosophy today is very weak against modern sophists. It is even most often the case that our great sophists – because there are great sophists – are regarded as great philosophers. [. . .] The modern sophist attempts to replace the idea of truth with the idea of the rule. This is the most profound sense of Wittgenstein's otherwise ingenious endeavor. Wittgenstein is our Gorgias, and we respect him as such. The ancient sophist already replaced truth

with a mixture of force and convention. The modern sophist seeks to contrast the
force of the rule, and more generally, the modalities of language authority of the
Law, with the revelation or the production of the true.[37]

In other words, for 'the sophists, there are only conventions and relations of force. And for Wittgenstein, only language games.'[38]

Perhaps we should note that all of these developments come from one particular work of Badiou's, *Conditions*, originally published in 1992. Similar developments can be found in Badiou's seminars from the same period, which have recently been published. While in them Badiou at first describes the sophist even as the philosopher's brother – 'enemy brother, however, a sibling of a philosopher'[39] – he is later requalified as the philosopher's opponent or adversary.[40] It seems that the work published earlier sharpens things, for in *Conditions* the sophist is qualified as a 'perverse double of the philosopher', which has to be 'assigned to his place', In addition, while Badiou in his seminar from the following year describes Nietzsche's typology as a 'generalized sophistry',[41] he still does not differentiate strictly between sophistics and anti-philosophy; he speaks, for instance, about the 'complicity of anti-philosophy and sophistics'.[42] He is well aware at that period of time that he should differentiate between anti-philosophy and sophistics, as is clear from one text on Lacan and Plato from that period: 'It is a question, once and for all, whether Lacan's proclaimed anti-philosophy is in our eyes necessarily a sophistical figure.'[43]

But that would have to wait a couple of years. The topics of sophistics in the early 1990s is pushed somehow to the foreground, since Badiou devotes the next three years of his seminar to three important anti-philosophers: Wittgenstein, Lacan and Saint-Paul. It would only be later that Badiou differentiates between sophistics (be it ancient or modern) and anti-philosophy: while they are both sceptical about the truth, their main difference lies in the fact that anti-philosophy is not a technique of persuasion. The main aim of anti-philosophy is an act conceived as an unconditional break, a transformation or a groundless leap into the new. An emphasis on novelty is common to anti-philosophy and Badiou's own philosophy (truth is nothing but fidelity to an event, the latter breaks with situation, encyclopedia, and *doxa*). It seems that this has consequences for Badiou's dealings with sophistics. While sophistics on the one hand became less similar to philosophy and therefore less dangerous, this resulted in more decisive action against it: from being 'assigned to its place' it had to be 'reduced to silence'. A very Aristotelian move indeed, Cassin would comment. That move came almost twenty years later, when Badiou once again devoted a lot of his energy and time to Plato. His seminar from 1989 to 1990 was namely devoted to Plato's *Republic*; however, twenty years later Badiou again spent three years of his seminar on the same topics (*Pour aujourd'hui:*

Platon!, 2007–2010). His became obsessed with re-translating the entirety of Plato's *Republic* into contemporary French, and after some time he really did so.[44] On the occasion of publishing the first chapter of the book in English, he wrote the short introduction to it. Therein he redefined, again, the relation between philosophy and sophistics:

> It is as if, for Plato (or rather his textual stand-in, Socrates), it were impossible to begin to think affirmatively without having first refuted the sophist. The word 'refute,' moreover, is not accurate. Rather, it is a question of defeating him, which means: reducing him to silence. The violence of that moment, which also involves a dark comedy of sorts, derives from the fact that all means are fair, once it's not so much a matter of being right as it is of winning. What is involved here, in a way, is a sort of struggle to the death, in the sense it takes on in Hegel, when the Master and the Slave confront each other in order to determine how thinking will continue. Here, too, the issue is one of determining how philosophy can become established, and in order for that to happen, the sophist – the man who places language at the service of personal interest and the established powers – must leave the public stage. The fact that this moment is a negative one is also owing to one key point: rhetoric, of which the sophist is the master, accompanies a thinking in which negation holds sway. Why should this be so? Because the sophist defends a thesis (an opinion) only insofar as he knows that he could defend the opposite thesis. This is the inevitable consequence of a thinking – actually an intellectual and verbal dexterity – that is made to serve not the invariance of a principle but rather the variability of opinions, which reflect power relations, localized desires and interests. The battle between Socrates and Thrasymachus is ultimately a battle between philosophy, the handmaiden of the eternity of truths, and rhetoric, the handmaiden of the opportunism of interests. Ontologically, it affords a potent version of the battle between two orientations in thought. [. . .] As far as Socrates is concerned, Thrasymachus is diabolical, albeit with no grandeur other than his sheer brutality. He is diabolical in Goethe's sense: the Spirit that always negates.[45]

So, the sophist in the end is not only 'assigned to his place' but also 'reduced to silence'. Even more, Badiou redefines the sophist. He is now someone who wants only to oppose and negate, he becomes a kind of resister by profession, eternal grumbler, complainer and faultfinder. He is not exactly a rabble-rouser, but very close to a 'professional againster' and almost an embodiment of 'a will-to-be-against'.[46] Obviously political and philosophical adversaries and rivals of Badiou have changed through time, they are no more Lyotard, Derrida, and the like, but are now 'democratic materialism', for which, as defined in *Logic of Worlds*, 'there are only bodies and languages'. It seems that the figure of the sophist can be associated with 'democratic materialism', since a sophist is obviously seen as a trickster, as someone with a full bag of tricks: 'Rhetoric, of which the sophist is the master, accompanies a thinking in which negation holds sway.' Even more, in Badiou's view, it seems that for philosophy to flourish, first a sophist must be defeated: it is 'impossible to begin to think affirmatively without having first refuted the sophist'. Why?

What is the exact status of this refutation? Hitherto, readers of Badiou were accustomed to the explanation that philosophy is possible when (and only when) four generic procedures of truth are present simultaneously. Or, in Badiou's own words: 'We shall thus posit that there are four conditions of philosophy, and that a lack of a single one gives rise to its dissipation, just as the emergence of all four conditioned its apparition. These conditions are: the matheme, the poem, political invention and love.'[47] Now we somehow get yet another condition – a refutation, even a violent gesture, a rather violent silencing of the sophist. Not only is this something Badiou had never presented thus far, it is also something he tried to avoid at all costs. While for Heidegger, for instance, the beginning of philosophy is simultaneous with the forgetting of Being, with the great Fall, Badiou's explanations[48] were far more down-to-earth, less dramatic, pompous and profane, secular even. With this new redefinition we get a violent and negative act at the beginning. This violence is something negative, while Badiou himself consistently insisted on his allegiance to affirmationism. So, not only is this inconsistent with Badiou's standard previous theses, it now somehow devalues his own arguments presented so far and paradoxically gives unexpected power and importance to the sophist, since the silencing of the latter becomes the condition *sine qua non* of philosophy.

However, this latest gesture of Badiou's is also problematic from yet another perspective: it literally repeats Aristotle's gesture of reducing the sophist to silence, a move countlessly decried by Barbara Cassin in her work. The 'long Aristotelian detour',[49] as she calls it, is a turning point in relation to philosophy as such and the relation thereof to language (and thus indirectly to sophistics). It has consequences for all of us today, too: 'Since nowadays we are Aristotelians, having suckled on the decision of meaning with our mother's milk, "sophistry" needs to be defined.'[50] As she has demonstrated in her book *La Décision du sens*, a translation of and commentary on book Gamma of Aristotle's *Metaphysics* co-written with Michel Narcy, for Aristotle, language use depends on the stability of words. For Aristotle, we should and must use words in the same way, with the same intentions – for this is precisely what distinguishes the human being as a rational animal. So, here we have a demand for univocity, a kind of decision on meaning, while on the side of the sophists we have equivocity:

Indeed, Aristotle makes the refusal of homonymy a weapon of mass destruction against sophistry. He bases his refutation of the adversaries of the principle of noncontradiction (the only demonstration of the first principle that is possible without a petition) on the necessity of univocality: in order to speak, one must say and signify a single thing, the same for oneself and others. A word cannot simultaneously have and not have the same meaning – 'hello' cannot mean 'go to hell' – the word is the first encountered entity to satisfy the principle of noncontradiction. The sense of a word, its definition, is the essence of the thing that the word names: 'man' signifies a man and means 'animal endowed with logos'. Either one yields to the decision of meaning, or one does not even speak, and as speech is the definition of man, one must be either a plant or a god.[51]

On the other hand, language is, for Gorgias, a powerful *pharmakon* that in the hands of a skilled rhetor can act as either a poison or a cure (or both at the same time). Or, as Gorgias observes in his *Encomium of Helen* (§8): 'Speech is a great master, which with the smallest and least perceptible of bodies performs the most divine of acts.'[52] Aristotle and an important majority of the philosophic tradition since then assume that a key function of the principle of non-contradiction is the separation of meaning from nonsense, a distinction which for the sophists was much more blurred – the line dividing black and white, true and false, is intrinsically blurred, and they played in many ways with ambiguities and homophonies. The pleasure of speaking, speaking to no avail, is something essential for the sophists, yet in that way they also nurture the creative, performative side of language. Here Cassin finds an ally in Novalis, who in his notebooks from 1798 wrote the following:

> Language is such a marvelous and fruitful secret – *because when someone speaks merely for the sake of speaking*, he utters the most splendid, most original truths. However, if he wants to speak about something definite, capricious language makes him say the most ridiculous and confused stuff. This is also the cause of the hatred that so many serious people feel toward language. They notice its mischief, but not the fact that the chattering they scorn is the infinitely serious aspect of language.[53]

Relying on Novalis, Cassin calls the approach to language that embodies this experience of its affective and performative function a *logology*. For Novalis, philosophy must aspire to logology, something the ancient sophists were very close to.

Hence the importance of sophistics as a 'fiction of philosophy'[54] and as an essential part of philosophy itself; it is its internal product and its 'effect of the structure'.[55] Sophistics 'in fact works as a way of delimiting philosophy'[56] and has many virtues of its own, especially due to its emphasis on words and performativity. However, the ambiguous and elusive status of the 'sophist' demands a different approach towards the question of truth and falsity. Here again, Cassin strongly opposes Badiou. If the latter in his fidelity to Plato emphasises the Idea and philosophical category of Truth, Cassin exposes the fetishisation of truth in (Badiou's) philosophy as well as the insistence of sophistics on the power of words in their performativity and inconsistency to reshape our world and the truth itself. In addition, while Badiou defines sophistics primarily as being organised around the statement 'there is no truth', Cassin emphasises: 'I would disagree that this is sophistry's statement of principle. A sophist knows that a destroyer is first and foremost a battleship. [. . .] The sophist's position is not in the relation to truth but with respect to discourse.'[57]

Discourse as a social bond is therefore the soil on which the sophists flourish. However, the sophists are not simply political agitators, rabble-rousers or only politically engaged. Speaking for the pleasure of speaking, speaking to no avail – and in this way producing something new – this is, in Cassin's eyes, where sophistics shows its virtues. Sophistical discourse is namely performative, it creates worlds, it is demiurgical, it makes worlds happen[58] – this is yet another lifelong thesis Cassin is committed to up to her most recent work: 'Being is an effect of saying, an act of a successful word, from Gorgias to Austin.'[59] Here, at the point of creation, the creation of the new, which is the sole purpose of philosophy, on the one hand (according to Badiou), and sophistics, on the other, we can find yet another unexpected agreement between Badiou and Cassin. At least in principle. It is true that for Badiou the aim is to produce the truly new and that is really the only thing that matters to him. However, philosophy for Badiou, strictly speaking, does not produce anything; the events are produced elsewhere, in generic procedures. Badiou – as a fervent opponent of the 'linguistic turn', of course – would strongly object that one could produce anything new through language. But that is not important for our purposes here, either. What is important is that the production of the new in Badiou – or rather, the emergence of an event – is for him something hazardous, lawless, something that in a strict sense does not serve any purpose. At that point it is close to Cassin's emphasis on 'speaking to no avail' or on '"pure" speaking for the sake of speaking'. Perhaps here Badiou comes dangerously close to the sophists, too. In what sense? In his *Second Manifesto of Philosophy*, namely, Badiou mentions a certain critique, a recent criticism by a journalist 'with regard to young students and misinformed teachers, this prosecutor stated, philosophers such as Slavoj Žižek or myself are nothing less than reckless. This is a standard theme intoned by the worst conservatives, from Antiquity right up until today: Young people run extremely grave risks if put in contact with "bad masters" who will divert them from all that is serious and honorable – namely, a career, morality, the family, order, the West, property, law, democracy and capitalism.'⁶⁰ Instead of avoiding such a characterisation and charge of 'corrupting the youth', Badiou openly embraces it:⁶¹ 'By definition, philosophy, when it truly appears, is either reckless or it is nothing. As the power of destabilizing the dominant opinion, it summons youth to those points where the continuous creation of a new truth is decided.'⁶²

However, here, precisely at this point, we made a full circle and we are back at the very beginning, here a philosopher is (again) dangerously close to a sophist. Badiou surely knows that here he is rehashing a very old reproach against Socrates, a reproach made by many contemporaries following Aristophanes in his *Clouds*. As was already pointed out at the beginning of the present *paper*, Plato spent a lot of his time and energy (and also a lot of his work, somewhere between a third and a half of it) in an effort to delimit Socrates from the sophists. This dilemma is very old and well known. Let us quote here only the basic contours as summed up by Kerferd:

> The very idea of including Socrates as part of the sophistic movement is at best a paradox and to many absurd. Plato seeks to present Socrates as the arch-enemy of the sophists and all that they stood for. Down the centuries the gulf between Socrates and the sophists, it would seem, has become even wider and more unbridgeable, as Socrates has become a symbol and a rallying-cry. However, on the other hand it is clear that Socrates was quite widely regarded as part of the sophistic movement. Through his well-known friendship with Aspasia it is likely that he was in fairly close contact with the circle of Pericles, and his intellectual and educational impact on the aspiring young men at Athens was such that in function he was correctly so regarded. The fact that he took no payment does not alter his function in any way. But were there no differences between him and the rest of the sophists? The answer requires an attempt to discover what was the method and what was the content of Socrates' teaching, and this is difficult.⁶³

The dilemma therefore does not concern only a question of accepting fees for teaching or, as summed up by Karatani in his unique concise style:

> At the time, those who advocated for Socrates sought to distinguish him from the Sophists, because he was being impeached as a Sophist. For example, Socrates accepted no fees for his teaching. Therefore, the argument went, he was not a Sophist. If one accepts the definition of a Sophist as one who teaches the arts of rhetoric for money, then clearly Socrates was not a Sophist. Yet, despite the fact that Socrates accepted no fees for his teaching, he was still seen by his peers as a typical Sophist.⁶⁴

So, is Socrates a philosopher or a sophist, or perhaps even both? Can we draw a line here? Do we have to choose between philosopher and sophist? Is there a choice? Do we have to make one? What if we do not choose? In what way could one understand Kerferd's proposition 'that Socrates should be treated as having a part to play within the sophistic movement'?[65] Both Badiou and Cassin know perfectly well that in a way it is difficult to draw a line here. Badiou at first proposes a kind of politically correct vision of coexistence with the sophist – 'the ethics of philosophy essentially inheres in retaining the sophist as adversary, in conserving the polemos, or dialectical conflict.' As we saw, he later shifts to more radical solutions here, too: from the sophist being 'assigned to his place' to his 'being reduced to silence'. Badiou retains a choice and he finally chooses, too. And while Cassin sees and shows the importance of sophistics for contemporary thought, she refuses to make such a choice, even more, she tries in a way to have her cake and eat it too. How? Her point is visible via the superposition of Heidegger and Arendt on Greece in *L'effet sophistique*. The details of the argumentation are not important for our topics here; however, what is important is that Cassin in the end presents us with a kind of division, an internal division. She presents Arendt's solution of dividing Socrates into a thinker and a citizen: 'As a thinker, he is rather the Socrates of Plato, a platonizing Socrates; as a citizen, he is rather a Socrates sophist.'[66] This division itself has problems of its own (Is a citizen not also a thinker? Is a thinker not also a citizen? etc.); however, it seems that instead of choosing one part of the choice ('either-or'), Cassin chooses *both*. She devotes a lot of space in her later work to developing arguments for this topic, such as speaking 'as', '*en tant que*', lying, etc. I can speak, she claims, as a philosopher as well as a woman simultaneously, depending on my choice and angle I want to point out.[67] Needless to say, the dilemma is not between only two of the elements, but rather presents us multiple, infinite choices. We cannot discuss the implications of this move more thoroughly here; let us only remark that the logic of 'speaking as' is today ubiquitous and was first developed by Deleuze's elaboration of the logic of the conjunction 'and':

> AND isn't even a specific conjunction or relation, it brings in all relations, there are as many relations as ANDS, AND doesn't just upset all relations, it upsets being, the verb... and so on. AND, 'and ... and ... and ...' is precisely a creative stammering, a foreign use of language, as opposed to a conformist and dominant use based on the verb 'to be'. AND is of course diversity, multiplicity, the destruction of identities. [...] Because multiplicity is never in the terms, however many, nor in all the terms together, the whole. Multiplicity is precisely in the 'and', which is different in nature from elementary components and collections of them.[68]

In this way, we have come unexpectedly, via Badiou and Cassin on sophistics, to completely new terrain, new topics that should be discussed further, but we cannot do so here. Even more, we made a full circle considering our topics, and yet we are again at the beginning. While our aim was predominantly to expose a certain fixion, a fiction concerning sophistics as sophistry, we have also come to a point that necessitates a different approach to the whole debate on it, which demands that different choices be made and presents us with different dilemmas. A hint at the end, perhaps, in which direction it would also be possible to go further. If we understand the very elusive nature of the sophist in terms of Lacan's *objet petit a*, it would be possible to understand why, first, the sophist returns again and again, why he or she returns in the figure of a contemporary, why he or she is in fact a certain 'stain' in the picture, which nonetheless as a 'clandestine passenger'[69] has to be excluded, extracted from the picture/fiction/history in order for the latter to make sense at all. Precisely as such, as excluded, extracted from the field (note that for Lacan the field of reality 'is sustained only by the extraction of object *a*, which nevertheless gives it its frame'[70]), the sophist also *frames* any future debate on sophistry, sophistics and philosophy.

Notes

1. This chapter is a result of the research program P6-0014 'Conditions and Problems of Contemporary Philosophy', the research project J6-9392 'The Problem of Objectivity and Fiction in Contemporary Philosophy', and the bilateral cooperation project BI-US/18-20-026 'Objectivity beyond the Subject-Object Dichotomy: Fiction, Truth, Affect' between the Research Centre of the Slovenian Academy of Science and Arts and the University of New Mexico, which are funded by the Slovenian Research Agency.
2. Jacques Lacan, *Autres écrits* (Paris: Seuil, 2001), p. 258.
3. Here, at the point of 'historical counterpart', too, things are far from being resolved once and for all. A number of scholars have struggled to explain the differences between sages, poets and sophists from the eighth century BC onwards; the differences between the fifth- and fourth-century sophists; the differences between Ionian philosophers and the sophists; the differences between particular sophists, etc. Furthermore, the very term pre-Socratics was introduced at the turn of the nineteenth century. (For a brief overview of that introduction, see André Laks, *The Concept of Presocratic Philosophy. Its Origin, Development, and Significance*, trans. Glenn W. Most (Princeton and Oxford: Princeton University Press, 2018), pp. 19–34.) So many unresolved issues and controversies concerning 'the sophists' are rather not surprising considering the very elusive nature and definition of a 'sophist'.

4. G. B. Kerferd, *The Sophistic Movement* (Cambridge: Cambridge University Press, 1981), p. 174.
5. Aristotle, 'Sophistical Refutations', 165b21–23. Quoted from Aristotle, *The Complete Works of Aristotle. The Revised Oxford Translation*, ed. Jonathan Barnes, Vol. 1 (Princeton and Chichester: Princeton University Press, 1984), p. 279.
6. Aristotle, 'Sophistical Refutations', 171b28, p. 291.
7. For a brief and instructional overview of the fees paid to poets, philosophers and sophists in ancient Greece see Kerferd, *The Sophistic Movement*, pp. 25–8.
8. For more on this, see Marcel Henaff, *The Price of Truth. Gift, Money, Philosophy*, trans. Jean-Louis Morhange with the collaboration of Anne-Marie Feenberg-Dibon (Stanford: Stanford University Press, 2010).
9. Michael Svoboda, 'It Takes an Empire to Raise a Sophist: An Athens-Centered Analysis of the Oikonomia of Pre-Platonic Rhetoric', in *Logos without Rhetoric. The Arts of Language before Plato*, ed. Robin Reames (Columbia: University of South Carolina Press, 2017), p. 120.
10. Alexandre Koyré, *Introduction à la lecture de Platon suivi entretiens sur Descartes* (Paris: Gallimard, 1962), p. 96.
11. Svoboda, 'It Takes an Empire to Raise a Sophist: An Athens-Centered Analysis of the Oikonomia of Pre-Platonic Rhetoric', p. 121.
12. Gilles Deleuze and Félix Guattari, *What Is Philosophy?*, trans. Hugh Tomlinson and Graham Burchill (London and New York: Verso, 2009), p. 63.
13. Deleuze and Guattari, *What Is Philosophy?*, p. 64.
14. See the title and developments in first chapter of Barbara Cassin, *Sophistical Practice. Toward a Consistent Relativism* (New York: Fordham University Press, 2014).
15. Alain Badiou, *Parménide. L'être I – Figure ontologique, 1985–1986* (Paris: Fayard, 2014), p. 130.
16. Rachel Barney, 'The Sophistic Movement', in *A Companion to Ancient Philosophy*, ed. Mary Louise Gill and Pierre Pellegrin (Oxford: Wiley-Blackwell, 2009), p. 78.
17. Plato, *Complete Works*, ed. John M. Cooper (Indianapolis and Cambridge: Hackett, 1997), p. 256.
18. It seems that Marcel Detienne too holds that view: 'Plato was correct to regard them as masters of illusion who presented men not with the truth but with fictions, images, and idols, which they persuaded others to accept as reality.' Marcel Detienne, *Masters of Truth in Archaic Greece*, foreword by Pierre Vidal-Naquet, trans. Janet Lloyd (New York: Zone Books, 1996), p. 118.
19. The logic here is exposed by Cassin in the following manner: 'if sophistics, if Lyotard, if Austin, then Trump.' Barbara Cassin, *Quand dire, c'est vraiment faire. Homère, Gorgias et le people arc-en-ciel* (Paris: Fayard, 2018), p. 231.
20. See two illuminating recent works on this topic: Étienne Balibar, *La crainte des*

masses: Politique et philosophie avant et après Marx (Paris: Galilée, 1997); Frank Ruda, *Hegel's Rabble: An Investigation into Hegel's Philosophy of Right* (London and New York: Bloomsbury, 2011).

21. For Karatani, for instance, this has nothing to do with the (ancient) sophists: '[T]he reduction of rhetoric to a set of techniques for domination was the view, not of the Sophists, but of the Athenians. The Athenians had no desire to learn anything from foreigners beyond this instrumental art of rhetoric.' Kōjin Karatani, *Isonomia and the Origins of Philosophy*, trans. Joseph A. Murphy (Durham, NC and London: Duke University Press, 2017), p. 123.
22. Barbara Cassin, *Sophistical Practice*, p. 39.
23. See André Lalande, *Vocabulaire technique et critique de la philosophie* (Paris: Quadrige/ PUF, 2018 (1st edn, 1926)), pp. 1010–11.
24. Quoted from the entry 'Sophism, sophist', in *Dictionary of Untranslatables*, ed. Barbara Cassin; trans. Steven Rendall, Christian Hubert, Jeffrey Mehlman, Nathaniel Stein, Michael Syrotinski; trans. ed. by Emily Apter, Jacques Lezra and Michael Wood) (Princeton and Oxford: Princeton University Press, 2015), p. 1007.
25. Barbara Cassin, *Plus d'une langue* (Montrouge: Bayard, 2019), p. 21.
26. Barbara Cassin, 'Introduction', in *Dictionary of Untranslatables*, p. xix.
27. Jacques Lacan, *The Seminar of Jacques Lacan, Book VII: The Ethics of Psychoanalysis, 1959–1960*, ed. Jacques-Alain Miller, trans. Dennis Porter (New York: W. W. Norton, 1992), p. 11.
28. See Barbara Cassin and Alain Badiou, *Heidegger: His Life and His Philosophy*, trans. Suzan Spitzer (New York: Columbia University Press, 2016); *There's No Such Thing as a Sexual Relationship: Two Lessons on Lacan*, trans. Suzan Spitzer and Kenneth Reinhard (New York: Columbia University Press, 2017); *Homme, femme, philosophie* (Paris: Fayard, 2019).
29. For the basic information on this debate, see the 'Introductory notes' of Kenneth Reinhard in Badiou and Cassin, *There's No Such Thing as a Sexual Relationship: Two Lessons on Lacan*, pp. IX–XXVII.
30. See Alain Badiou, *Lacan. Anti-philosophy 3*, trans. Suzan Spitzer and Kenneth Reinhard (New York: Columbia University Press, 2019).
31. Barbara Cassin, *Jacques the Sophist. Lacan, Logos and Psychanalysis*, trans. Michael Syrotinski (New York: Fordham University Press, 2020).
32. For the debate on this point, see the illuminating essays of Dolar and Zupančič: Alenka Zupančič, *What Is Sex?* (Cambridge, MA, and London: MIT Press, 2017), pp. 62–9; Mladen Dolar, 'Sophist's Choice', *Crisis and Critique* (special issue 'Jacques Lacan: psychoanalysis, politics, philosophy'), vol. 6, no. 1 (2019), pp. 66–85.
33. See in this context Judith Butler, *Subjects of Desire. Hegelian Reflections in Twentieth-Century France* (New York: Columbia University Press, 1987).

34. Deleuze and Guattari, *What Is Philosophy?*, p. 3.
35. Lacan, *Autres écrits*, p. 258.
36. Alain Badiou, *Conditions*, trans. Steven Corcoran (London and New York: Bloomsbury, 2017), p. 19.
37. Badiou, *Conditions*, pp. 5, 6, 7.
38. Badiou, *Conditions*, p. 168.
39. Alain Badiou, *Le Séminaire. Théorie du mal, théorie de l'amour, 1990–1991* (Paris: Fayard, 2018), p. 17.
40. Alain Badiou, *Le Séminaire. L'essence de la politique, 1991–1992* (Paris: Fayard, 2018), pp. 16–18.
41. Alain Badiou, *Le Séminaire. Nietzsche. L'antiphilosophie I, 1992–1993* (Paris: Fayard, 2015), p. 108.
42. Badiou, *Le Séminaire. Nietzsche*, pp. 148–9.
43. Alain Badiou, 'Lacan et Platon: le mathème est-il une idée', in *Lacan avec les philosophes* (Paris: Albin Michel, 1991), p. 136.
44. See Alain Badiou, *Plato's* Republic. *A Dialogue in Sixteen Chapters, with a Prologue and an Epilogue*, trans. Susan Spitzer (Cambridge: Polity Press, 2012).
45. Alain Badiou, 'Reducing the Sophist to Silence', trans. Susan Spitzer, *Lacanian Ink*, no. 35 (2010), pp. 85–6.
46. See the opening lines of the section 'Being-Against: Nomadism, Desertion, Exodus', in Michael Hardt and Antonio Negri, *Empire* (Cambridge, MA and London: Harvard University Press, 2001), p. 210.
47. Alain Badiou, *Manifesto for Philosophy*, trans. Norman Madarasz (Albany: State University of New York Press, 1999), p. 35.
48. In his seminar on Parmenide, for instance, he develops the thesis that philosophy is originally linked with the possibility of breaking with the narrative, *récit*, and of introducing matheme. (See Alain Badiou, *Le Séminaire. Parménide. L'être I – Figure ontologique, 1985–1986*, p. 258.)
49. Cassin, *Jacques the Sophist*, p. 24.
50. Cassin, *Jacques the Sophist*, p. 28.
51. Cassin, *Sophistical Practice*, p. 249.
52. Cassin, *Sophistical Practice*, p. 249.
53. Cassin, *Jacques the Sophist*, p. 33.
54. Barbara Cassin, *L'effet sophistique* (Paris: Gallimard, 1995), p. 11.
55. Cassin, *L'effet sophistique*, p. 9.
56. Cassin, *Jacques the Sophist*, p. 30.
57. Cassin, *Jacques the Sophist*, p. 37.
58. Barbara Cassin, 'Du faux ou du mensonge à la fiction (de pseudos à plasma)', in *Le*

Plaisir de parler. Études de sophistique comparée, ed. by Barbara Cassin (Paris: Minuit, 1986), p. 18.
59. Cassin, *Quand dire, c'est vraiment faire*, p. 125.
60. Alain Badiou, *Second Manifesto for Philosophy*, trans. Louise Burchill (Cambridge: Polity Press, 2011), p. 70.
61. And this is not just a single occasion, since on other occasions too Badiou starts, rather ironically of course, with his 'confession': 'my aim is to corrupt the youth'. See Alain Badiou, *La vraie vie* (Paris: Fayard, 2016), p. 8.
62. Badiou, *Second Manifesto for Philosophy*, p. 71.
63. Kerferd, *The Sophistic Movement*, pp. 55, 57.
64. Karatani, *Isonomia and the Origins of Philosophy*, p. 127.
65. Kerferd, *The Sophistic Movement*, p. 57.
66. Cassin, *L'effet sophistique*, p. 257.
67. For more on this topic, see Cassin, *Jacques the Sophist*, pp. 125; Alain Badiou and Barbara Cassin, *Homme, femme, philosophie* (Paris: Fayard, 2019), pp. 209–16.
68. Gilles Deleuze, *Negotiations*, trans. Martin Joughin (New York: Columbia University Press, 1995), p. 44.
69. We can perhaps here borrow Lacan's qualification of 'den' from his *L'Étourdit*: Lacan, *Autres écrits*, p. 494.
70. Jacques Lacan, *Écrits: The First Complete Edition in English*, trans. Bruce Fink (London and New York: W. W. Norton, 2006), p. 487.

8   On Rumours, Gossip and Related Matters
Mladen Dolar

PHILOSOPHY FAMOUSLY STARTED with a divide, by drawing a sharp opposition between what in Greek times was called *doxa* and *episteme*. *Doxa* is the regime of opinions (or beliefs). Anybody is entitled to an opinion, and there is no compelling necessity that opinions be firmly grounded; they depend on private views, tastes and preferences. As one cannot argue about tastes, so one ultimately cannot seriously argue about opinions, although one constantly does. One cannot seriously argue because they are based in one's personal stance – I think so, I feel so, I experience it this way, I believe so – and they are ultimately tautological – I think so because I think so, and my personal opinion is my right and my freedom, indeed the much celebrated freedom of opinion. As opposed to this, *episteme* is knowledge that has to be epistemologically grounded, not in some personal preferences or tautologies, but in the 'thing itself'. Knowledge aims at truth – this is its ambition – and truth is binding and universal, not a matter of mere opinion. Knowledge has to be legitimised, it has to be based on sound argument, factual evidence and impartial objectivity, with all this to be ultimately grounded in logos. Let's say that logos is the big Other that should vouchsafe for legitimate proper knowledge. Let's say that logos is the early Greek name for what Lacan, 2,500 years later, called the big Other, in the sense of the guarantee of knowledge in its universality and in its binding character. Logos is the authority we all have to assume when aiming at knowledge. The stark opposition between *doxa* and *episteme*, between opinion and knowledge, goes back to the Socratic foundations of philosophy, and Socrates famously spent his time dismantling people's opinions, destroying them, showing their lack of foundation, their ungrounded arbitrary nature. All it took was asking a couple of awkward questions; that was his favorite occupation.

    Now, rumours stand even lower in rank compared to opinions. One thing that can be said in favour of opinions is that at least people subscribe to them. They treat them as their cherished possession. They even take pride in them. They take them as self-expression. And, the freedom of expression is reputedly inalienable. By contrast, what defines rumours is that nobody quite subscribes to them. 'I heard that . . .,' 'people say that . . .,' 'it has been suggested that . . .,' 'rumour has it . . .'[1] Rumors have no author. They just circulate, anonymously, as if by themselves, impersonally, as the breeze of air stemming from nowhere and enveloping us, then passing on. And, on the way, the breeze easily turns into a tempest, a whirlwind – this metaphor actually became a running cliché about rumours throughout history.[2] Their expansion seems to present the case of *creatio ex* almost *nihilo*, a tiny speck grows into a magnificent creature by the mere movement. There is no assignable origin of a rumour. One just hears it and passes it on, as a relay, and it augments by being passed on. Of course, there are rumours that are intentionally invented and systematically spread. But, they only function as rumours as long they seemingly have no ascertained source. However, if rumours have no author, it doesn't follow that they have no authority – quite the opposite. By being impersonal and anonymous, with no origin, they carry all the more an unfathomable, inscrutable, intractable authority. There is something like a mysterious conversion, a transubstantiation, that takes place with rumours: there is no proof, no origin, no author, no guarantee, but, nevertheless, they are 'mystically' transformed into a formidable force that is very hard, virtually impossible, to combat. Being without foundation, they nevertheless work, with their efficiency standing in stark contrast to their lack of ground or support. 'Everybody knows' that this is a mere rumour, based on thin air, but one cannot stop oneself from lending it an ear and allowing it to work. Octave Mannoni, in a famous paper from 1964, proposed the notorious formula '*Je sais bien, mais quand même*', 'I know very well, but nevertheless . . .'[3] And, rumours present a vintage case of this formula: 'I know very well this is a mere rumor, but nevertheless . . . there may be something to it, or at least it's intriguing and entertaining, or some people may get into trouble because of it, so let me maliciously participate in this, although I know very well that there is ultimately nothing to it – or is there?' Furthermore, since nobody subscribes to them ('I am not maintaining this myself, this is just a rumour I heard,' with one being exempt from responsibility), they exactly fit another formula, elaborated by Robert Pfaller: 'beliefs without owners'.[4] There are beliefs circulating around that nobody quite believes in (one generally imputes them to others, the dupes), but they nevertheless produce effects. In Pfaller's reading, such beliefs are ultimately constitutive of social bonds and of culture at large.

It looks as if rumors present another face of the big Other: not the face of logos, knowledge and truth, but something that nobody quite believes to be true, yet it unfailingly works and is given a questionable credence and general currency. It's a matter of effectiveness and expediency, rather than (or as opposed to) truth. There is a kind of paradoxical reversal with this kind of big Other: the more it appears fickle, unfounded, untrustworthy, unsubstantiated, the more it presents the big Other in its pure form, overpowering precisely because of its lack of foundation, not despite it. It is given a space to rule against everyone's better knowledge. It is as if we have to do here with two opposing faces of the big Other, with no common measure: on the one hand, the big Other that can (and should) provide the epistemological foundation of proper knowledge, based on logos and aiming at truth; and, on the other hand, another big Other based on nothing but hearsay, on the wind, but nevertheless standing fast and sticking. This is the thing with rumours: they stick. They stick whether one wants them to or not; they leave their mark, which seems to be ineffaceable. Yet, despite the stark opposition between the two, could it be that the big Other is a Janus-faced creature, like Janus, the Roman double-faced deity, the god of boundaries and transitions, with the two faces inseparably grown together? Shall we say 'the big Other and its shadow?', 'the big Other and its double?'

Now, the career of Socrates was suspended in an iconic and exemplary way precisely between these two figures of the big Other. For, on the one hand, his principal ambition was to dismantle all unfounded opinions and firmly point them in the direction of the search for truth, the proper foundation of logos. But, on the other hand, the rumours were his undoing, the lever of his fall, the origin of his trial and ultimately of his death. When Socrates was standing in front of the Athenian tribunal (in 399 BCE), this is what he said at the beginning of his defence:

> There have been many who have accused me to you for many years now, and none of their accusations are true. These I fear much more than I fear Anytus and his friends [the present and identifiable accusers] [. . .]. Those who spread the rumors, gentlemen, are my dangerous accusers [. . .]. Moreover, these accusers are numerous, and have been at it a long time [. . .]. What is most absurd in all this is that one cannot even know or mention their names [. . .]. Those who maliciously and slanderously persuaded you [. . .], all those are most difficult to deal with: one cannot bring one of them into court or refute him; one must simply fight with shadows, as it were, in making one's defense, and cross-examine when no one answers. [. . .] Very well then. I must surely defend myself and attempt to uproot from your minds in so short a time the slander that has resided there so long.[5]

The situation is exemplary: Socrates, who fought false opinions and promoted the way to truth based on logos more than anyone else in history, to the point that he became the model and the beacon of this struggle, this same Socrates was powerless against the power of rumours that had been spreading against him for many years, rumours that had no basis whatsoever, yet resulted in the indictment, the trial, the sentence and death. He could easily fight the visible opponents. But, the ones he couldn't fight were the invisible ones who paved the way for the visible ones. It's like fighting shadows, but shadows won the day in the end. The other face of the big Other, based on rumours, hearsay and slander, got the upper hand over its glorious face of logos, truth and epistemology. It turned out that logos was helpless against rumours; the faceless anonymous avalanche won against the best of arguments. This is a vintage case: the other big Other is more powerful than the official and celebrated one; rumours, trivial and unfounded as they are, have the capacity to outwit logos, which seems to be no match for them. And, even the wisest of men (according to the Delphic oracle) had to concede defeat.

There is a Latin adage: *Audacter calumniare, semper aliquid haeret*. 'Slander boldly, something always sticks.' 'Spread rumors audaciously, some of it will always fasten.'[6] However unfounded they are, rumours always leave a stain, and the stain is virtually impossible to erase. There is a cynical calculation: one knows this may not be true and that there is no proof, but one also knows that it will stick, regardless of its falsity. And, there is a moment of enjoyment involved in the easy power this gives one – one can wield the weapon of rumours in quasi-certainty that it will always hit its mark, without sullying one's hands. There is a sort of magical thinking in the functioning of rumours, namely the belief that one can affect people (and things) with mere unfounded words. The words have the capacity to stain what they refer to even if they are completely inaccurate and unjustified; words start functioning as the property of the thing named. Whatever one ascribes to people in rumours will start functioning as their 'spectral'quality and no amount of argument can undo this smear. One is helplessly framed by the rumour, and one is 'always already' in the defensive position. With rumours, the referential function works as if by unconscious magic, affecting things with words by mere naming.

There is a long history which testifies to this indomitable and irresistible power of rumours, a history of bemoaning and lamenting the utter injustice of it. One is innocent. Then, the rumours are spread and one is suddenly in a position of protesting one's innocence in vain. For, even if 'everybody knows' that rumours are false, they have nevertheless managed to demolish and spoil one's innocence, without one doing anything wrong. They frame their victim in such a way that the victim cannot simply step out of this frame. 'Everybody knows', but also everybody secretly believes that there must be something to it. The word has the capacity not only to nominate its referent, but to produce (the spectre of) something that isn't there. The laments and complaints about this are countless in our cultural tradition, so let me briefly give you a few prominent examples marking different eras, like a brief course in the cultural history of rumours, the power of rumours, well, from Socrates to Trump. Leaving aside the beginnings in antiquity (and I guess the beginnings stretch back as far as mankind), I propose three stages which mark modernity.[7]

We cannot but start with Shakespeare. There are a dozen or so places where Shakespeare refers to rumours. But let me briefly mention just two memorable ones. First, most striking and most famous is no doubt a line in *Hamlet*. Hamlet talks to Ophelia after the grand scene of his soliloquy in a most peculiar dialogue where he keeps insulting and humiliating her. Among other things he says the following: 'If thou dost marry, I'll give thee this plague for thy dowry: be thou as chaste as ice, as pure as snow, thou shalt not escape calumny. Get thee to a nunnery, farewell' (3.1.135–9). This is a very harsh line: no amount of chastity and purity will save her; there is no way she could protect herself against calumny and rumours; and this is the only dowry that Hamlet can think of to give her for her possible future marriage. You shall be stained if you stay in this filthy world, stained by calumnious words and rumours, and it appears that the nunnery would then present a safe haven against this ubiquitous stain. But the situation is ambiguous and double-edged: does he really want to protect her innocence from calumnious filth, or isn't it rather that, by the very way of addressing her, he himself produces the calumny, the very stain that he is warning her about, the stain from which she will never recover? Isn't it rather that he, her lover, is the source of calumny he allegedly wants to protect her from? Treating her implicitly like a whore and sending her to a nunnery – how could she ever escape her fate? Nunnery, mentioned five times in the scene, functioned at the time as a euphemistic term for brothel, hence the utter ambiguity. Can one detect the allusive subtext that he may be sending her to the whorehouse where she allegedly belongs? Is she implicitly blamed for being a representative of womanhood such as epitomised by his mother? Isn't there an undertone of his jealousy at the prospect of her possible future marriage? All this – through the insinuating rumour masquerading as the protection against rumours. Virtue cannot escape calumny. But, by giving her this warning as her dowry, Hamlet actually thereby undoes her virtue himself, by being the first source of calumny. It's a poisoned dowry. The scene is violent and cruel, and in line with the figure of Hamlet riven by inner antagonisms coinciding with the emerging antagonisms of the modern age, a man of two minds. The cruelty and ambiguity of the scene seemingly epitomise the troubled modern mind through the odd spyglass of calumny.

Here is another Shakespearean example, of a very different tenor.[8] At the happy ending of *The Comedy of Errors*, his early play, when all the errors are dissipated and there is a general merriment of recognition, the Abbess says the following: 'The duke, my husband, and my children both, / And you the calendars of their nativity, / Go to a gossip's feast, and joy with me; / After so long grief, such felicity!' To which the Duke responds: 'With all my heart, I'll gossip at this feast" (5.1.404–8). Gossip's feast – what can this be? We must take into account the etymology of gossip:

> Old English godsibb 'sponsor, godparent,' from God + sibb 'relative' (see sibling). Extended in Middle English to 'a familiar acquaintance, a friend, neighbor' (*c* 1300), especially to woman friends invited to attend a birth, later to 'anyone engaging in familiar or idle talk' (1560s). Sense extended 1811 to 'trifling talk, groundless rumor.'[9]

So gossip refers to a company of people who are not related by blood; it refers to social networking beyond the immediate family ties. They form a 'spiritual' community. And what else does this spirit consist of, at a minimum, but gossip? Gossip, the tie beyond blood, family and social hierarchies, refers to the horizontal ties, propelled by the prospect of joy, indeed the feast, of gossiping. But, what appears here as partaking in the feast of a joyful community has the nasty tendency of sliding over into the other side of gossip. Alenka Zupančič briefly commented on this in her book on comedy (but only in the Slovene version), suggesting that gossip's feast, laid down by the early Shakespeare at the dawn of modernity, was inevitably heading towards the new horizon of meaning in the time of the postmodern big Other – 'Did the signifiers at that time long past already know the direction in which their new meaning would evolve?'[10] From 'the gossip's feast' to Facebook – and couldn't 'gossip's feast' serve as a fitting description of our agonising current predicament?

My second example, marking the second historic moment, stems from *The Barber of Seville*, 170 years later during the heyday of the Enlightenment.[11] *The Barber of Seville* was originally a comedy written by Beaumarchais (*Le barbier de Séville; ou, la précaution inutile*), first staged in 1775 as a huge success, indeed one of the most successful comedies of the eighteenth century, the paradigmatic enlightenment comedy from the time leading up to the French Revolution. But this original comedy was doubly overshadowed. First, it was overshadowed by Beaumarchais himself, who wrote a sequel to it, the notorious *Le mariage de Figaro*, *Figaro's wedding*, originally staged in 1784. This sequel outdid the first installment by its success and impact. It was one of the most explosive pieces of the time. And, if one is to believe Napoleon's (alleged) opinion, Figaro was already 'revolution in action' and there would have been no French revolution without it (but Napoleon's famous words are actually subject to rumours). Then, second, the original piece was overshadowed by its opera version, *Il barbiere di Sivigla*, written by Gioacchino Rossini in 1816, forty years later, which became one of the most successful and most frequently produced operas of all times.[12] But what interests me here is just one particular scene from this opera. Briefly, Don Bartolo, a lecherous old man who wants to marry his young protégée Rosina, has a formidable adversary in Count Almaviva, who is very much in love with her and pursuing her. So, in this scene, Don Bartolo seeks advice from his friend Don Basilio as to the best means to ruin his rival. And Don Basilio has but one piece of advice to give: calumny. Calumny can destroy anyone. And, in a famous aria, one of the most celebrated bass buffo arias in the classical repertoire, he sings great praise to the formidable force of calumny. (I cannot desist from giving you also the brilliant Italian original.)[13]

Calumny is a little breeze,	La calunnia è un venticello
a gentle zephyr,	un'auretta assai gentile
which insensibly, subtly,	che insensibile sottile
lightly and sweetly,	leggermente dolcemente
commenses to whisper.	incomincia a sussurrar.
Softly softly, here and there,	Pianno pianno terra terra,
sottovoce, sibilant,	sotto voce, sibilando
it goes gliding, it goes rambling.	va scorrrendo, va ronzondo;
Into the ears of the people,	nelle orecchie della gente
it penetrates slyly	s'introduce destramente,
and the head and the brains	e le teste ed i cervelli
it stuns and it swells.	fa stordire e fa gonfiar.
From the mouth re-emerging	Dalla bocca fuori uscendo
the noise grows crescendo,	lo schiamazzo va crescendo:
gathers force little by little,	prende forza a poco a poco,
runs its course from place to place,	scorre già di loco in loco,
seems the thunder of the tempest	sembra il tuono, la tempesta
which from the depths of the forest	che nel sen della foresta,
comes whistling, muttering,	va fischiando, brontolando,
freezing everyone in horror.	e ti fa d'orror gelar.
Finally with crack and crash,	Alla fin trabocca, e scoppia,
it spreads afield, its force redoubled,	si propaga si raddoppia
and produces an explosion	e produce un'esplosione
like the outburst of a cannon,	come un colpo di cannone,
an earthquake, a whirlwind,	un tremuoto, un temporale,
a general uproar,	un tumulto generale
which makes the air resound.	che fa l'aria rimbombar.
And the poor slandered wretch,	E il meschino calunniato
vilified, trampled down,	avvilito, calpestato
sunk beneath the public lash,	sotto il pubblico flagello
by good fortune, falls to death.	per gran sorte va a crepar.

If calumny ever had a eulogy, a panegyric, a song of praise, an anthem, then this is the one. It is a very funny aria, one of the great showpieces and one of the most famous bass arias in operatic history. It starts with a gentle piano, then develops in a snowballing crescendo to an overwhelming fortissimo climax (*'come colpa di canone*, like the outburst of a canon'), and then ends gently, cheerfully and maliciously, enjoying the inevitable downfall of the poor victim, his 'death' – indeed, calumny can kill. The musical directions (pianissimo, piano piano, rinforzando, crescendo, chorus) are actually given already in Beaumarchais's original prose text, which was just waiting to be put to music.

But this is the age of Enlightenment, its glorious height, and the revolution is just around the corner. So, the setting is very different from *Hamlet*. And given the optimism of the age, the power of calumny and rumours fails for once. The great irony of this piece is that, after extolling so persuasively the gigantic powers of calumny, this acclaimed calumny miserably fails in the end. True love wins. The pernicious and malicious stratagems of the depraved *ancien régime* are defeated – also with the help of the skills and intrigues of the shrewd servant Figaro, a self-made man for the new age. Where Socrates failed, there Figaro succeeded; Socrates couldn't fight the slanderous shadows, but Figaro could. The servant can defeat the Master; shrewdness and cleverness can defeat rank. The message is: calumny and rumours can be outwitted. And, no doubt, one can detect in this the ultimate faith in the triumphant powers of reason, which can be the match even for the invincible forces of calumny and gossip (associated with the forces of the *ancien régime*). One big Other wins over the other one; reason wins over its shady double. And, this could even serve as a makeshift definition of the ambition of the Enlightenment. Reason will prevail, even against such an indomitable adversary as rumours.

My third example is predictably less optimistic and brings us to modern times. If we open Kafka's *Trial* on page one and read the first sentence, this is what it says: 'Someone must have been spreading rumors about Josef K., for one morning, without having done anything wrong, he was arrested.'[14] 'Jemand mußte Josef K. verleumdet haben . . .' For *verleumden* the dictionary gives 'to slander, to calumniate, to vilify, to defame, to denigrate, to malign, to backbite'. This is one of the most famous opening sentences in the whole of world literature. So, in the beginning there was – not the Word, logos, as in the Bible, not the act, as with Faust – in the beginning, there was a rumour. Here we have in a paradigmatic form the two versions of the big Other: in the beginning there was logos versus in the beginning there was a rumour, which is, to be sure, also a word, but emphatically not the Word, logos, anything but. Two kinds of word face each other – in the beginning there was a word, but which word? Was it logos or rumour? – One could propose a 'dialectical synthesis' of the two: 'Rumor has it that in the beginning there was the Word.' Actually, if we look closer at this sentence, it already itself has this kind of structure. 'Someone must have been spreading rumors about Josef K.' – the sentence doesn't maintain that there actually were rumours spread; rumours are subject to inference, conjecture, surmise, hypothesis. One could propose the paraphrase: 'Rumour has it that someone has been spreading rumours . . .' There is something like a meta-rumour involved. The sentence, simple as it appears, turns out to be mind-boggling.

Rumours, by definition, have no author, so there is an unspecified 'someone', *jemand*, who can never be brought to light and identified. It starts with a word coming from nowhere, yet overpowering. One could say that the situation of Josef K. is somewhat analogous to that of Socrates: Socrates as well was the victim of rumours spreading anonymously for a long time, eventually resulting in the arrest, the charge and the trial. But, with Socrates, at least we know what the rumours were, or at least what the accusations against him were – corruption of youth, disregard for the deities of the City, etc. The peculiar thing with Josef K. is that we never learn what the allegations were, nor what he was charged with; indeed, he was never even charged and there was actually no trial (apart from one curious interrogation, with the title being a spectacular misnomer). Josef K. never had an opportunity to present his apology before the court, like Socrates. But, their separate fates come together in the end, at the point of execution, Socrates drinking the hemlock and Josef K. being slaughtered with a knife 'like a dog'. They were both killed in the end on the basis of something that started as a mere rumour. Slender cause, disastrous effects (or more aptly, 'sle/ander cause'). There is the stark discrepancy between cause and effect.

With Kafka, we have the darkest version of rumours: they stand at the origin, they stand for the absent origin, they don't need to be specified, spelled out, substantiated in any way. This is just a rumour as such, in its purest form, and all one can say about it is that it was in some way directed against Josef K. This is a rumour without content and without substance, rumour *schlechthin*, rumour *sans phrase*. This is the pure other face of the big Other: it doesn't need any content to work, it just works as an instigating moment, and it instigates a process (indeed *Der Prozess*) which is unstoppable. What was a mere slander, a very slender slander, is magnified by the Law, by the Court, becoming a whirlwind, against which there is no possible defense. How could one defend oneself if there is no charge? So, if the shadowy side of the big Other is overwhelming, then its first side, that of logos, has apparently gone into hiding. The Court is the institution which is supposed to be based on Law, and ultimately on logos, the harbinger of logos in chaotic social turmoil, the impartial big Other to resolve any dispute. Yet the Court is entirely taken hostage by the other side of logos, hostage of rumours. It is a receding entity, massively omnipresent but nowhere to be seen (like the Castle – both the Court and the Castle are 'subject to rumours', emphatically so). The two sides of the big Other have been amalgamated, not by some compromise or middle ground, but by one swallowing the other – the logos part becoming the extension of its shadow, the shadow overshadowing its alleged origin.

There is one more thing: The rumour, the calumny, the slander, *die Verleumdung*, which initiated it all, is mentioned only once, only in the first sentence. The novel never comes back to this, to the supposed origin of the trial. There are no clues whatsoever as to who this someone might have been. Moreover, there is something curious about this famous first sentence, namely the whole novel is written from the perspective of Josef K.; we see things only with his eyes – except for the first sentence.[15] The supposition of someone spreading rumours is not presented as K.'s own assumption; the sentence indicates that this is the suggestion of an objective narrator. This narrator also further affirms that Josef K. has done no wrong – or does he? If we look at the German sentence and its subjunctive mode, the sentence doesn't even maintain this much: 'ohne daß er etwas Böses getan hätte', more accurately rendered as 'without allegedly having done anything wrong'. K.'s innocence as well is subject to rumours. In any case, the objective narrator is there only to throw the first stone and then he disappears. From here on, we see things only through Josef K.'s perspective.

If we were to make a guess as to who it might have been that has been spreading rumours about K., then maybe the most interesting hypothesis would be that there can be no other than K. himself. This is the line of thought proposed by Giorgio Agamben in his paper 'K.'[16] where he also points out that the letter K may well stand for calumny, *kalumnia* in old Latin (spelled with a K), and that slanderous accusation was an abominable crime in Roman law, with the perpetrators being branded with the letter K on their forehead.[17] (Kafka, being himself a lawyer, was very knowledgeable about Roman law.) Thus Josef K. could very well himself figure as the great calumniator, branded as K for bringing the false accusation against himself. We are at one further remove from *Hamlet*: for Hamlet's warning about calumny ultimately hit Ophelia, under the guise of her alleged protection, whereas Josef K. may well be the originator of the calumny, if unwittingly, that hit nobody but himself, ruined him and brought about his end. In matters of calumny, the modern age has advanced since *Hamlet*.

Before coming to the present time, let me give you an example of a very different tenor. Most of the references to rumours fall into the category of laments about their crushing power against which reason, proofs and argument are helpless – to the point that this amounts to a recurring cliché. But this example takes things from a very different angle. It stems from Cervantes's *Novelas ejemplares*, *Exemplary stories*, published in 1613, eight years after the first part of *Don Quixote* and its huge success. The particular story I have in mind is called 'El casamiento engañoso', 'The deceitful wedding', and it contains a very famous part of 'The dialogue of the dogs', one of the showcases of Spanish literature. One of the protagonists of the story is in hospital, delirious, and, during the night, he overhears two old dogs having a conversation.

The two dogs, Scipio and Berganza, want to tell the stories of their lives to each other, in the idleness of the deep night. But, the two dogs are not like the animals from fables who can just talk without any further ado; they are both conscious that the gift of speech they have been given is very special. So, throughout the dialogue they keep reflecting on the nature of speech, its function and its peculiarities, on its mysterious powers and pitfalls. One dog, Berganza, is telling the story of his life to the other, recounting the adventures of his dog's life and the troubles with his past masters, etc. But he cannot quite refrain from engaging in slander, gossip and denigration, so he is constantly admonished and rebuked by the other dog to proceed carefully with this propensity of language. Then, in response, Berganza says the following:

> To be sure, Scipio, one has to be very wise and very circumspect if one wants to sustain two hours' conversation without one's words bordering on gossip. For I find in myself, although I'm an animal, that I've only to open my mouth a few times before the words come rushing to my tongue like flies to wine, and all of them malicious and slanderous. And so I repeat what I've said before: that we inherit our evil words and deeds from our earliest ancestors and we ingest them with our mothers' milk. This is clearly seen in the way a child has barely got his arm out of his swaddling clothes when he raises his fist as if to avenge himself on the person he thinks has offended him. And almost the first word he articulates is to call his nurse or mother a whore.[18]

To follow this suggestion, gossip (rumours, slander, etc.) is not some minor deplorable deviation from what speech usually is and should properly be but, rather, pertains to the basic function of speech and sneaks in already at its origin. There is no speech without gossip, from the moment one opens one's mouth. It usurps the origin, but there is no language without usurpation. There is no function of referring, of neutral description or of objective account, without gossip immediately sneaking in. If we extrapolate this suggestion, then it's rather the opposite of what is taken for granted: the usual function of speech, supposedly communication and information, is already premised on the basic stance of slander and insult. To speak is to speak maliciously, to speak is to gossip and to spread rumours, to speak is to denigrate. Indeed, where would we be if we were only to proffer confirmed information and sound statements? We wouldn't last a minute if we were confined to sentences like 'The cat is on the mat' that analytical philosophy is so fond of. Actually, we might well cease to be human.[19]

In this view, communication and information are but an attempt at taming, domesticating and downplaying what speech originally is, a cover-up of what speech is at its minimal, namely gossip. We don't primarily need language to impart information. We need language in order to gossip, the one thing that animals can't do. Roman Jakobson famously proposed six basic functions of language,[20] but one can't find the function of gossip on the list. I guess the linguists are too polite and too idealistic; they believe in communication and collaboration. Cervantes's dogs have a more realistic or, more precisely, cynical (in line with etymology, cynicism stems from *kynos*, the dog) view of things and are, if one may say so, capable of adopting a more materialist standpoint. On one view of language, people basically like each other, they want to communicate, to cooperate, exchange useful information – communication is ultimately the name of the game. On the other view of language, advocated by the two dogs, people basically hate each other, they use language as a weapon, they can hardly wait to gossip and slander, to throw insults at each other, to hurt and offend. So, who to follow, Jakobson or Berganza?

The dog suggests that the evil words and deeds, malice and slander, come naturally. We ingest them with our mother's milk; they stem from our 'earliest ancestors', *primeros padres*. What undoubtedly lurks at the bottom of this is the idea of the Original Sin, committed by Adam and Eve whose progeny we are. We are all heirs to the Fall, hence the propensity to slander. In the Slovene translation, there is an incredible footnote here helpfully pointing out that dogs, as animals, after all do not stem from Adam and Eve and are thus not prey to the Fall.[21] From this, we can extrapolate a basic thesis, namely that the gift of language, which Cervantes's dogs so heatedly debate, is what constitutes the Fall. Language and Fall coincide. Language is our Original Sin – hence its natural and spontaneous propensity to gossip and calumny. Since it coincides with the Original Sin, it's not surprising that its basic function is to spread unfounded malicious rumours, and that one cannot speak for any length of time without this 'zero function' coming to the surface, sneaking in, however much one tries to keep it at bay. No neutral communication, no neutral information, no language without gossip – ever since the Fall, but the Fall is language itself.

There is no language without gossip, but nowhere more than in Slovenia. In Slovenian, there is this peculiarity that the word for rumours, *govorica* (most often used in plural, *govorice*), is the same as the word for language. So there is this speculative unity (but only in Slovenian?) of the two sides, one word for both, language and rumour.[22] In Slovenia, the gift of speech coincides with the gift of rumours, to the point that one cannot tell them apart. Other languages need metaphors (like voice, shouting, calling, hearing), whereas, in Slovenian, language itself is the metaphor of rumours – or is it the other way round?

One should be careful to distinguish insults and gossip, which are amalgamated in the canine theory in the above quotation. Insults are launched at interlocutors, at the addressees of speech, like the infant calling his nurse or mother a whore. But gossip essentially concerns people who are absent; one cannot gossip about the interlocutor in his/her presence. Gossip is based on the community of speakers at the expense of the others who are absent and can therefore be gossiped about. Gossip is insult at one remove, an insult that has disentangled itself from the immediacy of the speech situation and has been relegated to referring to the absent. Gossipers form a community based on exclusion, and the reference to the third parties, conveniently absent, provides the safety, the protection against exposure, and the glue that ties together the gossiping community. Perhaps the humanising act is the transition of speech from insult to gossip, for it is only in gossip that language acquires the function of founding a community of speakers by the exclusion of some. Insults can still be taken as an extension of hostilities that animals launch at each other. But gossip appears as a specifically human function.

Looking back at what I have been proposing all along, the two sides of the big Other, its official and its shadowy side, the logos side and the rumours side, we can see that, according to the canine theory of language, the shadow comes first, preceding what it is supposed to be the shadow of, or at least sneaking in immediately, co-originary. There is no big Other that wouldn't be contaminated by its shadow from the outset. The official Other comes too late, trying to cover up the shadow that preceded it but never quite managing. It tries to present it as a mere shadow in the first place, a deviation of logos, its unfortunate straying away, a contingent nuisance. It tries to protest its own innocence, putting all blame on its malicious counterpart. The two dogs themselves have a theory of philosophy and its relation to rumours. Says Scipio in warning to Berganza:

> Be careful, Berganza, that this urge to philosophize which you say has come over you, is not a temptation of the devil, for gossip has no subtler veil to soften and conceal its dissolute wickedness than for the gossip-monger to claim that every word he utters contains the wisdom of a philosopher, that speaking ill of people is justifiable reproof, and exposing the defects of our fellows is a worthy and conscientious act.[23]

On this account, philosophy is a higher kind of gossip, gossip in disguise, pretending to be morally elevated and well founded. The temptation of the devil (who, in the first place, lured Adam and Eve out of the garden of Eden) is not merely to give in to gossip and its lures; there is an even greater temptation, the philosophical temptation, namely, to present gossip as philosophical wisdom, as logos itself, that has deceptively cut its umbilical cord with its gossipy origin and can reign free in its seeming universality and ideas. The devil's temptation is to rationalise and legitimise rumours, to purify them, rather than discard them as unworthy. Thus philosophy is the devil's subtlest veil. The problem with logos is its unavowed and disavowed enjoyment in gossip and rumors, its complicity with them, the impossibility to cut itself loose from them. Thus, the two sides of the big Other, seemingly in stark opposition, with no common measure, are actually secretly bound together and tacitly support each other. To make an abrupt aside into Lacanian theory: shouldn't one here be reminded of the Lacanian adage that 'there is no Other of the Other?' And, given the share of enjoyment that gossip provides and by which it is driven, couldn't one say that we have here an inherent link between two Lacanian adages: *ça parle* (it speaks) and *ça jouit et ça ne veut rien savoir* (it enjoys and doesn't want to know)? Isn't gossip precisely the mediator of the two, the 'it' of 'rumour has it?'

There is a very strange psychoanalytic postscript to this story. One of the earliest documents we have about Freud's youthful development is the correspondence with his friend Eduard Silberstein. Silberstein was Freud's classmate in gymnasium and later a colleague at university. Their correspondence started in 1871, when Freud was fifteen, and spanned ten years, until 1881.[24] This was a very close friendship and a very intense exchange, prefiguring Freud's later correspondence and close friendship with Wilhelm Fließ. The two young boys, who were already learning English, French, Latin and Greek at school, decided to learn Spanish by themselves from a primer. They established an Academia Española, with just two members (but with a seal and official documents),[25] and decided to conduct a correspondence in Spanish for practice. This was clumsy Spanish with many mistakes, but they improved as they went along. The textbook they used contained – what else? – a section from 'The Dialogue of Two Dogs'. So, they agreed to cast themselves in the role of the two dogs and signed their letters as Scipio (Freud) and Berganza (Silberstein). This is a youthful correspondence, involving everyday matters, discussing girls and first loves (Freud falling in love with a Gisela Fluss), and duly containing a fair amount of gossip, in line with the spirit of the story. But, gradually it moved to more serious topics of philosophy in their student days – we have there a testimonial of Freud's first engagement with philosophy and, in a famous letter, he recounts his meeting with Franz Brentano, whose lectures he attended and who was his major influence in philosophy. So, what we have here is a glimpse into the pre-psychoanalytic Freud, his very early development – could we say the birth of psychoanalysis out of the spirit of the two dogs? Is this the birth of psychoanalysis out of the spirit of gossip? The inseparability of the linguistic Other (in this case, literally as the grammar and vocabulary of Spanish) from its gossipy double? Is this the slide from mere gossip to philosophy as the higher kind of gossip?

There is an unbelievable postscript to this postscript. Later in life, the two close friends lost contact. Silberstein was a Romanian Jew and, after finishing his studies, he moved back to Romania. He later married and his young wife developed a mental illness. He was very concerned, and eventually decided to send her to Vienna to see Dr Freud, who by then had established his practice and garnered a reputation as a therapist. This was a desperate call for help to his friend from youth, ten years after the end of their correspondence. The young woman eventually got an appointment to see Freud, who had his office on the third floor (this was before he moved to Berggasse). So, walking up to his office, in May 1891, she threw herself out of the window and killed herself, before ever seeing Freud. This was a very gruesome ending to this story, which had such a hilarious beginning.

Where does this leave us? What does this amount to? What does it mean for our present predicament, shall we say the fourth stage in this roughly sketched historical progress (after Shakespeare, Beaumarchais and Kafka)? Now, there is a rumour going around that the big Other doesn't exist. It seems that psychoanalysis may well be at the origin of this rumour. This is what Lacan kept insisting on – the Other lacks, the Other is barred, there is a lack in the Other, ultimately the Other doesn't exist.[26] This is what psychoanalysis is ultimately supposed to teach us. Yet, one has to add, the Other may not exist, but this doesn't prevent it from having consequences and effects. We are bound by them. It's not that the lack of the Other gives us the free hand of 'anything goes'. Maybe the very fact that it is split in two, the Other and its shadow, is already a consequence of this lack. Or, could one say that rumours from the outset figured as the symptom of the Other of logos, inhabiting its lack, flaunting its lack, displaying its deficiency, its leakiness, the shaky nature of its foundations?

One very wrong conclusion to draw from this would be the cynical one: the big Other, the one based on logos and truth, doesn't exist, its reality is actually the spread of rumours, the gossip function of language, from which logos can never detach itself. And, let's admit it, we are all red under the skin, we all enjoy gossip and rumours, even though 'we know very well' (not 'even though' but all the more so since we know very well) that this has no foundation and no truth value. It displays its efficacy and, as opposed to truth, it produces enjoyment (like *Schadenfreude*). What is more, there should be no reason to feel bad, given that this is the basic function of language and sociality anyway. The philosophical logos is but its disguise, vainly pretending to be something else. So, all reality is ultimately the doggy reality (doggy, i.e. quite literally cynical), this is what it boils down to, there is gossip and malice, there is no big Other. This stance seems to be symmetrically opposed to the philosophical one, which traditionally maintained that only the true big Other of logos exists, while the shadowy big Other has no consistency, being just a contingent occasional deviation without a foundation, a mere shadow.

'The big Other doesn't exist' can be taken as a kind of slogan of our present times, or a starting point of their diagnosis, a shorthand for the process of decline that has marked modernity since the times of Figaro and the Enlightenment. If the Enlightenment and its (questionable) victory could be seen as the triumph of the Other of logos and reason, then the subsequent history of modernity could be seen as the long story of its waning, the dwindling of the big Other. The story of modernity could be summed up like this: the Enlightenment has done away with the traditional authorities of patriarchal fathers, priests, and sovereigns, laying down the laws and prescribing the rules and prohibitions, in order to install the proper big Other of reason, science, democracy, etc. But, then the authority of reason and knowledge that subtended the enlightenment itself waned, laws and moral precepts became negotiable, the transcendental guarantees faded. The difference between knowledge and opinion has gradually collapsed through the rise of modern media, which promised to be the formidable instrument of the Enlightenment. Opinions and knowledge, the two entities that philosophy starkly opposed at its birth, have both increasingly become like manifestations of the third entity, rumours, functioning as their middle term, their common ground, their mediator. One could sum up this diagnosis also in this way: we have been rumourised, rumours carry the day. Likewise, the distinction between the public (the traditional domain of the big Other) and the private has been increasingly collapsing, to the point that the Internet, now the main source of public and private information, functions as an indistinct mix of public and private, with rumours as the general backdrop. To be sure, I am extrapolating and simplifying a common account. Throughout the twentieth century, this process has been enhanced and magnified with the avalanche of media in all their shapes and sizes, and their increasing sway, the mediatisation of the world at large. It reached a new level with the Internet as the century was approaching its end, then reached its highpoint (so far) with social media, Facebook, Instagram, forums, blogs, YouTube, Twitter . . . There is nothing like the Internet and social media to spread rumours, instantly and in vast quantities (particularly with robots, one doesn't even need human agency, with statistically targeted audiences and carefully steered secret algorithms). The Internet, in its short history, seems to have rapidly run the course from logos (with the initial utopian promise of instant and massive access to information, unparalleled in history, with the enormously facilitated communication, the prospect of emancipation and democratisation) to the shadowy calumnious other side of the big Other, which seems, yet again, to be winning the day. In a remarkably short time, it accomplished the slide from Jakobson to Berganza, from the optimism of a new instrument of the Enlightenment to the most efficient propagator of rumours and conspiracy plots. It went from logos to logo. It looks like a new avatar of Janus, with the two faces of communication/information versus rumours, the latter again prevailing. With the Internet and the social media (as opposed to newspapers and TV, where there used to be a neat line separating the audience from the public content), we are dealing with the collapse of the lines public/private, actor/spectator, producer/consumer, opinion/knowledge, rumor/information. It can never acquire the proper stamp of the big Other; it rather consists in an infinite multiplicity of small others. But, however big their sum total, they can never amount to the big Other.

This cumulative whirlwind, this escalating vortex (in the press, with the slide from Citizen Kane to Rupert Murdoch, from TV to the Internet and Facebook, each next step adding an additional twist to the previous one), seems to be pointing in one single direction that could be summed up with this simple Lacanian shorthand: 'there is no big Other', 'the big Other doesn't exist', 'the big Other lacks'. Donald Trump, the loudest harbinger of this gospel, seems to be the biggest Lacanian around, for most of his pronouncements can be translated into a very simply adage, namely 'There is no big Other', 'The big Other lacks'.[27] Any inconvenient facts or information are immediately relegated to unsubstantiated rumours; for any facts, there are alternative facts, any lie can be sustained by thousands of other lies. Trump also seems to be the biggest Hegelian around. In a famous quip, when Hegel was criticised that facts contradicted his theory, he allegedly replied: 'Um so schlimmer für die Fakten', 'so much the worse for the facts'. (One can add that this famous adage itself is subject to rumours, since there is no source or proof.) So, now, what are we to do, at least those of us who are Lacanians and Hegelians, having such a formidable highly placed ally, such an enthusiastic supporter, seemingly practising Hegel and Lacan on a daily basis?

In conclusion, there is a final twist. The rumour about the demise of the big Other as the mark of modern times may well be another piece of 'fake news'. There is something wrong with this diagnosis, plausible as it seems; there is something amiss with this summing up of our predicament with the shorthand 'there is no big Other, it has collapsed'. Maybe our predicament is far bigger: not that the big Other has dwindled and lost all authority, but that it is alive and well and has become intractable, perhaps more than ever.[28] This is not the big Other of logos (of the symbolic order, of knowledge, reason, science, etc.), and also not the big Other of the Name of the Father, sovereignty and the patriarchal order. The rumourisation is not simply the victory of the shadowy side of the big Other that has prevailed over its other side and brought about its demise. Neither is it simply the symptom of the absence of the Other, its lack – but, rather, the symptom of its being repressed (or shall one say foreclosed?) and put beyond reach. What we have to deal with is an unfathomable big Other which inhabits our socio-economic order, sustaining its globalised power structure, the very framework of our capitalist universe, so that the more we lament that there is no big Other anymore, the more powerful it seems to become. The more any particular other can be reduced to rumours, the more the big Other rules supreme; the more it's flaunting its lack, the stronger it is. Here is how Alenka Zupančič lucidly put it:

> We are indeed dealing with a rather panicked conservation of the Other as utterly *inactive*, but also as utterly un-compromised, intact, absolute; the symbolic order (which is principally 'our' economic order) appears as a playground within which we are free to change anything we want, to play with different possibilities and endless variations, yet we are utterly powerless in relation to the crucial parameters of this socio-economic structure itself.[29]

Thus the deceptive adage 'there is no big Other' is the furthest away possible from what the Lacanian adage 'the big Other lacks' was after. The more we lament its demise, the stronger it is. And, in order to shatter it, we would need to invent a strategy which would go beyond playing the one side of the big Other against the other. Our task, if we take figures like Lacan and Hegel as our guides, is more difficult than ever.

As to objective fictions, let me propose two theses. First, the big Other is – always – an objective fiction. We, taught by psychoanalysis, know full well that the big Other lacks and is sustained only by its fictitious character gaining objective currency. And, second, there is a shift whereby the adage that the big Other lacks can function perfectly as an objective fiction, covering up the pernicious functioning of the big Other in our times. The more it flaunts its lack, the stronger it is.

Notes

1. Mark the curious structure of this common wording, 'rumour has IT', indicating that rumours may indeed have to do with the Freudian It. I owe this observation to Henrik Jøker Bjerre.
2. *Fama crescit eundo*, as the Latin proverb has it, rumour grows as it goes, it increases while spreading. The proverb stems from Virgil's lines in the *Aeneid* (IV, 174–5).
3. See Octave Mannoni, 'I know well, but all the same . . .', trans. G. M. Goshgarian, in *Perversion and the Social Relation*, ed. Molly Anne Rothenberg, Dennis Foster and Slavoj Žižek (Durham, NC: Duke University Press, 2003), pp. 68–92.
4. See Robert Pfaller, *On the Pleasure Principle in Culture: Illusions without Owners* (London: Verso, 2014).
5. Plato, *Apology*, 18b–19a, trans. G. M. E. Grube, in *Complete Works*, ed. John M. Cooper (Indianapolis: Hackett, 1997), p. 19.

6. The adage in this form stems from Francis Bacon (*De augmentis scientiarum*, 1623), but this is Bacon's paraphrase of a passage from Plutarch.
7. No doubt, there are countless examples of this in different cultures, so any choice is somewhat arbitrary. There is the danger of drawing up a catalogue of picturesque anecdotes that can be infinitely multiplied. But I will try to keep this to a small array of significant cases and to a theoretical red thread.
8. Apart from a handful of quotations which point in the same direction (e.g. 'Backwounding calumny the whitest virtue strikes' (*Measure for Measure*, 3.2.174, etc.), there is the striking instance of personified Rumour that opens Part II of *Henry IV* and which I must leave aside for lack of space.
9. *Online Etymology Dictionary* <https://www.etymonline.com/word/gossip>.
10. Alenka Zupančič, *Poetika, druga knjiga* (Ljubljana: Društvo za teoretsko psihoanalizo, 2004), p. 134.
11. There are many more examples to be considered. And given the present pandemic crisis, I have to mention at least Daniel Defoe's *A Journal of the Plague Year* (1722), where plague itself is preceded and at all times accompanied by the rumours about the plague – to the point that the plague can serve as a metaphor for rumours, or that the rumours are themselves a plague of sorts. However, Defoe's account, written almost sixty years after the event (1665), is not so much based on rumours, but is surprisingly accurate (in many ways better than the contemporary witness accounts), relying on serious research.
12. The sequel, *Figaro's Wedding*, was put to music by Mozart, *Le nozze di Figaro*, in 1786. So, paradoxically, there are two operas competing for the title of the most successful opera of all times, both based on Beaumarchais's Figaro comedies.
13. <www.murashev.com/opera/Il_barbiere_di_Siviglia_libretto_Italian_English>.
14. There are many English versions of this, e.g. 'Someone must have traduced Joseph. K.' (Willa and Edwin Muir); 'Someone must have been telling lies about Joseph K.' (David Wyllie); 'Someone must have slandered Joseph K.' (Breon Mitchell); 'Someone must have been telling tales about Josef K.' (Mike Mitchell); 'Someone must have made a false accusation against Joseph K.' etc. Let me keep 'rumours' for the present purpose. For the German: <www.digbib.org/Franz_Kafka_1883/Der_Prozess>.
15. I owe this observation to Alex García Düttmann.
16. Giorgio Agamben, *Nudities* (Stanford: Stanford University Press, 2011), pp. 20–36.
17. Cf. 'In Penal Colony', Kafka's story based on 'branding' the letter of the law onto the body.
18. Miguel de Cervantes, *Exemplary Stories*, trans. Lesley Lipson (Oxford: Oxford University Press, 2008), p. 263. I owe this reference to Aaron Schuster.
19. The idea that gossip is the basic function of language has its proponents among

serious anthropologists and psychologists. The most famous in this respect is Robin Dunbar, *Grooming, Gossip and the Evolution of Language* (Cambridge, MA: Harvard University Press, 1996). Grooming is a powerful agent in monkey societies for establishing social bonds and hierarchies. So, in this light, language would be 'grooming at a distance': 'Language thus seems ideally suited in various ways to being a cheap and ultra-efficient form of grooming' (p. 79). The use of gossip can be empirically researched:

> About two-thirds of conversation time is devoted to social topics. These include discussions of personal relationships, personal likes and dislikes, personal experiences, the behavior of other people and similar topics. [. . .] one of the most important things gossip allows you to do is to keep track of (and of course influence) other people's reputations as well as your own. Gossip [. . .] is all about the management of reputation. (p. 123)

The name of the game is social networking, establishing the in-groups and out-groups, and particularly 'reputation management', a very apposite concept – one should follow this line from its incipient forms forming the elementary social bonds to its flamboyant cancer-like expanse on Facebook and Twitter.
20. Roman Jakobson, 'Linguistics and Poetics', in *Style in language*, ed. Thomas A. Sebeok (Cambridge, MA: MIT Press, 1960), pp. 350–60.
21. Cervantes, *Zgledne novele*, trans. Anton Debeljak (Ljubljana: Slovenski knjižni zavod, 1951), p. 470.
22. More precisely, *govorica* is the more generic term which encompasses *jezik*, language, and *govor*, speech; it corresponds more or less to *le langage* in French. Slovenian seems to be unique in this respect, although I haven't done any thorough research. Other etymologies (in languages I am familiar with) are based on noise or shouting (English *rumour* from French *rumeur*, both from Latin *rumor*, likewise in other Romance languages), voice (Serbo-Croatian *glasine*), calling (German *Gerücht* from *rufen*, despite the popular etymology from *riechen*, smell; the same in Scandinavian languages, *rykte*, etc.), hearing (Russian *sluhi*). It seems that only in Slovenian language immediately coincides with rumours. The difference is most often drawn by the singular/plural divide (but not necessarily), like language/languages, so that the plural turns the unity of language into a multiplicity of rumours. Perhaps this can go a long way in explaining Slovenian history.
23. Cervantes, *Exemplary Stories*, p. 266.
24. *The letters of Sigmund Freud to Eduard Silberstein*, ed. Walter Boehlich (Cambridge, MA: Harvard University Press, 1990).
25. There is a most curious 'will to organisation', a drive, a push – why would two teenage boys learning Spanish need an organisational framework, with insignia and

all? Do they require the guarantee of the big Other? Is this something like a tiny premonition of the later fate of psychoanalytic associations?

26. Let me just quote one of Lacan's last public statements: '*L'Autre manque. Ça me fait drôle à moi aussi. Je tiens le coup pourtant, ce qui vous épate, mais je ne le fais pas pour cela.* [The Other lacks. I don't feel happy about it myself. Yet, I endure, which fascinates you, but I am not doing it for that reason.]' 'Dissolution', *Ornicar?*, vol. 20–1 (1980), p. 12. One can discern here something like a draft of an ethics of psychoanalysis: to endure in the face of the lack of the Other.

27. More precisely, there are at least three basic variations on this: 'to pretend as if there were no Other; to make oneself the mouthpiece of the Other; to identify the Other with one's charismatic persona'. Aaron Schuster, 'Beyond Satire', in *Sovereignty, Inc.*, ed. William Mazzarella, Eric L. Santner and Aaron Schuster (Chicago: University of Chicago Press, 2020), p. 190.

28. This is, from another perspective, what the Freudian concept of superego aims at – after the demise of paternal authority, the superego is prospering in unheard of and intractable ways. The obscene flipside has become the defining feature.

29. Alenka Zupančič, *Why Psychoanalysis?* (Uppsala: NSU Press, 2008), p. 55.

9 'There is no such thing as the subject that thinks': Wittgenstein and Lacan on Truth and the Subject
Paul M. Livingston

THIS CHAPTER IS part of a larger sequence, one aim of which is to articulate a bit what can still be said, in truth, about the 'being' of a subject – if one can be said to have any – within the scope of a formal approach to truth as having the structure of language.[1] It is a familiar point of the doxography of the twentieth century that such an approach, as taken for example by analytic philosophy after the 'linguistic turn', destabilises the psychological subject of thought and experience by displacing it from any constitutive position, either with respect to objects or meanings. What remains less well-marked is what results from this displacement with respect to the position from which these – objects and meanings – take their place in language and from which can then be articulated the knowledge of them that the structure of a language, as spoken, permits. I shall have recourse to the early Wittgenstein of the *Tractatus*, as well as the late seminars of Lacan, because of the way both locate this positional question in relation to the *totality* of what that structure allows to be articulated as known. I will be interested, especially, in the particular kind of complex organisation that both give to the structural field of what can be said, according to their own methods, and in the correlative kind of unity that this allows to be inferred in the position from which this articulation can be enunciated. This unity, I will argue, can be seen as having its point in the application it permits – an application that might, as I shall suggest, be called 'ethical' – to what speaks in the life of a speaking being, in default of agency, ego and consciousness, and in abeyance of the identity of thinking and being that these presume as their metaphysical guarantee. That the identity of thinking and being is here in abeyance means, as I shall suggest, that if the 'subject' or 'I' can indeed be specified as a 'linguistic' or 'grammatical' fiction, it is nevertheless not a 'subjective' being as opposed to an 'objective' one, but (as one that locates itself in being with respect to what can be articulated in language) comes to have there the sense of the undecidability of their alternative.[2]

I.

In the *Tractatus Logico-Philosophicus* at section 5.5421, appealing to considerations about the logical form of the possible relations between sentences, Wittgenstein draws the striking conclusion of the nonexistence of a psychological subject:

> *5.5421* This shows too that there is no such thing as the soul – the subject, etc. – as it is conceived in the superficial psychology of the present day.
> Indeed a composite soul would no longer be a soul.

Slightly later in the text, at 5.631, Wittgenstein repeats the conclusion, this time appealing to considerations about the form of a complete expression of the truths of the world:

> *5.631* There is no such thing as the subject that thinks or entertains ideas. [*Das denkende, vorstellende, Subjekt gibt es nicht.*]
> If I wrote a book called *The World as I found it*, I should have to include a report on my body, and should have to say which parts were subordinate to my will, and which were not, etc., this being a method of isolating the subject, or rather of showing that in an important sense there is no subject; for it alone could *not* be mentioned in that book.—

What is it that leads Wittgenstein, in both cases, to this striking denial of the existence of a subject capable of entertaining thoughts and ideas, of expressing judgments or of making assertoric claims about the world, of representing the world or its objects or facts in consciousness, or of possessing a knowledge of its circumstances or affairs? In the second case at least, despite the evident boldness of the conclusion, the argument is relatively straightforward. If I were to write a book that would include all and only the *facts* of the world as I can establish them, know them or express them, such a book could include (in addition to any number of banal empirical particularities of the distribution of matter or the happening of events) an indication of one particular body as 'privileged' – so to speak – that is, as under *my* volitional control and as the body whose pains *I* (the author of the book) feel. But such an indication would be no *description*: there would be, and could be, no sentence in the book that *describes* a subject that is privileged in this sense. Nor indeed would it be possible for any sentence in the book to describe the form of this 'privilege' itself:

that is, although the book would indeed include many descriptions of the activities of persons (including those of the author of the book), and although I can say that there is a person that is privileged as the author of *this* book itself, there is nothing in the world that corresponds to what I will feel to be *my* subjectivity, agency or selfhood. Assuming only the identification, maintained throughout the *Tractatus*, between the world as a whole and the totality of what can truly be said ('The world is all that is the case'), the conclusion follows directly: as there is nothing that can be said of the subject or self, and hence nowhere for 'it' to be found, there is in all rigour no 'it' at all.

Since the argument thus turns on language, it might be resisted on these grounds. Could there not, even granting the validity of the argument, still be a subject whose being or essence necessarily identifies it as *beyond* the possibility of linguistic expression – no subject or self *in* the world of facts, but (so to speak) nevertheless one that takes up its distinctive position – that from which it speaks, judges, understands or perceives – outside it? This suggestion is worth taking seriously, and is even motivated by the once-influential line of interpretation of the *Tractatus* that drew on biographical and historical detail to ally what is effectively the *Tractatus*'s own position of enunciative demonstration with that of a 'transcendental' subject in the Kantian mould and its agency with the noumenal will that Schopenhauer treated, in idealist fashion, as constituting the 'inner' nature of the world itself.[3] But the most we can say about such a noumenal subject, given the *Tractatus*'s project of the delimitation of language, is that *nothing* could be said about it. Or, accordingly, *from* its position. To suppose a structural truth about the world to be discernible from its (imagined) perspective would be to assume there to be such an 'outside' perspective from which the structure of the world could be viewed. But the visual metaphor aside, it is clear that there could then be *no* possible articulation in language of any truth of this position itself.[4]

Where, then, do we speak from, if what speaks in us is not locatable anywhere within the being of what-is? Or more broadly and formally: if we cannot, in view of the linguistic argument, place ourselves who speak within the world that we can speak about, what speaks in us when we speak in the first person? If a unitary sense of the being that speaks can be sustained, positionally, only by rejecting any possible characterisation of what holds it in being, then the unitary source or sense of a speaker's intentions or presentations can be sustained only by obscuring a radical and basic incommensurability between this position and that of anything about which anything can, in truth, be said. But the anonymity that necessarily then appears to characterise the position of enunciation whose positive description was frustrated by our insight into the form of the world might also be taken as a positive indication, having, on the level of a formalism indicative of the structure of truth, its own purely positional sense.

As I shall argue, such a formalism is indicative not with respect to 'the' being of the subject but with respect to the structure that ultimately supports the kind of unitary being that a subject is *supposed* to have – and, in this way, indicative of a characteristic desire, what we might express – speaking 'metaphysically' – as the desire to occupy a position outside of the world. In addition, however, this already suffices to indicate the relevant desire as the only one that Wittgenstein ever indicates positively to characterise the motivation of ethics. In the concluding sentences of the 1929 'Lecture on Ethics', Wittgenstein asserts the form of this desire, while at the same time insisting on the complete futility of its pursuit, as that of our inclination to 'run against' the boundaries of language:

> My whole tendency and I believe the tendency of all men who ever tried to write or talk Ethics or Religion was to run against the boundaries of language. This running against the walls of our cage is perfectly, absolutely hopeless. Ethics so far as it springs from the desire to say something about the ultimate meaning of life, the absolute good, the absolute valuable, can be no science. What it says does not add to our knowledge in any sense. But it is a document of a tendency in the human mind which I personally cannot help respecting deeply and I would not for my life ridicule it.[5]

That the sense of ethical desire can yield nothing other than the nonsense that it inevitably produces at the point of its attempt to locate for itself a substantive unity of its being: this is what is shown by the examples that Wittgenstein adduces, in the lecture, in arguing that the attempt to express the 'absolute' position of the sense of the world must fail. This attempt has the form, for example, of the attempt to express in language the 'miracle' that there should be a world at all, and thus to find in the being of language a positive support for what appears miraculous in the fact of its existence. But the attempt to characterise those experiences which should bear witness to such a miracle inevitably fail. For these experiences too are, if anything, expressions of what happens at a particular time and not at others, and as such cannot express – as all expressions of facts cannot – the sense of an absolute. The recognition that the subject has no being beyond the relationship it here seeks with the dissimulated totality of language as a whole, then suffices to expose that the real support of this operation – the only support it can have – lies in just this dissimulation of the flat formal structure of language itself.

II.

Whence, then, what must in fact and all truth stand revealed as the illusion of a subject of thought and experience, the constantly maintained appearance, pursued throughout the career of the life of a speaking subject and at the root of the constitutive fictions that are societies and cultures, communities and values? Here, the argument leading to the conclusion of 5.5421 is more revealing, and can be put in summary form as showing that all of these illusions, along with the underlying illusion of the 'intentional' relationship itself, are *uniformly* the outcome of a falsified mode of unity, in particular of a distinctive mode of the falsification of the unification of sentences in truth. This is the way that this argument, like the first one, turns on the structure of linguistic truth, and more specifically on the formally flat unicity of its expression in sentences. But let us move closer.

The conclusion reached at 5.5421 of the necessary simplicity of a subject and hence the nonexistence of any subject follows from considerations in 5.541 and 5.542 concerning the real form of sentences appearing to report the beliefs, thoughts or assertions of a subject – sentences, that is, such as 'A believes that p is the case' or 'A thinks p' – and from the underlying claim (5.54) that a sentence can only appear significantly within another one if the two are connected by means of a *truth-functional* operation. This claim itself follows from the recognition that truth-functions are interdefinable (and indeed uniformly definable in terms of a single operation, the operation of joint negation or neither-nor) and finally from the overarching claim, at the plenary remark 5, that all propositions are truth-functions of elementary propositions.

More important, for the current argument, than the logical atomism and reductionism implicit in these remarks is the formal requirement they effectively place on the composition of truths and on the forms of combination that can appear within them. There is no form of combination of truths that is not directly compositional, no way for a being of truth to appear that is not comprised by the unitary and wholly decidable law of the formation of more complex sentences from simpler ones.[6] Thereby Wittgenstein excludes any mode of the composition of truths that is, so to speak, itself 'substantive': that is, any mode of the combination of truths that would have, or require, a being of its own. The exclusion is itself licensed by the underlying formal flatness of the world as the totality of facts: for if there were any such substantive function of combination, the fact of its being or its truth would necessarily find expression only in the superlative forms of exceptionality that the logical apparatus of the *Tractatus* would itself discern as nonsensical.[7]

Given this, the argument of 5.5421 follows directly. Sentences containing 'verbs of intentionality' (such as 'believes', 'has the thought that', etc.) and having a propositional complement appear at first to relate a subject to a proposition. But that relationship, if it existed, would be non-truth-functional: there is, for example, in general no way of inferring from the truth value of p to that of 'A believes that p', or conversely. Given, then, that a sentence can appear within another sentence *only* truth-functionally, this cannot be their real form. The appearance that such a sentence asserts a relationship between a subject and a sentence is thus misleading: whatever the actual form of these sentences may be, they cannot be taken to be descriptive of the changing and variable attitudes or intentional acts of a thinking subject. The point is general, bearing against any conception on which the being of a subject of thought, experience, judgment or assertion is understood through its purported relations or capacities to relate to the 'objects' or 'contents' of that thought, experience, judgment or assertion. From this, Wittgenstein accordingly concludes that there is and can be no such thing as the soul or subject that thinks or experiences. Indeed there is no coherent conception of a soul that is 'composite' in the sense that it entertains or holds differing contents over time, while remaining (in whatever sense) self-identical.

Formally speaking and with respect to the structure of truth, the commitment to there being only truth-functional combinations of sentences amounts to the commitment to a general *extensionalism*: all genuinely meaningful sentences can be replaced, without change of truth value, by equivalent sentences whose referring terms refer to the same objects. Since intentional sentences apparently reporting the attitudes of subjects towards propositions fail of this requirement, they are often rejected in the course of an extensionalist accounting for truth and meaning overall. For many projects, such as Quine's, this goes along with an *eliminativist* conclusion on the level of total ontology: intentional 'attitudes' in general, and indeed intentionality itself, are to be eliminated from a scientifically motivated accounting for the totality of what there is.

But Wittgenstein's aim is not a total ontology in this sense, and the positive aspect of what a subject of language might nevertheless be taken to be begins to emerge if we consider rather the implications of what he characterises as the *real* form of the (apparently) intentional sentences. These sentences do not, as we have seen, have the form of asserting a relationship between a subject and another proposition. But, significantly, they are *not* meaningless:

> 5.542 It is clear, however, that 'A believes that p', 'A has the thought p', and 'A says p' are of the form '"p" says p': and this does not involve a correlation of a fact with an object, but rather a correlation of facts by means of the correlation of their objects.

This positive suggestion has a partial basis in the 'picture' theory announced earlier in the *Tractatus*, according to which sentences in general have their meaning in virtue of the structural isomorphism between the names in a sentence and the objects in the state of affairs (whether actual or only possible) for which it stands. This sufficiently ensures that the coordination envisioned here – that of the fact of a sentence as written or spoken with the fact for which it stands – is possible only insofar as the two share a structure, and thereby that the reality of an act of asserting or believing is essentially and fully determined by structure in this sense. In this sense, structure is the reality of meaning in that there is no possible act of asserting, believing, meaning or thinking except that which takes its place, and sense, within the structure of a language. But in addition, it ensures that any such act has, primarily, the structure of a propositional *saying*: no thought that such-and-such, no believing or imagining it, no denying or doubting it either, unless there is a *saying that* such-and-such: unless, that is, there is a structural possibility that it be said at some time by someone. What can be said: that is what can be the case, but it is also what can be thought, believed, asserted or maintained. But what is it that can be said? Evidently, what can be the case: but to say that it is the case is just to say it.[8]

By making all intentional meaning a matter, at basis, of this structural isomorphism between the sentence 'p' and the fact that p, Wittgenstein thus simultaneously suggests that there is no sense outside the formal structure of disquotation: no meaning, that is, except as it exists in the movement from 'p' to p and back again. But it is also here that, formally and decisively, what may be characterised as the structure of truth can be seen to enter the analysis. For it will be noted that the disquotational analysis of meaning, which analyses the meaning of 'p' quite simply, by associating it with the circumstance that p, is formally identical with the criterion that Tarski proposed in 1933 for an extensionally adequate and formally correct theory of truth:

'p' is true if, and only if, p.

As a long series of analyses in the analytic tradition bear out, the schema is fruitful despite its simplicity. In particular, as Tarski discovered, it suffices to demonstrate that any language that includes the resources to describe its own sentences, and that is semantically 'closed' in the sense that it does not require the position of a metalanguage from which to characterise its structure, will be subject to inevitable contradictions that systematically render truth axiomatically indefinable and the truth-conditional sense of its sentences undecidable. Though I cannot go into detail here about the implications of this structural undecidability, it is perhaps to be noted that, given it, Wittgenstein's analysis of the real disquotational form of the (apparently) intentional sentences effectively can then already be seen to show the possibility of a formal anomalousness of the intentional and mental with respect to determinate causation, and that this formally demonstrable anomaly appears, at least, analogous to the antinomical structure that, for Kant, opens the possibility of a subject's freedom.[9] In any case, it thus appears on the level of the semantic analysis of truth for a language as a whole, that the schema which captures it already suffices to demonstrate the inability of such a language to ensure, without contradiction, the closure of its world, and thereby, also, to the formally paradoxical situation of whatever operates or figures the operation of an agent of that attempted closure.[10]

III.

Here, however, I would like to suggest in a more limited way simply that if we take the disquotational schema, as Wittgenstein's analysis suggests, to operate as a general and minimal schema of linguistic presentation as such, this is not without consequences for an analysis of the subject insofar as it can be grounded in truth. The schema is itself, obviously, devoid of subjectivity or agency. As far as the schema *itself* is concerned, it is not a subject, or 'the' subject, that speaks when it is asserted that-*p*. The only evident 'agent' of assertion is, rather, the sentence '*p*', or its sense, itself. If we generalise this over-hastily, we will be tempted to suppose that the schema witnesses something like a *total* capture of truth in essentially anonymous sentences, each of which would be wholly objective: an impersonal annunciation of the whole of being from no position at all. But if we may indeed take the schema as a *general* form of presentation, we may also ask – and this is the key, as I shall argue, to that understanding of the truth of a subject's position that we can hereby reclaim – *how* and *by whom* the schema is applied.

For if, as the schema bears out, every speaking is thus, as such, structured so as to bring the whole structure of a language to bear, it is also to be noted here that there is no such thing as a speaking that does not take place somewhere, or at some time. This recognition corresponds to a formal one which, to anticipate a little, Lacan also makes an axiom of his project: namely, that there is no metalanguage. This means that there is no position from which one can articulate the structure of one's language in a way that does not also bear on the language in which that articulation itself takes place. But the reflexivity of this self-application is also quite evidently central to the *Tractatus*'s project and elucidatory method. Famously, this method culminates, in the penultimate and final remarks of the text, with a decisive recognition that the propositions of the work are, by the light of its own theory, nonsense. The 'ladder' is thus to be kicked away if we are to 'see the world aright', and all that is left, after this, is the silence of proposition 7. In response to this, Russell had imagined, in his introduction to the *Tractatus*, that there might be some escape from the paradoxical character of the book's final conclusions by means of an open hierarchy of distinct languages, each capable of delimiting the previous one but having no final summation into a totality. But it is clear that Wittgenstein does not consider this a real possibility: the theory of the *Tractatus* is indeed to be applied to *all* that can be said, and the self-application of the semantic results to the (seeming) propositions of the work is itself essential to the intended demonstrative outcome, the possibility of seeing the world *as a whole* in a clarified way.

What is said, is said by someone at some time. But what can be said by someone (or, rather, written) can, in principle, capture the *totality* of what is the case. Far from this seeming paradox being an objection to Wittgenstein's analysis, it is in fact the formal core of the *positive* theory of a subject – this time, of what he terms 'metaphysical' subject – that Wittgenstein goes on, immediately after the remark about *The world as I Found it*, to propose.

According to this theory, as stated at 5.641:

> ... there really is a sense in which philosophy can talk about the self in a non-psychological way [*in welchem in der Philosophie nichtpsychologisch vom Ich die Rede sein kann*].
>
> What brings the self [*das Ich*] into philosophy is the fact that 'the world is my world'.
>
> The philosophical self is not the human being, not the human body, or the human soul, with which psychology deals, but rather the metaphysical subject, the limit of the world – not a part of it [*die Grenze – nicht ein Teil – der Welt*].

How can we understand a self – an 'I' or, perhaps, 'ego' – that is nowhere *in* the world but is rather the boundary of it? Evidently, there is no possibility of *directly* attributing to such a 'self' anything like intentionality, agency or thought. Despite this, as Wittgenstein says, there *is* a sense in which the limit-structure of language that becomes evident through the disquotational schema, as applied, effectively reintroduces the position of the speaker, and indeed clarifies its status on a radical formal ground.

How, then, *does* the 'I' that speaks in the position of enunciation enter the totality of structure that it speaks about? Put another way, how does a structure of enunciation that articulates the meaning of presentation in general – that suffices formally for the saying of all that is, or can be, the case – enter, even necessarily, into any possible act of saying, any possible phenomenon of temporally unfolding discourse?

As Wittgenstein says, it enters in the precise sense that 'the world is my world'. At 5.62, he specifies this further: 'The world is *my* world: this is manifest in the fact that the limits of my *language* (of the language which alone I understand) mean [or refer to -P.L] the limits of *my* world.'[11] That is, the sense in which the world is limited for me is the same as the sense in which my language is. But why speak about 'my world' or 'my language' here at all? The decisive consideration, I think, is again this: that there is no such thing as a language that is not spoken and understood; that is, there is no language, as we may now say, that is not someone's. And thus, no truth except that which can be articulated at a point where such a one can find itself. For, at any rate, if Wittgenstein *had* written, instead of 'the limits of my language . . . mean the limits of my world', rather 'the limits of *language* mean the limits of *the* world', he would thereby have invoked, necessarily, something about which the least or first question we should ask would be what possible support it could have, in all sense and truth, for *its* kind of being, if this support is not ultimately to be located in the dynamic reality of discourse – in the life of speaking beings – itself.[12]

But that there is no such thing as language-as-such is not only, then, the evidently necessary source of the articulation of the 'I' that alone bears philosophical relevance to that dynamic reality of human discourse and life, but also equally necessary for the sense of what any kind of structural reflection on it can have for that life. Contrary to the many interpretations that have taken the *Tractatus* (often in supposed distinction to what is purported to be the contrasting 'use-theory' of meaning of the *Investigations*) to be theorising the logical structure of language 'as a whole' from the austere and abstract point of view that its visual metaphor induces, Wittgenstein's method does not ignore this positionally necessary co-articulation of truth and life but rather, and centrally, affirms it. Indeed, as I have suggested, this is what makes it possible for that method to operate, not indeed as the metaphysics of a subject or the repetition of idealism's promise to ground an identity of thinking and being, but rather, in default of any such identity, as the potential dissolution of the problems of a life through the radical clarification of its sense.[13]

IV.

If the preceding analysis is correct, there is no possibility of thought, belief, assertion or judgment except as structured by the linguistic schema of disquotation: that is, except that which is to be located strictly within the movement from '*p*' to *p* or back again. This means that that the privilege and unity of the 'I' that is purported to think, judge or assert has nothing other than a *positional* ground in relation to what its imagination figures, in its own discourse, as the whole of language: the totality of all that can be said. There is no subject but that which takes up its place within the linguistic structure that disquotational truth effectively delimits: no place, in truth, for the subject's saying but that whose place is already laid by this structure itself, and which a speaking being sometimes comes to occupy. This means that a living being's saying, as discourse, is always structured by the dynamics that this structure imposes, or that it holds itself in being as such only as it can effectively situate itself with respect to this total field that defines truth, but this also does not preclude, as we have seen, its entry into this field, at the limits, or the potential transformation of its total relation to it.

I should now like to consider briefly the relationship of this to Lacan's most consistently maintained 'definition' of the subject, as that which 'slides in a chain of signifiers' or that which one signifier presents to another.[14] This will operate as a kind of prolegomenon – and that is all it can be – to considering how the formal structure of truth can be seen, in terms both Lacanian and Wittgensteinian, as articulating the linguistic field that Freud radically opened to our understanding with his discovery of the unconscious and within which psychoanalysis moves. It will also have consequences, as well, for the question of the way in which Wittgenstein's and Lacan's own discourses effectively maintain themselves, and thus for the kinds of illumination, insight or transformation these discourses offer to provide.

In his seminar session of 21 January 1970, Lacan devotes several pages to the *Tractatus*, by way of illuminating what he is there theorising as the discourse of the analyst by contrast with the other three he introduces in seminar XVII (namely those of the master, the university and the hysteric).[15] Lacan emphasises, in particular, the way in which Wittgenstein's project in the *Tractatus* casts light on the way that truth is structurally situated within the 'effects of language taken as such' and how this situation points to the reality of the unconscious as it is uncovered by analysis. Crucial to this uncovering, Lacan emphasises from the start, is that it operate by treating the value of 'truth' *only* as it can appear within the constraints of a propositional logic: that is, as reduced to the inscription of its symbol (the capital letter 'T' (or 'V')). Lacan describes Wittgenstein, along these lines, as:

> ... the author who has given the most forceful formulation to what results from the enterprise of proposing that the only truth there is is inscribed in a proposition, and from articulating that which, in knowledge as such – knowledge being constituted on the basis of propositions – can in all strictness function as truth.[16]

For Lacan, the result of Wittgenstein's exceptionally forceful operation will be to draw out the consequences of what he (Lacan) calls the factitiousness [*le factice*] of language: the consequences, in other words, of Wittgenstein's recognition that, while there is no truth outside of propositions – and therefore no truth outside the single composite proposition expressing the totality of facts that constitute the world as such – the true proposition is already, structurally and as such, on the other hand so constituted as to assert a fact.[17] It follows, as Wittgenstein notes and Lacan underscores, that there is no logically coherent possibility of signifying an act of assertion or judgment, separate from the inscription of the proposition asserted or judged-true itself. Given that 'an assertion declares itself to be the truth', Wittgenstein's operation accordingly allows no sense for the act of assertion – indeed for the 'intentional' act in general – other than that which is already involved in the marking of propositions with the empty inscriptions 'T' or 'F.' But this marking, as applied to the elementary propositions that form, for Wittgenstein, the scaffolding of all truths, is sufficient to determine the world as a whole.

The negative consequences of this, for the placement of anything like a subject in the world, are those we have already seen. There is no place in truth, nowhere within the world whose truth is the totality of true propositions, for a subject *capable* of thinking or experience. There is thus no place for a psychology of the ego, or even for a philosophy of 'the' self. Indeed, as Lacan notes, this suffices to indicate the whole philosophical development of the self-identical and transcendental 'I' as rather an exemplary, and ultimately illusory, product of the *university* discourse, which seeks to harbour truth in the form of the signifier of the master, S_1.[18] The analyst's discourse that Wittgenstein's operation of factitiousness is shown to articulate, by contrast, locates in the position of truth the whole battery of signifiers S_2 – that is, what articulates and defines the totality of possible knowledge as articulated in linguistic signs – thereby to occupy no agency but that of the structurally 'lost' object small-a: for this discourse, for which there is no object but what can be described in propositions, there is only the possibility of articulating propositionally, and subject to the constraints of the logic that imposes itself here, whatever of knowledge can be asserted as truth. And to mark this articulation formally is just to realise, in one's own discourse, the structure of truth insofar as it speaks in what language – *my* language – allows to be said.[19] Absent from the world and without character, the subject that would organise the activities and events of a life leaves behind only the effective possibility of this self-articulation, at the limit of the sense of sentences, of what their structure formally permits.

What can we then say about the way that this absence and this possibility can be said to organise the field of human desire, the point at which we can presumably then locate any 'ethical' significance they might be seen to have? Commenting on the simple 'stupidity' [*betise*] of isolating the factitiousness of the simplest of sentences – the impersonal 'it is day' – Lacan specifies this precisely as the pivot to the detection of what is concealed in the desire of the subject and is thereby exposed by means of the way it puts in relief the topology of the position from which its language speaks:

> The stupid thing, if I may say so, is to isolate the factitiousness of 'It is day.' It is a prodigiously rich piece of stupidity, for it gives rise to a leverage point, very precisely the following one, from which it results that what I have used as a lever-

age point myself, namely that there is no metalanguage, is pushed to its ultimate consequences.

There is no other metalanguage than all the forms of knavery [*toutes les formes de la canaillerie*], if we thereby designate these curious operations derivable from the fact that man's desire is the desire of the Other [*que le désir de l'homme, c'est le désir de l'Autre*]. All acts of bastardry [*Toute canaillerie*] reside in the fact of wishing to be someone's Other, I mean someone's big Other, in which the figures by which his desire will be captivated are drawn.

Thus this Wittgensteinian operation is nothing but an extraordinary parade, the detection of philosophical skullduggery [*qu'une détection de la canaillerie philosophique*].

The only sense is the sense of desire. This is what one can say after having read Wittgenstein. The only truth is the truth of what the aforesaid desire hides about its lack, so as to pretend to make nothing of what it finds [*Il n'y a de sens que du désir. Voilà ce qu'on peut dire après avoir lu Wittgenstein. Il n'y a de vérité que de ce que cache le dit désir de son manque, pour faire mine de rien de ce qu'il trouve.*][20]

In the absence of the metalanguage position or the transcendental subject that would occupy it, Lacan suggests that the only possible way for sense to be constituted is as an effect of desire, in particular the desire which – as all desire is the desire of the Other – operates in particular as that of the constitution of the (big-'O') Other for another. The movement of this desire is then recognisable: it is the imaginary production of the illusion of the totality of language, the truth of the world as a whole. But if sense is constituted by this desire, we can also read in it, diagnostically, the temptation to try to speak outside language, the desire that produces, as Lacan says, all the forms of mischief [*canaillerie*], endemic to our human self-reflection, that the Wittgensteinian critique of language suffices to root out.

By means of the critique, these forms of philosophical mischief are, uniformly, shown to be grounded in an illusion: the illusion of the Other, which does not exist. But at the same time, if Lacan's reading is correct, their production is diagnosed as the outcome of a structure of human motivation that is inherent to the life of the speaking being, insofar as it speaks.

This means that the disillusion that consists in the clarification of the sense of life cannot have the significance that I come to stand outside the world, but only that I locate myself differently with respect to truth: that I no longer can situate myself in relation to a truth that I think to correspond to being as a whole, but that I come to orient myself differently *within* the chain of signifiers that effectively positions me in being. This disorientation has, and can only have, a positional sense with respect to the illusory or contradictory totality of structure by means of which the appearance of the Other subsists. The nonexistence of the Other thus means, in these terms, that I cannot rely on any assumption of the unity of thinking and being, because a position from which this unity could be maintained does not exist. There is thus no synchrony between them: not only does an 'I think' fails to ground an 'I am', but the same can be said of all the forms in which what Lacan calls the 'I-cracy' of the university discourse proposes to ground truth and knowledge in the activities and agency of a subject, be it as transcendental a one as one likes. But that there, where I think, I am not, or at any rate my being cannot be assured: this, as Lacan points out, effectively defines a task, predicated on the movement of the subject's place of enunciation itself.

With this, we can perhaps venture to return, without, of course, seeking to endorse anything like maxims for action or principles of conduct, to what might be said to be 'ethical' dimensions of what the project of the *Tractatus* effectively inscribes in the life of a speaking being. Famously, this project culminates with the enjoined silence of proposition 7, which commentators have seen as having the form of a prohibition that effectively creates the field from which access is thereby barred, whether of (it is supposed) mystical insight into what cannot be said or the nameless surplus of an impossible pure *jouissance*.[21] But rather than following either of these suggestions, I would prefer instead, cleaving to the clear Lacanian instruction according to which 'structure is the real', to return to the main structural suggestion of the 'Lecture on Ethics', about the form of ethical motivation. This is the suggestion according to which it is the *same* desire that moves us, uselessly, to run up against the boundaries of language, or to speak nonsense there where, realising that no propositions can express what we want to mean, we see that we can no longer speak sense.

In Lacanian terms, we can now recognise this desire as the desire to place oneself in the position of someone's Other, and, acknowledging, with Wittgenstein, the *complete* futility of the attempt to fix ethics in propositions, we can nevertheless understand differently the significance of the characteristic activity it involves. The desire that animates this activity is, as we have seen, the desire to speak in the locus of another. But if it cannot yield ethical propositions or truths, nevertheless we can say something more of where this desire moves us: to where the subject tries to establish itself in being. We have seen that 'it' cannot do that: as Wittgenstein says, here any attempt to finally fix the ethical position of the subject in the medium of the absolute can only yield nonsense. But in abeyance of any possible *existing* subject of thought or experience, it remains open to investigate the logico-grammatical form of the attempt, and perhaps to find in this investigation the possibility of a clarification of its sense.

In 'The Freudian Thing', Lacan specifies the task of psychoanalysis by interpreting what he calls Freud's 'last will and testament', the penultimate sentence of lecture 31 of his *New Introductory Lectures*: 'Wo Es war, soll Ich werden.' Resisting the usual translation of 'id' and 'ego', Lacan emphasises that there is nothing in this formulation that suggests, in either case, a definite article. The question is rather that, as Lacan suggests, of a 'locus of being': in that place where the 'Es' – the subject – was, there must I come to be. We saw that, though there is no place for a subject in the world, there is nevertheless a distinctive entry of the 'I' into the world, in the *Tractatus*, one that I can make through the reflective analysis of the position from which I speak. We find our way to this entry, or renew it, when we practise the clarification of our language, the language that is our own and is the form of our life. The suggestion would be that this entry – just that which Wittgenstein treats as the entry of the 'metaphysical subject', propounding from its position a discourse which, like the analyst's discourse as Lacan defines it, removes itself from its field of knowledge in order to let that of its knowledge which appears as truth support its agency – then can operate the radical clarification of life that a critical reflection on language offers it to practise.

Notes

1. See also Paul M. Livingston, *The Politics of Logic: Badiou, Wittgenstein, and the Consequences of Formalism* (New York: Routledge, 2012), especially chapters 2 and 9, and Paul M. Livingston, 'Science, Language, and the "Truth of the Subject": Lacan and Wittgenstein', *Crisis and Critique*, vol. 5, no. 1 (2018), pp. 237–59.
2. Compare Wittgenstein, *Philosophical Investigations* § 307: '"Aren't you nevertheless a behaviorist in disguise? Aren't you nevertheless basically saying that everything except human behavior is a fiction?" – If I speak of a fiction, then it is of a *grammatical* fiction.' (Ludwig Wittgenstein, *Philosophical Investigations*, German text with English translation, trans. G. E. M. Anscombe, P. M. S. Hacker and Joachim Schulte, Revised 4th edn (Oxford: Blackwell, 2009).)
3. See, for example, P. M. S. Hacker, *Insight and Illusion: Wittgenstein on Philosophy and the Metaphysics of Experience* (London: Oxford University Press, 1972), chapters 1 and 3, who sees the 'metaphysical self' of the *Tractatus* as essentially a 'transcendental' self and Wittgenstein's Tractarian position as a whole in terms of a transcendental idealism inherited from Kant and Schopenhauer, later to be rejected in the *Investigations*.
4. Here I follow the so-called 'resolute' interpretation, suggested by Cora Diamond, 'Ethics, Imagination, and the Method of Wittgenstein's *Tractatus*', reprinted in Alice Crary and Rupert Read (eds), *The New Wittgenstein* (London: Routledge, 2001); and James Conant, 'Elucidation and Nonsense in Frege and Early Wittgenstein', reprinted in Alice Crary and Rupert Read (eds), *The New Wittgenstein* (London: Routledge, 2001), among others, which balks at the idea of a thinkable but not sayable 'content' of what can only be shown.

5. Wittgenstein, *Tractatus Logico-Philosophicus*, trans. and ed. D. F. Pears and B. F. McGuinness (London: Routledge & Kegan Paul, 1974) (henceforth: *TLP*), pp. 11–12.
6. Decidable, at any rate, as long as we restrict ourselves to the truth-functional calculus of propositional logic without treating quantification; there are, of course, well-known inadequacies in the *Tractatus*'s account of quantification which I do not go into here. For a helpful treatment, see, however, Diego Marconi, 'Predicate Logic in Wittgenstein's Tractatus', *Logique et Analyse*, vol. 38, no. 152 (1995), pp. 179–90.
7. This is also closely connected to what Wittgenstein calls at 4.0312 his 'fundamental idea': that the signs for the logical truth-functions (AND, OR, IF-THEN and NOT) do not represent anything, and more generally, that there can be no signs that represent the underlying logical structure of facts.
8. For this reason, Wittgenstein says at 4.064 that assertion [*Bejahung*] is not external to propositions and indeed that a proposition asserts, precisely, its sense.
9. The analogy is suggested, though cautiously, by Donald Davidson in 'Mental Events', reprinted in Donald Davidson, *Essays on Actions and Events* (Oxford: Oxford University Press, 2001).
10. For some suggested connections between the formal structure of cosmological antinomies and the structure of Kantian freedom, see, for example, Anonymous, 'Politics, Subjectivity, and Cosmological Antinomy: Kant, Badiou, and Žižek', *Crisis and Critique*, vol. 1, no. 2 (2014), pp. 23–50.
11. As G. E. M. Anscombe (*An Introduction to Wittgenstein's* Tractatus (South Bend, IN: St Augustine's Press, 1971), p. 167), points out, this should be read (according to a correction in Wittgenstein's own hand to a copy of the first edition of the *Tractatus*) as having the sense of 'the only language I understand' rather than 'the language that only I understand': the sense is not then of a radically private language (what is perhaps envisioned critically in the *Philosophical Investigations*' later attack on that idea), but only of the first-personal orientation I must necessarily take toward any language I can understand at all.
12. Here I am indebted to Maria Balaska's perceptive argument (in Maria Balaska, *Wittgenstein and Lacan at the Limit: Meaning and Astonishment* (Palgrave Macmillan, 2019)) for the ethical significance of what, drawing on Lacan and Wittgenstein, she terms the 'merits of being involved in meaning'.
13. Compare, especially, *TLP* 6.52 and 6.521.
14. For example:

    The signifier, as I have said, is characterized by the fact that it represents a subject to another signifier . . . The subject is nothing other than what slides in a chain of signifiers, whether he knows which signifier he is the effect of or not. That effect – the subject – is the intermediary effect between what characterizes a signifier and another signifier, namely the fact that each of them, each of them, is an element. We know of no other basis by which the One may have been introduced into the world if not by the signifier as such, that is, the signifier insofar as we learn to separate it from its meaning effects.

Lacan, *On Feminine Sexuality: The Limits of Love and Knowledge: The Seminar of Jacques Lacan, Book XX, Encore 1972–1973*, trans. with notes Bruce Fink (New York: Norton, 1999), p. 48.

15. 'To say that the true is inseparable from the effects of language, considered as such, is to include the unconscious within them.' Jacques Lacan, *The Seminar of Jacques Lacan, Book XVII: The Other Side of Psychoanalysis*, trans. with notes Russell Grigg (New York: W. W. Norton, 2007), p. 70.

16. Lacan, *Seminar XVII*, p. 66.

17. As in *TLP* 4.21: 'The simplest kind of proposition, an elementary proposition, asserts the existence of a state of affairs.'

18. The transcendental I is what anyone who has stated knowledge in a certain way harbors as truth, the S_1, the I of the master ... The myth of the ideal I, of the I that masters, of the I whereby at least something is identical to itself, namely the speaker, is very precisely what the university discourse is unable to eliminate from the place in which its truth is found. From every academic statement by any philosophy whatsoever, even by a philosophy that strictly speaking could be pointed to as being the most opposed to philosophy, namely, if it were philosophy, Lacan's discourse – the *I-cracy* emerges, irreducibly. (Lacan, *Seminar XVII*, pp. 70–1)

19. Compare Lacan's 'The Freudian Thing', under the heading 'The Thing Speaks for Itself':

> But now the truth in Freud's mouth takes the said bull [*bête*] by the horns: "To you I am the enigma of she who slips away as soon as she appears, you men who try so hard to hide me under the tawdry finery of your proprieties. Still, I admit your embarrassment is sincere, for even when you take it upon yourselves to become my heralds, you acquire no greater worth by wearing my colors than your own clothes, which are like you, phantoms that you are. Where am I going, having passed into you? And where was I prior to that? Will I perhaps tell you someday? But so that you will find me where I am, I will teach you by what sign you can recognise me. Men, listen, I am telling you the secret. I, truth, speak.

Jacques Lacan, *Écrits: The First Complete Edition in English*, trans. Bruce Fink in collaboration with Héloïse Fink and Russell Grigg (New York: W. W. Norton, 2006), p. 340.
20. Translation slightly modified from the translation by Grigg; in addition to the French original, I have also consulted Gallagher's translation.
21. Compare, for example, Žižek in *The Sublime Object of Ideology* (London: Verso, 2008), pp. 184–5:

> If we define the Real as such a paradoxical, chimerical entity which, although it does not exist, has a series of properties and can produce a series of effects, it becomes clear that the Real par excellence is *jouissance*: *jouissance* does not exist, it is impossible, but it produces a number of traumatic effects. This paradoxical nature of *jouissance* also offers us a clue to explaining the fundamental paradox which unfailingly attests the presence of the Real: the fact of the prohibition of something which is already in itself impossible. The elementary model is, of course, the prohibition of incest; but there are many other examples – let us cite only the usual conservative attitude toward child sexuality: it does not exist, children are innocent beings, that is why we must control them strictly and fight child sexuality – not to mention the obvious fact that the most famous phrase of analytic philosophy – the last proposition of the *Tractatus* – implies the same paradox: 'Whereof one cannot speak, thereof one must be silent.'

10　The Awful Truth:
　　　Games and Their Relation to the Unconscious
　　　Amanda Holmes

THE ESSENTIAL RELATIONSHIP between truth and chance is brilliantly compressed in a line from Leo McCarey's screwball comedy *The Awful Truth* (1937). The line is delivered by the character Lucy Warrener in response to her suspicious husband Jerry. Just as Jerry has come home to find Lucy in some compromising circumstances she explains, 'I've just been unlucky, that's all. You've come home and caught me in a truth and it seems there's nothing less logical than the truth.' The relation between luck and truth is mediated by a certain logical error, by the failure of logic to maintain its place in truth.

The logical error that Lucy invokes is the same we find in the very first year of Jacques Lacan's Seminar when he says that 'error is the habitual incarnation of truth'[1] and that truth's nature 'is to propagate itself in the form of error'.[2] The point we find in this inaugural year of Lacan's teaching sets up the dimension of truth as it is revealed by psychoanalysis: one that problematises any simple opposition between truth and error or between a truth and a lie. Psychoanalysis shows how truth erupts within the very order of error and the lie, in misrecognition and negation.

The problems entailed in the simple opposition between a truth and a lie are evinced in the 'awful' truth between Lucy and Jerry in McCarey's film. The truth trap in which Lucy is caught when she offers up this riddle is set up by the fact that Jerry has just come home expecting to tell a few little lies of his own. There is evidence that Jerry had been preparing several rather elaborate covers for his illicit affair. When he comes home and is greeted with Lucy's lack of suspicion, Jerry himself is left to take up the jealous distrust he had been expecting to encounter. Jerry thus greets Lucy by receiving his own message in an inverted form and any truth that Lucy tells can only be received as a lie.

The solution to being 'caught in a truth', this comedy of re-marriage goes on to show, is to play a little game with it. In order to get out of the truth trap one must know how to lie truthfully. There is a certain relation between being 'caught in a truth' and the famous liar's paradox, in which the phrase 'I am a liar' offers a logical problem for considering the validity of its assertion; for if I really am a liar, how can I truthfully say so? Lacan famously provided a solution to the liar's paradox by identifying the split between the subject of the statement (*sujet de l'énoncé*) and the subject of enunciation (*sujet de l'énonciation*), pointing out that 'the *I* of the enunciation is not the same as the *I* of the statement [and so . . .] from the point at which I state, it is quite possible for me to formulate in a valid way that the *I* – the *I* who, at that moment, formulates the statement is lying.'[3] The dilemma Lucy Warrener finds herself in presents a similar problem precisely because the truth presents itself as a lie. The split between the subject of enunciation and the subject of the statement is reduplicated in the structure of truth in the marriage of Jerry and Lucy. Lucy is actually caught not in a lie, but in a truth just like the liar in the liar's paradox who can only tell the truth by saying he is lying. In both cases of the liar's paradox and being 'caught in a truth', we find a trap set up by the ill fit between logic and truth. To be caught in a truth is to find oneself at the limits of the logical.

To be 'caught in a truth' reveals that the dimension of truth is itself predicated upon a lie. As Lacan puts it, 'In the first instance, it is as establishing itself in, and even by, a certain lie, that we see set up the dimension of truth, in which respect it is not, strictly speaking shaken, since the lie as such is itself posited in this dimension of truth.'[4] That is to say that the world of truth is organised according to the structure of the signifier, a structure which we have to accept as setting up also the essential possibility of the lie. This is the lie that sets up the order of the Symbolic. The illogic that sets up the trap of truth is neither a mistake, nor a flaw in truth, the illogic is rather that which grounds truth. This same logical error is truth's cornerstone. In short, we find that a foundational element of truth is nothing other than a certain lie.

The constellation of truth, luck, illogic and the lie that characterises the trap in which Lucy Warrener is caught brings us right to the heart of psychoanalysis and to the question of truth's peculiar objectivity, an objectivity which is not reducible to being either the simple correlate of subjectivity, nor to the cold, hard facts of realist assertions about the objective world. The situation in which being unlucky leads to being 'caught in a truth' bears a certain resemblance to the psychoanalytic scenario in which truth is closely tied to chance. In psychoanalysis, Lacan explains, 'We try to get the subject to make available to us, without any intention, his *thoughts*, as we say, his comments, his discourse, in other words, that he should intentionally get as close as possible to chance.'[5] Psychoanalysis plays with the constitutive intermingling of truth and chance. If psychoanalysis is a praxis in which the seemingly contingent aspects of free association reveal the determinations of unconscious structures, psychoanalysis is itself the practice of letting oneself get 'caught in a truth', not so much in order to break free of it but in order to identify the structures in which we are always already snared. The place of truth in psychoanalysis is grounded then not in necessity and universality but in chance, in the chance of the symptom. 'Because the symptom is in itself, through and through, signification, that is to say, truth, truth taking shape.'[6] Psychoanalysis thus grounds truth in a certain kind of chance and sets up the rules in which we can play a little game with this truth. It is this imbrication of the psychoanalytic notions of truth and chance that compels the present study on the important place of games in psychoanalytic theory.

One can easily find several important references to various games in Lacan's writing and throughout his Seminar. Lacan's allusion to the game of bridge, for example, provides an imaginary support for setting up the L Schema and the place of the 'dummy' in bridge provides a model for what Lacan calls the subject at the place of 'the foreclosed position that enters into the game of signifiers'.[7] Elsewhere, it is the game of odds and evens which opens Lacan's famous reading of Edgar Allen Poe's story *The Purloined Letter*. Finally, we find at the heart of Lacan's intervention into the temporal assumptions of logical structures the strange logic game in a particular version of the prisoner's dilemma in his essay on 'Logical Time and the Assertion of Anticipated Certainty'. In short, Lacan makes frequent use of games in order to develop his thinking and the game is a persistent metaphor for the Symbolic Order and the play of signifiers. But we need go no further than Freud's seminal discussion of the *fort/da* game in *Beyond the Pleasure Principle* to see that the game as such has always been an important site of study for psychoanalytic theory. As part of the everyday material with which psychoanalysis works, games exhibit something about the nexus of pleasure, repetition, identification, displacement and revenge.

Neither Freud nor Lacan explicitly thematised the concept of the game *qua* game; that is, we do not get a theory of games from Freud in the same way that we get a theory of jokes in his text on *Jokes and Their Relation to the Unconscious*. The game nevertheless is there, not so hidden and definitely in plain sight throughout some of the most important conceptual developments of psychoanalysis. We find it at one of the origin stories of symbolic formation in the *fort/da* game; we find it at the heart of Lacan's first major intervention regarding the temporal structuration of logic; and finally we find it in Lacan's critique of the notion of inter-subjectivity in his analysis of the game of odd or even. The wager of this *paper* is that if we look for the conceptual unity among these various examples of games, we find a concept of the game that underlies the thought of both Freud and Lacan. This concept of the game, I argue, is fundamental to Lacan's initial formulation of truth and it reveals the essential relation between truth and chance, at least as it is played out in the early formulations of truth in Lacan's thinking up until the mid 1950s.[8] Just as jokes reveal something essential about the structure of the unconscious, as Freud makes clear in his book on the topic, games reveal something essential about the structure of truth in psychoanalysis.

Before turning to the instances of the game in psychoanalytic theory, it will be useful to say a few things about games in a more general sense. To borrow and revise a set of theses on games from Roger Caillois's scrupulous text *Man, Play and Games*, we can identify five elements that define the game as we will be conceiving it:

- First of all, the element of pleasure is inextricable from the game. The *raison d'être* of games is pleasure; they have 'a joyful quality as diversions'.[9]
- Second, games entail the carving out of a place in reality that is separate from reality. The game has a delimited space and time that sets it apart from the reality of so-called 'real life'.
- Third, in this separate realm of the game, the contingent elements of reality are crystallised. This contingency is precisely the element of chance as it is played out in the game. Depending on the game, there will be an uncertainty about who will win the game, for example, or how the cards will fall. Who wins the game will be determined by 'a combination of chance, strategy, and the players' own initiatives'.[10] It is the play of these contingent elements that will distinguish any given round of the game from any other.
- Fourth, a game is not productive. It creates 'neither goods, nor wealth, nor new elements of any kind; and, except for the exchange of property among the players, [the game ends with the same, larger structural] situation identical to that prevailing at the beginning of the game.'[11]
- Fifth and finally, the game offers a distilled form of relation that is guided by certain rules but the status of these rules is distinct from that of the law. These rules are either an extension of the law or a suspension of the law. The game is thus set apart from the law in an important sense.

These five defining characteristics of games reveal why the game is such fruitful ground for psychoanalysis because it sets up the place of the game as the site of playing with the boundaries of the law at the behest of the pleasure principle. Moreover, we can begin to see the relationship between the concept of the game and the concept of truth as we think through the idea that the game distils a larger structure from reality or so-called 'real life' into a simplified form that exposes some element of the truth of that larger reality. What the game gives us, in short and to paraphrase Lacan, is truth 'carried out under the innocent conditions of fiction'.[12] The game offers up a form of fiction in reality whose crucial structures are determined by none other than the pleasure principle. Games thus reveal the way in which the pleasure principle responds to the reality principle, in Freudian terms. Transferred into the realm of Lacan's thinking, the game shows a dimension of play at the order of the Imaginary, which reveals the determinations of a Symbolic order, and it is a certain slippage between the play and the game which exposes the dimension of the Real.

In order to develop a unified concept of the game in psychoanalysis let us now take up three examples, two from Lacan and one from Freud. It is useful to note that each of these games represents a different kind of game. We will address the game of even and odd, which is a guessing game, what Lacan calls a game of chance; we will then turn to the game in the prisoner's dilemma, which is a logic game; and finally we will turn to the game of *fort/da*, which is a game of representation and recognition. Let us now take up each game briefly and in order.

Odd or Even?

Before Lacan's seminar on *The Purloined Letter* became *the* 'Seminar on *The Purloined Letter*', Lacan turned to Poe's short story in the second year of his Seminar for an analysis of a game that he said illustrated the limits of the notion of 'inter-subjectivity'. 'Inter-subjectivity' is a concept which names an initial formulation of the imaginary structures of the subject in the *between* of subjects. This game of odd or even shows us how to think beyond inter-subjectivity, beyond the Imaginary structuration of the subject's constitutive relation between itself and an other, precisely because the pleasure of this game is derived from playing with the illusion that is set up by this inter-subjective structure. The pleasure of this game is derived from playing at the limits of the Imaginary.

The game of odd or even is a sort of guessing game with two players; one player takes a random number of marbles in hand and the other guesses whether the number of marbles is odd or even. If the guess is correct, the guesser gets a marble; if incorrect, he loses one. While this game may not seem particularly exciting – it does not even have the allure of the bluff that we find in poker or the complexity of the 'tell' that we find in a game of bridge – the game of odd or even becomes interesting when we begin to conceive of the strategy at play in the principle of guessing. Something important reveals itself when we inquire into the principles behind what Lacan himself calls this 'game of chance'.[13] Lacan cites the following description of the strategy behind the game from Poe's story, out of the mouth of the great Dupin himself. Dupin tells the story of a schoolboy who was very good at this game of odd or even:

> *Of course he had some principle of guessing; and this lay in mere observation and admeasurement of the astuteness of his opponents. For example, an arrant simpleton is*

his opponent, and, holding up his closed hand, asks, 'Are they even or odd?' Our schoolboy replies, 'Odd,' and loses; but upon the second trial he wins, for he then says to himself, 'The simpleton had them even upon the first trial, and his amount of cunning is just sufficient to make him have them odd upon the second; I will therefore guess odd;' –he guesses odd, and wins. Now, with a simpleton a degree above the first, he would have reasoned thus: 'This fellow finds that in the first instance I guessed odd, and, in the second, he will propose to himself upon the first impulse, a simple variation from even to odd, as did the first simpleton; but then a second thought will suggest that this is too simple a variation, and finally he will decide upon putting it even as before. I will therefore guess even;' he guesses even, and wins. Now this mode of reasoning in the schoolboy, whom his fellows termed 'lucky' – what, in its last analysis, is it?[14]

Dupin's interlocutor, the narrator of the story, then responds '*It is merely* [. . .] *an identification of the reasoner's intellect with that of his opponent.*'[15] With the diagnosis of the role of identification in the game, we can immediately see how the strategy behind this so-called game of 'chance' is relevant to Lacan's inquisition into what is *beyond* the principle of inter-subjectivity. 'At first glance, it is a matter of simple psychological penetration, a kind of ego-miming,'[16] as Lacan puts it. On the face of it, this game seems to illustrate the Imaginary relation of subjectivity as constituted by other subjects, 'That the subject should think the other to be similar [*semblable*] to himself, and that he reasons as he thinks the other must reason.'[17] We can locate this game easily at the level of the Imaginary; the game gives us the perfect image of a mirrored relation between two players, each considering what the other might be thinking, as the paradigm of what we might at first be satisfied to call 'inter-subjectivity,' identifying a set of rules and patterns of behaviour that are co-determined according to a set of principles of identification between the two players. But what Lacan goes on to show is that the game of odd or even is marked not by this inter-subjectivity, not by the uncanny ability of the mythological schoolboy to correctly measure the astuteness of his opponent and mirror it, but by something that is *beyond* the inter-subjective relation. As Lacan says 'the heart of the matter lies in a completely different register from that of imaginary inter-subjectivity.'[18] It lies instead in the register of the Symbolic.

At this point, Lacan introduces the idea that one might play this game of even and odd with a machine.[19] If one plays such a game with a machine, the inter-subjective dimension is not lost but gains a new status: instead of an Imaginary relation between two opponents, what gets emphasised through the patterns of repetition in each round of the game is the Symbolic dimension. Lacan turns to theories of probability in order to show the more complex networks of signifiers that begin to develop as the game goes on. Instead of being a simple back and forth repetition of a game that takes place in the Imaginary relation of identification between the players, patterns begin to emerge as a series is formed, probabilistic structures are created that allow for a Symbolic determination. So, for example, Lacan explains that there is a 50/50 chance that one can guess correctly, or for that matter incorrectly, in the first round of the game. But as soon as we are on to the second round, the chances are only 25 per cent that one will have the same result, win or lose, as one had on the first round. The chances drop to 12.5 per cent on the third round, decreasing each time as the game goes on. As sets are formed in time and as a sequence develops, the probabilities for guessing become more determinate within a Symbolic matrix. It is the sequential ordering of the game's rounds that develop this Symbolic matrix around how the game will be played out and that introduce certain probabilities.[20] Further, when one begins to order the sequences themselves, various matrices of signification begin to emerge from the simple binary of even and odd.

Things get even more interesting, however, when we realise that, in spite of the Symbolic formations that emerge in the series, there is another element of the play: each time the game of odd or even is played there remains a 50/50 chance that one will make the right guess, even though there will also be another level of Symbolic determination at the level of probabilistic structuration. Lacan explains that this difference exposes the distinction between the Symbolic and the Real. At the order of the Real, there is a 50/50 chance either way, each time a round is played, that one will guess correctly.[21]

Lacan returns to the discussion of this game at several points throughout his Seminar and again in his essay on *The Purloined Letter*. The analysis he offers is much more complex than we need to establish here as Lacan goes on to explain the emergence of a diachronic series of Symbolic organisations out of this simple binary opposition between even and odd (+/−). For the purposes of this chapter, what is of interest is that the game of odd or even exposes that truth is itself the split between the orders of the Symbolic and the Real and that this split has something to do with the location of chance and the limits of the Imaginary. At first, it looks like the game is located at the level of the Imaginary identification between the players but it turns out that there is instead happening, a play of sorts, between the Symbolic and the Real. The truth of the game emerges as split among these orders. It is not that these are two different truths, a truth of the Real and a truth of the Symbolic; rather there is a truth that is itself set up precisely between the chance of the Real and the determinations within the Symbolic Order. The dimension of truth is rent asunder by the fact that on one level, if I win the game of even or odd three times in a row, the chances that I will win a fourth time are only 6.25 per cent and yet, taken as a single round, I still have a 50 per cent chance either way. 'From the point of view of the Real, on each occasion there are as many chances of winning as losing. The very notion of probability and chance presupposes the introduction of a symbol into the real. It's a symbol you're addressing, and your chances bear only on the symbol.'[22] So, there are multiple levels of chance at play in this game and it is the way in which the determinations of chance do not match up between the orders of the Symbolic and the Real that opens onto the domain of the truth of the game. It might be tempting to understand this point as suggesting that the Real is simply the sheer contingency of the guess, 'odd or even', which then shapes the Symbolic matrix as the sequence builds, but that is not quite it. The point is rather that the very structure of the sequence itself, at the level of the Symbolic which lies at the level of significations derived out of probability, is always retroactively shifting in its structuration by the Real. Truth in this game shows that 'nothing happens by chance'[23] but that does not mean that it is simply a proof of determinism. Rather, it is proof of the distinction introduced by the placing of chance between the Symbolic and the Real.

The Prisoner's Dilemma

We now turn from a game of chance, which illustrated the place of probability in thinking about the formation of Symbolic structures out of the development of a seemingly random series, to a logic game. This logic game, on the other hand, shows the limits of Symbolic formations. In his essay 'Logical Time and the Assertion of Anticipated Certainty' Lacan develops an account of the following 'game':

A prison warden summons three prisoners and announces to them the following:

For reasons that he does not disclose, he is able to free one of the prisoners. In order to decide which, he has devised a little game.

There are three prisoners and the warden has five disks differing only in colour: three white and two black. Without telling the prisoners which colour disk, he will fasten one to each of the prisoners between the shoulders. The disks are outside of their direct visual field and indirect ways of getting a look at the disk are excluded by the absence of any means by which the prisoners can see their own reflection. The prisoners are left alone and can see each other's disks as they are fastened on their backs. They are told to consider each other and their respective disks, without being allowed, of course, to communicate among themselves what they see. The first to be able to deduce the colour of his own disk will be the one to benefit from the discharging measure of the warden. But his conclusion must be founded upon logical and not simply probabilistic grounds. Keeping this in mind, it is agreed that as soon as one of the prisoners is ready to formulate such a conclusion, he will pass through the door to the warden's office so that he may be judged individually on the basis of his response.

Once the rules of the game are clear, each prisoner is adorned with a white disk; no use is made of the black disks, of which there were, let us recall, only two.

How can the subjects solve the problem?[24]

Before we turn to Lacan's solution to this game, it is interesting to note that this game does not quite fit with many of the criteria for the elements of the game as defined earlier. We said that the purpose of a game is pleasure and that games have a joyful quality as diversions. Unless we count that the game might be enjoyable for the warden who devises it, it is difficult to see this as a game of pleasure and enjoyment. Second, we said that the game does not produce anything. Here, there is a certain ambiguity because the game does in fact aim to produce a decision about the freedom of one of the three prisoners. Finally, we said that the game entails a suspension of the law in some sense. The game in the prisoner's dilemma depends upon the players already being excised from the law precisely in their role as prisoners. So, this fits with the idea of the suspension of a law but only insofar as the prisoners are outside the law and because of this they are subjected to the rules of the game as determined by the whim of the warden. We might formulate, however, that the real game in Lacan's account of the prisoner's dilemma is not the one that the prisoners themselves play in this little story but rather the game that one enters into upon having heard the puzzle. The game is what the fiction makes possible for those who hear it. This is then a kind of game within a game, not unlike the dream within a dream, which 'points to a closer relation to the real'.[25]

So, what to make of this game within a game? If what we learned about the relation between truth and chance in the game of odd or even was that truth is that which is beyond the Imaginary inter-subjective relation, that it is predicated on the place of chance between the Symbolic and the Real, what the game of the prisoner's dilemma illustrates is something beyond the Symbolic. The game of the prisoner's dilemma plays instead with the parry between the Imaginary and the Real. This parry is revealed in the solution Lacan offers. He develops what he calls the perfect solution to the problem, which entails that each of the players arrive at the same conclusion, at the same time. Each player would be able to reason the following:

> I am a white, and here is how I know it. Since my companions were whites. I thought that, had I been a black, each of them would have been able to infer the following: 'If I too were a black, the other would have necessarily realised straight away that he was a white and would have left immediately; therefore I am not a

black.' And both would have left together, convinced they were whites. As they did nothing of the kind, I must be a white like them. At that, I made for the door to make my conclusion known. All three thus exited simultaneously, armed with the same reasons for concluding.[26]

Lacan's perfect solution takes into account that each player will begin to solve the puzzle by considering not simply what each of the other prisoners is thinking but what each of the prisoners think another is thinking in relation to a third. However, the emphasis here is not on the Symbolic matrix that is created in what each of the prisoners see, rather the inaction of the other prisoners gives the clue which is the final piece of the puzzle. It is what Lacan calls 'suspended motion'. Each of the prisoners is able to solve the problem because of the element of time. Looking around at one another and realising that the other prisoners too are not able to solve the puzzle with which they are confronted very quickly, it is this identification with one another through the third that sets up an Imaginary relation which allows for the solution to emerge.

Lacan calls this solution a sophism because the solution incorporates something beyond the logical process used to solve it. Namely, it incorporates the suspended movements of the prisoners, it incorporates the element of time. The forms of classical logic, Lacan tells us 'never give us anything which cannot already *be seen all at once.*'[27] And in this solution, the essential piece of the puzzle is the hesitation of the prisoners, a hesitation which signals the piece of information that each requires to solve it. While classic logic games would entail a reasoning that is fundamentally spatial, this game:

> In complete opposition to this, [shows] the coming into play as signifiers of the phenomena here contested makes the temporal, not spatial, structure of the logical process prevail. What the suspended motions disclose is not what the subjects see, but rather what they have found out positively about what they do not see: the appearance of black discs.[28]

Lacan goes on to explain that the truth of the sophism reveals itself precisely in this relation of time, in the temporalised reference of oneself to another. And here is where the truth of the game comes in. 'The truth of the sophism thus only comes to be verified through its *presumption*, so to speak, in the assertion it constitutes. Its truth thus turns out to depend upon a tendency that aims at the truth.'[29] That is, truth here is shown to be something that depends upon a certain conjecture, a presumption depends on a confirmation. But truth as it is usually conceived is of course the opposite of what we might think of as 'mere' conjecture. Lacan goes on to explain that this is 'a notion that would be a logical paradox were it not reducible to the temporal tension that determines the moment of concluding'.[30] That is, truth's contingency is the dimension of time and this is what the game of the prisoner's dilemma shows us.

The game within a game that we find in Lacan's version of the prisoner's dilemma plays with that which goes beyond the Symbolic that is established in the game. Lacan's solution plays at the limits of the Symbolic structures determined within the game. What shows up only as absence (time and the black disks) offers clues to the logical, rather than probabilistic, relation between chance and truth. The play here is one between the Imaginary and the Real insofar as the solution is formed on the basis of several absences: the absence of black disks and the hesitation of the other prisoners. It is a play between the Imaginary identifications of the prisoners with one another that allows for this dimension of absence to emerge in its signifying function.

Fort! Da!

We have now come to our final game: the game of *fort/da*. We have so far seen that the game of odd or even showed a play between the Symbolic and the Real, showing what is beyond the Imaginary. Then the prisoner's dilemma offered a play between the Imaginary and the Real, showing what is beyond the Symbolic. Now, turning to the game of *fort/da*, we find a play between the Imaginary and the Symbolic.

In Freud's *Beyond the Pleasure Principle*, the *fort/da* game proves fruitful ground for an investigation into pleasure and what is beyond it; it evinces the phenomenon of the repetition compulsion and offers an example of the tendency to turn unpleasant, passive experiences into active ones through the mechanism of the game. As is well known and often repeated, this story is one from Freud's own family: it was a game played by his grandson. Freud discovers that the boy doesn't cry or protest when his mother leaves him, instead he plays the *fort/da* game, a game that the child himself seems to have invented in which he throws a small wooden reel over a cot and says the word '*fort*' or 'gone' and then, using the string to which the reel is attached, pulls it back into view and says '*da*' or 'there'. It is a game of disappearance and return, a sort of object oriented peek-a-boo, in which Freud finds evidence of the 'great cultural achievement'[31] of sublimation in an instinctual renunciation of the satisfaction of being with the mother that finds its substitute in the game.

Freud turns to this game because it represents a certain kind of child's play that poses a problem for too quick an assumption of the pleasure principle. He points out that many children's games entail the repetition of unpleasant events. The *fort/da* game is an example of this as it repeats the presumably unpleasant event of the mother's departure. 'How', Freud asks, 'does [the] repetition of [a] distressing experience as a game fit in with the pleasure principle?'[32] In other words, if a game is fundamentally something that is motivated by pleasure, how is it that the game can seem to aim at something beyond pleasure?

The first answer that Freud gives is that the unpleasant experience is a passive one and by repeating this event in the form of a game, the child becomes an active participant in the experience. 'As the child passes over from the passivity of the experience to the activity of the game, he hands on the disagreeable experience to one of his playmates and in this way revenges himself on a substitute.'[33] Here, we see that this game does in fact abide by the pleasure principle insofar as it pursues the pleasure of mastering what had before been a merely passive experience. What this explanation suggests is that the pleasure we find at play in the *fort/da* game is not only the sweet pleasure of revenge but is also the pleasure of representation as such. It is the play of identification between the Symbolic ordering of an Imaginary relation, to the reel and to the mother. Lacan references this game of *fort/da* in his analysis of the game of odd or even and the connection between the two is precisely in their determinations ending in the Symbolic Order.

> This game, in which the child practices making an object (which is, moreover, indifferent by its very nature) disappear from his sight, only to bring it back, and then obliterate it anew, while he modulates this alternation with distinctive syllables – this game [. . .] manifests in its radical traits the determination that the human animal receives from the symbolic order.[34]

The play we find set up in the game of *fort/da* is a game that plays with the formation of the Symbolic out of the Imaginary structures of infantile identification. The fun of this game is derived from the back and forth play between the Symbolic and the Imaginary as a way of dealing with the encounters of absence that come from the domain of the Real.

Conclusion: *Same! Different!*

To conclude, we return to *The Awful Truth*. We find in the film's conclusion one last game for our analysis. This is a slightly different kind of game than the ones we have so far encountered but it nevertheless bears some resemblance to them. This is another game within a game, one that plays with the repetition compulsion, and that is not without its strategy. It is a play on words that shows up at the end of a larger game that makes up the play of the film: a game of divorce that entails various moves informed by rather complicated strategies. At this point at the end of the film, we find a game of a simple play on words, a game that shows the play of the signifier in its true dimension, that of love.

In the final scene of the film, Lucy and Jerry are just minutes away from the finalisation of their divorce. This is their exchange:

> *Lucy*: It's funny that everything's the way it is on account of how you feel.
> *Jerry*: Huh?
> *Lucy*: Well, I mean, if you didn't feel the way you do, things wouldn't be the way they are, would they? I mean, things could be the same if things were different.
> [A little while later . . .]
> *Jerry*: You're wrong about things being different because they're not the same. Things are different except in a different way. You're still the same only I've been a fool . . . but I'm not now. So long as I'm different don't you think that . . . well maybe things could be the same again only . . . a little different?

This word play brings Lucy and Jerry's game of divorce to an end and makes possible another round of marriage. What we see here in the couple's reunion is that the little game that plays with the signifiers 'same' and 'different' generates a certain possibility, it shows the way out of their truth trap. The example of Lucy and Jerry shows that playing a game is a serious affair: through the game they establish a repetition that holds the promise of the new.

Notes

1. Jacques Lacan, *The Seminar of Jacques Lacan, Book I: Freud's Papers on Technique*, ed. Jacques-Alain Miller, trans. John Forrester (London and New York: Norton, 1991), p. 263.
2. Lacan, *Seminar I*, p. 263.
3. Jacques Lacan, *The Seminar of Jacques Lacan, Book XI: The Four Fundamental Concepts of Psychoanalysis*, ed. Jacques-Alain Miller, trans. Alan Sheridan (London and New York: Norton, 1998), p. 139.
4. Lacan, *Seminar XI*, p. 138.
5. Jacques Lacan, *The Seminar of Jacques Lacan, Book II: The Ego in Freud's Theory and in the Technique of Psychoanalysis*, ed. Jacques-Alain Miller, trans. Sylvana Tomaselli (London and New York: Norton, 1991), p. 296.
6. Lacan, *Seminar II*, p. 320
7. Jacques Lacan, 'On a Question Prior to and Possible Treatment of Psychosis', in

Écrits: The First Complete Edition in English, trans. Bruce Fink (London and New York: Norton, 2006), p. 461.

8. I have limited the scope of this paper to the early and middle period of Lacan's thinking. This scope allows for a more focused study on what is at stake in the relation between truth and chance in the discussion of games as they reveal a helpful lens through which we can think the relation between the Imaginary and the Symbolic.
9. Roger Caillois, *Man, Play and Games*, trans. Meyer Barash (Urbana, IL and Chicago: University of Illinois Press, 2001), p. 10.
10. Caillois, *Man, Play and Games*, p. 10.
11. Caillois, *Man, Play and Games*, p. 10.
12. Jacques Lacan, 'Logical Time and the Assertion of Anticipated Certainty', in *Écrits: The First Complete Edition in English*, trans. Bruce Fink (London and New York: Norton, 2006), p. 163.
13. Lacan, *Seminar II*, p. 295.
14. Edgar Allen Poe 'The Purloined Letter', in *Selected Prose and Poetry*, revised edition with an introduction by W. H. Auden (New York: Holt, Rinehart & Winston, 1961); *cf.* Lacan, *Seminar II*, pp. 179–80.
15. Poe, 'The Purloined Letter'; *cf.* Lacan, *Seminar II*, p. 180.
16. Lacan, *Seminar II*, p. 180.
17. Lacan, *Seminar II*, p. 181.
18. Lacan, *Seminar II*, p. 181.
19. We find at this point in Lacan's discussion of the game of odd and even a certain flirtation with American game theory, cybernetics and information theory. Lydia Liu has traced out a thorough intellectual history surrounding Lacan's relation to what she develops as 'American theory', a term which names game theory, cybernetics and information theory coming out of the United States in the 1950s. See Lydia Liu, 'The Cybernetic Unconscious: Rethinking Lacan, Poe, and French Theory', *Critical Inquiry*, vol. 36, no. 2 (Winter 2010), pp. 288–320. Liu makes a provocative claim that Lacan actually derived many of his fundamental theses about the structure of language from American theory and that 'A great deal of what we now call French theory [in the United States] was already a translation of American theory before it landed in America to be reinvented as French theory' (p. 291). Although it is not the central concern of this chapter, I disagree with Liu's analysis and try to show why Lacan's treatment of the game was an extension of some of the ideas that were foundational to psychoanalysis as Freud himself formulated it, namely in the game of *fort/da*.
20. For a very helpful explication of Lacan's analysis of this game, see Bruce Fink's 'The Nature of Unconscious Thought or Why No One Ever Reads Lacan's Postface to the Seminar on "The Purloined Letter"', in *Reading Lacan's Seminars I and II:*

Lacan's Return to Freud, ed. Richard Feldstein, Bruce Fink and Marie Janus (Albany: SUNY Press, 1996).
21. Lacan, *Seminar II*, p. 182.
22. Lacan, *Seminar II*, p. 182.
23. Lacan, *Seminar II*, p. 295.
24. Lacan, 'Logical Time and the Assertion of Anticipated Certainty', pp. 161–2.
25. Jacques Lacan, 'Kant with Sade', in *Écrits: The First Complete Edition in English*, trans. Bruce Fink (London and New York: Norton, 2006), p. 648.
26. Lacan, 'Logical Time and the Assertion of Anticipated Certainty', p. 162.
27. Lacan, 'Logical Time and the Assertion of Anticipated Certainty', p. 166.
28. Lacan, 'Logical Time and the Assertion of Anticipated Certainty', p. 166.
29. Lacan, 'Logical Time and the Assertion of Anticipated Certainty', p. 173.
30. Lacan, 'Logical Time and the Assertion of Anticipated Certainty', p. 173.
31. Sigmund Freud, *Beyond the Pleasure Principle, The Standard Edition of the Complete Psychological Works of Sigmund Freud*, vol. 18, trans. James Strachey, Anna Freud et al. (New York: Vintage Books, 2001) p. 15.
32. Freud, *Beyond the Pleasure Principle*, p. 15.
33. Freud, *Beyond the Pleasure Principle*, p. 17.
34. Jacques Lacan, 'Seminar on the Purloined Letter', in *Écrits: The First Complete Edition in English*, trans. Bruce Fink (London and New York: Norton, 2006), p. 35.

| 11 | The Objective Construction: Freud and the Primal Scene
Tadej Troha

The observer of the soul cannot penetrate into the soul, but there doubtless is a margin where he comes into contact with it.

F. Kafka

IN FREUD'S FIVE major case histories, there is a fragmentary but consistent train of thought concerning the potential of a single analytic case to serve as the ultimate case, the one case that would give us crucial insights into the universal laws of the psychic apparatus while retaining its irreducible singularity.[1] Freud's concern, then, is not at all with another, albeit upgraded, version of the quest for generalisation of the particular, but with making the particular appear in its totality as the complete representation of the functional principles of *any* psychic apparatus. In this perspective, the fundamental rule of psychoanalysis, which originally refers to the patient, should eventually be applied to the psychic apparatus as the proper object of psychoanalysis. The ultimate task of the analyst, then, is to create the conditions for the object to appear on its own terms – that is, to appear objectively.

In the *Fragment of An Analysis of a Case of Hysteria*, the case history better known as 'Dora', this tendency is readily apparent, for Freud chose a case whose inherent characteristics would allow, or rather compel, the reader to focus attention on the structural dynamics of hysteria instead of dwelling on the spectacle of symptom formation.

> More interesting cases of hysteria have no doubt been published, and they have very often been more carefully described; for nothing will be found in the following pages on the subject of stigmata of cutaneous sensibility, limitation of the visual field, or similar matters. I may venture to remark, however, that all such collections

of the strange and wonderful phenomena of hysteria have but slightly advanced our knowledge of a disease which still remains as great a puzzle as ever. What is wanted is precisely an elucidation of the *commonest* cases and of their most frequent and typical symptoms.[2]

At this stage, however, the general value of a single, even the commonest, case is still considered to be very limited. A single case is not only incapable of covering *in toto* the material with which psychoanalysis is concerned; it cannot, moreover, serve even as the ultimate case of a particular form of neurosis.

> A single case history, even if it were complete and open to no doubt, cannot provide an answer to all the questions arising out of the problem of hysteria. It cannot give an insight into all the types of this disorder, into all the forms of internal structure of the neurosis, into all the possible kinds of relation between the mental and the somatic which are to be found in hysteria. It is not fair to expect from a single case more than it can offer.[3]

The two case histories that followed in 1909, 'Little Hans' and the 'Rat Man', represent two possible approaches to the further development of the strategy of minimal distortion established in 'Dora'. In 'Little Hans', the epistemological wager of the case is, strictly speaking, a by-product of the central therapeutic goal: by getting to the root of the neurosis at a time when it is still evolving and not yet subject to various secondary mutations, the analyst may have found not only the easiest way to cure the existing psychic affection, but also to prevent it from recurring in the future, thus giving the patient a lifelong immunity. In this way, however, Freud enters the zone where the foundation of the particular neurosis begins to appear as the possible foundation of every neurosis.

> Strictly speaking, I learnt nothing new from this analysis, nothing that I had not already been able to discover (though often less distinctly and more indirectly) from other patients analysed at a more advanced age. But the neuroses of these other patients could in every instance be traced back to the same infantile complexes that were revealed behind Hans's phobia. I am therefore tempted to claim for this neurosis of childhood the significance of being a type and a model, and to suppose that the multiplicity of the phenomena of repression exhibited by neuroses and the abundance of their pathogenic material do not prevent their being derived from a very limited number of processes concerned with identical ideational complexes.[4]

In contrast, the universal contribution of the 'Rat Man' case is not so much a product of Freud's deliberate quest for the possible universal origin of neurosis; rather it coincides with his assessment of obsessional neurosis as such, which was based primarily on the analysis of this particular case. The fact that obsessional neurosis is 'a dialect of the language of hysteria' which is 'more nearly related to the forms of expression adopted by our conscious thought' and which 'does not involve the leap from a mental process to a somatic innervation [. . .] which can never be fully comprehensible to us'[5] brings with it an important advantage for the analyst, since it gives him unmediated access to 'the all' (or better, to the 'not-all') of the patient's psychic apparatus. In consequence, the discussion of obsessional thinking would be, for Freud:

> of extraordinary value in its results, and would do more to clarify our ideas upon the nature of the conscious and the unconscious than any study of hysteria or the phenomena of hypnosis. It would be a most desirable thing if the philosophers and psychologists who develop brilliant theoretical views on the unconscious upon a basis of hearsay knowledge or from their own conventional definitions would first submit to the convincing impressions which may be gained from a first-hand study of the phenomena of obsessional thinking. [. . .] I will only add here that in obsessional neuroses the unconscious mental processes occasionally break through into consciousness in their pure and undistorted form, that such incursions may take place at every possible stage of the unconscious process of thought, and that at the moment of the incursion the obsessional ideas can, for the most part, be recognized as formations of very long standing. This accounts for the striking circumstance that, when the analyst tries, with the patient's help, to discover the date of the first occurrence of an obsessional idea, the patient is obliged to place it further and further back as the analysis proceeds, and is constantly finding fresh 'first' occasions for the appearance of the obsession.[6]

In spite of all the objective advantages of obsessional neurosis – total articulation of the mental processes in the mental sphere itself; discursive proximity between the conscious and the unconscious; occasional direct and undistorted intrusion of the unconscious into consciousness; virtually self-driven progression of the obsessional idea towards its origin – the fact remains that in the 'Rat Man' case history Freud failed 'in completely penetrating the complicated texture of a severe case of obsessional neurosis',[7] ostensibly because he gave priority to the practical goal of successful treatment.

> The patient recovered, and his ordinary life began to assert its claims: there were many tasks before him, which he had already neglected far too long, and which were incompatible with a continuation of the treatment. I am not to be blamed,

therefore, for this gap in the analysis. The scientific results of psycho-analysis are at present only a by-product of its therapeutic aims, and for that reason it is often just in those cases where treatment fails that most discoveries are made.[8]

Having been – for obvious reasons – relieved of this dilemma in the Schreber case, Freud seized the opportunity to reflect at length on the underlying mechanisms of symptom formation and repression, revisiting the key concept of fixation as a dispositional point – which is not only 'the precursor and necessary condition of every "repression"', but also determines the manifestation of the *failure* of repression, 'of *irruption*, of *return of the repressed*'. This irruption, Freud argues, 'takes its start from the point of fixation, and it implies a regression of the libidinal development to that point'.[9] This theoretical contribution is of critical importance because it establishes a direct bridge between the presubjective origin of the *Neurosenwahl* and the modes of its appearance in the present state – and it is precisely this bridge that would prepare the ground for the final great case history, the case of the 'Wolf Man'.

In 'Wolf Man', we can find two explicit epistemological reflections. The first one, which appears in the last part of the text, adopts a standard tone.

> It is obvious that a case such as that which is described in these pages might be made an excuse for dragging into the discussion every one of the findings and problems of psycho-analysis. But this would be an endless and unjustifiable labour. It must be recognized that everything cannot be learnt from a single case and that everything cannot be decided by it; we must content ourselves with exploiting whatever it may happen to show most clearly. There are in any case narrow limits to what a psycho-analysis is called upon to explain. For, while it is its business to explain the striking symptoms by revealing their genesis, it is not its business to explain but merely to describe the psychical mechanisms and instinctual processes to which one is led by that means. In order to derive fresh generalizations from what has thus been established with regard to the mechanisms and instincts, it would be essential to have at one's disposal numerous cases as thoroughly and deeply analysed as the present one. But they are not easily to be had, and each one of them requires years of labour. So that advances in these spheres of knowledge must necessarily be slow.[10]

In principle, nothing seems to have changed since the publication of 'Dora'. As before, an individual case is regarded as having a limited potential of conveying a universally valid insight, and like any science, psychoanalysis must also be content with slow progress. However, the second epistemological reflection, which is part of the introductory remarks, opens up a completely different perspective regarding the epistemological and ontological status of a single case.

> Naturally a single case does not give us all the information that we should like to have. Or, to put it more correctly, it might teach us everything, if we were only in a position to make everything out, and if we were not compelled by the inexperience of our own perception to content ourselves with a little.[11]

Not only this particular case, but every possible case, i.e. every concrete manifestation of a psychic apparatus, embodies the totality of the latter, and is to be regarded in itself as the nucleus of all possible knowledge which psychoanalysis would ever be capable of gaining, if only the analyst were able to adjust their perceptual faculties fully to the specific mode of appearance of this peculiar object.

In what follows, we will attempt to show that Freud's response to the task of a possible objective representation of an individual case in the 'Wolf Man' is to reconfigure the position of the observer himself. When the analyst assumes the position of outside vis-à-vis the patient, the objectivity of the case remains merely potential; but if he somehow manages to integrate himself provisionally into the patient's psychic apparatus, if he is able to transform it provisionally into a collective substance and to situate himself within this collective sphere that temporarily suspends the idea of a possible outside, something may eventually emerge that will gradually demand to be perceived as objective within this provisionally constructed common field. Freud's term for this objective phenomenon that refuses to be reduced to fiction – despite at the same time being one – is, of course, the primal scene. As for the subjective impression of undeniable clarity it evokes in the observer, however, the primal scene is by no means the first phenomenon of its kind, and to understand the appeal it had for Freud a detour into the prehistory of psychoanalysis is indispensable.

Hypnosis Revisited

It is a commonplace in the history of Freudian thought that psychoanalysis proper began at the moment Freud finally abandoned the technique of hypnosis. Therefore, it comes as no surprise that it was Freud himself who in his own account of the history of the psychoanalytic movement set the ground of what was to become a *doxa*.

> The theory of repression is the corner-stone on which the whole structure of psycho-analysis rests. It is the most essential part of it; and yet it is nothing but a theoretical formulation of a phenomenon which may be observed as often as one

pleases if one undertakes an analysis of a neurotic *without resorting to hypnosis*. In such cases one comes across a resistance which opposes the work of analysis and in order to frustrate it pleads a failure of memory. The use of hypnosis was bound to hide this resistance; *the history of psycho-analysis proper, therefore, only begins with the new technique that dispenses with hypnosis.*[12]

Even in this conventional understanding of the constitutive rupture, there is a hint of continuity. Hypnosis, as he put it in another text from the same year, deserves gratitude 'for having brought before us single psychical processes of analysis in an isolated or schematic form', thereby giving 'us the courage [. . .] to create more complicated situations in the analytic treatment'.[13] In this perspective, the new technique would not only prove to be an improvement over the failures of hypnosis, but could at the same time be seen as a further development of the latter, one that assumed all of its essential objectives and thus allowed Freud to leave the archaic, undeveloped stage in the past.

There is, however, an alternative line of thought present in Freud's texts, one in which hypnosis keeps reappearing, reminding Freud of the fact that the development of psychoanalytic theory is just as non-linear as is the development of the psyche of his patients. In its most condensed form, it is given in 'Analysis Terminable and Interminable':

> Hypnotic influence seemed to be an excellent instrument for our purposes; but the reasons for our having to abandon it are well known. No substitute for hypnosis has yet been found.[14]

It is quite telling that this remark relates to the 'Wolf Man' case, precisely the one we would expect to display the accomplished stage of the new technique. The case that should have become the ultimate proof of its effectiveness proved to be a demonstration of its inherent hazard – the hazard of becoming static, of closing itself, of turning itself inward.

According to Freud, the patient 'remained for a long time unassailably entrenched behind an attitude of "obliging apathy". He listened, understood, and remained unapproachable.'[15] As the Wolf Man himself put it in his memoires, he 'felt [himself] less as a patient than as a co-worker, the younger comrade of an experienced explorer setting out to study a new, recently discovered land.'[16] The patient was obviously convinced that he was part of an unbinding theoretical dialogue, an equal partner in what he conceived of as scientific communication. However, the Wolf Man failed to notice that the other partner in the dialogue had already disappeared and mutated into a mere material support of his own *objet a*. The effects of transference therefore manifested only after Freud's additional gesture, i.e. after his announcement that he would bring to a close the apparent dialogue, to eliminate the remaining minimum of his own personal presence.

> I determined – but not until trustworthy signs had led me to judge that the right moment had come – that the treatment must be brought to an end at a particular fixed date, no matter how far it had advanced. I was resolved to keep to the date; and eventually the patient came to see that I was in earnest. Under the inexorable pressure of this fixed limit his resistance and his fixation to the illness gave may, and now in a disproportionately short time the analysis produced all the material which made it possible to clear up his inhibitions and remove his symptoms. All the information, too, which enabled me to understand his infantile neurosis is derived from this last period of the work, during which resistance temporarily disappeared and the patient gave an impression of lucidity which is usually attainable only in hypnosis.[17]

Here, Freud suggests a somewhat unexpected analogy between the brand-new technical measure and the old, long-abandoned technique – which, also, seemed to find a way to bypass the resistance and to isolate the pure historical cause of the present condition. However, there is an important difference between the two. In hypnosis, the absence of resistance was limited to the state of hypnosis itself, while in the second case, the absence produces a situation which is much more difficult to keep under control, for the latter is, in principle, interminable – despite the disappearance of the resistance being only temporary.

Freud was certainly aware of the contrast, so the analogy amounts not to the absence of resistance as such but to the *lucidity* that emerged as a result of this opening and which not only relates to an unexpected ability to reproduce the past cause – like it did in hypnosis – but also pertains to the continuous production of the material in the present. It is worth repeating that the decision to determine the fixed time limit by which analysis would end was based on previously establishing and managing the transference. Whereas hypnosis functioned as an auxiliary technique, as an instrument of treatment that was substantially isolated from the treatment as such, transference expands over the whole treatment and can be thought of as coextensive with the analytic situation, or better, as its organisational principle. In this view, the history of psychoanalysis begins with the abandonment of hypnosis; the history of psychoanalysis proper, however, is nothing but the process of conceptualising the transference.

With the Freudian sequence of this history being condensed in the five great case histories, it is hardly surprising that the problem of transference already appears in the first case, in 'Dora'. However, it is crucial to note that its recognition and theorisation appears as belated, only in the postscript, as a theoretical compensation for Freud's practical oversight: 'I did not succeed in mastering the transference in good time,' Freud admits. 'Owing to the readiness with which Dora put one part of the pathogenic material at my disposal during the treatment, I neglected the precaution of looking out for the first signs of transference, which was being prepared in connection with another part of the same material a part of which I was in ignorance.'[18] It was, in fact, not Dora herself but the transference that was one step ahead of Freud at this point – and it was precisely this delay that Freud was eager to prevent in the later analyses. The almost triumphant tone that accompanied his description of setting the fixed time limit in the Wolf Man case could thus be explained by his belief in finally being able to master the transference and himself being the one to use transference as the means to bring the analysis to a conclusion. Considering this, it is quite telling that the 'heroic gesture' is in fact an almost verbatim reproduction of Dora's words in the last session:

> She opened the third session with these words: 'Do you know that I am here for the last time to-day?' – 'How can I know, as you have said nothing to me about it?' – 'Yes. I made up my mind to put up with it till the New Year. But I shall wait no longer than that to be cured.' – 'You know that you are free to stop the treatment at any time. But for today we will go on with our work.'[19]

The heroic gesture of fixing the time limit is therefore a repetition of the ending of Freud's first great case history. In his first reaction to the given ultimatum, he still managed to keep up with his position. Later in the session, however, the plural pronoun 'we' he used in his response was increasingly revealed to be nothing but a wishful phantasy. The more the session approached the end, the longer Freud's interventions were becoming, and finally it was in fact him 'going on with their work'. The end of the analysis is thus a full page-long, rather delirious and almost comical monologue that attempts to provide a convincing interpretation of what Dora's illness was about. To give an extract, it goes like this:

> May you not have thought that [. . .] And that now he [. . .] But you told me yourself [. . .] So you too wanted to wait for him [. . .] I imagine that this [. . .] You have not even got the right to assert [. . .] After all, you did not let him finish his speech [. . .] And I think that is why [. . .] So it must have been [. . .] You will agree that [. . .] I know now – and this is what you do not want to be reminded of – that you did fancy that Herr K.'s proposals were serious, and that he would not leave off until you had married him.[20]

One could well argue that it was precisely this ending that pushed Freud towards recognising the significance of 'transferences' (transference then still being a plural concept) as the 'inevitable necessity' of any analytic situation. 'It is easy', Freud argues, 'to learn how to interpret dreams, to extract from the patient's associations his unconscious thoughts and memories, and to practise similar explanatory arts: for these the patient himself will always provide the text.' Transference, however, is the segment of the analytic situation that first has to be detected, or better, which first has to be constructed as an object.

> Nevertheless, transference cannot be evaded, since use is made of it in setting up all the obstacles that make the material inaccessible to treatment, and since it is only after the transference has been resolved that a patient arrives at a sense of conviction of the validity of the connections which have been constructed during the analysis.[21]

At this early stage of theory, the conviction of the validity can only be arrived at after the transference has been resolved. Transference, strictly speaking, is thus nothing but an instrument for establishing new connections, whereas the conviction itself is a function of the external reality. In contrast, the later notion of analytic construction is precisely an attempt to think transference and construction as homologous: transference is itself already a construction, the construction is internal to transference, its internal repetition, and consequently, the conviction of its validity can only appear from within the transference.

The 'Ultra-Clear' Recollections

The general Freudian response to the question of the validity of the analytic construction is well known. The patient's 'yes' counts only if it is given indirectly, only if it is followed by an immediate acceleration of the production of new memories that supplement and expand the construction. However, in the last part of the 1937 'Construction in Analysis' paper, he adds some remarks 'which open up a wider perspective':

> I have been struck by the manner in which, in certain analyses, the communication of an obviously apt construction has evoked in the patients a surprising and at first incomprehensible phenomenon. They have had lively recollections called up in them – which they themselves have described as 'ultra-clear' – but what they have recollected has not been the event that was the subject of the construction but details relating to that subject. For instance, they have recollected with abnormal

sharpness the faces of the people involved in the construction or the rooms in which something of the sort might have happened, or, a step further away, the furniture in such rooms – on the subject of which the construction had naturally no possibility of any knowledge.[22]

To this remark we should add some further remarks. Firstly, the opening of a wider perspective should not be understood separately from his general response. This 'surprising and at first incomprehensible phenomenon' is only the most extreme version of the indirect confirmation. Secondly, the patients' description of recollections as 'ultra-clear', *überdeutlich*, is not simply a predicate of these recollections, but rather signifies the impossibility of giving any substantial predicate as regards their truth value. Thirdly, it is obvious that Freud himself is not convinced of how to evaluate these phenomena.

> These recollections have themselves led to nothing further and it has seemed plausible to regard them as the product of a compromise. The 'upward drive' of the repressed, stirred into activity by the putting forward of the construction, has striven to carry the important memory-traces into consciousness; but a resistance has succeeded, not, it is true, in stopping that movement, but in displacing it on to adjacent objects of minor significance.[23]

This judgment nevertheless holds true only as long as one remains within the register of interpretation. In order to grasp the excess of their significance over the meaning, or better, in order to express the *je-ne-sais-quoi* of these phenomena, Freud opts for another discursive strategy. In line with his usual procedure when faced with phenomena that he feels cannot be adequately represented in the usual scientific fashion, he introduces an analogy.

> These recollections might have been described as hallucinations if a belief in their actual presence had been added to their clearness. The importance of this analogy seemed greater when I noticed that true hallucinations occasionally occurred in the case of other patients who were certainly not psychotic.[24]

When he yields to this line of thought, this leads him to the question of whether hallucinations themselves might perhaps relate to an actual event in the patient's earliest childhood, so that 'there [would] not only [be] method in madness, as the poet has already perceived, but also a fragment of historical truth.' However, we should perhaps steer this line of thought in the other direction and contaminate 'normality' with the elements of psychosis. In this sense, the 'ultra-clarity' of the recollections itself, which cannot be interpreted or taken as a sign of belief, can be taken as an intra-mnemonic hallucination, which bears witness to another subject within the subject – not to the subject of belief in the reality of memory, but to the subject of the certainty of its current presence. Although the patient is well aware that what it concerns is a memory of a past event, he perceives the recollection as factual, as if it were occurring in the present. And it is precisely the certainty thereof, the sense of reality, *Wirklichkeitsgefühl*, which is of another order, unattainable by conventional memory. These recollections affirm the construction – however, not by adding new content, but by repeating its very formal mechanism. And as far as we hold to the hypothesis that construction is an inner repetition of transference, we seem to be faced with a series of paradoxical formations that have three features in common: it is impossible to determine their author/agent; it is impossible to install them in the frame of linear time – they are simultaneously in the present and in the past (perhaps this is the ultimate meaning of Freud's 'timelessness' of the unconscious); and their mode of existence is repetition.

Afterwardsness Redoubled

How, then, are we to understand the primal scene from the Wolf Man case from this perspective? The primal scene was constructed – by both the analyst and the analysand – on the basis of a dream that occurred at the age of four and which, again, was marked by the same 'lasting sense of reality' we have just discussed and which, according to Freud's dream theory, attests 'to an occurrence that really took place and was not merely imagined'. The dream of the wolves sitting on the tree actually plays a double role: on the one hand, the analysis of the dream triggers the emergence of the construction in the course of the treatment; on the other hand, the dream is not simply a recollection of the primal scene but the means of its activation.[25]

Freud's discovery of this double causal link between the dream and the primal scene corresponds to his decision, in the published record of the treatment, to focus exclusively on the *infantile* neurosis – despite the fact that the material at his disposal could only have been the Wolf Man's current condition, which, in turn, was 'to be regarded as a condition following on an obsessional neurosis which has come to an end spontaneously, but has left a defect behind it after recovery'.[26] To put it differently, the current condition had no autonomous determination but was essentially a *Folgezustand nach einer spontan abgelaufenen, mit Defekt ausgeheilten Zwangsneurose*, a sequela of the infantile neurosis, i.e. a further complication that followed its faulty recovery. The instalment of *Nachträglichkeit*, 'afterwardsness', as the inner momentum of the primal scene nicely demonstrates Freud's break with his views in the period of cathartic treatment, presented in *Studies on Hysteria*. While the cathartic treatment aimed at intervening in linear causality by erasing the effects of the original trauma, the analytic construction – as the means of intervening into retroactivity – argues for the absolutely binding and irrevocable character of the *intrinsically retroactive* trauma.

The retroactive character of the primal scene 'in the interval between the ages of one and a half and four years' is fully recognisable in the following sentences:

> What was essentially new for him in his *observation* of his parents' intercourse was the conviction of the reality of castration – a possibility with which his thoughts had already been occupied *previously*. (The sight of the two girls micturating, his Nanya's threat, the governess' interpretation of the sugar-sticks, the recollection of his father having beaten a snake to pieces.) For now he saw with his own eyes the wound of which his Nanya had spoken, and understood that its presence was a necessary condition of intercourse with his father.[27]

While other parts of the text seem to imply that the primal scene is split between the *observation* of coitus and its deferred understanding at the age of four, in this case observation itself adopts a retroactive quality. All the events Freud listed in brackets happened after the scene took place but logically precede the observation, the paradox being that the 'reality of castration' chronologically precedes the possibility: by observing the event at the age of one and a half, the Wolf Man recognises the reality of castration, the possibility with which his thoughts had already been occupied *previously* – but in fact later. In the register of the primal scene, *reality* is a condition of the possibility of *possibility*.

In this perspective, two further elements from the analysis are of major significance. One can recall that at one moment in the period before the introduction of the primal scene, a memory of the seduction by his sister emerged, which Freud interpreted as an event that offered the patient a passive sexual aim. The obvious reading of this event as one disturbing the linear development, supposedly aiming at the active sexual aim, seems entirely plausible.[28] Its role, however, is more ambiguous. It seems, namely, that we should view his seduction by his sister as the affirmation of his already passive attitude in observing the primal scene. This allows Freud to locate the derailment of the patient's sexual development already in the primal scene, which he defines – in line with its retroactive character – as the *second* seduction:

> [The sexual development of the patient] was first decisively influenced by the seduction, and was then diverted by the scene of observation of the coitus, which in its deferred action operated like a second seduction.[29]

It appears then that the observation of the scene is essentially passive. However, towards the end of the treatment – i.e. after the time limit has been determined – a 'kind of recollection' emerged from a very early age, 'timidly and indistinctly',[30] of a nursery maid, and which soon produced a proper recollection of a scene of the maid, Grusha, 'kneeling on the floor, and beside her a pail and a short broom made of a bundle of twigs; he was also there, and she was teasing him or scolding him.'[31] The further material, produced in the analysis, 'fitted together spontaneously'[32] and filled in the gaps: her scolding being the threat of castration, reacting to him having micturated on the floor. Freud's analytic translation, moreover, provides a significant turn of perspective regarding the primal scene:

> When he saw the girl on the floor engaged in scrubbing it, and kneeling down, with her buttocks projecting and her back horizontal, he was faced once again with the posture which his mother had assumed in the copulation scene. She became his mother to him; he was seized with sexual excitement owing to the activation of this picture; and, like his father (whose action he can only have regarded at the time as micturition), he behaved in a masculine way towards her. [. . .] The action of the two-and-a-half-year-old boy in the scene with Grusha is the earliest effect of the primal scene which has come to our knowledge. It represents him as copying his father, and shows us a tendency towards development in a direction which would later deserve the name of masculine.[33]

Still, if the action in the scene with Grusha is the first effect of the primal scene, it is by no means its realisation – it is, strictly speaking, not an effect of the primal scene we have been discussing, i.e. the one that was activated at the age of four. It might be that this recollection served Freud as confirmation of the reality of the primal scene. However, such 'active' interpretation of the scene (where the observer sees himself as the seducer-to-be) is just as insufficient as its 'passive' counterpart.

In the specific case of the Wolf Man, a patient marked by strongly ambivalent character traits, the primal scene itself had to be structured like the Wolf Man, to paraphrase Lacan. According to Freud, the patient's psyche was characterised by three fundamental traits: (a) 'his tenacity of fixation'; (b) 'his extraordinary propensity to ambivalence'; and (c) 'his power of maintaining simultaneously the most various and contradictory libidinal cathexes, all of them capable of functioning side by side'.[34] In order to produce a material record of the formation of the subject's disposition, then, the primal scene had to be structured in such a way that it corresponded to the above-mentioned traits – yet in a different register. The Wolf Man's tenacity of fixation found its echo in the inherent 'afterwardsness' inscribed within the primal scene itself. His propensity to ambivalence was presented as originating in the more structural ambivalence of the active and the passive. And lastly, his ability to simultaneously maintain the contradictory libidinal cathexes turned out to be a consequence of the oscillation between identification with the father and the mother in observing the primal scene. It is, again, crucial to keep in mind that the primal scene is a construction, and is, as such, essentially resistant to any interpretation. Yet this feature is nothing but another expression of its ability to capture the peculiarities of the case, which 'were revealed by the psycho-analytic treatment but were not further elucidated'.[35]

The Ultimate Analogy

No further clarification is possible: theory has reached its limit, and in the capacity of 'producing the impression' only analogies can come close to the construction. According to Freud, the last fundamental trait of the patient's psyche – or better, the trinity of all fundamental traits – belongs to 'the general character of the unconscious, which in his case had persisted into processes that had become conscious'.[36] Not only is the unconscious of the Wolf Man unconscious – even the conscious part of his psyche acts in accordance with the same principles:

> So it was that his mental life impressed one in much the same way as the religion of Ancient Egypt, which is so unintelligible to us because it preserves the earlier stages of its development side by side with the end-products, retains the most ancient gods and their attributes along with the most modern ones, and thus, as it were, spreads out upon a two-dimensional surface [*in eine Fläche ausbreitet*] what other instances of evolution show us in the solid [*zu einem Tiefengebilde wird*].[37]

The essence of the Wolf Man can only be described with the ultimate analogy, the one encompassing the unconscious as such. Considering the magnitude of this claim, it is hardly surprising that Freud tries to relativise the analogy, reducing it such that it related merely to the affective dimension of the patient's psychic apparatus, while 'in the region of pure logic he betrayed, on the contrary, a peculiar skill in unearthing contradictions and inconsistencies'.[38]

The attempt to relativise its scope, however, is compensated for by yet another analogy. In the very last paragraphs, after he had already reached the end of what he had to say about the case, Freud offers an analogy, which seems to serve him as the universal correlate to the former, to the one that articulated the pure singularity of the case.

> If one considers the behaviour of the four-year-old child towards the reactivated primal scene, or even if one thinks of the far simpler reactions of the

one-and-a-half-year-old child when the scene was actually experienced, it is hard to dismiss the view that some sort of hardly definable knowledge, something, as it were, preparatory to an understanding, was at work in the child at the time. We can form no conception of what this may have consisted in; we have nothing at our disposal but the single analogy – and it is an excellent one – of the far-reaching instinctive knowledge of animals.[39]

Above, we have already shown that the construction is able to produce an ultra-clear recollection of a sort comparable to hallucination. Moreover, another analogy – the one we presented at the beginning – demonstrated the proximity of the reaction to the setting of the time limit and the state produced by the long-abandoned technique of hypnosis. The latter analogy, however, proves to be more than coincidental. Let us recall the passage from the *Introductory Lectures* in which Freud draws attention to the problem brought by the local liberation of the material from resistances occurring in hypnosis:

> That state was precisely able to withhold the existence of the resistance from the doctor's perception. It pushed the resistance back, making a certain area free for analytic work, and dammed it up at the frontiers of that area in such a way as to be impenetrable, just as doubt does in obsessional neurosis.[40]

A very similar metaphor appears once again in 'Analysis Terminable and Interminable', relating precisely to the Wolf Man case. The success of the employment of the 'heroic measure' of fixing the time limit, now called the 'blackmailing device', proved to be an illusion. Freud writes:

> [The 'shrinking up' of his resistances] cannot guarantee to accomplish the task completely. On the contrary, we may be sure that, while part of the material will become accessible under the pressure of the threat, another part will be kept back and thus become buried, as it were, and lost to our therapeutic efforts.[41]

While the first metaphor shows how avoiding the resistance in hypnosis deceives us as to the insistence of resistance – as it was dammed up at the frontiers and hence ceased to function as resistance, the second metaphor makes an even further point. The subject in question is no longer resistance but the fate of the material itself. Again, in the first metaphor the material condensed itself in the resistance-free area, and nevertheless remained 'whole' – despite being falsely articulated, while in the second metaphor a certain part of the material becomes buried and lost for good. In the first case the loss is provisional and temporary, still allowing for a proper articulation at some future point; in the second case, it becomes irreversible. Some part of the material is *verschüttet*, remains 'blocked', 'entombed', 'buried alive' – and will only appear as 'spilling' over the other part of the material, thus 'overwhelming' the entire psyche.

This view finds support in a further metaphor. We have already called attention to Freud's understanding of the patient's current neurosis as *Folgezustand*, as the secondary complication of the provisional recovery. At the time of writing 'Analysis Terminable and Interminable', he already knew that his former view of the case was over-optimistic.

> The patient has stayed on in Vienna and has kept a place in society, if a humble one. But several times during this period his good state of health has been interrupted by attacks of illness which could only be construed as offshoots of his perennial neurosis. Thanks to the skill of one of my pupils, Dr. Ruth Mack Brunswick, a short course of treatment has on each occasion brought these conditions to an end. [. . .] Some of these attacks were still concerned with residual portions of the transference; and, where this was so, short-lived though they were, they showed a distinctly paranoid character. In other attacks, however, the pathogenic material consisted of pieces of the patient's childhood history, which had not come to light while I was analysing him and which now came away – the comparison is unavoidable – like sutures after an operation, or small fragments of necrotic bone. I have found the history of this patient's recovery scarcely less interesting than that of his illness.[42]

The perennial neurosis and its offshoots, residual portions of transference, pieces of childhood history, tearing like small fragments of necrotic bone: here, Freud manages to summarise all three phases of the case (the childhood neurosis and its sequela, the treatment and the recovery from the treatment itself), which find embodiment in strange objects that are at the same time necrotic and buried alive, dead and undead.

However, it would be false to interpret this outcome as the product of constructing the primal scene, but rather of Freud's attempt to use the primal scene as an instrument to bring the analysis to a definite end. Should he rather withdraw from making another step? Should he rather recognise the primal scene – the singularity of the most singular case – as the only possible form of the 'independent existence of the scheme' that he is searching for in the field of phylogenetics? Perhaps he should simply affirm the patient's subjectivisation of the primal scene in all its ambivalence, and resist the temptation to impose on the Wolf Man its 'active' or 'passive' interpretation. Instead of forcing the end, Freud should perhaps do what was even more unexpected and even less in line with his standard procedures. Perhaps he should go a step further in imitating Dora and instantly quit the analysis himself, thus forcing the patient to contemplate the only image that he – otherwise a painter, drawing landscapes and still lifes – produced collectively, in the analysis, together with Freud.

Notes

1. This contribution was written in the framework of the scientific project J6-9392 'The Problem of Objectivity and Fiction in Contemporary Philosophy' and the programme P6-0014 'Conditions and Problems of Contemporary Philosophy', financed by the Slovenian Research Agency. An earlier version of this *paper* appeared in the journal *Lamella* (Aarhus: Aarhus Universitet, 2021).
2. Sigmund Freud, 'Fragment of an Analysis of a Case of Hysteria', in *The Standard Edition of the Complete Psychological Works of Sigmund Freud, Vol. VII*, trans. James Strachey (London: Vintage, 2001), p. 24.
3. Freud, 'Fragment of an Analysis of a Case of Hysteria', p. 13.
4. Sigmund Freud, 'Analysis of a Phobia in a Five-Year-Old Boy', in *The Standard Edition of the Complete Psychological Works of Sigmund Freud, Vol. X*, trans. James Strachey (London: Vintage, 2001), p. 147.
5. Sigmund Freud, 'Notes upon a Case of Obsessional Neurosis', in *The Standard Edition of the Complete Psychological Works of Sigmund Freud, Vol. X*, trans. James Strachey (London: Vintage, 2001), pp. 156–7.
6. Freud, 'Notes upon a Case of Obsessional Neurosis', pp. 228–9.
7. Freud, 'Notes upon a Case of Obsessional Neurosis', p. 156.
8. Freud, 'Notes upon a Case of Obsessional Neurosis', pp. 207–8.
9. Sigmund Freud, 'Psycho-Analytic Notes on an Autobiographical Account of a Case of Paranoia', in *The Standard Edition of the Complete Psychological Works of Sigmund Freud, Vol. X*, trans. James Strachey (London: Vintage, 2001), p. 68.
10. Sigmund Freud, 'From the History of an Infantile Neurosis', in *The Standard Edition of the Complete Psychological Works of Sigmund Freud, Vol. XVII*, trans. James Strachey (London: Vintage, 2001), p. 105.
11. Freud, 'From the History of an Infantile Neurosis', p. 10.
12. Sigmund Freud, 'On the History of the Psycho-Analytic Movement', in *The Standard Edition of the Complete Psychological Works of Sigmund Freud, Vol. XIV*, trans. James Strachey (London: Vintage, 2001), p. 16.
13. Sigmund Freud, 'Remembering, Repeating and Working-Through', in *The Standard Edition of the Complete Psychological Works of Sigmund Freud, Vol. XII*, trans. James Strachey (London: Vintage, 2001), p. 148.
14. Sigmund Freud, 'Analysis Terminable and Interminable', in *The Standard Edition*

of the Complete Psychological Works of Sigmund Freud, Vol. XXIII, trans. James Strachey (London: Vintage, 2001), p. 230.
15. Freud, 'From the History of an Infantile Neurosis', p. 11.
16. Muriel Gardiner (ed.), *The Wolf-Man and Sigmund Freud* (London: Penguin, 1973), p. 158.
17. Freud, 'From the History of an Infantile Neurosis', p. 11.
18. Freud, 'Fragment of an Analysis of a Case of Hysteria', p. 118.
19. Freud, 'Fragment of an Analysis of a Case of Hysteria', p. 105.
20. Freud, 'Fragment of an Analysis of a Case of Hysteria', pp. 107–8. Dora's response translated comedy into a melodrama: 'Dora had listened to me without any of her usual contradictions. She seemed to be moved; she said good-bye to me very warmly, with the heartiest wishes for the New Year, and – came no more' (pp. 108–9). And as is well known, the melodrama repeated itself as a *Witz*:

    On a date which is not a matter of complete indifference, on the first of April (times and dates, as we know, were never without significance for her), Dora came to see me again: to finish her story and to ask for help once more. One glance at her face, however, was enough to tell me that she was not in earnest over her request. (pp. 120–1)

21. Freud, 'Fragment of an Analysis of a Case of Hysteria', p. 116.
22. Sigmund Freud, 'Constructions in Analysis', in *The Standard Edition of the Complete Psychological Works of Sigmund Freud, Vol. XXIII*, trans. James Strachey (London: Vintage, 2001), p. 266.
23. Freud, 'Constructions in Analysis', p. 266; emphasis added.
24. Freud, 'Constructions in Analysis', pp. 266–7.

25. We shall further bear in mind that the activation of this scene (I purposely avoid the word 'recollection') had the same effect as though it were a recent experience. The effects of the scene were deferred, but meanwhile it had lost none of its freshness in the interval between the ages of one and a half and four years. We shall perhaps find in what follows reason to suppose that it produced certain effects even at the time of its perception, that is, from the age of one and a half onwards. (Freud, 'From the History of an Infantile Neurosis', pp. 44–5)

26. Freud, 'From the History of an Infantile Neurosis', p. 8.
27. Freud, 'From the History of an Infantile Neurosis', pp. 45–6; emphasis added.

28. But his seduction gives the impression not merely of having encouraged his sexual development but of having, to an even greater extent, disturbed and diverted it. It offered him a passive sexual aim, which was ultimately

> incompatible with the action of his male genital organ. At the first external obstacle, the threat of castration from his Nanya, his genital organization, half-hearted as it still was, broke down (at the age of three and a half) and regressed to the stage which had preceded it, namely to that of the sadistic-anal organization, which he might otherwise have passed through, perhaps, with as slight indications as other children. (Freud, 'From the History of an Infantile Neurosis', p. 108)

29. Freud, 'From the History of an Infantile Neurosis', p. 47.
30. Freud, 'From the History of an Infantile Neurosis', p. 90.
31. Freud, 'From the History of an Infantile Neurosis', p. 91.
32. Freud, 'From the History of an Infantile Neurosis', p. 92.
33. Freud, 'From the History of an Infantile Neurosis', pp. 92–4.
34. Freud, 'From the History of an Infantile Neurosis', pp. 118–19.
35. Freud, 'From the History of an Infantile Neurosis', p. 118.
36. Freud, 'From the History of an Infantile Neurosis', p. 119.
37. Freud, 'From the History of an Infantile Neurosis', p. 119.
38. Freud, 'From the History of an Infantile Neurosis', p. 119.
39. Freud, 'From the History of an Infantile Neurosis', p. 120.
40. Sigmund Freud, 'Introductory Lectures on Psycho-Analysis (Part III)', in *The Standard Edition of the Complete Psychological Works of Sigmund Freud, Vol. XVI*, trans. James Strachey (London: Vintage, 2001), p. 292.
41. Freud, 'Analysis Terminable and Interminable', p. 218.
42. Freud, 'Analysis Terminable and Interminable', p. 218.

12 (From the Lie in the Closed World to) Lying in an Infinite Universe
Frank Ruda

'Mundus vult decipi, ergo decipiatur.' ['The world wants to be deceived; therefore it should be deceived.']

(Petronius)

'Your bait of falsehood takes this carp of truth . . .'

(W. Shakespeare, *Hamlet*, 2.1.62)

IN 1942, THREE years before the end of the Second World War Alexandre Koyré, the great French philosophical historian of science, at this time working from his New York exile, wrote a text on a peculiar form of altering objectivity, namely on lying. The great historian of the break constitutive of modern science and thus also of a break that can be read as foundational for the modern concept of objectivity, addresses therein the peculiar form of language-usage that appears to be, at least according to a familiar trope, specific to man.[1] Since 'man is defined by his faculty of speech, inherent in which is the possibility of the lie.'[2] Speaking does potentially always mean lying. This view is shared by many, for example by Martin Heidegger. In a lecture in 1930 Heidegger noted that 'man is the hearth [*Herd*] of falsehood, of dissimulation [*Verstellung*], of the lie, of deception, of error, in short: of all kinds of untruths.'[3] Man is the dissembling hearth of an entire universe of untruths and therefore it may seem 'as if . . . the lie was itself the essence of human society.'[4] This is already a toned down version of the famous Nietzschean trope that the 'art of dissimulation reaches its peak in man: here deception, flattery, lying and cheating . . . playacting before others and before oneself . . . nothing is as incomprehensible as how an honest and pure drive to truth could have arisen among men.'[5]

At origin and foundation man is the lying animal for Nietzsche. More cautiously, for Koyré man is the animal able to lie. Humans are capable (and thus are at least potential) liars. And 'man has always lied to himself and to others,'[6] Koyré notes as if thinking of the Psalms' (115:11) 'omnis homo mendax.' Humans can lie, this is what they always did. They lie to others. Maybe they can even lie to themselves. But this is just a maybe. Since not everyone would immediately agree that one can lie to oneself. Some – to whom I will return below – consider it impossible, because we would then need to be able to become co-conspirators in a conspiracy against ourselves. Yet, if it were possible to lie to oneself, there would immediately arise a whole new dimension of combinatoric, of (not) lying to others while (not) lying to oneself.[7] Against the background of these general remarks, it is worth noting that Koyré's text does not consider and examine lying as such, even though its original French title could suggest such an approach – since it directly would translate as 'Reflections on Lying'.[8] Effectively, Koyré neither seeks to examine lying as general human capacity from an anthropological, philosophical or linguistic standpoint[9] nor is he interested in formulating any 'phenomenology of the lie'.[10] His aim is to conceptualise the contemporarily dominant forms of lying and his is a today unavoidably overshadowed by politics. Koyré's text, to be more precise here, seeks to examine what its English title addresses as the function – note this mathematical term – *the political function* of the lie under present, destructively modern conditions: it thus addresses *the political function of the modern lie*.

There are many reasons that prohibit any direct comparison of the historical background that motivated Koyré's diagnosis and the present times. But, with due caution, one can detect resonances between the two. This may be because our conjuncture has also been characterised as one whose 'truth . . . is war',[11] even if though this more apparently pertains to Koyré's situation. But, and more pertinently, Koyré's analysis clearly speaks to a present situation wherein political lying seems to have gained a renewed actuality.[12] Lying in politics is widely perceived – obviously not for the first time in history – as a real problem. Lying has (re-)entered the centre stage of what is presently deemed to be world politics and thereby also got a leading role in almost all present-day media coverage. Yet, the present moment comes with a twist of its own. When the media started covering the increase in political misrepresentations of objective reality – and these misrepresentations are what it then referred to as lying – it came itself under attack for presenting fake news and especially so when it was reporting on political lying. 'Fake news' was the term coined to (mis-)represent when there was supposed mass mediatic lying about political lying. When reporting on lying can itself be turned into and be perceived as potential lying, we advance an additional step in the understanding of the intimate entanglement of truth-telling and lying.[13] Telling the truth can sometimes be perceived or even operate for the sake of a lie, lying can sometimes be a way of telling the truth. It is such a complication of the difference between truth-telling and lying that is also at stake in Koyré's text. But this raises several questions.

Is this just a complicated interlinkage or can the distinction between the two also be undone? If so, does this provide sufficient justification for those who see the stability of the entire political universe threatened by the existence of 'fake news'? Is politics not constitutively universal only because its truth is brought about from a particular and hence partisan position? One could also assume that there are no neutral news and fact in politics, simply because there is no neutral political universe and politics thereby is unavoidably the art of organised collective side taking? On the other hand, what if the distinction could be destabilised? Would this not necessarily mean that it must have been unstable from the very beginning? How could we then appropriately historicise it (so that we could evaluate that now is better or worse than before)? Are there for instance epochs where this instability of this distinction is more or less apparent? How to measure this visibility? Do we encounter limits when we try to dissolve or historicise the distinction between truth-telling and lying, so that something transhistorical comes to the fore, a *mentior ergo sum*?

Once Jacques Derrida argued that it is impossible to lie to oneself.[14] This claim is rather surprising, as it implies that ultimately we cannot but be truthful to ourselves. There is no self-deception possible. I cannot believe the lies I am trying to tell myself when I at the same time know that they are lies and I am lying. But I also cannot lie if I do not know what I do. Otherwise, I am ill-informed or deceived and thus still trying to tell the truth. Lying implies knowledge of what I do, Derrida claims. Therefore the moment I am lying to myself and cannot but know that I am lying, I cannot lie to myself. This Derridean claim stands in continuity with Aristotle's critique of Plato's *Hippias Minor*, wherein the former asserted that lying must be distinguished from merely getting the facts wrong.[15] Lying – as Derrida does not tire from noting – is not making an error, but an intentional act. It always comes with the intention to lie and it provides the stable ground on which one can distinguish telling the truth, making an error and lying. The far-reaching implication of Derrida's claim that there is no possibility of lying to oneself is that there is also no possibility to bracket or obliviate the knowledge one has about one's intention to lie. One cannot lie to oneself and one thus can also not lie to oneself about lying to oneself. The distinction is as stable as it gets. *Mentior, ergo scio*.

From this perspective what appears to be specifically human is thus the impossibility to lie to oneself. Yet, Derrida thereby identifies a spellbinding, unavoidable and unchangeable auto-transparency at the bottom of all lying-practices. The condition of possibility of my lying to others is the condition of impossibility of me lying to myself. Thus the distinction between lying and truth-telling seems now much more stable than we previously assumed. If so, is there no real historicity to this distinction? Derrida at least asserts in the same spirit: 'It is difficult to believe that the lie has a history.'[16] But if lying is unable to be historical, it seems to transform from a potentially extra-moral into a genuinely moral problem or category. If we always know what we do when we lie and cannot lie to ourselves, we can raise the question if we should treat others in a way we would and could never treat ourselves. We just seem to have found a stable moral standard. Everything now revolves around the intention to lie or not to lie. To lie or not to lie, this is the moral question. There can no longer be any consideration of truth-telling or lying in a Nietzschean extra-moral sense. And this is the basis against which Derrida deems all positions who claim to see a historical development within which lying becomes more and more radical, widespread and total ultimately untenable – a type of position of which Koyré appears to be a clear representative.[17] This is why this Derrida-discussion is conceptually instructive for what is at stake with the discussion of Koyré's text. What becomes untenable is the claim that lying could be total. But if there were nothing but lying, we would also need to lie to ourselves. This we cannot do. There can thus be no totalisation of the lie and, in this sense, no worsening in the history of lying.

But can one really not imagine a fetishist disavowal operative on the depicted level of self-transparency – in the sense that I know very well (that I know something is a lie), but nevertheless (I believe I am not lying to myself)?[18] Is it not the case, as the early Plato's Socrates put it once, that 'the ignorant person would often involuntarily tell the truth when he wished to say falsehoods'?[19] Can't there be a parapraxis even in lying? And a parapraxis in telling the truth? Might not the possibility of a parapraxis in both provide a common ground? Is failing to be true to oneself always an error in one's self-perception and self-understanding? Imagine a liar who only lies to those who do not lie to themselves (because they cannot), does she lie to herself or not? If she does not (because she cannot), she has to lie to herself (even though I cannot), but if she lies to herself (even though she cannot), she must (but she cannot). Such a liar, this seems to be Derrida's point, therefore does not exist (but so does woman, Lacan might add). Is lying not sometimes about claiming the impossible, even though knowing it is not true?

To start again from a different angle: if there were no lying to oneself, there could never really be any history of the lie, because something in lying never changes and thus the only thing we would be able to get is a structural analysis of this very practice. Lying then would have a transcendental structure. How does one then explain the impression that there is or can be an increase in lying, say in a political conjuncture? Is this simply an error, a misperception or, worst case, a lie? There is certainly a temptation of those born later or latest to think that whatever they live through is new, more dramatic, relevant, world-historic or cause for concern than anything that happened before. But is the other extreme not to assume that nothing ever changed about practices of lying? To say something meaningful about this would presuppose to observe that something changed about lying? This question is one that occupied Koyré. Since he claims there has been a transformation, linked to and therefore specific to the 'totalitarian regimes'.[20] They transformed the operativity and framework of the modern practice of political lying. This means that for Koyré lying in fact has a history, a history that is more than just a fabrication, more than an ackamarackus, not only made-up, but cracked-up, broken, divided, determined by transformations, modifications or intensifications. So, what is the difference between lying in politics in 1942 and lying before?

Koyré identifies 'some mighty innovations'[21] that have taken place within the realm of the untruthful. Even if what happened cannot be classified as 'a deep revolution which changed the very framework and patterns of our thinking' – this is how he describes the break induced by modern science – what he identifies is nevertheless 'a destruction of the Cosmos',[22] at least of the previous political world(-order).[23] These innovations make a move from lying in a closed world to lying in an infinite universe, through the destruction of the former. It seems that with or in the aftermath of a new conception and practice of science – and thus of truth-telling – co-emerges also a new sense of lying. Politics is the field in which this new sense produces its effects: 'Never before has there been so much lying as in our day. Never has lying been so shameless, so systematic, so unceasing.'[24] What is new, and here not in opposition to Derrida, is at first only the enormous quantitative increase. But lying turning non-stop did, and here different from Derrida, thereby produce a qualitative transformation of lying itself: it becomes more shameless and systematic.[25] It is not the persisting (quantitative) hair loss that at one point (qualitatively) transforms the hairy into a bald head, it is the abundance of naked lying empires that when piling up endlessly transforms the universe. This is lying's leap from quantity into quality.

Lying through its multiplication now acquired 'total a character'.[26] Koyré in 1942 believes what is, *inter alia*, totalitarian about totalitarian regimes is the totalisation of lying. This comes with implications similarly paradoxical to the Cretan liar's paradox. If there were total lying, would it still be lying (this was Derrida's critique)?[27] In Koyré, the history of the lie moves from finite to infinite, from lying within a closed space to lying in an infinite universe (of lying). It seems in modernity the lie is everywhere and becomes everything: 'Modern man . . . bathes in the lie, breathes the lie.'[28] The lie is the water we use to cleanse ourselves and the air that we breathe. It has become modern man's life-element, her vital principle. With the move into the era of mass consumption and mass-media-output, lying became a modern elementary medium. Now human beings started to live in a society that perceived itself as being kept alive through a bond of potential lies.

A particular human feature – the capacity to lie – was thus turned into *the* very (invisible) material of any social bond. During an age in which 'the sciences have a privileged claim on truth' and where 'the truth of science goes without saying',[29] human political life and lying can, nonetheless, become almost indistinguishable. There are jokes trying to encapsulate this historical transformation. Like the following one: 'Washington couldn't tell a lie. Nixon couldn't tell the truth, and Reagan couldn't tell the difference.' But Koyré does not share this diagnosis. For him, the history of lying does not end in abolishing the difference between truth and lie altogether. This is not, different from Derrida's assumption, the effect of the totalisation of the lie. The immense quantitative increase of lying generates a qualitative leap. This leap appears as a decay in quality. Quantity transforms regressively into quality: 'The quality of the modern lie has deteriorated as the volume has increased.'[30] It has become the modern water and air, but both are rather dirty and polluted. Such discursive climate change results from 'an absolute and total contempt for truth' that manifests in the omnipresent belief that there is no truth, at least none that is universal. People no longer believe that there is 'a single objective truth valid for everybody',[31] because they cannot imagine it emerges from a one-sided perspective.

The quantitative-qualitative leap of lying is thus linked to a transformation that does not only affect the lie, but truth as well. It transforms our relation to the 'the past and the present', to past and present 'truths' that come now to be regarded as merely subjective and relative beliefs (as if regressing from logics to metaphysics). The totalisation of the lie is, for Koyré, the flipside of a de-universalisation and de-absolutisation of truth. Ultimately, this means that any truth of and in the past and the present as well the idea of truth as such is no longer considered 'a light, but a weapon'.[32] For Koyré, every truth can become a weapon if you use (and understand) it wrongly. Truth does then no longer orient but become a means of warfare. The expansion and multiplication of lies led to a repurposing, a weaponisation of the very concept of truth. Truths are now perceived as only being regional, local, particular and relative. They are no longer in 'agreement with reality, but [in] agreement with the spirit of a race or nation or class . . .'[33] They are instrumentalised by liars everywhere as their own truths. That – or if – a liar can take charge of truth means that the liar's sovereignty becomes redundant and lying turns total.[34] There are still lies and truths, but truths no longer have anything to do with 'discovering reality as it is'. They rather are directed 'toward what is not'.[35] Truths now force reality to become the reality of these very truths and this is why they work like weapons.

When lies are everywhere, truth does not simply disappear, *pace* Derrida, but it changes its function (recall Koyré's title). This is what it means to assume that there is an entanglement between truth-telling and lying, but that there is also a history of both. A 'totalitarian regime' does never fully suspend 'the distinction between the true and the false', but repurposes it by reconceiving of it under the '*primacy of the lie*'.[36] If lying is what there is, the truth is (and is no longer) the truth of what there is. Truth is turned problematically partisan. There is a suspension of truth through the very ways in which it is kept alive. Truth-telling can thereby become a tool of lying, it can be instrumentalised. How was this possible? Koyré notes that even though lying has been inexorably condemned in all religions, apart from Kant's and Fichte's severe rejection of lying, philosophers have in general been less strict when it comes to lying. Overall, they took a 'more human' approach, admitting that sometimes it may be better not to tell the truth, or 'at least not always to everyone'.[37] The problem is thus not that the philosophers demonstrated the impossibility of lying to ourselves, but rather that there is always and thereby too many good reasons to lie. If lying can be justified because of concrete particular circumstances, there is a history of lying.

Certainly, 'a lie is not uttered in the void' and thus always specific and particular because 'every word is always addressed to someone in particular'.[38] One subject is lying to another subject by means of language and this implies that 'lying can in no way be reduced to a dual relationship between the subject who utters the ('untruthful') message and the subject who receives it. The moment two subjects are addressing each other by means of signifiers, we are always dealing with an irreducible third dimension or instance.'[39] In Koyré's reading, philosophy understands that lying is always a concrete act and thus necessitates a concrete analysis of concrete situations that must bear in mind this third instance.[40] Yet, what the philosophers on Koyré's account have insinuated regarding the ethics of lying is that, because it is always concrete, symbolic and conjunctural, it is ultimately unproblematic 'as long as it is "harmless" and does not interfere with the smooth function of social relations'.[41] Philosophy is consequentialist: well-founded exceptions make the rule. No one anticipated that quantity can transform into quality and that massive lying can have an impact on the concept of truth. This is the problem with arguing that as long as lying does not create a conjuncture that destroys all conjunctures, lying can be tolerated – when it reached its tipping point, there is no going back. It is simply too late for complaints when we identify the former.[42] If lying becomes total, it becomes the substitute or the new form of the social bond and this repurposes the locus of lying. Lying is then no longer an inner exception to the norms of social conduct, but the norm a group uses for its comportment to another.

It seems difficult to avoid the insight that a 'lie is a weapon' of which 'it is legitimate to use it in struggle'[43] – and this struggle then also and unavoidably turns out to be a struggle about what counts as a lie. This is one of the reasons why diplomats have never been considered principled truth-tellers,[44] neither have businessmen or advertisers for that matter. So, when humans were still living in a closed world, this world was, by definition, a shared world within which it was possible to detect conditions for the exception of lying, for example in a situation of war. This changed when the world became an infinite universe. It might just be that the transformation brought about by modern science (that in turn led to a transformed concept of truth) prepared the conditions for the very quantitative-qualitative increase in lying (since this is what made the change from the closed world to the infinite universe possible). Within these conditions, the common ground has turned into a whirlpool and whirlwind of (large and small) infinities that we do not share but that separate us from one another. If war was the paradigm case for the justified and excusable exception beforehand, all things change when the state of exception, as others will repeat Koyré diagnosis later, has become 'permanent and taken for granted'.[45] We thus move from a closed world wherein exceptions are organised under the primacy of truth-telling to a situation where the exception is the rule and 'the lie, once an emergency measure, now becomes the norm'.[46]

Lying is thereby objectively massified: it is everywhere once the objective exceptional condition (i.e. struggling with the enemy) becomes the determining feature of the subjectivised infinite universe. Lying is for a group what appears in the first half of the last century as the common ground when there is no common ground. It is what creates cohesion where there otherwise is none. It is that from which everything that holds together a collective political life is conceived of. At this stage of his argument Koyré adds an important twist: any group 'surrounded by a world of unbending and irreconcilable foes', assuming 'the enemy to be all-powerful', would be able to identify an infinite 'abyss between itself and them', so that there exists 'no tie or social obligations'.[47] What enables the social bond is lying collectively to those who are infinitely different; it is the stuff of which the bond is made when all bonds are placed in an abyss of infinity. Against such a background – within an infinite universe of infinitely different all-powerful enemies – lying 'would become obligatory and be transformed into a virtue'[48] because the 'enmity' has been 'rendered absolute, total'.[49] Lying becomes total when in an infinite universe difference becomes so infinite, enmity becomes absolute and hence cohesion and solidarity is per se fictitious and made up. What a political collective that identifies an infinity separating it from its enemy does, when the latter is represented as being infinitely powerful, is to 'take refuge in the dark of secrecy'.[50]

If the enemy is too mighty and no negotiations or mediations are possible, then secrecy is presented as the only way to maintain the existence of the collective. Thereby 'the lie . . . will become a condition of sheer existence, a primary and fundamental rule of behavior'.[51] We only remain who we are if we lie collectively, if we individually lie ourselves into a collective. The social bond is thus a form of collective secrecy, transparent opacity and see-through misrepresentation. If the enemy must be duped, it is best to dupe her in pretending to disappear altogether, in duping her to believe one does not even exist. This is what is common to lobbyists, gangsters, conspiracy theorists, and one might be able to add a few more. This is to say a social group, to quote Forrester commenting on Koyré, 'given a hostile environment, necessarily constitutes itself anew not as a secret society, but as something more profound – what Koyré calls "une société à secret," a society *of* the secret, a society whose existence is now predicated upon the secret.'[52] Forrester derives from this the claim and question that 'complete loss of foundation seems to follow from here. Does it exist?'[53] But as should be clear from the discussion thus far: the loss of foundation is not a consequence but stands at the ground of the society of the secret. It is not an effect of but enables the proper historicity of the lie; if not the vacillating of the distinction between lying and truth-telling, then at least their reshuffling and repurposing. But what precisely does it mean that the society of the secret has experienced a loss of foundation?

It does not mean that the organisation simply replaces the foundation with a secret. It rather means that it does replace the lack of foundation with a collective form of a shared practice of lying. This collective practice of lying is also a practice of lying about one's foundation and, in this sense, it is a shared lying about lying and the collective form of lying to oneself and the other(s). Every member is initiated into it and understands the implicit rules of this lying collective. The society of the secret emerges as an original, primordial lie, as *proton pseudos*. This in consequence produces far-reaching effects that Koyré sees becoming visible in the regimes of the 1940s. On the one side, this leads to the effect that whoever is initiated into such a society will therefore assume that whatever their leader says publicly is not to be believed because it is addressed to the enemy.[54] Because the society always seeks to deceive its infinitely powerful enemy, it never shows itself as what it is publicly and this implies its leader(s) will never tell the truth. '[A]ny statement made is a falsification. Every word, at least every word uttered in public, is a lie.'[55] The foundational secretive practice of collective lying, this specific organisation of the primacy of the lie, overdetermines the way each lie appears in public. It means for each member of the society to have specific reading glasses on, glasses one gets when becoming a member of the society. But there is another side to this. It is here, on the other side, that Koyré's argument shows is true contemporary significance. He points out that it is crucial to see how the secrecy of the secret groups does not at all stand in contradiction with another feature of the 'totalitarian regimes',[56] their surprising honesty.

It is not the case that these regimes ever hid their agendas so that only the initiated would know them. Rather something happens as an effect of the totalisation of the lie in an infinite universe: there is a peculiar recursive loop at work in the perception of the public appearance of representatives of a collective (practice of lying). One in advance assumes she will be lying. But in fact, the secret organisational principle, the shared practice of lying, does not suggest that anyone would need to keep their actual political agendas secret. Quite to the contrary – and this makes it interesting for contemporary eyes – the secret totalitarian organisation '*conspires in broad daylight*'.[57] How and why is a society of the secret able to conspire right in front of everyone? The society with a secret appears to be a society with an open secret and yet does thereby not at all become an open society. Maybe it is even hard to imagine an open society without an open secret. The society of the open secret openly tells everyone what it is about, it speaks out in public about their goals and ends. It thereby organises 'an open conspiracy',[58] and precisely this makes the difference between a secret society and a society with a secret quite visible.[59] A secret society conspires but shies away from the daylight, whereas a society with a secret does everything it does out in the open, in open public view, precisely because its founding principle is a shared practice of collective lying. Now, how does this work? The society with the secret knows that sometimes the best hiding place from the enemy is in plain view. Sometimes, when one knows that everyone assumes that whatever the leader says is a lie, this allows for actually telling the truth. The society with a secret is a society with an open secret when it initiates even their enemy into the reading protocol of its public discourse. It determines the way in which its own discourse is read by the others and thereby it can speak openly, yet everyone will take it as a disguise. It is possible to directly and publicly say the truth, even a horrible truth, if everyone believes it to be a lie or strategy of diverting everyone's attention anyhow.

What this second side introduces is thus a further twist on what it means to understand any public statement made as a falsification. Because everyone believes that what is said publicly is a lie, this assumption can be used to make the 'rhetorical move' that one can call 'the double lie'[60] – it is a form of lying about lying, a public feigning to feign, of lying to lie. It has a similar structure to the famous Jewish joke told by Freud: 'Why are you telling me you are going to Lemberg, when you are actually going to Lemberg?' Here this could be rendered as: 'Why are you telling me you are telling the truth' – because I cannot but assume that you are lying – 'when you really are telling me the truth?' This truth-telling works under condition of the primacy of the lie.[61] The moment the other, be it the enemy, the masses or whoever, is not a part and thus outside the society with a secret is made to assume that a society's public discourse cannot be taken at face value, this very society already started determining the entire field of the perception of this very discourse. Koyré's surprising and important diagnosis is thus that precisely in times that operate under the primacy of the lie, there emerges the dangerous possibility for a society with a secret to actually tell the truth that no one identifies as such. And it is precisely here that one must listen carefully. One can tell the truth, even though it might be unbearable if the other thinks it is a lie and thereby one might become able to say the impossible and publicly utter the otherwise unspeakable. It is precisely in times when lying appears to be everywhere that the most dangerous, the naked truths, are made invisible through their over-visibility and transparency. It alters the objective condition of the appearance of truth. Telling the truth can thus appear very different when it is done in the form of lying to lie (in the eyes of the others). Because then a true statement can at the same time veil and unveil its own truth (and horror). The political function of the modern lie is to veil such unveiled truth. This is an important lesson to be learnt.

Notes

1. It is certainly not entirely arbitrary that three important texts (Jankélevitch, Koyré and Sartre) on lying were written in the same period, Vichy France.
2. Alexandre Koyré, 'The Political Function of the Modern Lie', *Contemporary Jewish Record*, Vol. III (New York: American Jewish Committee, 1945), p. 290.
3. Martin Heidegger, 'Vom Wesen der Wahrheit. Vortrag am 5. Dezember 1930 in Marburg a.d.L. und am 11. Dezember 1930 in Freiburg i.Br.', in *Gesamtausgabe*, vol. 80.1. Vorträge. Teil 1: 1915–1952 (Frankfurt am Main: Klostermann, 2016), p. 389. My translation. It would be a longer discussion if and if so in what sense lying and deception is a genuinely human trait. This discussion gets more intricate when one takes into account that human beings are beings able to 'feign feigning', they can pretend to pretend, lie that they are lying. Some argued that this is a unique feature (cf. Jacques Lacan, 'The Subversion of the Subject and the Dialectic of Desire', in *Écrits* (London and New York: W. W. Norton, 2012, p. 683), others problematised this assumption (cf. Jacques Derrida, *The Beast and the Sovereign, Vol. 1* (Chicago: University of Chicago Press, 2011), pp. 97–135). For the present purposes, I will not revisit this debate about the lie and the human but rather problematise assumptions about the former alone.
4. Miguel Abensour, 'Rire des lois, du magistrat et des dieux', in *Jean Borreil. La raison de l'autre* (Paris: L'Harmattan, 1995), p. 93.
5. Friedrich Nietzsche, 'On Truth and Lies in a Nonmoral Sense', in *On Truth and Untruth. Selected Writings, Friedrich Nietzsche* (New York: Harper Perennial, 2010), pp. 20f.
6. Koyré, 'The Political Function', p. 290.
7. A pointed elaboration of crucial complexities can be found in: Alenka Zupančič, 'Lying on the Couch', *Problemi International*, vol. 1, no. 1 (2017), pp. 99–115. For an instructive overview of the prominent positions, see: *Lying and Truthfulness*,

ed. Kevin DeLapp and Jeremy Henkel (Indianapolis, IN and Cambridge: Hackett, 2016).
8. The text was first published in French under this title in a journal of the École Libre de Hautes Études (*Renaissance*).
9. He could otherwise have been tempted to see, like the early Wittgenstein, in language itself the reason for why thought presents itself in disguised form and not as itself. For an analysis of the linguistics of lying, cf. Harald Weinrich, *The Linguistics of Lying and Other Essays* (Seattle: University of Washington Press, 2005), pp. 3–80.
10. Koyré, 'The Political Function', p. 290.
11. Alain Badiou, *The Meaning of Sarkozy* (London and New York: Verso, 2008), p. 14.
12. I do not want to insinuate that today there is overall more lying than before. There is, for example, also the contrary diagnosis that there we witness less and less 'authentic lying' (Derrida) and even 'the death of the lie' in politics, as Albin Kurti called this in a conversation (e.g. traditional lying that attempted to protect the lie as well as the reason for lying from coming out seems to have been replaced by a type of lying that is easily discernible as such and even became indifferent about its own coming out.)
13. This discussion must certainly be closely connected to the grandiose recent work by Mladen Dolar. Cf., for example, his 'Gossip's Feast. Politics in the Time of Rumours', at <https://www.youtube.com/watch?v=bs55DaqjubA>.
14. Cf. Jacques Derrida, 'History of the Lie: Prolegomena', in *Without Alibi* (Stanford: Stanford University Press, 2002), p. 31. In this text, Derrida also criticises Koyré (and Arendt) for missing this point.
15. Aristotle, *Metaphysics* (Indianapolis, IN and Cambridge: Hackett, 2016), Δ 29, 1025a1, p. 96.
16. Derrida, 'History of the Lie', p. 31.
17. Derrida, 'History of the Lie', pp. 58ff.
18. Surprisingly, throughout his essay, Derrida seems to counter Nietzsche who famously claimed: 'Man forgets, of course, this is how things are; he therefore lies in this way unconsciously . . .'. Nietzsche, 'On Truth and Lies in a Nonmoral Sense', p. 30.
19. Plato, *Lesser Hippias*, in *Complete Works*, ed. John M. Copper (Indianapolis, IN and Cambridge: Hackett, 1997), p. 926 (367a).
20. Koyré, 'The Political Function', p. 290.
21. Koyré, 'The Political Function', p. 290.
22. Alexandre Koyré, *From the Closed World to the Infinite Universe* (Baltimore: Johns Hopkins University Press, 1957), pp. vii and 7.
23. Koyré speaks in a different context also of 'another world' that already emerged with Machiavelli. Cf. Alexandre Koyré, 'La pensée moderne', in *Études histoires de la pensée scientifiques* (Paris: Gallimard, 1973), p. 21.

24. Koyré, 'The Political Function', p. 290. Over sixty years later, one finds a similar diagnosis and the claim that 'lying never lay so heavily on an entire country as on Germany under Hitler's dictatorship.' Weinrich, *The Linguistics*, p. 6.
25. Whereas Derrida, when discussing Hannah Arendt, suggests there is merely a 'mutation'. Cf. Derrida, 'History of the Lie', p. 40.
26. Koyré, 'The Political Function', p. 291. This is relevant because Derrida critiques Arendt for assuming that the movement of history culminates in 'a hyperbolic growth of the lie . . . in short, the absolute lie: not absolute knowledge as the end of history, but history as the conversion to the absolute lie.' Derrida, 'History of the Lie', p. 40.
27. Derrida claims that when the lie becomes absolute the distinction between lying and truth-telling collapses: 'The absolute lie . . . *can always* survive indefinitely without anyone knowing anything about it or without anyone being there any longer to know it or remember it.' This as a logical possibility only, because absolute lying would eradicate any stable definition of lying altogether. Koyré, 'The Political Function', p. 293. For Arendt's position that I am not discussing, cf. Hannah Arendt, 'Lying in Politics: Reflections on the Pentagon Papers', in *Crises of the Republic* (New York: Harcourt, 1972) and 'Truth and Politics', in *Between Past and Future. Eight Exercises in Political Thought* (New York: Viking, 1961).
28. Koyré, 'The Political Function', p. 291. This a diagnosis that one can also find articulated by analysts of modern lifestyles (cosmetics, veils, masks, clothing in general). Cf., for example, Karl E. Scheibe, 'In Defense of Lying: On the Moral Neutrality of Misrepresentation', cited in Martin Jay, *The Virtues of Mendacity. On Lying in Politics* (Charlottesville, VA and London: University of Virginia Press, 2010), p. 29. There was also the famous 'credibility-gap' in the 1960s in American politics, which became a well-known phenomenon in Western democracies. Already Adorno noted that 'the less the people believe in political integrity, the more easily can they be taken in by politicians who rant against politics.' Cf. Theodor W. Adorno, 'Democratic Leadership and Mass Manipulation', in *Gesammelte Schriften*, Vol. 20.1: Vermischte Schriften, I (Frankfurt am Main: Suhrkamp, 1986), p. 271.
29. John Forrester, *Truth Games. Lies, Money and Psychoanalysis* (Cambridge, MA: Harvard University Press, 1997), p. 7.
30. Koyré, 'The Political Function', p. 291.
31. Koyré, 'The Political Function', p. 291.
32. Koyré, 'The Political Function', p. 291.
33. Koyré, 'The Political Function', p. 291.
34. Ernst Bloch remarked comparably that 'the false does not want that one speaks the truth about it. Which is why no idiom about the lie is true.' Ernst Bloch, 'Die Fabel des Menenius Agrippa oder eine der ältesten Soziallügen', in *Politische Messungen,*

Pestzeit, Vormärz (Frankfurt am Main: Suhrkamp, 1970), p. 172. Can there be a true discourse about lying?

35. Koyré, 'The Political Function', p. 291.
36. Koyré, 'The Political Function', p. 291.
37. Koyré, 'The Political Function', p. 292. For an instructive overview, cf. Jay, *The Virtues of Mendacity*.
38. Koyré, 'The Political Function', p. 292.
39. Zupančič, 'Lying on the Couch', p. 102.
40. Carl Schmitt will read this as what objectively grounds 'the dialectic of power and impotence' which necessitates that in view of this 'infinite tidal-sea of truth and lie, reality and possibility' someone else but the sovereign must choose what can be assumed to be true and what not. Cf. Carl Schmitt, *Dialogues on Power and Space* (Cambridge: Polity, 2015), p. 34.
41. Koyré, 'The Political Function', p. 292.
42. Along these lines, Sartre claimed that lying is an essentially affirmative act in which 'consciousness affirms that it exists by nature *as hidden from the Other*'. This is to say, what I share with the other is what will necessarily remain hidden from him and this hiddenness comes to the fore through the act of lying. Jean-Paul Sartre, *Being and Nothingness: A Phenomenological Essay on Ontology* (New York: Philosophical Library, 1956), p. 88.
43. Koyré, 'The Political Function', p. 293.
44. Koyré, 'The Political Function', p. 293. For this cf. Alexander Stagnell, *Diplomacy and Ideology: From the French Revolution to the Digital Age* (London and New York: Routledge, 2020).
45. Koyré, 'The Political Function', p. 293.
46. Koyré, 'The Political Function', p. 293.
47. Koyré, 'The Political Function', p. 293.
48. Koyré, 'The Political Function', p. 293.
49. Koyré, 'The Political Function', p. 294.
50. Koyré, 'The Political Function', p. 294.
51. Koyré, 'The Political Function', p. 294.
52. Forrester, *Truth Games. Lies, Money and Psychoanalysis*, p. 17.
53. Forrester, *Truth Games. Lies, Money and Psychoanalysis*, p. 17f.
54. And Koyré will point out how this even determines the inner structure of the collective:

> The initiated know it, the initiated and those worthy of being so. They will understand and decipher, they will penetrate the veil that masks the truth. The others, the enemy, the masses, including the organization's own rank and

file, will swallow the public pronouncements as the pure truth, and by this token reveal themselves unworthy of sharing in the secret truth, of belonging to the elite. (Koyré, 'The Political Function', p. 298)

This is complicated by the subsequent aspect.
55. Koyré, 'The Political Function', p. 295.
56. Koyré, 'The Political Function', 296. It is a longer discussion if the label 'totalitarian' is really appropriate. For this cf. Slavoj Žižek, *Did Somebody Say Totalitarianism? Five Interventions in the (Mis)Use of a Notion* (London and New York: Verso, 2011). Derrida convincingly remarks that what Koyré describes with this term should be expanded to also account for the working of the 'capitalistico-techno-mediatic power' that the news agencies generate. Cf. Derrida, 'History of the Lie', p. 56.
57. Koyré, 'The Political Function', p. 297.
58. Koyré, 'The Political Function', p. 297.
59. The open conspiracy functions thereby similar to a symptom, because there is always a 'true lying of the symptom'. Cf. Jacques-Alain Miller, *Pièces détachées – Cours no. 1, 17.11.2004*, at: <2004-2005-Pièces-détachées-JA-Miller.pdf> (jonathanleroy. be), p. 9. This is to say it veils what it unveils.
60. Forrester, *Truth Games. Lies, Money and Psychoanalysis*, p. 18.
61. Here Koyré's diagnosis might need some actualisation as he states:

> The point could well be made that far from concealing and dissembling their immediate or long-range aims, the totalitarian governments have always proclaimed them *urbi et orbi* as no democratic government has ever had the courage to do, and that it is absurd to pin the lie on someone like Hitler who made public his entire program in *Mein Kampf*, and proceeded to realize it point by point.

Even democratic governments seem to have learnt something since Koyré's time. Koyré, 'The Political Function', p. 296.

13   A Short Essay on Conspiracy Theories
Alenka Zupančič

LET'S BEGIN WITH a fairly obvious fact: conspiracies certainly exist.[1] The designation 'conspiracy theory' is often used simply as a means of discrediting certain perfectly rational suggestions about something not being such as presented by official authorities, about there being more to it that meets the eye, about the existence of other hidden motivations and agendas. However, we somehow also feel that there is a difference between (hitherto) unproved suspicions and assumptions about hidden manipulations or agendas and conspiracy theories in the strict sense of the term. Even though it is sometimes hard to tell what exactly this difference would be, and it seems that conspiracy theories simply cease to be considered conspiracy theories when they turn out to be true. This would suggest that we are dealing with a relationship similar to that between the potential and the actual: conspiracy theories are like a reservoir of numerous hypotheses and possibilities, only some of which turn out to be true (and, in so doing, losing the status of being conspiracy theories). Yet, it is clear that this kind of distinction somehow misses the essence of what is at issue with conspiracy theories. For the latter carry in themselves a real, *factual* surplus of theory, which cannot be reduced to, or absorbed into, the difference between theory and actuality. In other words, the question is not simply that of actuality (existence) or non-actuality (non-existence) of some conspiratorial plot, but at least as much that of a specific actuality, reality, of the *theory* itself. The investment, the passion, involved in 'conspiracy theories' is not simply on the side of conspiracies and their revealing, but at least as much on the side of fabricating, forming, producing the theory, assembling or recognising the things that attest to it, interpreting and connecting the clues.

When it comes to conspiracy theories we could thus use the paradigm of Lacan's famous commentary on jealousy: even when our partner is, in fact, cheating on us, there is still something pathological about our jealousy; there is a surplus that the 'correspondence with facts' cannot fully absorb. We could similarly say that even though some conspiracies really exist, there is still something pathological that pertains to conspiracy theories, some surplus investment that is not reducible to these or those facts. On the other hand, it is important to stress that the 'pathology' at stake here is never simply an individual pathology, but rather registers as a social pathology. As Frederic Jameson beautifully argued in his seminal study of conspiracy films of the 1970s and 1980s, conspiratorial thinking functions as an important means of cognitive mapping in late capitalism – it could be seen as almost the only way left to think about the social as *totality* and about the collective (as opposed to the individual).[2]

Yet, our focus here will be not so much on the possible subversive aesthetic of conspiracy theories as on their epistemological passion and its limit, that is on 'theory'. Within a more generalised feeling of anxiety related to (im)possible presentations of social totality, an almost imperceptible shift of emphasis occurs with conspiracy theories: the emphasis shifts from the reality described by some conspiracy theory ('in truth, the facts are such and such'), to conspiracy, deception, as such. This accounts for the so-called 'paranoid' aspect of conspiracy theories: someone is deliberately manipulating us, doing everything in order to – not simply gain from it – but to *deceive* us, divert us from how things really stand. There are many shades of this, some of them clearly classifiable as serious pathology, with a reference to 'Them' remaining as the only consistent thread, whereas everything else dissolves into a rather messy bulk. A good example is the following testimony of one of the passionate Flat Earthers who gets the chance to explain his convictions in the Netflix documentary *Behind the Curve*:

> And then I found out that it's actually, that biblical cosmology is a geocentric cosmology, then I realised why they are hiding the truth. It's because they don't want anyone to know anything. They want people dumb, blind, deaf to the truth, so they can inject you with their vaccines, and their public schooling and this heliocentric model, which is basically forced sun worship.

It soon becomes all about *Them*, who want us to be become so and so, to do and believe this or that. The agent of conspiracy – even if it remains vague and undefined – is in the foreground, omnipresent and implied in a series of bizarre metonymical shifts concerning the content (vaccinations, public schooling, paganism), the logical connection between which seems clear to the speaker, but much less so to the listener (in our case, it seems to be taken randomly from the evangelist repertoire). In this respect, narratives of conspiracy theorists can often strike us as akin to the logic of dreams and the connections established by what Freud called the dream-work: they seem perfectly logical and self-evident to the dreamer, but when the latter wakes up, they appear very strange and illogical. And Freud of course was right to insist that there nevertheless *is* a logic involved in the dream-work.

Something else about conspiracy theories is interesting and resembles dreams. For the most part, we can say that they do involve or touch some real, or that, with their incredible narratives, they propose a deformed and displaced articulation of something that could be called, with Lacan, '*le peu du réel*', a little piece of the real. Let's take the example of a quite popular theory according to which the moon landing was staged in a film studio and never really happened. As Jodi Dean has nicely shown,[3] during the period of the Cold War, the entire American space programme had been intrinsically linked to its own television presentation. The rooting and implementation of the TV culture (TV as the new big Other, as the modern focal point, the 'home fire' of every family) had taken place simultaneously and in close relationship to the development of the space programme; from the very outset, the presentation of this programme had been targeting TV audiences, and this included the criteria for choosing and presenting the key protagonists (astronauts) and their families. Could we not infer from this that television and the moon landing were, in fact, materially bound together in a kind of surplus overlapping or fusion, and that it is the real of this fusion that, in a displaced form, propels and surfaces in theories according to which the landing never really happened and was entirely studio staged. This does not mean that the surplus of TV staging involved in NASA's moon expedition 'explains' this particular conspiracy theory or that the latter can be reduced to it. There are many more things at stake, but we can say that the investment in its TV staging, and in the wholesome presentation-production of the expedition, functions as the 'little piece of the real' – probably not the only one – at work in this conspiracy theory.

In any case, conspiracy theories are a complex and interesting phenomenon which cannot simply be dismissed with disdain. Even less so in these times when some of the most bizarre of conspiracy theories seem to be forcefully entering the public space, the mainstream, even official politics. (The most striking example here is probably the link between QAnon and the politics and person of Donald Trump; according to some sources more than thirty-five candidates for congress adhered to this conspiracy theory, which we'll look into in more detail later.) And this is an important shift in the social status of conspiracy theories compared to their marginal and positionally subversive status in the 1970s and 1980s. There are many reasons for this march of conspiracy theories from the social margins to its centre, and they are situated on many different levels.

For example, one often points the finger at what appears in our contemporary Western society as a kind of vulgar and generalised postmodern realisation of 'Nietzscheism': the decline of objective truth as value and as epistemological category. In this vein, one likes to attribute the fact that 'it is no longer possible to distinguish truth from fiction' to the influence of modern and postmodern theory, to the deconstruction of the notion of the original, to the undermining of different authorities and to the general promotion of relativism and nominalism . . . But, in this enthusiasm of rediscovered realism, one also tends to forget a very realistic fact that it is often quite *objectively* hard to distinguish between the two. Counterfeits and 'fakes' are in fact getting better and better; technology has produced some astonishing and disturbing effects in this regard. Our social relations in late capitalism are excessively fictionised, in order for the *reality* of capital to be able to follow its course. And, this is not a question of theory, but of real material configurations that include and necessitate such fictions.[4] 'Postmodern' questioning and undermining of the original has long since moved to reality itself, and is no longer simply 'a question of perspective', of a theory or an 'ideology' of the multitude of different perspectives.

We can, of course, agree that the supposedly democratic relativising and levelling of different claims, with scientific claims appearing as just one of many 'language games', appear today as a considerable social problem, as does the dissolution of the 'public' as a general or common platform that has long played the role of the shared big Other and its replacement with particularised and privatised truths. Yet, even if we accept this rather simplistic thesis according to which it was 'relativism' that paved the way for conspiracy theories to enter the mainstream, this by no means implies that conspiracy theories swear by relativism. On the contrary, they take the category of truth very seriously. They believe that there is Truth; they are just convinced that this truth is different or other than the official one. The paradigmatic idea of conspiracy theories is not that 'there are many truths', but that *there exists another Truth*.

Critical Theory and Conspiracy Theories

In this precise point conspiracy theories do not so much resemble a 'Nietzschean relativism' as they come close to a certain tradition of critical theory, of 'critique' – as Bruno Latour waggishly observed some time ago:

> Let me be mean for a second. What's the real difference between conspiracists and a popularized, that is a teachable version of social critique inspired by a too quick reading of, let's say, a sociologist as eminent as Pierre Bourdieu (to be polite I will stick with the French field commanders)? In both cases, you have to learn to become suspicious of everything people say because of course we all know that

they live in the thralls of a complete *illusion* of their real motives. Then, after disbelief has struck and an explanation is requested for what is really going on, in both cases again it is the same appeal to powerful agents hidden in the dark acting always consistently, continuously, relentlessly. Of course, we in the academy like to use more elevated causes – society, discourse, knowledge-slash-power, fields of forces, empires, capitalism – while conspiracists like to portray a miserable bunch of greedy people with dark intents, but I find something troublingly similar in the structure of the explanation, in the first movement of disbelief and, then, in the wheeling of causal explanations coming out of the deep dark below. [. . .] Of course conspiracy theories are an absurd deformation of our own arguments, but, like weapons smuggled through a fuzzy border to the wrong party, these are our weapons nonetheless. In spite of all the deformations, it is easy to recognize, still burnt in the steel, our trademark: *Made in Criticalland*.[5]

Latour concludes from there that the pertinence of critical theory (which he has been himself part of) may be running out, and critique should be set on different foundations, should change profoundly. In other words, his essay is also a programmatic text that accompanies his own philosophical turn to ontological realism or 'practical metaphysics', as he calls it in his book *Reassembling the Social*. This is, of course, not the place to engage in the discussion of Latour's work and his version of metaphysics. What is interesting for our present purposes is perhaps the following, which makes the landscape we are dealing with rather more complex: Latour's turning away from critical theory moves, in fact, in the direction of radical *relativism*, of affirming the existence of multiple contradictory worlds and claims, which are all of the same ontological value. Put in the simplest form, the fundamental Latourian thesis is this: there exists no basic structure of reality, but, instead, a plurality of realities ('words') which shall all be considered of equal ontological weight, all considered as 'objective'. There are no subjective facts. Similarly, we need to take seriously (and literally) the claims of different actors about what motivates them, instead of always looking for another, truer explanation.

So, paradoxically, Latour uses the comparison of critical theory with conspiracy theories to argue a point which, in its consequences, sounds like a universalisation of conspiracy theories: to every actor her conspiracy theory. What he deems problematic in the logical modality of conspiracy theories (as well as in critique or critical theory) is only the fact that these theories believe in truth at all and in a possibly different reality (different from what seems to be the case), in the existence of a basic structure of reality, in the possibility for things – including what we get as 'facts' – *to be explained* (in another way) *by any interpretation, narrative or theory*. This then is the point that critical theory shares with conspiracy theories: they both believe in the existence of another, different truth. Contrary to this, Latour's metaphysics is radically opposed to the very modality of interpretation and of sceptical attitude. We could say that, in Latour's metaphysics, conspiracy theories are one of the multiple worlds (or several of them) which enter as such into interaction with other worlds. They are not problematic because of their views or what they hold to be true, but merely because of their 'critical' epistemological point of departure, which is, in fact, 'dogmatic' (there exists a basic structure of reality which we can establish). One should also not forget that the target of Latour's essay is, in fact, 'critique' and not conspiracy theories, the latter appearing as a means of discrediting the epistemological presuppositions (and ontological consequences) of critique on account of its proximity to conspiracy theories. Yet, this is above all a rhetorical manoeuvre which, in its implications, nevertheless seems to be much too simplistic.

What is attributed to 'critique' in this perspective is paradoxically what Nietzsche attributed to classical metaphysics: the belief in the existence of two worlds, one apparent and one true, whereby the 'critique' involves interpreting the world according to the automatic presupposition that appearances are always deceiving and that there exists another, truer explanation. Sceptical attitude and hermeneutical passion, 'passion for interpretation', are in this sense also and obviously quite different from the claim that 'there are no facts, only interpretations', since interpretation is here driven by the conviction that it operates in the service of the truth (in the singular), that it leads somewhere and that it matters where it leads. Latour's main target is thus the conviction that there even exists such a thing as a right explanation. In this sense, he is indeed much closer to 'postmodernism' than to critical theory. In his endeavour to undermine the perspective of 'critique', relativism is not Latour's enemy, but his ally. This is useful to keep in mind when reading the following observation, with which we could otherwise fully agree.

> In which case the danger would no longer be coming from an excessive confidence in ideological arguments posturing as matters of fact – as we have learned to combat so efficiently in the past – but from an excessive *distrust* of good matters of fact disguised as bad ideological biases! While we spent years trying to detect the real prejudices hidden behind the appearance of objective statements, do we now have to reveal the real objective and incontrovertible facts hidden behind the *illusion* of prejudices? And yet entire Ph.D. programs are still running to make sure that good American kids are learning the hard way that facts are made up, that there is no such thing as natural, unmediated, unbiased access to truth, that we are always prisoners of language, that we always speak from a particular standpoint, and so on, while dangerous extremists are using the very same argument of social construction to destroy hard-won evidence that could save our lives.[6]

The efficiency of this argument resides in explicating the turn which we probably all experience as very true: on many levels of our society, we are witnessing lately a massive discrediting of different facts (for example: of scientific evidence of climate change, of the existence of the COVID-19 virus, of the safety of the vaccines, of the credibility of public media . . .), so that many different actors, starting with conspiracy theorists, no longer trust these facts and see them as the embodiment of prejudices, as ideological fog, illusion, manipulation. In the present context of the COVID crisis, we can, in fact, also see how a considerable part of the so-called 'critical public' (and theory) at least partly overlaps in their views with conspiracists. However, when greeting Latour's diagnosis with approval, we must not forget that his point and 'solution' is not at all a return to and reaffirmation of 'true facts' (for example, scientific facts) and their defence against the 'dangerous extremists' he evokes, but, on the contrary, a radicalisation of relativism, with the difference between illusion and reality becoming utterly irrelevant. In other words, Latour does not suggest that we should start revealing the objective and provable facts which are now hidden behind the *illusion* of prejudices (hidden in their *appearing* as prejudices), but that we should completely abandon the very (epistemological and ontological) apparatus of *distinguishing* between the two. Everything that exists is an objective and relevant fact. Facts are not the opposite of illusion or fiction – the latter also constitute facts.

We propose to take Latour's suggestion from the above quotation more literally, as a useful identification of the change that has occurred in the relationship between illusion and actuality. But we are not willing simply to give up on the epistemological value of this distinction between illusion and actuality which, moreover, cannot be reduced to the distinction between a true and an apparent world. And, I hope it is needless to stress that we find within the tradition of critical theory powerful currents and works that strongly resist this oversimplified distinction between two worlds (true and apparent), which can be said to actually miss the essence of 'critique'. Of course, this essay cannot be an occasion for analysing critical theory and its relationship to Latour's theory, which we are leaving behind at this point. We'll simply take the suggestion about a conspicuous similarity of the 'first reflex' (scepticism) that conspiracy theories share with critical theory as a starting point for exposing some of their important differences. This will then hopefully help us shed some new light on several fundamental structural traits of conspiracy theories.

The Subject Supposed to Deceive (Us)

Let's start with the automatism of doubting everything that presents itself as official fact, that is to say with the principled and pronounced sceptical attitude. For example, the key point of the ideology critique is that it is not enough to define ideology as 'false consciousness' and that one needs to carefully examine the ways in which this 'falseness' materially exists in reality and in our everyday practices. Scepticism takes place primarily with respect to symbolic authorities, with respect to 'power', to the supposed self-evidence of general consensus or simply with respect to everything 'official'. However, while critical theory examines the means and ways in which, for instance, the 'manufacturing of consent' takes place, and hence focuses its critical lenses upon consensus reality, upon the way in which certain facts are being produced as facts, upon their inner structuring and dialectics, upon the workings of ideology (mechanisms that usually operate right before our eyes, on the surface, and are inseparably bound up with a given reality), a conspiracy theory immediately jumps to what is behind, to hidden depths, to another reality. It never really deals with (critical) analysis of facts and of reality in their inner structure, but simply sweeps them away as false examined seriously – and *thus irrelevant*. The basic assumption of any critical theory worthy of its name, on the other hand, is that precisely as 'false' these facts are extremely relevant for the analysis and have to be taken and examined seriously. This basic move from the problematic character of facts and reality to their resulting *irrelevance* represents indeed – in a quite literal way – the first step towards the 'loss of reality' characteristic of conspiracy theories. The interrogation of why and how illusions appear and structure our reality gets immediately solved/dismissed by evoking the Agent of alleged conspiracy, which 'explains' everything at once. It seems that this Agent of conspiracy, with all the often very complex machinations it is purportedly orchestrating, has only one fundamental agenda: to deceive us, to keep us in error – not so much to deceive us *about* this or that, but to deceive us, full stop. It is usually also not very clear why It does this: deception as such seems to be the main and sufficient motive. Of course, we often get hear about 'Their' interests, 'Their' profiting from it . . . But these interests and profit habitually remain rather unclear and uncertain, especially if we take into consideration all the incredible efforts and expenses put into deception. Take, for example, the efforts (and costs) that would have been needed for 'Them' to sustain the illusion of a round earth rotating around the sun, if the earth were, in fact, flat: any possible interest, profit or gain dissolve in the face of what appears as a much stronger and primordial Interest or Will: to deceive us.

Conspiracy theorists thus have a very interesting and intricate relationship to what Lacan calls the agency of the big Other. On the one hand, they are convinced that a big Other very much exists (they believe in in the existence of an agency which is in itself consistent, operates purposefully, pulls all the strings and coordinates them). Yet they also believe that this agency is fundamentally and deliberately deceiving. We could say that they believe in the existence of Descartes's hypothetical evil genius or demon from the beginning of the *Meditations*, who deliberately deceives us about everything. Could we conclude from this that we are basically dealing with a desperate attempt to preserve the agency of the big Other in the times of its disintegration into a generalised relativism, an attempt that can succeed only at the price of moving the big Other to the zone of malevolence and evil? The consistency of the big Other (its not being 'barred') can no longer manifest itself in anything else but in the Other successfully deceiving us. A consistent big Other can only be a big Deceiver (a big Fraud or Cheat), an evil Other. A consistent God can only be an evil God; nothing else adds up. Yet better an evil God than no God.

Yet to explain this by the 'need for a big Other' does not seem to exhaust the phenomenon and the meaning of the assumption shared by all conspiracy theories, namely that there exists a Subject or Agent who is deliberately deceiving us. The libidinal emphasis is not merely on the existence of the Other (better an evil Other than no Other at all); the deceptiveness and evilness of the Other rather seem to be *constitutive* of His existence, not just the price of this existence. The presupposition is thus somewhat stronger and could be formulated in this way: the big Other can only be deceiving/malevolent, or else It does not exist. Deceitfulness and malevolence seem to vouch from within for the consistency of the big Other – the consistency that remains utterly untouched in the midst of all the allegedly 'radical critique' and scepticism at work in conspiracy theories. The Other *is* almighty. We can certainly detect here an inner limit of the critical attitude and scepticism on which conspiracy theorists like to pride themselves. They are not at all too critical or too sceptical, but, rather, not critical and sceptical enough. They don't believe anyone or anything, they are sceptical of every 'fact', yet they believe in a big Other deceiving us consistently, systematically and unfailingly at all times. Related to this is another feedback loop of conspiracy theories, their blind spot that appears as tautology and as their inner limit. If a conspiracy theory turns out to be 'true' and thus becomes the official version of events, this throws a dubious light on the figure of the almighty Deceiver, who thus turns out to be less mighty and consistent than we have claimed. Conspiracy theorists often invest great efforts in proving their theories. Yet, if they succeed with these proofs, this puts their original presuppositions in a bad light: was this then really a Conspiracy, or just an (unsuccessful) attempt to cover up certain facts? The condition of existence of a Conspiracy is, in a way, that it can never really become the official version of events. If this happens, it itself provides grounds for suspicion: maybe this is a new, even more perfidious tactic (a double game), involving a deeper level of Conspiracy . . .

Let's imagine for a moment that an objective investigation would, in fact, confirm that the moon landing was staged and filmed in a studio. Would the supporters of this theory be triumphantly opening campaigns, celebrating that their theory prevailed and that they have been *right* all along? I think it is safe to say that this would not be the case. This is because what they want to be 'right' about in this whole matter is not the question whether or not man has indeed stepped on the moon, but the claim that 'They' are systematically deceiving us about that. The moment conspiracy theories turn out to be 'right,' they also turn out to be wrong, since the (successful) deception is over. Conspiracy theories are right about the authorities systematically and deliberately deceiving us only insofar as the deception fully works. At least partly related to this is yet another distinctive feature of conspiracy theorists: that they can easily let go of one conspiracy theory and embrace another, that they tend to rotate between different conspiracy theories (often believing in several at once). The emphasis is not so much on the content, as it is on the modality of conspiracy, that is on the fact that there is a conspiracy going on. What follows from there is that, in their insisting on *another truth*, the emphasis is not so much on truth as it is on 'another', other, different. More exactly, otherness constitutes here an inherent moment of truth; truth is always other (than official) –hence its plasticity and slipperiness.

Conspiracy does not exist only on 'Their' side, on the side of the deceiving Other(s); there is also something conspiratorial that exists on the side of conspiracy theorists. It is not only that Conspiracies are supposedly planned and carried out in secret locations, where the evil and powerful meet and rule the world; conspiracy theorists also keep to secret, dark locations, away from the sunlight (for example, in the depths of the Internet), and there is certainly something like a conspiratorial 'complicity' that exists between them: a certain tie, an initiation into and sharing of some surplus knowledge – yet a surplus knowledge that exists only so long as there exists a Conspiracy on the other side.

Conspiracy theorists are usually caught in a mirroring, imaginary relationship with the (deceitful) Other. On the one hand, there is 'us' (who know what is *really* going on), and on the other side are 'Them' (who, of course, also know what is going on, since they are the agents of all the machinations). In between are the naive, blinded masses of people who, with their belief in the 'official version' of events propagated by 'Them', actually testify to the existence and the colossal dimension of conspiracy. What most people believe does not appear in this configuration as a 'reality check' that could make the conspiracy theorists pause and perhaps doubt their beliefs, but, on the contrary, appear as proving the rightfulness of the conspiracy theorists' beliefs.

We mentioned above the *surplus knowledge*, which also constitutes an important element of this configuration. 'Our' surplus knowledge, our knowledge about how things really stand, functions as a direct guarantee (testimony about) the consistency of the big Other, of the big Deceiver. Or, perhaps more precisely: our surplus knowledge is in a way a worldly appearing, embodiment of this consistency, its 'extimate' core. The key to the consistency of the big Other dwells outside Him; it dwells in us, who are able to see it, and to take care of it with our theories and interpretative efforts.

The Delirium of Interpretation

Related to the preceding is a specific 'delirium of interpretation' at work in conspiracy theories. Paradoxically, the interpretation is fuelled here by knowledge of the solution, of the end result: the basic question is how to read and interpret what takes place or appears in this world in such a way that we'll get a result given in advance (existing in the basic claims of a conspiracy theory), and which differs from the 'obvious' explanation. In this respect, conspiracy theories resemble what is known from the history of science (particularly astronomy) as 'saving the phenomena' – with the 'choice' between the Ptolemaic system and the heliocentric model as the most famous example. The Ptolemaic system, based on the presupposition of the earth as the centre of the universe, around which other planets circulate, started to be confronted at some point with a growing mass of empirical telescopic observations of planetary movements which did not appear as circular. In response to this, the Ptolemaic astronomers developed a very complex theory of epicycles and eccentric orbits, which would be able to reconcile the observation results with the basic presumption (that the earth stands motionless and the planets circulate around it), and hence to account for the discordant 'facts'. The heliocentric hypothesis was able to account for these facts better and in a much simpler way, but it required a radical change of the most fundamental cosmological presuppositions. Conspiracy theories often strike us as similar to this practice of 'saving the phenomena': they introduce additional hypotheses and much more complicated explanations of the same events in order to justify their version of reality, which they believe in and take as their starting point.

In addition to the figure of the big Other as the big Deceiver, there also exists in some conspiracy theories a more specific instance of a specular, mirror-image big Other: a big Other that is on 'our' side, a good big Other, the carrier of Truth and Light. This is a feature that brings some of these conspiracy theories close to religion. The good, truthful Other differs considerably, in its inherent structuring, from the big Other of the consistently deceptive narrative. It functions as a sort of Oracle, as a Grey Eminence of enigmatic messages, which as such do not (yet) form a consistent narrative. It falls to us to construct this Narrative. This is the figure of the good big Other that we encounter, for example, in what is probably the most popular political conspiracy theory today: QAnon.

On 28 October 2017, 'Q' emerged from the primordial swamp of the Internet on the message board 4chan, and quickly established his legend as a government insider with top security clearance (the co-called Q-clearance) who knew the truth about the secret struggle for power between Trump and the 'deep state'. Since then, he has posted more than 4,000 times, and moved from posting on 4chan to posting on 8chan in November 2017, went silent for several months after 8chan shut down in August 2019, and eventually re-emerged on a new website established by 8chan's owner, 8kun.[7] Though posting anonymously, Q uses a 'trip code' that allows followers to distinguish his posts from those of other anonymous users (known as 'Anons'). Q's posts are cryptic and elliptical, enigmatic. They often consist of a long string of leading questions designed to guide readers towards discovering the 'truth' for themselves through 'research'. The beauty of this procedure is, of course, that when a concrete prediction fails to come to pass (which happens fairly often), the true believers quickly adapt their narratives to account for inconsistencies. For close followers of QAnon, the posts (or 'drops') contain 'crumbs' of intelligence that they 'bake' into 'proofs'. For 'bakers', QAnon is both a fun hobby and a deadly serious calling. (Here we can see again how 'bakers' resemble in their functioning what Freud called the dream-work, composing a seemingly 'consistent' narrative out of bits and 'crumbs' of realty.)

This particular theory, for which many hold that it is more than a conspiracy theory (a worldview akin to a new religion or a new political movement), thus involves a hierarchical structure, at the centre of which stands 'our', good, big Other, fighting from the underground against the evil big Other who rules the world and keeps us prisoners of all kinds of illusions. The iconography of 'resistance movement' that stands at the heart of one of the most reactionary conspiracy theories is in itself very interesting in instructive. The movie *The Matrix* presents us with a kind of 'leftist' version of a very similar configuration: a smaller group of 'freedom fighters' is resisting the big Other who keeps the world caught in a gigantic illusion of life and reality; from the underground the freedom fighters try to break this spell and fight for emancipation. The key figure for the success of this fight is called – the Oracle.

In QAnon Q functions indeed as an oracle: thanks to his supposed access to the highest secrets he is an embodiment of the absolute surplus knowledge, the 'crumbs' of which fall among his followers who then 'bake' stories out of them – they bake and compose these narratives based on their own research and interpretation. It probably goes without saying that the passion involved in this research is in itself a considerable satisfaction and hence reward for the bakers' efforts. In some ways, we are dealing with a challenge and a passion similar to that involved in a whole range of games, except that here the lines between game and reality are obliterated from the very outset and the stakes so much the higher. For to be good in this game means to know more about the (true) reality of the world. Besides 'bakers' and the most fervent followers, there is also a big crowd of 'ordinary' believers who simply take these narratives, this *work* (of conspiracy theory) *in progress*, seriously. But also with these 'ordinary people,' we can detect an unmistakable passion for interpretation, a considerable amount of self-initiative in researching and establishing all kinds of connections, which can also vary considerably – within the general narrative framework of QAnon – depending on the local environment and personal obsessions.

Opposite the big Other of conspiracy, the big Deceiver thus stands in this conspiracy theory as an oracular big Other; the latter does not tell us the Truth (except, of course, in its vaguest contours), but it helps *us* guess it, dig it out or 'reconstruct' it, fully spell it out by ourselves – and, hence, subjectivise it, take it for our own and, if needed, defend it passionately. We could recall here Lacan's remarks concerning the function and functioning of enigma. Taking as an example the enigma that the Sphinx posed to Oedipus who, by answering it, became the king (and, hence, fixed his destiny), Lacan points out that Oedipus could have answered differently to the Sphinx's question ('What it is that first goes on four feet, then two and finally on three?'). But, in this case, he wouldn't be the Oedipus we know:

> I think you can see what the function of the enigma means – it's a half-said [*mi-dire*], just as the Chimera appears as a half-body, with the risk of disappearing altogether once the solution has been found.
>
> If I insisted at length on the difference in level between the utterance [*énonciation*] and the statement [*énoncé*], it was so that the function of the enigma would make sense. An enigma is most likely that, an utterance, I charge you with the task of making it into a statement. Sort that out as best you can – as Oedipus did – and you will bear the consequences. That is what is at issue in an enigma.[8]

When solving this kind of enigma, we sort of stake ourselves as a wager; we get involved in the reality that we are deciphering; we become a guarantee of this reality. This explains well the investment, the zeal, one can observe in conspiracy theorists – including those conspiracy theories that do not involve any oracular figure and where the enigma consists in putting together different pieces of the world in such a way that they would accord with the utterance describing an alternative reality (a flat earth, for example).

In this sense, the truth that we establish based on our own 'research' and deciphering of enigmatic, oracular messages is, of course, much more strongly subjectivised; for in a way, it *is* the truth of the subject. One cannot have a neutral, indifferent stance towards it. It is also much more militantly efficient than a truth simply told or revealed. This is because we spend hours, days, years looking for and establishing certain connections, moving our 'knowledge' from the register of supposedly 'better knowledge' to the register of a considerable 'occupation' of this knowledge. We are personally invested in it, since it binds knowledge to our very Being, a being which we are ready to pawn for this knowledge (for deciphering the truth). The subjective investment has, of course, many practical and – in the case of QAnon, politically objective – consequences.

At issue is also an extremely 'productive' type of link between knowledge and belief, which looks like a caricature of what psychoanalysis conceptualised with the notion of *transference*. The blind faith in some of the basic claims (and/or their heralds) is the condition or trigger of the mass production of (surplus) knowledge. In other words, involved here is not just a blind faith in a certain conspiracy's dogmas or truths, but also the fact the *we* personally (and 'autonomously') dig out and reconstruct the truth through our own labour and research. This is based on an infallible faith which already contains the end result. The research and the knowledge based on it are, in this sense, like pieces of a puzzle the design of which already exists in its contours, although it also remains 'plastic' and ambiguous in many ways. Yet, this description is still too simple. For we need to pay attention to an important spin, a circular redoubling that we can see in many testimonies of fervent followers of different conspiracy theories. Many emphasise that the first step is not belief, but scepticism. As a rule, it all starts with disbelief: people hear about some conspiracy theory and are very sceptical about it, frequently finding it absurd. Yet something about it (sometimes its very 'absurdity') attracts their attention enough for them to start looking into it some more, to do some research and to – often with fascinated disbelief – plunge into the reading of related literature and websites, which sends them straight down the 'rabbit hole'. In this process, scepticism and disbelief are gradually replaced by fervent Belief in the knowledge thus obtained, the Belief that is all the more absolute because they have themselves come to this knowledge, in spite of their original scepticism and based on their own research and establishing the right connections. The scepticism that we find at the origin of practically all conspiracy theories is the inherent condition of true faith. Yet this scepticism is not only scepticism regarding the official versions of events and official authorities, but also scepticism concerning the conspiracy theory itself; it constitutes the inner condition and the first step towards absolute belief in it.

In this respect, conspiracy theories come indeed very close to the configuration of the unconscious knowledge, 'knowledge that doesn't know itself', that Lacan also points out in relation to enigmas. It is as if, from the very outset, its supporters *knew without knowing*, without knowing that they know. What attracts them immediately in a conspiracy theory, in spite of their scepticism, is ultimately that, in a way ('unconsciously'), they already know. Or, as Peter Klepec formulated this following a different path: 'We could say that the firmness of their conviction or belief springs from what is unconscious in the psychoanalytic sense of the term.'[9]

The beliefs the rightness of which we establish and vouch for ourselves, personally, and that are fortified on the level of the unconscious, are special kind of beliefs, and the subjective investment is involved here in a particularly strong way, making of doubt the main fuel of certainty. The (more or less paranoid, albeit not always unjustified) attitude, according to which we can believe no one and nothing and can rely only on ourselves, thus starts to function in a dialectical turn as the inner condition and pillar of the blind and unshakable belief in most bizarre, incredible things. We can indeed wonder how people who believe no respectful media, no authorities, no scientific proofs – people who, in sum, meet all the segments of the 'official' explanation of reality with utter scepticism – can immediately believe that aliens are kidnapping humans, that the earth is flat, that George Soros runs a child trafficking network, that the COVID-19 virus does not exist . . . The list is very, very long and very picturesque. The more bizarre the idea, the more credible it seems; the actual credibility of a theory is inversely proportional to its spontaneously perceived credibility. This is not so surprising, since spontaneity is, in this perspective, nothing but prejudice systematically produced by the media. What we *spontaneously*, automatically believe is thus most certainly wrong or, as Alhusser would put it, it is a hallmark of ideology. Yet what is very different from any kind of Athusserian 'critical' perspective is this additional move that we find in conspiracy theories, the move in which the element of bizarreness and incredibility becomes itself an immediate epistemological criterion of truth, proof of the theories' claims.

The Enjoy-meant

We have so far kept aside the fact that conspiracy theories also carry in themselves a strong libidinal component, the problem of enjoyment. In conclusion, we'll now try to sketch out briefly the logic of this component. An element of excessive enjoyment often appears in conspiracy theories as their instigator or bait: something that first catches our attention. A typical example of this kind of excessive, fantasmatic bait is QAnon's hijacking of the #SaveTheChildren hashtag. It is also in many other aspects that QAnon's manipulative big Other swarms with surplus enjoyment. QAnon's supporters believe, among other things, that a cabal of Satan-worshipping Democrats, Hollywood celebrities and billionaires[10] runs the world while engaging in pedophilia, human trafficking and the harvesting of a supposedly life-extending chemical from the blood of abused children. Besides this last motive, which is a traditional anti-Semitic commonplace, anti-Semitism is at work already in the initial claim. The idea of the all-powerful, world-ruling cabal comes straight out of the Protocols of the Elders of Zion, a fake document purporting to expose a Jewish plot to control the world that was used throughout the twentieth century to justify anti-Semitism.

The Other as the place onto which get projected different fantasies and excessive and bizarre enjoyment, is something that we find in all conspiracy theories. Yet its presence is not equally strong in all of them, and does not 'interpellate' all the followers in the same way. We could say that, although conspiracy theories always incorporate a *structural place* of the Other who indulges in some sort of 'impossible enjoyment', who is stealing our enjoyment or enjoying at our expense, who, with his enjoyment, embodies the quintessential Foreignness with respect to us – this is nevertheless not what primarily defines conspiracy theories. The notions about the stealing of enjoyment (by the Other), as well as about the Foreign character of this enjoyment, constitute a somewhat more general category or fantasmatic structure,[11] which can be found, for example, in all racisms and, of course, at the very core of anti-Semitism. So, maybe we should reverse the perspective here and say: the significance and the presence of the enjoying Other in a conspiracy theory is proportional to the role and significance held in it by racism, anti-Semitism, feelings of being threatened by Foreigners . . .

In theories such as, for example, the flat earth theory or theories about the moon landing being staged, this component is present to a much lesser degree or left up to the individual psychological traits of the followers. Yet, this does not mean that the layer of enjoyment is absent; it means that we need to look for it elsewhere. Indeed, there is something that we can find in *all* conspiracy theories and that is inherently connected with enjoyment – connected with what Lacan called *joui-sens* (a word play with *jouissance* [enjoyment]), 'enjoy-meant' or the enjoyment of meaning. Many already have noted that conspiracy theories are kinds of hermeneutic machines – we could call them 'Meaning games', paraphrasing the title 'Hunger games'. One of the fundamental rules of these 'games' is that everything that happens has a meaning, that there are no coincidences, no contingencies. Everything that happens is up for interpretation that will lead to its true Meaning. With Lacan, we come to a perhaps surprising connection between this generating of meaning and enjoyment. *Qui n'en a le sens avec le joui?* Says Lacan in one of his famous word plays – 'who doesn't "get" the meaning [*sens*] along with pleasure [*joui*]?'[12] The phrase is difficult to translate, but we could also say: who doesn't make (produce, generate) meaning with pleasure, who doesn't enjoy making sense/meaning? At issue is not only enjoyment in meaning, enjoyment taken in producing/recognising meaning, but also the act of producing, generating, 'making' sense *of* enjoyment, making it 'mean' something.

One of the basic driving forces of conspiracy theorists could be identified precisely as making sense of enjoyment, *jouissance* – and this insofar as *jouissance* is meaningless, serves no purpose, doesn't make any sense and strikes us as superfluous (as something that need not be there). To repeat: the vector here *simultaneously* points in both directions, from enjoyment to meaning (interpretation as making sense and use of something that appears as meaningless, useless) and from meaning to enjoyment (enjoyment in producing meaning).

From this perspective, the conspiratorial presumption that 'there are no coincidences' could be seen as another way of saying that 'there is no enjoyment', that is to say, as signalling the repression of enjoyment in its status of being a meaningless, useless X. As far as conspiracy theorists are concerned, there are no coincidences, no contingencies, therefore no enjoyment – not on their side, at least. Every shoot of enjoyment (of which there is certainly no lack) gets immediately processed into meaning, drives the hermeneutic machine, and overtakes the quest for truth as the driving force of interpretation. In this respect, conspiracy theories are like a manufacturing industry of enjoyment, a manufacturing industry in the sense of 'processing products from raw materials'. It is a manufacturing industry of enjoyment that relies heavily on (the work of) the unconscious. Yet the enjoyment thus processed into meaning doesn't stop coming back; it keeps returning with the enjoyment in 'making sense', the enjoyment in meaning. And this calls for more (conspiracy) theory. In this way, conspiracy theories are kept closed within their own vicious circle on account of this circle never being able actually to close – for what keeps pouring into it, together with the welcome familiarity of meaning, is a strange, heterogeneous element of enjoyment.

Notes

1. This chapter is a result of the research programme P6-0014 'Conditions and Problems of Contemporary Philosophy', the research project J6-9392 'The Problem of Objectivity and Fiction in Contemporary Philosophy' and the bilateral cooperation project BI-US/18-20-026 'Objectivity beyond the Subject-Object Dichotomy: Fiction, Truth, Affect' between the Research Centre of the Slovenian Academy of Science and Arts and the University of New Mexico, which are funded by the Slovenian Research Agency.
2. Frederic Jameson, *The Geopolitical Aestethics* (Bloomington and London: Indiana University Press and British Film Institute, 1992).
3. Jodi Dean, *Aliens in America. Conspiracy Cultures from Outerspace to Cyberspace* (Ithaca: Cornell University Press, 1998).
4. See Slavoj Žižek's paper in this volume.
5. Bruno Latour, 'Why has Critique Run Out of Steam? From Matters of Fact to Matters of Concern', *Critical Inquiry*, vol. 30, no. 2 (Winter 2004), pp. 228–30.

6. Latour, 'Why has Critique Run Out of Steam?', p. 227.
7. Julia Carrie Wong, 'QAnon explained: the antisemitic conspiracy theory gaining traction around the world' (2020) available at <https://www.theguardian.com/us-news/2020/aug/25/qanon-conspiracy-theory-explained-trump-what-is> accessed 15 February 2021.
8. Jacques Lacan, *The Seminar of Jacques Lacan, Book XVII: The Other Side of Psychoanalysis*, trans. Russell Grigg (London and New York: W. W. Norton, 2007), pp. 36–7.
9. Peter Klepec, 'Kaj spregleda "teorija zarote"?', *Časopis za kritiko znanosti*, no. 266 (2016), p. 68.
10. Here are some of the names that keep coming up: Hillary Clinton, Barack Obama, George Soros, Bill Gates, Tom Hanks, Oprah Winfrey, Chrissy Teigen and Pope Francis.
11. For a more detailed account of this and of some related questions see Mladen Dolar, 'The Subject Supposed to Enjoy', in Alain Grosrichard, *The Sultan's Court: European Fantasies of the East* (London and New York: Verso, 1998), pp. ix–xxvii.
12. Jacques Lacan, *Television. A Challenge to the Psychoanalytic Establishment*, trans. Joan Copjec (London and New York: W. W. Norton, 1990), p. 16.

Index

absolute knowing, 20
abstract labour, 25, 26–7, 37, 39, 93
abstract labour time, 36, 38
abstract social labour, 38
Adorno, T. W., 86, 87, 103n
agalma, 76
Agamben, G., 153
Alcibiades, 76
alienation, 16, 17, 94, 96
allegory of the cave, 1
Ambassadors (Holbein), 33, 34, 35, 36
analogies, 211–14
'Analysis Terminable and Interminable' (Freud), 8, 203, 212, 213
analytic meta-psychology, 8
anamorphosis, 33, 34–7
 and social hieroglyphic, 37–40
anti-philosophy, 132
anti-Semitism, 246–7
apperception, 95
Arendt, H., 138, 229n
aristocratic evaluation, 121
Aristotle, 88, 125, 130, 134–5, 219
Arthur, C., 19
ascetic ideal, 114
atom bomb, 67
Awful Truth (McCarey), 183–4, 194–5

Bacon, F., 67
Badiou, A., 124, 127, 130, 131–4, 136–7, 138
bank loans, 14–15
Barber of Seville (Beaumarchais/Rossini), 149–51
Beaumarchais, P. A., Caron de, 149
Behind the Curse, 233
being, 165, 178; *see also* subject
beliefs, 145, 169, 171, 174, 245–6; *see also* opinions
Bentham, J., 3, 4–7, 8, 9, 10
Beyond Good and Evil (Nietzsche), 108, 113, 116
Beyond the Pleasure Principle (Freud), 185, 193–4
big Other, 2, 16, 22
 conspiracy theories, 239–40, 242–3, 244
 demise of, 158–61
 illusion of, 177–8
 lack of, 158, 164n
 as logos, 144, 151, 153, 156, 157, 158, 159
 public as, 235
 as rumours, 145–6, 147, 151, 152–3, 156, 157
 and surplus-value, 40
 and truth, 10–11n
 TV as, 234

Birth of Biopolitics (Foucault), 24–8, 41n
Bloch, O., 7
Boutroux, É., 75, 83n
brain science, 21
Brandom, R., 16
Brentano, F., 157
Brown, N. O., 50
Bruno, G., 65

calumny, 150–1, 153
capital, 14–15, 30, 37
  human, 24, 25–8, 38
  logic of, 20
  see also interest-bearing capital (IBC)
Capital (Marx)
  capitalist production, 19
  capitalist reproduction, 13–14
  commodity fetishism, 56, 72–3, 93
  human labour, 22
  money, 43n, 46
  movement of capital, 20
  nature and humans, 17–18
  utilitarianism, 3
  value, 38
capitalism, 4, 26, 80
  commodification, 86–7
  conspiracy thinking, 233
  fictitious prehistory of, 72
  history of, 73
  reality principle, 98
  social relations in, 235
  value of, 77–8
  and waste, 79
capitalist (anti-)sociality, 77–80, 84n
capitalist logic, 97
capitalist reproduction, 13–14, 15
Carson, R., 15
case histories, 198–202
  analogies, 211–14
  primal scene, 208–11
  transference, 203–6
  'ultra-clear' recollections, 206–8

Cassin, B., 124, 127, 129, 130, 134–6, 138
castration, 47–9, 51, 55, 209
cathartic treatment, 208–9
cave, allegory of, 1
certainty, 110–11
Cervantes, M. de, 153–7
chance
  game of, 187–90
  and truth, 183–6, 189–90, 191
child's play, 193–4
Chomsky, N., 16–17
Christian Scholastics, 88–9
civilisation, 78–9
Civilisation and Its Discontents (Freud), 78
class consciousness, 104n
cognitive science, 21
collective lying, 225–6
Comedy of Errors (Shakespeare), 148–9
commodification, 87
commodities, 38, 86
commodity fetishism, 2, 13, 19, 38–9
  Lacan, 45–6, 50, 52–3, 57
  money, 53–4, 56–9; *see also* economic fetishism
  objective fictions, 72–3
  psychoanalysis, 55
  and the Symbolic, 52–3
commodity form, 40
commodity, use- and exchange-value, 93–4, 102–3n
  exchange abstraction, 97
communication, 155
communism, 15, 16, 17, 18, 40, 78
concepts, 94, 96
  Hegel, 90–1
  Kant, 89–90, 92, 95
  Sohn-Rethel, 93
conceptual personae, 126, 127
conceptualism, 85–9, 92, 96–7, 99–100, 100n
confidence, 14–15
conjunction ('and'), logic of, 138
consciousness, 111, 112

conspiracy theories, 232–48
    and critical theory, 235–8
    delirium of interpretation, 242–6
    enjoyment of, 246–8
    scepticism, 238–42, 245
conspiracy theorists, 85
conspiracy thinking, 233
constant capital, 30
'Constructions in Analysis' (Freud), 206–7
content, 90–1
Copernicus, N., 65
cosmology, 74
cosmos, 65
counter-movement, 110
COVID-19, 238
critical theory, 235–8, 239
critique of objectivity, 106–12
    monopoly over the truth, 113–21
Critique of Pure Reason (Kant), 74, 89–90, 96
culture, 78
curtain/veil, 51

Dean, J., 234
debt, 15
Defoe, D., 162n
Deleuze, G., 121, 126, 131, 138
delirium of interpretation, 242–6
democratic materialism, 133–4
democratic society, 119, 120
Derrida, J., 219–20, 229n
Descartes, R., 65, 67, 73, 81n, 95, 239
desire, 47, 52, 53, 177, 178
Dialectic of Enlightenment (Adorno and Horkheimer), 103n
Dialectical Materialism and Psychoanalysis (Reich), 98
Dictionary of Untranslatables (Cassin), 129
Dictionnaire étymologique de la langue française (Bloch and von Wartburg), 7
disbelief, 245
discourse, 7, 28–9, 136, 174–5, 176, 178, 179

disinterested contemplation, 113–14, 116
disquotation schema, 171, 172, 174
'Doctrine of Being' (Hegel), 90–1
'Doctrine of the Concept' (Hegel), 91
Dolar, M., 1–2, 34–5
'Dora' (Freud), 198–9, 205–6, 214, 215n
double lies, 226
doxa, 144
dream theory, 208
dream-work, 234, 243
Duns Scotus, J., 88

ecology, 18, 20
economic amnesia, 72–3
economic fetishism, 81–2n
economic growth, 77
economic production, 71–2
Einstein, A., 7, 8
empirical concepts, 89
Encyclopedia Logic (Hegel), 90–1
enigmas, 244, 245
enjoyment
    conspiracy theories, 246–8
    games, 191
    gossip, 147, 157, 158
    reality principle, 98
    renunciation of, 72, 83n
    see also surplus-enjoyment
Enlightenment, 89, 151, 159
entropy, 32, 42n
environment, 18
episteme, 29, 144
epistemic production, 71–2
epistemology, 106, 118
Eros v. death-drive, 78
ethics, 168, 178, 223
exchange *see* commodity, use- and exchange-value
exchange abstraction, 97
Exemplary stories (Cervantes), 153–7
exploitation, 31
expressive subjectivity, 17

fabulous entities, 6–7
facts, 160, 166
fake news, 218, 219
fallacy, 128
false appearance, 27–8, 31, 32, 33
false consciousness, 87
fetishism, 45, 47–50, 51, 55–6; *see also* commodity fetishism; economic fetishism
feudalism, 32, 37, 98
fiction, 1, 2, 9, 21–2, 124, 131; *see also* objective fictions
fictitious capital, 14–15
fictitious entities, 5–7, 8, 9, 10
Figaro's wedding (Beaumarchais), 149, 162n
film, 51
fixation, 201
flat earth theory, 247
Flat Earthers, 233
Flynn, T., 26
form, 90–1
Forms, 88, 89
fort / da game, 185, 193–4
Foucault, M., 24–8, 41n
Fragment of An Analysis of a Case of Hysteria (Freud), 198–9
freedom, 15, 16–17, 19, 21
Freud, S.
  capitalism, 78
  case histories, 198–202: analogies, 211–14; primal scene, 208–11; transference, 203–6; 'ultra-clear' recollections, 206–8
  dream-work, 234, 243
  fetishism, 47, 55, 58
  fort / da game, 185, 193–4
  friendship with Silberstein, 157–8
  hypnosis, 202–3
  Lustgewinn, 76
  lying, 226
  metapsychology, 8
  modern physics, 65

mythology, 7
pleasure principle, 70
psychoanalysis, 97, 98
surplus-objects, 77
'Freudian Thing' (Lacan), 178–9, 181n
frustration, 48, 49
fundamental idea, 180n

game theory, 196n
games, 185–7
  Awful Truth (McCarey), 194–5
  fort / da game, 185, 193–4
  Meaning games, 247
  odd or even, 185, 187–90, 196n
  prisoner's dilemma, 190–3
Gegenbewegung (counter-movement), 110
General-Ansturm gegen die Erkenntniß (Nietzsche), 106
God, 240
'God is dead', 105–6
gold, 46, 52
Gorgias, 125, 134–5
gossip, 2, 148–9, 154–6, 162–3n
Grenze, 19
Guattari, F., 126, 131

hallucinations, 207–8, 212
Hamlet (Shakespeare), 148, 153, 217
Hardt, M., 15
Hegel, G. W. F., 10, 89, 90–3, 97, 127, 130, 131, 160
Hegelian dialectic, 18–21, 100n
Heidegger, M., 67–9, 69, 72, 110, 134, 217
Hippias Minor (Plato), 219
historical nominalism, 24, 26–8
History of the World, 91
Horkheimer, M., 86, 87, 103n
human capital, 24, 25–8, 38
humanity, 6
Hume, D., 75
hypnosis, 202–3, 204, 212
hysteria, 198–9, 200

Ideas as ideal forms, 1
ideology critique, 238–9
Il barbiere di Siviglia (Rossini), 149–51
illusion, 238, 239
Imaginary, 6, 48, 49, 130, 187–9, 191–2, 193–4
Imaginary organisation, 66, 73, 74, 79
immonde, 71–2, 73–4, 75–6, 80
incarnations of theory, 69
individuality, 91–2
infantile neurosis, 208, 215–16n; *see also* 'Wolf Man' (Freud)
inner perception, 95
insults, 156
Intellectual and Manual Labour (Sohn-Rethel), 92–3
intentionality, 145
interest fetishism, 54
interest-bearing capital (IBC), 46, 50, 52, 53, 56–7
Internet, 159–60
interpersonal relations, 14–15, 15
interpretation, delirium of, 242–6
inter-subjectivity, 187, 188
intuition, 74
investments, 16
irony, 17

Jakobson, R., 5, 155
Jameson, F., 233
Janus, 146
jealousy, 232–3
Jewish joke, 10–11n, 226
Johnston, A., 104n
Jokes and Their Relation to the Unconscious (Freud), 185, 186
joui-sens, 247
jouissance, 7, 35, 247–8
  surplus-*jouissance*, 28, 35, 36, 37–8, 40
Journal of the Plague Year (Defoe), 162n
judgements, 91

Kafka, F., 151–3, 198
Kant, I.
  abstractions, 93, 94
  concepts, 89–90, 92, 95
  intuitions, 74
  objective knowledge, 111, 112
  reason, 96
  schematism, 103n
Kapital (Marx) *see Capital* (Marx)
Karatani, K., 137, 141n
Karl Marx's Ecosocialism (Saito), 17–19
Kerferd, G. B., 137
Klepec, P., 245–6
Klossowski, P., 111
'know-how' *see savoir-faire*
knowledge, 82n
  ancient Greece, 144
  and belief, 245–6
  critique of, 106
  and modern science, 64–9
  objective, 105, 106, 108, 110, 111, 112
  and opinion, 159
  practical, 29, 36
  scientific, 21, 29, 36, 81n
  subject of, 112
  surplus-k., 66, 71, 72, 241–2
  theory of, 106, 107, 111–12
  see also absolute knowing; *savoir-faire*
Koyré, A.
  critique of the sophists, 126
  incarnations of theory, 69
  lying, 217, 218–19, 220: in an infinite universe, 224–5; totalitarian regimes, 221–3, 225–6
  modern physics, 70
  modern science, 68, 71
  modernity, 64
Kuhn, T., 70

labour
  abstract, 25, 26–7, 37, 39, 93
  Marx's definition, 22

paid, 31–2; *see also* wage labour
semblance of, 31
social, 38, 40, 43n
as spurious infinity, 20–1
surplus-l., 27, 29, 31, 36
unpaid, 27, 28, 31–3
labour power
  as abstract labour, 38
  as commodity, 15, 30
  value of, 31, 32, 33, 36, 37, 39
'Labour Theory of Suture' (Johnston), 104n
labour theory of value, 26–7, 29–34; *see also* surplus-value
labour time, 25, 26–7, 29, 31, 32, 33, 36, 37, 38
Lacan, J., 3, 4–5, 6
  *agalm*a, 76
  anamorphosis, 33, 34, 35
  Badiou on, 130, 132
  big Other, 2, 16: conspiracy theories, 239–40; illusion of, 177–8; lack of, 158, 164n; as logos, 144; and truth, 10–11n
  capitalism, 77–8
  Cassin on, 130
  cosmos, 65
  *discour*s, 7
  enigmas, 244, 245
  entropy, 32, 42n
  fetishism: castration, 47–9, 55; commodity fetishism, 45–6, 50, 52–3, 57; and the curtain/veil, 51
  fiction, 9, 124, 131
  'Freudian Thing', 178–9, 181n
  games, 185–6: *fort / da* game, 194; odd or even, 187–90, 196n; prisoner's dilemma, 190–3
  *immond*e, 71–2, 73–4, 75–6, 80
  jealousy, 232–3
  *joui-sen*s, 247
  *jouissanc*e, 7, 247–8: surplus-*jouissanc*e, 28, 35, 36, 37–8, 40
  on Kant, 74–5
  language, 129, 175–9
  le peu du réel, 234
  liar's paradox, 184
  master-slave dialectic, 28–9, 37–8
  meaning, 247
  metalanguage, 172, 177
  object a, 33, 75, 76–7, 80
  rivalry, 130–1
  science, 66–7, 69, 70–2, 81–2n
  signifiers, 39
  surplus-labour, 36, 37
  surplus-value, 82n
  truth and error, 183
  truth and subject, 165, 174–9
  waste, 78–80
Lady-Thing, 76
Lalande, A., 128
language
  Aristotle, 134–5
  Bentham, 5–6
  and gossip, 155, 162–3n
  and irony, 17
  Lacan, 129, 175–9
  translation, 128–9
  troubadour lyrics, 76
  Wittgenstein, 167–8, 169–74, 180n
lathouse, 72, 75
Latour, B., 235–8
Le mariage de Figaro (Beaumarchais), 149, 162n
le peu du réel, 234
Lebrun, G., 20
'Lecture on Ethics' (Wittgenstein), 168, 178
legal fictions, 7
liar's paradox, 184; *see also* lying
linguistic fictions, 7
'Little Hans' (Freud), 199
Liu, L., 196n
loans, 14–15
logic games, 190–3

'Logical Time and the Assertion of
    Anticipated Certainty' (Lacan), 185,
    190–2
logology, 135
logos, 144, 151, 153, 156, 157, 158, 160
Lustgewinn, 76
lying, 184, 217–27
    in an infinite universe, 224–5
    Sartre, 230n
    totalitarian regimes, 221–3, 225–6
    and truth-telling, 229n

Man, Play and Games (Caillois), 186
Mannoni, O., 47, 55, 56, 57, 145
market competition, 22n
Marx, K.
    alienation, 16, 94
    on Bentham, 3
    capitalism, 4
    capitalist reproduction, 13–14
    commodity fetishism, 2, 13, 38–9, 45–6,
        53, 56: cure, 57–9; objective fictions,
        72–3; psychoanalysis, 55; Universals
        and Particulars, 19
    commodity form, 40
    commodity, use- and exchange-value, 93
    communism, 78
    economic amnesia, 72–3
    fictitious capital, 14–15
    Foucault's (mis)reading of, 24–8
    labour theory of value, 26–7, 29–34; *see
        also* surplus-value
    materialist thesis, 86
    money, 46, 50
    necessity v. freedom, 17
    political economy, 8
    surplus-enjoyment, 77
    surplus-population, 77, 79
    see also Capital (Marx); *Karl Marx's
        Ecosocialism* (Saito)
Marx-Hegel relation, 19–22
Marxist Psychoanalysis, 97–9

masters, 129–30
master-signifier, 40
master-slave dialectic, 28–9, 37–8, 131
materialist traditions, 2–3
mathematics, 65–6, 67, 69, 73
Matrix, 243
meaning, 171
Meaning games, 247
mechanistic worldview, 65, 73
media, 159, 218
metalanguage, 172, 177
metaphysics, 236, 237
metapsychology, 8
method, 113
modern physics, 64, 65, 70
modern science
    epistemic production, 71–2
    and knowledge, 64–9
    and reality, 73
    scientific amnesia, 69–72
    and truth, 222, 224
    see also cognitive science
modernity, 64, 66, 72, 159, 221
money, 14, 20, 46, 50, 53–4
    as interest-bearing capital (IBC), 46, 50,
        52, 53, 56–7
moon landing, 234, 240–1, 247
Moses, 91
Musk, E., 16

names, 90, 97
natural sciences *see* modern science; science
nature, 17–18, 20, 67–8
necessity, 17, 105
negative freedom, 16–17
Negri, A., 15
neoliberalism, 24–8
neurobiology, 21
neurosis, 199–201, 204, 208, 213
New Introductory Letter on Psycho-Analysis
    (Freud), 7
Newton, I., 73

Nietzsche, F.
　critique of objectivity, 105–12: monopoly over the truth, 113–21
　lying, 217
　metaphysics, 237
'Nietzscheism', 235
nominalism, 1, 2–3, 10, 88, 89
　historical, 24, 26–8
Novalis, 135
Novelas ejemplares (Cervantes), 153–7
numbers, 90, 91, 101n

object *a*, 33, 34–5, 36, 38, 75, 76–7, 80, 203
objective fictions, 2–3, 10
　big Other, 161
　in capitalism, 4
　commodity fetishism, 72–3
　Foucault, 27–8
　in modernity, 66
　science as, 70
　surplus-objects, 77
　unpaid labour, 32–3
　workers, 87
objective knowledge, 105, 106, 108, 110, 111, 1112
objective man, 108, 113, 114–16, 118, 119
objectivity, 2, 3, 4
　Nietzsche's critique of, 105–12: monopoly over the truth, 113–21
　of truth, 184
objects, 85, 86
obsessional neurosis, 200–1
odds and evens, game of, 185, 187–90, 196n
Oedipus, 244
official science, 69
On the Genealogy of Morality (Nietzsche), 113–14
opinions, 144–5, 159
Original Sin, 155

paid labour, 31–2; *see also* wage labour
paralogisms, 95–6

particularity, 91–2
particulars, 19, 88, 89, 90
patriotism, 17
penises, 47, 48
perception, 74
　inner, 95
personal freedom, 15
personal identity, 85
perspectivism, 106, 110
Petronius, 217
Pfaller, R., 145
phallus, 47–50
phenomenanalysis, 71
phenomenology, 71
Phenomenology of Spirit (Hegel), 21, 103n, 131
philosophical critique, 107
philosophical labourers, 116
philosophy
　as gossip, 156–7
　lying, 223
　objectivity in, 105, 106
　and science, 115–21
　of the self, 176
　and sophistics, 125, 130–7
　see also anti-philosophy
physics, 64, 65, 70
picture theory, 170–1
Plato
　*agalm*a, 76
　allegory of the cave, 1
　lying, 219, 220
　metaphysical realism, 88
　sophistics, 125, 126, 127, 128, 131, 132–3, 137
　Truth, 86
pleasure, 186, 191, 193
pleasure principle, 70, 98, 187, 194
poetry, 76
Poincaré, É., 75
political economy, 8, 13, 20, 24–5, 26–7, 39, 81–2n

political lying, 218–19
  in an infinite universe, 224–5
  totalitarian regimes, 221–3, 225–6
political-economic amnesia, 72–3
pollution, 75–6, 79–80
positive freedom, 17
positivism, 105
postmodernism, 70, 85, 234–5, 237
power, 115, 120, 147–8; *see also* labour power
practical knowledge, 29, 36
practical metaphysics, 236, 237
prejudices, 238
primal scene, 202, 208–11, 213
primitive accumulation, 72
prisoner's dilemma, 190–3
privation, 48, 49
probability, 188–90
production, 66, 68, 71–2
profit, 14, 27, 30, 31, 32, 53
proletariat, 20, 77
psychoanalysis
  big Other, 158
  case histories, 198
  fetishism, 55
  Foucault, 41n
  games, 186
  Lacan, 52, 178–9
  Marxist, 97–9
  symptoms, 45
  transference, 245
  truth and chance, 183, 184–6
  see also Freud, S.
psychoanalytic metapsychology, 8
psychology, 97
Ptolemaic system, 66, 242
pure concepts, 89
Purloined Letter (Poe), 185, 187–8, 189

QAnon, 234, 242–4, 245, 246–7

Rangverschiebung, 116–21
'Rat Man' (Freud), 199–201

Real, 189, 190, 191
Real abstractions, 3–4, 30, 38, 43n, 94
realism, 1, 2–3, 10, 85–9, 92, 96–7, 99–100
reality
  absolute knowing, 20–1
  Bentham, 9
  games, 186
  mathematisation of, 65–6
  modern physics, 65
  modern science, 73
  modernity, 72
  postmodernism, 70
  thing in itself, 74, 75
reality principle, 98, 187
reason, 96
Reassembling the Social (Latour), 236
recollections, 'ultra-clear', 206–8
recollective-recognitive structure of trust, 16
Reich, W., 98
relativism, 235, 236, 238
renunciation of enjoyment, 72, 83n
repression, 201, 202–3
Repulic (Plato), 132–3
Ricoeur, P., 97
rivalry, 130–1
Rosenthal, J., 19
Rossini, G., 149–50
Ruda, F., 20
rumours, 2, 144–61
  Barber of Seville (Beaumarchais/Rossini), 149–51
  Comedy of Errors (Shakespeare), 148–9
  Hamlet (Shakespeare), 148
  in modern times, 159–61
  Novelas ejemplares (Cervantes), 153–7
  power of, 147–8
  Slovenian, 155, 163n
  Socrates, 146–7
  Trial (Kafka), 151–3
Russel, B., 172

Saito, K., 17–19
Sartre, J.-P., 230n
savoir-faire, 29, 36, 37
scepticism, 238–42, 245
schematism, 89–90, 103n
Scholastics, 88–9
Schopenhauer, A., 167
Schranke, 19
science
   and philosophy, 115, 116–21
   see also modern science
science fiction, 66, 67, 68, 69, 70–1
Science of Logic (Hegel), 4
scientific amnesia, 69–72
scientific artifices, 69
scientific knowledge, 21, 29, 36, 81n
scientific objectivity, 113
scientific revolution, 64–6, 73; *see also* modern science
scientific thinking, 69–70
Second Manifesto for Philosophy (Badiou), 136
secrecy, 224–5, 226
self-cleaning/self-laundering fetish, 53–4
self-deception, 219
semblance of labour, 31
Seminar IV (Lacan), 49
Seminar V (Lacan), 46, 52
Seminar VII (Lacan), 9, 34
Seminar VIII (Lacan), 50
Seminar XI (Lacan), 7, 34, 51
Seminar XVI (Lacan), 9, 46
Seminar XVII (Lacan), 28
Seminar XVIII (Lacan), 45
Seminar XX (Lacan), 9
sentences, 169–71, 176
sexual cosmologies, 82n
sexual development, 209–10
sexual fetishism, 45
Shakespeare, W., 148–9, 217
shoe fetishism, 51
signifiers, 39, 40, 175, 176, 185, 195

Silberstein, E., 157–8
slander, 151, 152, 153, 154, 155
slave morality, 121
slavery, 32; *see also* master-slave dialectic
slave's knowledge, 36; *see also savoir-faire*
Slovenian, 155, 163n
Smith, A., 25
social alienation, 16
social bonds, 78, 222, 223, 224–5
social hieroglyphic, 37–40
social labour, 38, 40, 43n
social media, 159, 160
social reality, 21
social relations, 77, 235
Socrates, 1–2, 76, 126, 137–8, 144, 146–7, 152, 220
Sohn-Rethel, A., 92–3, 94, 95, 97, 98
sophisms, 128, 192
Sophist (Plato), 127, 128
Sophisterei, 128
sophistics, 124–39
   Aristotle, 125, 134–5
   Badiou, 131–4, 136–7, 138
   Cassin, 134–6, 138
   Hegel, 127, 130
   key figures, 125–6
   Plato, 125, 126, 127, 128, 131, 132–3, 137
   in post-Hegelian philosophy, 127–8
   terminology, 128
Sophistik, 128
sophistry, 124, 125
Spanish, 157
speech, 154–5, 167–8
spurious infinity, 20–1
stock exchange, 16
structure, 171
subject, 165, 166–70, 172–4, 175–9
subject of knowledge, 112
subject of thought, 111
subjectivity, 2, 3, 4, 16, 17, 95, 188
success, 99
surplus-enjoyment, 76, 77, 80, 82n

surplus-*jouissance*, 28, 35, 36, 37–8, 40
surplus-knowledge, 66, 71, 72, 241–2
surplus-labour, 27, 29, 31, 36; *see also* unpaid labour
surplus-population, 77, 79
surplus-production, 78
surplus-products, 76, 80
surplus-value, 14, 27, 28–34
   anamorphic structure, 36–7: and social hieroglyphic, 37–40
   and money, 50
   rate of, 43n
   and surplus-enjoyment, 76, 77, 80, 82n
   v. profit, 53
Svoboda, M., 126
Symbolic alienation, 16
Symbolic castration, 49
Symbolic determination, 189
Symbolic fictions, 21, 22
Symbolic Order, 16
   and games, 185, 187: *fort / da* game, 193, 194; odd or even, 188–9, 190; prisoner's dilemma, 191, 192, 193
   truth trap, 184
   see also big Other
symptoms, 45

technology, 67
Ten Commandments, 90–1
Theory of Fictions (Bentham), 3, 4, 5, 6, 7, 9, 10
Thing, 76
thing in itself, 74–5
things, 90–1, 96, 97; *see also* word and thing
thinking, 69–70, 95–6, 165, 171, 178; *see also* conspiracy thinking
thinking self, 111
Thus Spoke Zarathustra (Nietzsche), 114
time, 192
totalitarian regimes, 221–3, 225–6
Tractatus (Wittgenstein), 165, 166–74
   Lacan on, 175–9

traditionalism, 85
'Transcendental Dialectic' (Kant), 95
transcendental idealism, 90, 92
transcendental subject, 167
transcendental subjectivity, 94, 95
transference, 203–6, 208, 213, 245
translation, 128–9, 133
Trial (Kafka), 151–3
trickery, 124, 128, 129
troubadour lyrics, 76
Trump, D., 160, 234, 243
trust, 14–15, 16
truth
   Badiou, 132, 136
   and chance, 183–6: odd or even game, 189–90, 191
   Heidegger, 72
   and knowledge, 144
   Lacan, 9, 10–11n, 165, 175–9, 184, 189, 191, 192–3
   logic games, 192–3
   monopoly over, 113
   Plato, 86
   and political lying, 218, 219: totalitarian regimes, 222–3
   in postmodernism, 235
   relative standards of, 85
   Socrates, 1–2
   Wittgenstein, 165, 166–7, 169–72, 174–5
truth trap, 183–4, 195
truth-telling, 218–20, 221, 222–3, 224, 225, 226–7, 229n
TV culture, 234

'ultra-clear' recollections, 206–8
Understanding, 21
universality, 91–2, 105
universals, 19, 26, 88–9
university discourse, 176, 178
unpaid labour, 27, 28, 31–3; *see also* surplus-labour
utilitarianism, 3, 4–5, 7, 121

value/values, 110, 113; *see also* labour theory of value; surplus-value
variable capital, 30
veil/curtain, 51
verbal reality, 6, 9
von Wartburg, W., 7

wage labour, 27, 28, 31, 32
wage labourers, 37, 38
wage system, 40
'Wages, Price and Profit' (Marx), 30, 43n
Walter of Mortagne, 88
waste, 78–80
'We Scholars' (Nietzsche), 108, 113, 116
Weltanschauung see worldview
Western society, 234–5
What Is Philosophy? (Deleuze and Guattari), 131

Wittgenstein, L., 165, 166–74, 180n
'Wolf Man' (Freud), 201–2, 203–4, 208–13
word and thing, 85–6, 90, 91–2, 96
word play, 195
work, 77
world
  end of, 64, 67, 71, 73
  Lacan, 177
  negation of, 73–4
  polluted, 75–6, 79–80
  Wittgenstein, 166, 167, 173–4
worldview, 74
  mechanistic, 65, 73

Žižek, S., 3–4, 127
Zupančič, A., 28, 149, 161

EU representative:
Easy Access System Europe
Mustamäe tee 50, 10621 Tallinn, Estonia
Gpsr.requests@easproject.com

www.ingramcontent.com/pod-product-compliance
Lightning Source LLC
Chambersburg PA
CBHW052047220426

43663CB00012B/2479